From Yalta to Glasnost

From Yalta to Glasnost

The Dismantling of Stalin's Empire

Agnes Heller and Ferenc Fehér

Basil Blackwell

First published 1990
First published in USA 1991

Basil Blackwell Ltd
108 Cowley Road, Oxford OX4 1JF, UK

Basil Blackwell, Inc.
3 Cambridge Center
Cambridge, Massachusetts 02142, USA

British Library Cataloguing in Publication Data
A CIP catalogue record for this book is available from the British Library.

Library of Congress Cataloging in Publication Data

Heller, Agnes.
From Yalta to glasnost: The dismantling of Stalin's empire/Agnes Heller
and Ferenc Fehér.
    p.   cm.
First published in Great Britain in 1990.
ISBN 0–631–17772–8
1. Europe, Eastern—History—1945–1989. I. Fehér, Ferenc, 1933–. II. Title.
DJK50.H45 1991
947—dc20   90-447
                                                                                     CIP

Typeset in 10/12pt Plantin by
TecSet Ltd, Wallington, Surrey

Printed in Great Britain by
T.J. Press (Padstow) Ltd, Padstow, Cornwall

Contents

Preface

From Yalta to Glasnost is a collection of essays written between 1979 and 1989 which, combined, provide the dramatic chronicle of the process that the authors term 'Eastern Europe's long revolution against Yalta'. Since the authors themselves were, before their forced emigration from Hungary in 1977, political actors, occasionally participating in the forefront of the events they describe, they never commented on the twists and turns of events from a purely academic stance. They were analyzing and recounting the single chapters of the great drama as they occurred, and they did not nurture the hope, not even in their most sanguine dreams, ever to be able to sum up a positive conclusion – relative as it is. But with the revolutions of the historic year of 1989 in Hungary, East Germany, Czechoslovakia and Romania, preceded by the victory of Poland's decade-long upheaval, this (relative) positive conclusion of the story has now arrived. When the authors looked, during the stormy days of the collapse of Stalin's East European empire, at their earlier comments on the various stages of the process, they were most surprised to realize that these analyses fit smoothly together and yield a continuous chronicle of the demise of the 'Yalta system' in Eastern Europe.

The inverted commas around the term 'the Yalta system' indicate the major enigma of the narrative. In the political literature as well as in the journalism of the postwar decades, the most heterogeneous and incompatible meanings have been attributed to this term. Some observers denied any reasonable signification of the term 'Yalta' altogether while others understood it as the acronym for the darkest conspiracy story of modern history. The authors tried to strike a realistic balance between the two extremes in recounting the original story, the historic meeting in Yalta, February 1945, its varying interpretations by the various powers, the initially devastating consequences of these interpretations, and the emergence of the anti-Yalta movements gradually gathering momentum.

The book is full of predictions made in the course of appraising the events as they took place. Once again, the authors were most astounded to realize how many of their political forecasts had come literally true. In a period when the Western press was infatuated with Kádár's regime, allegedly the maximum of moderation those people 'down there' could dream of, and when Western analysts made frantic efforts to blot out the story of the Hungarian revolution of 1956 from the annals of history, the authors took an 'inexcusably romantic' position in 1981. They hailed the great revolution as the supreme effort to destroy a totalitarian regime from within, and as an attempt to question the tacit premises of the Cold War in East and West alike. They predicted in 1979 that the coming decade would be one of revolutions in the area with its epicenter being in Poland. Amid vehement protests and repeated statements about their 'political naîveté' and their 'dissidents' zeal', the authors called attention to the gradual awakening of German nationalist movements donning various guises in the early eighties which, despite their Aesopic language, had one unambiguous strategic objective: the unification of the two German states and the formal closure of the war in a peace treaty. The authors had, and still have, an ambiguous relation to this process. On the one hand, they regard the Germans' right to restore their national unity and conclude the war in a formal peace treaty as incontestable. On the other, they have never ceased to criticize this movement's self-delusions, its hypocritical forms and, above all, those of its aspirations which potentially endanger the European equilibrium and the interests of the nations east of the Elbe which have suffered so terribly from German imperialism. In an ongoing string of comments for four years, the authors have been following, initially entirely critically, later with a growing understanding but without ever abandoning the critical stance, the gradual unfolding of the 'Gorbachev phenomenon'.

Although it has a relative conclusion and an internal coherence, *From Yalta to Glasnost* has not been written from the Hegelian position of 'the end of history'. It was written *in history*, as a comment on history and as an ongoing narrative. Both the given single event recounted by the authors and their attitude to the event stood in the historical process, and therefore their judgments, despite their unexpected predictive value, shared the relativity of all judgments made in the course of history. If there is now an almost epic conclusion to their story, as the authors believe, it has been granted by this mysterious entity termed 'History' which, for once, turned a smiling face toward this part of the world which has suffered so much. It is the authors' belief that from now on, it is, in the main, the responsibility of the East Europeans what kind of conclusion they will add to their long story of defeats, martyrdom and sudden victory.

Agnes Heller and Ferenc Fehér
New York

Acknowledgements

The authors and publishers wish to express their gratitude for permission to reprint the following: 'Eastern Europe's Long Revolution against Yalta', to the University of California Press (originally published in *Eastern European Politics and Societies* II, 1, Winter 1988, pp. 1–34); 'Eastern Europe Enters the Eighties', to the editor of *Telos* (originally published in *Telos*, 45, Fall 1980, pp. 5–19); 'Soviet Strategy before Gorbachev', to M. E. Sharpe, publisher, and to the editors of *New German Critique* (originally published in *Doomsday or Deterrence?*, 1984, apart from the section on 'The option of a new Rapallo', published in *New German Critique*, 37, Winter 1986, pp. 7–58); '*Red Square*', to the editor of *Telos* (originally published in *Telos*, 61, Fall 1984, pp. 167–81); 'The Gorbachev Phenomenon', to Polity Press (originally published in F. Fehér and A. Arato, eds, *Gorbachev – The Debate*, 1988); 'Crisis and Crisis Management under Gorbachev', to the editors of *Thesis Eleven* (originally published in *Thesis Eleven*, 21, 1988).

The authors also wish to express their gratitude to their editor, Ann Bone, for her highly conscientious and competent work on their manuscript.

Part I

Introduction

1

Eastern Europe's Long Revolution against Yalta

THE MEANING OF YALTA

What was Yalta? Is it possible to identify a phenomenon in the past or present world of political affairs which deserves the appellation 'Yalta system'?

In a literal sense, 'Yalta' was the meeting of February 4–11, 1945, of the 'Big Three', Churchill, Roosevelt and Stalin, which took place in the Crimea in a holiday resort near Yalta. This meeting had been preceded by a 1943 conference in Teheran and was soon to be followed by the third and last summit of the War Alliance in Potsdam, in August 1945.[1]

The documents issued at the end of the Yalta conference provide us with at least a partial record of the agenda. The Big Three discussed the problems which were related to the creation of the United Nations Organization, a project to which the American party had attributed extreme importance, and during this discussion they resolved the hotly debated technical issue of voting. The conference also discussed the 'German problem'. While the meeting upheld the demand for unconditional surrender and reached agreement, furthermore, concerning the future zones of occupation, it only nominally proclaimed the 'dismemberment' of Germany, which had earlier served as the cardinal thesis of the Allied Powers. In fact, the Big Three remained thoroughly divided on this very issue. Furthermore, the conference could not even nominally resolve the dilemma of German reparations for war damages. The most vehemently and frequently debated issue at Yalta was that of Poland and her future under Soviet rule. On this issue, the Big Three only apparently agreed. In a similar fashion, after a much more superficial debate, a consensus seemed to have prevailed among them concerning Yugoslavia. The situation of Iran and the Turkish Straits were also discussed. Finally, the summit at Yalta also brought agreement, this time a genuine and secret one, on the issue of the Far East. The latter included a promise by the Soviet government to enter the war against Japan after the military defeat of

Germany. It also involved some territorial concessions to the USSR made by the United States to the detriment of Nationalist China, a war ally whose government was neither consulted nor advised about this decision. Equally unmentioned in the final communiqué remained the informal, but crucial, debate on the future role of France. With respect to this issue, stubborn British support achieved the concession, despite Roosevelt's reluctance and Stalin's hostility, that the role of a big power should be conferred upon France by acknowledging France as one of the occupying powers after the defeat of Germany.

Even the most seemingly value-free and matter-of-fact description of the agenda at Yalta is likely to deepen that bitter discord which was to characterize subsequent evaluations of the conference. For those who defended the 'Roosevelt tradition' (a group which consisted mostly of politicians who had personally participated in the work of the conference), 'Yalta' meant a single diplomatic act without the suggestion of a 'system' of any kind. In addition, 'Yalta' was thought to signify a successful summit meeting. Understandably, this is the position taken by Edward Stettinius. However, even as late as 1951, by which time the great expectations of Yalta had turned into fairly catastrophic realities, Charles Bohlen, who had acted as a diplomatic expert and President Roosevelt's official interpreter at the meeting, defended the relative merits of Yalta during the Senate hearings on his nomination as ambassador of the United States to Moscow.[2]

A completely different view of the summit is presented by British politicians and chroniclers. Their position may best be summarized by Chester Wilmot, who regards Yalta as Stalin's greatest victory. According to this analysis, the decisions made as a result of the negotiations at Yalta represented the victory of the American position over the British and the defeat of the former in the face of Stalin's inflexibility. In Wilmot's view, the American campaign against the British empire, having been launched earlier with the Atlantic Charter and the lend-lease agreement, resulted at the very least in a divided Western political and military strategy. In fact, American strategy often seemed to imply an outright support of Soviet duplicity. The fateful result of this strategy was general impotence and final capitulation before the Soviet onslaught.[3]

The wave of 'revisionist historiography' in the 1960s in the United States rejected both New Deal optimism and bitter British criticism concerning Yalta. The revisionists, like the others, looked back to Yalta to understand the roots of the grave postwar international situation. For these writers, the real cause of the catastrophe seemed to lie in an economically motivated American expansionism which, in its fear of a new postwar cycle of depression, did everything within its suddenly increased military power to dominate the world market. This economic expansionism thwarted the spirit of genuine reconciliation and collaboration with the Soviet Union, and therefore led directly to the Cold War.[4]

Finally, there is the crucial 'underground' assessment of Yalta which has remained unrecorded, that of the East European political actors. The difficulties in referring to such an elusive testimony are enormous. The memoirs and statements of non-communist or anti-communist statesmen in exile have been understandably toned down. Dependent on the West, these statesmen could not afford to launch a frontal assault on governments whose predecessors had signed the Yalta agreement.[5] But all those who have lived in the region are aware of the oral testimonies about this East European assessment.

The East European oral assessment of Yalta underwent two distinct phases. In the first period (1945–8), the illusions of which only vanished after 1956, even the most well-informed actors tended to believe, owing to the general secrecy which had surrounded the Big Three's negotiations, that more guarantees had been obtained at Yalta by the Western powers for the East European nations than was in fact the case. From the indubitable fact that Stalin was pushing ahead with his policies of sovietization even in countries (for example Czechoslovakia) where Western politicians entertained some hope for the future, anti-communist or non-communist East European politicians in exile or at home drew a totally false conclusion. The inauthentic propaganda campaign of the era of John Foster Dulles – Secretary of State and architect of American strategy in the fifties – about 'rolling back the iron curtain' only served to increase the unfounded expectations that, despite appearances to the contrary, certain unequivocal, temporarily concealed Western guarantees for Eastern Europe had been achieved in Yalta.[6] However, in direct proportion to the exhaustion of optimistic expectations, the oral testimonies of East European public opinion increasingly began to mention 'betrayal' and discuss a *system* of Yalta. Roosevelt's shortsightedness as a rule has held the seat of blame in these disheartened Eastern European circles, and Yalta, generally but without foundation, came to be identified with the infamous bargaining between Churchill and Stalin in Moscow in October of 1944.[7]

It is from the melding of this East European 'oral public opinion' with certain Western extremist positions that the *Yalta myths* have emerged.[8] The most frequent and perhaps the most popular version of these is the one which assumes that regular and continual behind-the-scene negotiations were conducted between the consecutive US administrations and Soviet leaderships. In these secret deals, it is assumed, the Yalta agreements were scrupulously and reciprocally honored, perhaps even complemented by new, equally secret and equally treacherous deals between the two superpowers.[9]

Both in the literature on Yalta and in what we are calling oral public opinion, a widespread guessing game, an exercise in hypothetical history, has been played continuously. Timothy Garton Ash recently made the following apposite remarks about these exercises in hypothetical history:

The question 'what should "the West" have done differently?' underlies virtually all discussions of cold war origins. . . . Hypothetical options here range from, at one extreme, a separate peace with Hitler . . . to, at the other, a full and swift recognition of Soviet claims to the Baltic states and the Polish eastern territories, and a determined effort at full alliance with the Soviet Union, both in the conduct of war and in postwar planning . . . If Britain and the United States had singlemindedly concentrated every ounce of their resources on preparing for landings in France in 1943, if no troops and landing craft had been siphoned off to the Mediterranean on the one side and the Pacific on the other, if the landings had been successful and if Western armies had then pushed forward as remorselessly toward the heart of Europe from the West as the Red Army did from the East, if the Soviet and American soldiers had shaken hands, not on the Elbe, but on the Oder, the Vistula, or even on the Bug, then the balance of power in Central Europe would have been very different – and another 100 million Europeans might today be free . . . . If, if, if . . . .But we who muse on the mountains above Marathon and dream that Prague might still be free have to recall something else as well. Even if a D-day in 1943 had been successful, even if Western armies had fought their way to the heart of Europe, it is scarcely imaginable . . . that this success could have been achieved without British and American casualties, two, three, perhaps five or ten times greater than those actually incurred.[10]

What we would like to propose, by contrast, is a totally different approach to Yalta, one which does not need this kind of hypothetical thinking. In terms of this conception, 'Yalta' denotes more than a single event. To use Arthur Schlesinger's happy term, it was a *universalist experiment with world government*, which failed (and which, for structural reasons, was doomed to failure from the start) but which had both antecedents and sequels in the politics of modernity. Its two major antecedents had been the Holy Alliance and the Versailles system, the latter being the brainchild in common of President Wilson and Prime Minister Clemenceau. As a sequel to Yalta, Kissinger's diplomacy may be mentioned. This policy was self-consciously modeled along the principles of Metternich and was regarded by its author as a more or less permanent (albeit improvised and perforce not institutiona-lized) system of governing the world by those with the power and wisdom for such an enormous task. Yalta, as a projected system rather than a single diplomatic meeting, was meant to be the prelude to a permanent (albeit also improvised and non-institutionalized) world government by at least one of its instigators (the Americans), and the idea was later reluctantly, conditionally and temporarily agreed to by the Soviets and British. Ultimately, one has to bear in mind that even the longest of experiments with world government, namely the system of the Holy Alliance, served its founders for no longer than a decade.[11]

It is undeniable that at least two of the Big Three, Roosevelt and Stalin, subscribed in their political planning to the kind of universalist conceptions which have been mentioned by Schlesinger. Roosevelt's universalism first appeared in his obsessive designing of a new edition of the League of Nations, the United Nations Organization, which in the first years of American belligerence had been unequivocally conceived by the United States administration as a future coercive world authority with armed forces at its disposal.[12] Furthermore, Roosevelt left little doubt concerning his conviction that the policies of the world organization should be those of the big powers. During the Yalta conference all three world leaders made sufficiently explicit their contempt for the small powers and the latter's share in conducting world affairs.[13]

In order to demonstrate to what extent Yalta may be correctly characterized as an exercise in world government, the following facts may be recounted. For one, during the conference the United States and the Soviet Union entered into a secret pact on crucial East Asian issues which remained hidden not only from hostile powers, but also from their closest ally, Britain, which was itself a Far Eastern power. More surprising perhaps is that not even Nationalist China, a favorite of Roosevelt and one of the allied governments, whose territory was the object of the deal, was apprised of it. The Big Three widely discussed not only France's share in the occupation of Germany, but also whether France should be granted again the rank of *la grande nation* after her humiliating performance in the war – at a time when the Soviet Union was Hitler's ally! True enough, the politics of the 'spheres of influence' was publicly condemned by the United States at the time as well as later. However, during the debates on Poland Stalin made several remarks with the explicit intent of demonstrating how loyally he stood by his agreement with Churchill by remaining silent about British politics in Greece. Thus the agreement on the 'spheres of influence' entered the system of world government and became a *de facto* recognized subsystem. There was an inconclusive debate about which of the neutral governments had the right to declare war on Germany (!) and thus become a 'primary signatory' of the Declaration of the UNO. If one adds the concealed campaign of the United States against the British empire (under the cover of the politics of trusteeships) and the fact that time and time again a confused debate was generated in Yalta on Latin American countries and their respective moral virtues, one can see that this conference, allegedly organized around immediate strategic emergencies, in fact took quite significant steps toward constructing an effective 'government of the world'. Perhaps the most conspicuous proof of the common intention of all great powers to govern the world collectively and indefinitely after military victory rests with one scarcely analyzed lacuna: the almost total absence of discussions concerning the principles of *future peace treaties*. From this suspicious silence on the one hand, and from the brutally imperialist projects with respect to Germany on the other, one can only infer that the underlying motive of these world governors was to create an indefinite administrative-colonial regime in Germany (and obviously in Japan as well), instead of entering into peace treaties and restoring German and Japanese sovereignties.[14]

The design of a benevolently authoritarian (and not necessarily tyrannical) world government should not be mistaken for some conspiracy of the power elite or alternatively for a brainstorm of those suffering from delusions of grandeur. Its intermittent recurrence warrants careful attention even where the opposition to it is firm and resolute, for such recurrence throughout history indicates lasting needs for an institution. When *et altera pars auditur*, several arguments for the design can be presented with at least a certain amount of persuasive force. To begin with, in the context of a general global war drawing to its end, both the topicality of the blueprint and its relative modesty should be emphasized. The whole plan was the exact opposite of Hitler's *Wahnsinn* (lunacy). It was based instead on the double consideration that global order had hopelessly broken down and someone had to set it right if civilization was to be saved, and that no *single* power was alone capable or authorized to impose its own order on the world. This is why a collective effort of the Big Three was needed. Furthermore, nations which had been facing the very real threat of wholesale extermination, rather than the usual humiliating experience of a military debacle, could not have mustered the extreme efforts necessary for victory unless the eschatological promise of a totally new world, based on the idea of a 'wise world government' and on the utopia of eternal peace (a correlative postulate of the Enlightenment project), could be held out to them.[15]

The view of Yalta proposed here would help to eliminate a number of confusing elements from the treatment of the problem, even if one sides with the victims rather than the designers of the system. There would no longer be a need for the 'if game'. 'Yalta' would be understood in this conception in terms of what it was intended to be, and not in terms of what it ought to have been, had its designers risen to the required level of grandeur. Nor would it then be necessary to unearth conspiracies from behind every cynical document of contemporary *realpolitik*. 'Yalta', as our conception suggests, certainly has not survived in the sense of a continuous and thickly veiled conspiracy by those governing the world. But it has survived in the sense that the powerful of the world still feel themselves appointed to make ultimate and supremely rational decisions for the rest of us. As a result they feel, irrespective of their political affiliation, a certain awe for the work once it has been performed. On the basis of this newly proposed thesis the character of Yalta, the concrete causes of its fiasco as well as the relative legitimacy of all revolts against the Yalta system, may now be analyzed in an objective manner.

AN ANALYSIS OF YALTA

The pivotal point is the heterogeneous and in fact totally incompatible types of political dynamics that were combined in the Yalta experiment. Two 'universalistic' aspirations and strategies, not only distinct from one another but even hostile, had from the outset been on a collision course in the project (although this absolute irreconcilability between them had only been apparent to the Soviets and not to the Americans).[16]

As far as American universalism is concerned, the positions of both William Appleman Williams and Arthur Schlesinger seem to us to be equally one-sided, but the two theses can be reconciled. The revisionist thesis of economic expansionism as the key to American universalism faithfully accounts for the role of the United States as 'imperial republic' but not for the global American crusade for freedom. The latter was inconsistent and at critical points hypocritical, but it was an undeniable fact that this great objective also served as a stimulus for American behavior in foreign politics.[17] The thesis of ideological universalism, on the other hand, gives a convincing account of the flare-up of 'Wilsonianism' among American policy makers (already an important ingredient of their political culture), but not for the deep, compromising and reactionary concessions made by each and every American administration to American financial interests.[18] If we interpret American policies in Yalta as the combination (and, more often than not, the unintentional and confused melange) of a sincere, committed and at times even enthusiastic ideological universalism (a crusade for 'freedom') on one hand, with economic expansionism on the other, we can then properly grasp all facets of this deeply contradictory, and ultimately failed, policy.

For the second time in the life of one generation, the historical opportunity lent itself to universalization of the American blueprint for a free republic as *constitutio libertatis*. This project was regarded by Hannah Arendt as an enterprise superior to the French revolutionary fiasco but one which had been treated by Europeans throughout the nineteenth century as a parochial solution.[19] In particular, three inherent features of the American project seemed to make it an adequate panacea for the open wounds of a bleeding and suffering world. Despite the terrible shock of a large-scale and extremely brutal civil war, the United States never had a culture based or focused on military valor. Throughout its history, the American republic had been free of Bonapartism and military dictatorship. Therefore it was the country *par excellence* of 'eternal peace'. Secondly, as is well known, the colonial origins of the United States made that republic the anti-colonial state *sui generis*. Given the Japanese erosion of the colonial system during the war, and the wartime impotence of the traditional colonial empires, there could be no doubt whatsoever that rapid decolonization was going to be at the top of the

agenda in the immediate postwar world. Insofar as the American administration pushed the cause of decolonization, hostile British critics could already
detect in the Atlantic Charter that the United States cast itself in the role of a
natural world leader. Thirdly, the United States was a federalist state,
exempt from those ethnic and national conflicts which had been poisoning
the lives of so many nation-states all over the world, and which had, of course
not independently from the influence of American doctrinaire principles in
Versailles, played such a crucial role in triggering the Second World War.

The British position was the only non-universalist one among the Big
Three. British statesmen had traditionally regarded their mother country,
this nucleus of the empire, as a historical singular rather than a universal.
The British political class never believed that British parliamentary liberalism
was an adequate system even for the rest of the European countries, much
less the colonies. Since the mother country had to reconcile its interests with
those of other liberal and illiberal nation-states within a system of continental
equilibrium, the empire could only be one among others, preferably the
largest and the most powerful. The British position therefore was one of
global interests and global vision but of no universalist projects, illusions, and
ambitions.

Precisely for that reason, the British delegation at Yalta acted more
consistently than critics of the conference normally assume and, relatively
speaking, was more successful than the American delegation. (The later
collapse of the British strategy was caused by the delay in recognizing
Britain's economic decline as a result of the war as well as the unpredictably
rapid melting away of the empire.) The British delegation at Yalta mistrusted
both its partners, if not to the same degree. By the time of the conference, all
tactically motivated attempts at appeasement with regard to Stalin had
evaporated from British politics.[20]

Churchill therefore fought more doggedly than the Americans for at least
symbolic Western satisfaction amidst real frustration, namely, for the empty
Soviet promise of free Polish elections; at the same time, he had incomparably fewer illusions about its success. In the traditional vein of British
imperial king- and country-makers, Churchill had no qualms about 'shifting
Poland westward' (in fact, the very term stems from him). With his historic
vision focused on centuries, and not simply on years, Churchill regarded
Russian supremacy in all matters pertaining to Poland as an 'open-and-shut'
case. The real trenches where the British delegation dug itself in lay
elsewhere. They no longer intended to accept, still less to promote, the policy
of destroying Germany as an industrial power and a potential military ally
(although they did not care much about German sovereignty). Therefore,
they effectively sabotaged all serious discussions on the 'dismemberment' of
Germany and, in unplanned complicity with the Americans, on German
reparations. The British in Yalta definitively stuck to their side of the bargain

with respect to the issue of spheres of influence, which had previously been presented by Churchill to Stalin in Moscow in October of 1944.[21] The British delegation also strongly and successfully supported the restoration of France to the rank of a (second-rate) big power, and this was deliberate: a renewed, 'strong-again' France was an indispensable factor for the new continental equilibrium.

The Soviet position also consisted of a kind of universalism, but one of a different order. The Soviet system, with its command economy, is the carrier of a modernizing trend; its integrating principle of rationality is that of growth neither triggered by nor limited to profit-oriented considerations, but rather driven by the dual trend of maximization and control. This system, as might be said of Marxist socialism in general (of which it is a degenerate offspring), claims for itself a rationality and validity far greater than its capitalist counterpart.[22] Given the character of Soviet universalism, which is irreconcilable with the American variant, the genuine question becomes why Stalin joined in the negotiations at all, even for the duration of three meetings. But in fact there *were* reasons for his temporary cooperation. Not even supreme Soviet ideological and state cynicism could, in 1945, totally neglect the deepest wish of the whole world for a new world order. Just as decades later Soviet leaders would skillfully manage to travel on the waters of pacifism, this time they could make good tactical use of the universal wish for a new, 'real' democracy precisely in the months when their armies, local satraps and newly created secret police forces were perpetrating wholesale butchery in East European countries (above all Poland and Bulgaria) as well as implementing, with Western approval, the mass deportation of Germans, in order to lay foundations for the periphery of the Soviet empire. Secondly, Stalin was a convinced Machiavellian who believed in unbridgeable economic and interest conflicts among the capitalist powers which, in due course, would undermine their universalistic pathos and war alliance. To be present at Yalta in fact also meant to exploit such potential conflicts. And Stalin, no doubt, was an ironical observer of the only public sense of indignation at the conference, Churchill's outburst against the American proposal of including the policy of trusteeship, this anti-British, anti-colonial American invention, in the documents of the conference.[23]

Stalin, who was of course the same man in Yalta as he had been 24 years earlier in his capacity as political commissar of Tukhachevsky's army, became during the Yalta debates exclusively Russian and patriotic.[24] The domination of Poland was a matter of Russian national security, Stalin repeatedly asserted, because Poland had already served twice as an avenue of invasion against his country. He made the first uncertain steps towards achieving a global expansionism in his secret bargaining with President Roosevelt on Far Eastern issues. He tested the liberal politicians of the West as he had earlier tested Hitler, only this time with greater self-confidence.

Had they abandoned him to do with his booty whatever he intended, in exchange he too would have been prepared temporarily to allow them to do whatever they wished with the revolutionary movements within their orbit. (Greece is the convincing proof in this case.) On this basis it would have been worthwhile for him to remain for some time within the framework of the 'Yalta system' which then could have operated as a genuine world government. This new world authority would have provided an official blessing for Stalin's conquests and while he could dispense with the Western figleaf, American and English *fiat* could have offered some propaganda value. It would also have spared him certain conflicts and efforts, by convincing the prospective victim that there was no hope for a serious resistance. However, given that in the actual event the Western politicians, much to Stalin's surprise and contempt, stuck to their 'democratic phrases' (though, as Stalin shrewdly understood, they had already resigned themselves to watch him get away with his booty), 'Yalta' could offer no significant use value for him.

In any event, Yalta, not just as a single diplomatic meeting but above all as a system, proved to be a complete fiasco. Yet the failed attempt at a collective world government at least had enough life in it to leave behind the seeds of discord. Without unjustifiably stretching our thesis, we propose to read many of the major postwar moves on a global scale as revolutions against the Yalta system, with or without this intent as their explicit objective.[25] France under de Gaulle drew the necessary conclusions from the role of second fiddle which had been allotted to her in Yalta. The seemingly irrational anti-Americanism of the de Gaulle era can be explained in part at least by the strong French Gaullist anti-Yalta sentiment.[26] Perhaps the other larger and more conspicuous cause of this attitude rested with French fears of German rearmament within Nato, and thus was also related to the yields of Yalta.

A second series of anti-Yalta revolutions took place in China over two decades. Both postwar governments of China, the Nationalist and Communist alike (if not to an equal degree), had a share in these revolutions. American advisors who were attached to Chiang Kai-shek often criticized the latter's unmanageable behavior which in their view led to his defeat. But they failed to understand the deep resentment of Nationalist China which had been caused by the humiliating treatment received in Yalta, and which in part explained this seemingly unmanageable behavior. The Kuomintang's half-hearted attempt to 'go it alone' in its war against the communists was, among other things, a reaction to Yalta. But paradoxically, China became the country of the anti-Yalta revolution under communist rule. Almost all postwar steps taken by Chinese communism, and several crucial decisions of their foreign policy after the seizure of power, can be explained exactly in terms of this hostility to, and gradual self-distancing from, the Yalta-created superpower hegemony. Already the decision in 1947 to begin an offensive policy was, as is well known, a radical departure from Stalin's advice and thus from the Yalta framework. There is unfortunately scant knowledge concerning the background circumstances of China's role in the Korean war, yet certain signs of independence from or even opposition to Stalin's strategic plans are nevertheless unmistakably present. And ever since the historic break with the USSR in the sixties, the rejection of Yalta 'hegemonism' in all hues and colors may be viewed as an abiding feature of Chinese politics.

The defeated powers, Japan and Germany, have been staging their own respective 'long revolutions' against the Yalta system for the past forty years. Japan has chosen the less theatrical way: the course of a meteoric rise to the rank of an economic world power, which is now seriously threatening American supremacy in the industrial and financial world. Germany remained politically paralyzed for a long while, despite *Wirtschaftswunder* (the economic miracle) and the distinguished role of the *Bundeswehr* as the largest conventional army of Western Europe. But in the seventies the dormant German volcano began to erupt anew. Neonationalist movements, first on the left, later toward the center, and more recently on the right, in surprising unison have begun to question the role of the Federal Republic as a bastion of the West, for the latter is not capable of restoring German unity and leaves German sovereignty (in the absence of a peace treaty) permanently incomplete. Since we have summed up our views concerning at least one type of German anti-Yalta movement below, it will suffice to register here the recurrence of a fateful Central European dialectic.[27] Similar to 1848, in the period when national revolutions in the center of Europe had set about to destroy the 'world government' of the Holy Alliance, one finds that today two main trends, the German and the East European movements, are once again headed on a collision course. But there is no 'historical necessity' that would bind the two actors to this collision course.

EASTERN EUROPE'S REVOLUTION AGAINST YALTA

Three methodological remarks are necessary by way of introduction to the issue of Eastern Europe's revolution against Yalta. First, the term 'anti-Yalta revolution' of Eastern Europe is not meant to imply a secret, coordinated and synchronized master plan operating in the East European nations. In fact, Yalta is rarely mentioned in the documents of its opposition, and social upheavals never understand themselves in terms of an 'anti-Yalta revolution'. The reasons for preserving this silence are obvious. An open challenge to 'Yalta' implies for each Soviet leadership a direct assault against the postwar conquests, an attempt to alter the borders created in 1984, and even a risk of European war. The term 'revolution' means here a 'reconstruction in retrospect' of separate and diverse events which in our view display common trends. Secondly, the anti-Yalta trend is not simply identical with the nationalist tendencies which are so clearly in evidence in the East European countries. Since Yalta imposed on East European nations not only dependence on the USSR, but also a particular social structure, social as well as national upheavals are included in this analysis. Thirdly, what follows will be a pattern of interaction that includes a description of those sustaining the 'Yalta system' as well as those opposing it, with the underlying premise being that the two must be understood together.

The anti-Yalta revolution had four distinct phases in Eastern Europe. The first phase took place in the immediate postwar period in which the groundwork of the Stalinist system was laid. The second spanned the three to four years immediately following Stalin's death in 1953. The third, long period included Khrushchev's last years of power and the whole Brezhnev era which, with respect to Yalta alone, show a remarkable degree of similarity. Finally, the fourth phase of the anti-Yalta revolution may be said to consist of the era we are presently living in.

Phase One

The immediate postwar years (1945–7) were characterized by a tremendous confusion in the vast area north of Greece, south of Finland and east of the Elbe. Almost the only clear fact was the Soviet military and political supremacy over the region. At the same time, the pro-Soviet and anti-Soviet actors alike were indulging in wild speculations concerning the potential longevity and the possible future forms of this supremacy. The confusion is usually explained in terms of Stalin's internal hesitation between pushing ahead with sovietization or instead transforming these countries into so many Finlands, that is, buffer states with internal liberalism but foreign political servility towards the Soviet Union. These alleged hesitations, which perforce remain an eternal puzzle to us, might serve as a trigger for yet another round of 'if games'. Instead, we believe it would be more fruitful to examine the main actors on the scene and their actual explicit intentions, and to proceed from there to a catalogue of options, only some of which were realized.

Despite his alleged nocturnal *monologues intérieurs*, Stalin is the least mysterious actor of them all. In our view, there is not the slightest foundation for reading Stalin as anyone else but the paradigmatic Bolshevik revolutionary with a total lack of moral inhibitions and with a sufficient degree of pragmatic realism. He could patiently wait when a forward march was not possible, but he never gave up, nor for that matter did he ever reconsider, his ultimate objectives. We simply see no corroboration for the assumption that Stalin would have been pondering the possibility, much less desirability, of any regime other than Soviet 'real socialism' for the countries of the area. Therefore, the only mystery still awaiting elucidation is the fate of Finland, and not what happened to the rest. The relatively slow progress of sovietization can in our view be accounted for by the following factors. First, in the collective enterprise of 'the hermeneutics of Yalta' Stalin's 'reading' of the text was resolute, free from internal doubts and completely authoritarian. His major premise was the assumption that in Yalta one fundamental principle had been agreed upon: *cuius regio, eius religio* (whoever has the territory imposes the religion). A loose translation of this dictum would be that the armies in a particular region prescribe the social systems to be imposed upon the countries of that region. However, in the meantime a significant change in the American administration had taken place. While the ultimate intentions of the new administration were not immediately apparent, the fact was that nuclear weapons gave the US an unexpected edge over the Soviet Union. Fathoming the intentions of the new administration and drawing the final conclusion that it was politically impossible for any American administration to deploy nuclear weapons against the Soviet Union took some time. Secondly, it was in Stalin's own interest to engineer the radical transformation as smoothly as possible – hence the wide and complex game of ideological deception, the ongoing hairsplitting concerning the character of the tautology 'people's democracies', the use of non-communist parties and politicians as Trojan horses, these all were ultimately so many self-created obstacles for a unicolor communist regime. The military outcome of an eventual armed conflict with East European resistance of any kind was never in question for an army that had so soundly defeated Hitler.[28] And yet, a large-scale and protracted civil war embracing the whole of Eastern Europe would have had incalculable effects on the one actor whose possible reactions Stalin had to take into consideration, the American administration. Finally, the actual forms of sovietization which might be imposed upon the region may have remained in doubt, but the determination to impose the Soviet system on them never was. The example of the Baltic states, swiftly reunited with the 'mother country', demonstrated that it was far from out of the question that *all* the countries that had ever been part of the Russian empire (Estonia, Lithuania, Latvia, Poland and Finland) might become republics of the USSR. A further dilemma was presented for Stalin by possible regional confederations (a southern Slav confederation, the confederation of Poland and Czechoslovakia, and the like). There was some short-term vacillation between alternative scenarios by the Soviet leadership, but the major long-term goals were clear.

Facing such a ruthless and unchallenged superpower which instilled fear not just in its enemies, but in its allies as well, and without themselves having the support of a single serious ally, East European actors of all political hues and colors were in considerable disarray. George Schöpflin correctly observed a primary feature of the immediate postwar situation: a power vacuum in Eastern Europe.[29] There was a simple explanation for this power vacuum. Almost all non-communist parties in almost all countries of the region (Poland being the obvious exception) – liberals, conservatives, populists, even social democrats – had either become accomplices to Hitler's war or, at the very least, had been incapable of putting up a serious resistance to Nazi Germany. These survivors of inglorious times therefore vegetated rather than boldly challenging the victor against whom they lacked moral justification.

Furthermore, Yalta created a geopolitical entity, 'Eastern Europe', which as a polity or a community of destiny had never before existed. Certain nations or ethnic groups of the geographically defined region had had a long prehistory of political sovereignty, while others had always been integrated into larger conglomerates of countries or regional monarchies. The history of some of these nations had been unfolding exclusively in the Habsburg empire (for centuries the Czechs had been the prime example of this), while others had been equally and exclusively determined by the internal history of the Ottoman empire. There were close historical, political, dynastic, diplomatic and cultural ties between some nations (for example between Poland and Hungary), while between others there were none. Never before had Bulgarian politics had to react to events in Bohemia or Poland, and vice versa. Some, such as Bulgaria, had always held close and amicable ties with historic Russia in a religious or political sense; others, above all Poland, were traditionally national, religious, and political enemies of Moscow. Some of these countries had been living at a fairly high level of urban culture for centuries (Bohemia, Poland, northern Hungary) while others (Albania, parts of Yugoslavia) still had strong tribal social structures. The latter sometimes lived in symbiosis with Moslem cultures which had little in common with the history of the diverse Christian nations and groups of the region north of the old Ottoman border.[30] In a crucial hour when the various national parties and political actors of 'Eastern Europe' ought to have acted in a supranational space, this proved to be an impossible task, given that there was so little experience with such action, so little mutual contact, and even insufficient knowledge of each other's respective languages. The resulting disarray of the possible national centers of resistance greatly assisted Stalin's master plan of homogenization.

As a rule, there was no unity even within the individual nations. While with the possible exception of Czechoslovakia (and, as Hugh Thomas assumes, Bulgaria)[31] the communists had no chance whatsoever of gaining even a temporary electoral majority, they did however have a considerable electorate in each country, since they were advocating issues of modernization long overdue in these backward areas.[32] The almost unanimous rejection of Soviet supremacy and communist rule as an agency of this supremacy, as it was to transpire in 1956 both in Hungary and Poland, was nowhere in evidence in the East European countries in the immediate postwar years.

As we now know with the benefit of hindsight, there was one actor who could have become an obstacle to the sovietization of Eastern Europe: the national communist. This assumption is more than mere conjecture. Tito's challenge to Stalin and Churchill's 'percentages agreement', and finally to the Yalta system as a whole, was perhaps the single most dramatic event in the annals of the East European anti-Yalta movements. Furthermore, there were 'dormant' national communist trends in other East European communist parties as well.[33] Whether or not the national communist alternative to Yalta would have meant a more tolerable existence for the East European countries (the example of Yugoslavia seems to corroborate, those of Romania and especially Albania thoroughly refute such a thesis), one fact hardly seems to be in doubt. In reality, Stalin had to accept the Yugoslav deviation from the pattern. However, he simply could not have afforded to tolerate a broader, concerted national-communist opposition to his war conquest. A historical loss of face of this magnitude had to be avoided even at the cost of a major East European war.

Our thesis is therefore, in contrast to the general conjectures to be found in the literature on the topic, that the *least* and *not* the most fecund period in which to produce alternative solutions to the Yalta system was precisely the immediate postwar era. The oppositional forces faced deep internal divisions within their respective nations and they lacked contact with one another in the artificially created supranational space of 'Eastern Europe'. They had no serious moral and political prestige accumulated in the war; often the exact opposite was the case. The non-communist actors were heavily sedated by illusions about the Western powers' willingness and capability to act on behalf of Eastern Europe. They were also entangled in a social struggle, and sometimes in a civil war, with the communists. The Soviet system seemed to offer a viable alternative to the tremendous prewar backwardness of the region, an alternative that temporarily attracted a considerable part of the populace. National unity against Yalta on this basis was not possible. Still less conceivable was any kind of confederation of the anti-Yalta forces among the single nations. Under such circumstances, the anti-Yalta forces – the Polish Home Army engaged in a civil war, the dormant national communists secretly dreaming about their own 'separate ways of the dictatorship of the proletariat' or hatching stillborn plans of supranational confederations, non-communist and anti-communist parties without support from the West – were all fighting a losing battle.

Phase Two

Stalin's governments of terror managed to compress half a century's work into five short years. But immediately after the tyrant's death in 1953 the anti-Yalta revolutions resumed their dynamic, though under modified circumstances. The uniform systems of Stalinist domination had reduced the diverse cultures, natural and social conditions of various countries to one common denominator of misery and fear. The fate they had been collectively sharing had generated in them a sense of community. Almost overnight, 'East European consciousness' had been born. Of course, this remained a deeply schizophrenic mindset. Bulgarians now had reason to watch with inquisitive eyes whatever was happening on the Polish scene, and Poles followed the revolt in Berlin with understanding anxiety. Yet this community of destiny did not in the least imply the obsolescence of reciprocal chauvinistic tendencies.

A further important change, which occurred as a result of the violent Stalinist uniformization of diverse cultures and histories, was a forced national unity against the all-embracing regime of oppression. By that time, a nationwide consensus had obtained solid objective grounds. The old, prewar social structures had been violently and successfully destroyed by the communist apparatuses. The previous division of East European societies into 'upper' and 'lower' classes now irrevocably belonged to the past. Those masses which less than a decade earlier had supported the communist program of modernization were by the time of Stalin's death gripped by the same kind of dissatisfaction or hatred as those who had always remained unreconstructed enemies of communism. On the other hand, a good deal of these reforms had been absorbed by history in the meantime; they constituted, so to speak, a natural background of social life in the region whose necessity not even old-time enemies disputed any longer. On the whole, communism no longer appeared as a vehicle or motor of modernization, but rather as an obstacle to it.

Between 1953 and 1956, the landscape strongly resembled that of the historically significant year of 1848 in Eastern Europe. In that year, national and social aspects of revolutionary dynamics were inseparably intertwined. Nations and ethnic groups which never for a moment ceased to feel enmity and distrust for one another made the first awkward attempts at synchronizing their struggle for emancipation. The peak of the revolution was achieved for a few days in 1956 when Hungary, led by a multi-party government, which had support in the workers' committees embracing the whole country, declared the country neutral and left the Warsaw Pact.

In the sense of a pragmatic *realpolitik*, for which only success counts, those commentators are undoubtedly correct who emphasize that the Soviet leadership could live with a lot of 'provocations' coming from Hungarian leaders and crowds, but not with desertion from the Warsaw Pact.[34] Leaving aside for the moment the problem of whether this is absolutely true, if it faithfully accounts for at least part of Soviet behavior, then the Hungarian revolution of 1956 appears as a revolutionary and unambiguous challenge to the Yalta system, just as Kossuth's short-lived republic of 1849 had been to the Central European equilibrium guaranteed by the Tsar.

The formula of neutrality with which Imre Nagy's government confronted Andropov, then Soviet ambassador and proconsul in Budapest, deserves further comment. It can of course be interpreted as a mere figleaf in the face of the genuine intentions of the deserters who in fact wanted to join the Western alliance but also knew that this would not be tolerated. However, serious arguments can be raised against this Machiavellian interpretation of Hungarian neutrality. There are explicit references in Nagy's private documents from 1955 (published in the West after his execution) that for a considerable amount of time prior to the revolution he had been pondering a non-bloc option for Hungary. Bibó, a prudent realist, did not want to make concessions on the neutrality issue either, not even after defeat. He offered the Soviet government guarantees, which were of course never seriously considered. One of the guarantors of neutral Hungary's goodwill would have been Tito's Yugoslavia, another deserter from the Yalta system which never joined the Western alliance either.[35]

Despite the superior wisdom of *realpolitik*, it seemed then, as it still seems now with the sobering perspective of hindsight, to be perfectly reasonable for actors of social change to push ahead aggressively both in Hungary and Poland. The horizon was full of encouraging signs. The Soviet politburo, then in the throes of a dramatic, and at times violent leadership and legitimation crisis, was clearly uncertain about which course to follow. Naturally, there was a limit to their hesitation. Neither the future status of Poland nor their domination over East Germany could for a moment be in doubt. (This is why the June 1953 uprising in Berlin stood no chance of success whatsoever; this is why furthermore Gomułka, with his clearly drawn line in 1956 beyond which he was not prepared to go, was for a moment the supreme realist.) But almost everything else seemed to be open and fluid. As rumors had it then, Beria, immediately before his downfall and execution, had put out feelers for a deal with the Western powers in which East Germany would have been swapped for German neutrality and perhaps for a considerable Western loan – and these rumors have never been refuted.[36] The armistice agreement in Korea, apparently totally unfeasible as long as Stalin lived, was signed shortly after his death. The conclusion to be drawn from the various interpretations of this act remains that, at least for the time being, the Soviet Union was not prepared to move beyond the 'Yalta line', but that still left much room for change.

More was achieved after the first summit in Geneva. Quite unexpectedly, the peace treaty granting independence and neutrality to Austria was signed in 1955 and this was without doubt a concession made by the Soviet Union. The Austrian peace treaty included several facets, all extremely important, for the anti-Yalta dynamic in Eastern Europe. First, the status accorded to Austria was better, larger and more flexible than the one that had been allotted to Finland. Secondly, with Austria having become neutral, Hungary ceased to be a 'frontline' country. We now know that in all deliberations concerning possible Western moves during the Hungarian revolution, Austrian neutrality, and the fact that the country could not be used as an avenue for military action, served as a moderating influence on Western temperament. The Austrian situation could also have played a certain role in the hours when Hungarian neutrality was debated and accepted in the Imre Nagy government. By the elimination of the Western zones of occupation in Austria, Hungary was no longer geopolitically in a position to join Nato, and this could have been an assurance for the Soviet Union, had its leaders seriously contemplated compromises with revolutionary Hungary. On the other hand, the very fact that Austria had been accorded that treaty suggested that perhaps Soviet leaders were indeed contemplating general concessions. The Soviets had abandoned a zone they had occupied for a decade, their first retreat in Europe.

At the other end of the map, China's unexpected (but not inexplicable) role as moderator was rising. During the dramatic days of the Hungarian revolution, the communiqué of the Chinese government advocating non-intervention and mutual respect in the relationship of 'socialist countries' was widely interpreted as a restraining influence over rash Soviet wishes for a quick mopping-up of the Hungarian rebellion. Less well known is the fact that this attitude had a prehistory. From Ochab, who was then Polish First Secretary and regarded in his own country as a highly inadequate reformer but by Moscow's standards as a potentially subversive factor, we learn that he deliberately sought and was believed to have received, support for a relative autonomy of action by the Chinese leadership during the summer of 1956 when he was visiting the Eighth Party Congress in China.[37]

The most crucial event during this period without doubt was the unexpected and spectacular reconciliation of the Soviet Union with Yugoslavia. This sudden shift in attitude was understood as a promising sign as far as the social structures of the separate East European regimes were concerned. But let us take a look for a moment at the event from the perspective of the anti-Yalta revolution. Yugoslavia's disobedience in 1948 in the face of Moscow's dictates was the clearest possible challenge to, and rejection of, the Yalta system to date. Both the West and the Soviet Union had interpreted this breakdown in the same manner. 'Rehabilitation' of Yugoslavia as a state, which was an incomparably more important event than would have been the rehabilitation of the Yugoslav communist party, objectively implied the questioning of the very principles of Yalta. Khrushchev was apparently not fully aware of these implications of his grand scheme. However, his Yugoslav bargaining partners did nothing to counsel him about this. For a year, the

Yugoslav leadership had unprecedented latitude in all matters of Eastern Europe. Since the Soviet reformers eagerly wanted to lure Tito and his group back into the 'socialist camp', they were for a while putting up with Tito's ever increasing demands, and even making partial concessions.[38] Unfortunately the Yugoslav leadership inexcusably wasted this unique opportunity at a time when their prestige stood at its zenith in Eastern Europe. Instead of launching a wholesale and principled campaign against the main culprit, the Yalta system, they indulged in a petty vendetta (admittedly against murderers and tyrants); thus they turned what was a matter of collective East European emancipation into a litigation over the Yugoslav claims to compensation. This happened because they were in part too self-centered, in part too conservative, with misgivings about the avalanche they might have ultimately set in motion. They crowned their shortsighted and selfish policies with both secret and public endorsement of the Soviet oppression of the Hungarian revolution. This gesture, which truly deserves the name 'betrayal', and which was triggered by second thoughts about the multi-party system emerging out of the Hungarian anti-Yalta revolution, set a precedent that might eventually become dangerous for the Yugoslav leadership. More importantly, perhaps, it also spelled the end of Yugoslav prestige in Eastern Europe. Here was a crucial actor with real avenues of opportunity left unexplored.

The other actor with more room for maneuver than it in fact realized was the United States. It is quite possible that American diplomacy was caught unawares by the suddenly accelerating storm in Eastern Europe.[39] Whatever the explanation, the fact remains that neither the reconciliation between the USSR and Yugoslavia, nor the slowly gathering storm in Hungary which took three years to reach the point of explosion, nor finally, the somewhat quicker Polish events, was ever accompanied by a *single* major American diplomatic campaign to renegotiate 'Yalta'. The secret message of John Foster Dulles at the peak of the Hungarian crisis, one handed to Khrushchev by Bohlen, stated only that the United States did not intend to recruit the newly neutral Hungary for Nato.[40] But this overly laconic message was clearly not adequate in the face of the unique historic moment.

The result was predictable. Most of the masses participating in the Hungarian revolution held the seemingly plausible belief that they would receive Western aid. In fact this revealed that the mystery of Yalta had not been fathomed by East European public opinion. But both American inactivity during the crisis and the theatrical and inauthentic debates in the United Nations afterwards taught certain lessons to East European actors which they are not likely to forget. The memorandum by István Bibó on the Hungarian revolution, addressed to the 'conscience of the world', is perhaps the best and most acutely conscious document of this general sobering attitude of the East European political actors. This paragon of the

Hungarian revolution has survived not as a memento of a 'mistake' (as the petty theorists of *realpolitik* would have it) but rather as the peak of the anti-Yalta movements in the region, although certainly not as a guide or manual for future actors.

Phase Three

The long third period that spanned the 25 years between the Hungarian revolution and the Polish revolution of Solidarity witnessed the degeneration of the anti-Yalta movement on the one hand, and the unsentimental and unhesitating brutality of the rulers in imposing their system, preferably in a Stalinist form, on the other. The only serious reformist movement, the Prague Spring of 1968, was too timid, too irresolute and from the start too heavily surrounded by aggressive enemies to raise, even indirectly, the problem of Yalta. The Czechoslovak republic was one of the major victims of the consequences of Yalta. Yet the fears for Yalta which even the irresolute Czech attempt triggered in the Brezhnev leadership are for this reason worth analysis.

In the first place, Brezhnev seemed to harbor genuine concerns about the complete dissolution of the Soviet sphere of influence that had been built up by Stalin. Therefore, at the first sign of the Czechoslovak events getting out of hand, he conjured up what was to be called the 'socialist community', turning the Warsaw Pact, which was initially a 'defense treaty', into a consultative political body. This was a major innovation, a creative act in several respects which had not been expected from such a mediocre person as Brezhnev. First, by the common military action of the Warsaw Pact armies (in which only two dissidents, Albania and Romania, refused to participate) Brezhnev institutionalized 'Yalta' in the form of a regional Holy Alliance. Secondly, the newly created 'socialist community' was the exact, and perhaps deliberate, reversal of the community-in-progress of anti-Yalta forces between 1953 and 1956. This shrewd move robbed the opponents of Yalta in the region of the feeling of having a new community of destiny against their collective fate. Finally, in his bargaining with an intimidated but still reluctant Dubček leadership, he presented his ace card, President Johnson's letter on the validity of the Yalta agreements. In acting against Dubčekist Czechoslovakia at an early stage, without waiting for overt 'counterrevolutionary' symptoms to emerge, Brezhnev was being neither irrational nor overly rash. Rather it was the Soviet leadership's realistic appraisal that the damaged edifice of Yalta could not bear the strain of yet another overt challenge (after Hungary in 1956), not to mention an outright desertion, *à la* Tito.

It is not without significance that at every juncture, when the system of Yalta is exposed to a direct threat, the 'Baltic solution', the incorporation of the rebellious states into the USSR, becomes one of the options of crisis management. Brezhnev shocked the Czechoslovak leadership with his furious outburst asserting that, as a result of the victory in the war, the borders of Czechoslovakia are at the same time the borders of the USSR, and shall remain so for all eternity.[41] When in May of 1969, during his last week in office, Dubček was conspicuously visited by Marshall Grechko, Commander in Chief of the Warsaw Pact armies, there was no mistake in Eastern Europe about the message being sent forth. Either Dubček's immediate resignation or the formal rule of the Soviet military over Czechoslovakia – these were the only alternatives. (Later Jaruzelski would claim that the same alternatives existed for Poland – martial law or loss of national sovereignty.)

In this period there was also a degeneration of the anti-Yalta movement as this worthy cause found champions it did not deserve: Hoxha's Albania and Ceaușescu's Romania. In both cases Stalinist motives had triggered an opposition to Stalin's system. The Romanian story is well known. Gheorghiu-Dej and his confidant were frightened by Khrushchev's adventurous criticism of Stalin and boycotted his course. In the sixties, being opposed to Khrushchev's assimilationist trends within the Comecon, the Romanian leaders stumbled upon the correct strategy: a combination of the advocacy of national egoism and the preservation of their oppressive regime. Self-serving considerations also led Hoxha to break relations with the USSR and formally abandon the Warsaw Pact in 1968, amidst the storms of the Soviet invasion of Czechoslovakia. His murderous regime was kept in hermetic separation from the rest of the world, almost as a third world enclave within Europe. With these new allies, the anti-Yalta movement seemed to have been hopelessly compromised.[42]

A deep and abiding parallel between the third and the first periods of the Yalta system arose. In the third period the Soviet apparatus regained its temporarily lost self-confidence, leaving behind all hesitations and experiments. Due to its regained equilibrium, the Soviet apparatus was once again on top of the process, and made decisions on time and without paying the slightest sentimental attention to international reaction of any kind. The opposition, on the other hand, stood there as if it had forgotten all the lessons learned from earlier periods. It was divided, it was maneuvering exclusively within national frontiers instead of reaching out for allies in the entire region, and the national dimension of the cause was strictly separated from the social dimension in its actions.

Phase Four

The fourth period is the one in which we are now living; all statements about it therefore warrant extreme caution. The period begins with Poland's revolution, only temporarily and partially defeated, and with the war in

Afghanistan. But rapid and significant changes in the Soviet leadership have as yet brought no change in the politics of the Yalta system.

The war in Afghanistan marked the end of the Brezhnev era of the Yalta system, but initially displayed all the same features of Brezhnev's characteristic management of the system. These days it has been conveniently forgotten that the invasion was not initially launched against any kind of counterrevolutionary insurgency, but rather against a dissident communist regime, an Asian version of Titoism.[43] In resorting to military action, Brezhnev simply duplicated his own strategy in Czechoslovakia. He forgot, however, about his own caution in the case of Albania and Stalin's prudence in the case of Yugoslavia. First, he neglected to consider what he (and Stalin) had already once learned: in a mountainous area with more or less tribal ways of life, protracted resistance to foreign invasion is much more likely than among a city-dwelling populace. This is so not because of a difference in the degree of courage between tribal warriors and city dwellers (as the Warsaw uprising in 1944 demonstrates), but because urban ways of life are more vulnerable. In the second place, in Afghanistan Brezhnev dismissed that factor of restraint which he had so closely observed when Albania defected from the Warsaw Pact, namely that certain steps, unproblematic as they are from the aspect of military strategy, involve the strategist in the gravest political consequences. Landing troops in Albania in 1969, or even a swift incursion into Pakistan to cut the supply lines of the Afghan guerrillas and bring them to capitulation would not have presented irresolvable problems for the Soviet army. However, the likely reaction of all Mediterranean powers in 1969, and that of China and the United States in 1980, would together have brought the world closer to an all-out war than it had been since Cuba.[44] What seemed in 1979 to this champion of Yalta a matter to be resolved without excessive efforts, proved instead to be a political impossibility outside the sphere of influence granted by Yalta.

The strategy of the anti-Yalta movements in the fourth period has been defined by the following features. First, all illusions about Western intervention on behalf or in support of East European anti-Yalta movements have vanished. With the thematization of Yalta as a system, the public interpretation of its meaning along these lines has now gotten under way, especially in the writings of the Polish and Hungarian opposition. Secondly, East European anti-Yalta movements had to realize in the late seventies, and even more so in the early eighties, that Nato is in the process of gradual disintegration. West Germany, the second largest Western military power (with France standing apart), has been for almost a decade now establishing her own new anti-Yalta strategy, one which is for the time being very much on a collision course with East European anti-Yalta movements.[45] Thirdly, the explicit premise of all anti-Yalta movements today is that, at least for the time being, the revolutionary method of the Hungarian example cannot be imitated.

A quotation from Adam Michnik will advise us on the closer meaning of this new strategy:

An assessment of the current international situation requires a cool appraisal of our aspirations and capabilities, of potential losses and potential gains . . . it constitutes the central problem for all Polish strategies, including the 'long march' strategies. This strategy is based on the assumption that the ruling elite is almost chronically incapable of learning from its postwar experiences, and that the stationary war between an organized civil society and the power apparatus will last a long time. In the meantime, significant changes may take place in the USSR – changes that are difficult to predict but also difficult to count on. Regardless of such changes, Poland will remain the political focus of every Russian State . . . And the Poles will have to figure out what relations to have with any such state . . . Let us . . . remember that as a point of departure for analysis of Polish–Russian relations we might take another look *at the contents of the Yalta agreements*, which, while placing Poland in the Soviet sphere of politico-military influence, leave to the Poles the choice of their system of government. The Yalta agreement does not stipulate the rule of the PUWP – that rule is merely a consequence of terror, rigged elections, and *Stalin's violation of the agreement.*[46]

All necessary elements for understanding the new strategy of oppositional movements, outside of Poland as well as within, can be found in this extremely lucid statement. For once, the movements overtly take up the issue of Yalta as a system for a new point of departure. Michnik suggests that there can be no serious oppositional strategy without clarifying what Yalta has been and what it represents today. Further, the proposed strategy is anti-Yalta in a qualified sense. Apparently, this strategy is aiming at a compromise with the USSR, as the big power of the region. It logically follows from all strategies of compromise that Hungarian radicalism *à la* 1956 will be relegated to the background. Both socially and nationally, it remains the paradigm but it does not serve as a blueprint for any foreseeable future action. Proceeding from here, Michnik embarks on a hermeneutics of Yalta, a close reading of what was and was not included in the texts of the historical Yalta conference which, as Michnik suggests, remains valid. In the Polish view, Stalin violated the texts of Yalta. The latter had indeed provided for a 'Soviet politico-military influence' but not for the present communist governments which came to power through the terror of the Stalin era.[47]

It must by now have become abundantly clear that in our opinion, Michnik's and the Polish opposition's initial thesis is either self-delusory or 'ideological' or both. Instead the following proposition may now be formulated. As with every text, the text of Yalta too (the general framework of which the Polish opposition accepts) allows for several readings. Stalin had imposed his own reading on the region. But the text naturally may be read differently. Furthermore, Soviet leaders themselves have been criticizing several aspects of Stalin's policies. Why then would Stalin's reading of the texts of Yalta be exempt from the same criticism?

However, once we demand a re-reading of the texts of Yalta, we set in motion a long-term strategy which, in Michnik's version, has two main antagonists: the communist-dominated state and civil society. This strategy has a minimum and a maximum program. The minimum program is tantamount to the de-totalization of society, to emancipating various ways of life, the whole range of cultural activities, the institutions of civil society (above all, the institutions of education) from the ideological intervention of the state. The maximum program would result in a change in the forms of government. But not even this distant change would affect the Yalta system, the strategic interests of the USSR.

This is then nothing else but a strategy of 'self-Finlandization' of East European countries. Whatever the actual future of this strategy, which has been ingeniously, and almost simultaneously, devised by Hungarian and Polish dissidents, it nevertheless holds several advantages in its favor. It can be pursued separately in each country of the region. In fact, this strategy has already traveled a long distance in the two countries of its invention. It is also the natural strategy of the Czechoslovak opposition, one that requires the anonymous and long-term heroism of many militants but not one that would impose unbearable sufferings on the whole of the populace. It is a *modus operandi* against which the apparatuses ultimately have no other weapon save that of forcible population transfer, or put simply, mass deportations. However, the latter would require a revolutionary self-transformation of the (fairly comfortable) way of life of the apparatus. It is, further, a master plan which can be followed without secret centers and conspiratorial methods in the individual countries. And it is, finally, a blueprint which would show such deep affinities that the nations, otherwise divided by their governments and mutual chauvinistic hatreds, could recognize their common cause.

Winter 1988

NOTES

1   There are several well-documented descriptions and analyses of the Yalta conference. In terms of a traditional scholarly representation, perhaps the best of them is Diane Shaver Clemens, *Yalta* (Oxford: Oxford University Press, 1970), although one should beware of the tendency in her arguments to engage sometimes in outright Jesuitic casuistry. Cyrus L. Sulzberger, *Such a Peace: The Roots and Ashes of Yalta* (New York: Continuum, 1982) is entertaining reading,

as well as an accurate chronicle. The personal account by Edward R. Stettinius, Jr., *Roosevelt and the Russians: The Yalta Conference* (New York: Doubleday, 1949) serves as a crucial document but for obvious reasons is clearly a biased, partisan account by the then Secretary of State, which should therefore be handled with caution. The same proviso may also be offered in the case of Winston Churchill, *The Second World War*, vol. 6, *Triumph and Tragedy* (Boston: Houghton Mifflin, 1972).

An American historian, William H. McNeill gives the following account for the fact that Yalta, and not the other two meetings became the symbol of wartime summits:

At Teheran, military strategy had dominated the discussion; by the time of the Potsdam Conference, on the other hand, the relations between the Russians and the West had so hardened that there was little to be done but ratify the existing fact by agreeing to disagree. At Yalta, on the other hand, the Big Three seemed . . . to have a wider margin of choice. They met at a time when each country's post-war role was yet to be clearly formulated; at a time when it seemed possible to turn their respective policies either towards agreement or towards conflict with one another. (William H. McNeill. 'The Yalta Conference, 4–11 February 1945', in Richard Fenno Jr., ed., *The Yalta Conference* (London: D.C. Heath, 1972). p. 3.

Based on our own understanding of the events which took place at Yalta however, McNeill's position is, at the very least, open to argument. There can be cogent arguments supporting an understanding of the three meetings together serving as a continuous and loosely institutionalized form of political decision-making. In this sense, then, Yalta is only the symbolic label for what in fact was a larger political process.

2   Stettinius's defense was that the Russians had made more concessions during Yalta than the Americans, *Roosevelt and the Russians*, p.6. Bohlen appeared incomparably more skeptical during his hearing, but nevertheless maintained that the negotiations were the only course open and, as such, that the United States had therefore made the correct choice. See Charles E. Bohlen, 'Testimony concerning nomination as ambassador in Russia', in Fenno, *Yalta Conference*, pp. 135–7.

3   Chester Wilmot, 'Stalin's greatest victory', in Fenno, *Yalta Conference*. Here the historian serves as the mouthpiece of the British political class, the members of which had identical or similar feelings but were compelled to silence or at least to cautiousness by the overwhelming reality of the postwar alliance.

4   The most concise rendering of this position can be found in William Appleman Williams, 'The nightmare of depression and the vision of impotence', in Fenno, *Yalta Conference*.

5   This self-restrained but unequivocally accusatory tone is perhaps best exemplified by the political biography of Stanislaw Mikolajczyk, *The Rape of Poland* (New York: McGraw-Hill, 1948). Not the individual statements perhaps, but rather the overall general narrative of Mikolajczyk's book makes the degree of irresponsibility and lack of comprehension with which both Roosevelt and Churchill had treated the Polish question clearly evident – if this behavior is assessed from the point of view of the Polish political forces in exile. In

Mikolajczyk's barely concealed view, the subsequent results of Yalta had been presaged by the attitudes of Roosevelt and Churchill.

6 The solid roots of such illusions may be seen from the testimony of the arguably most lucid and sober realist of East European political thought, István Bibó. In his appeal to the conscience of the world after the defeat of the Hungarian revolution in early 1957 he speaks of 'repeated promises of active support' by the Western powers in case the nations of Eastern Europe were ready, as the Hungarian nation indeed was, to act on their own behalf. István Bibó, 'Magyarorszag helyzete és a világhelyzet' (The situation of Hungary – the situation of the world), 1957, in *Magyar Füzetek*, 4 (Paris, 1979), p. 143.

7 This frequently cited episode is to be found in Churchill, *Triumph and Tragedy*, pp. 196–7. One example of this one-sided assessment which identifies Yalta with the Churchill–Stalin 'percentages agreement' is to be found in Ferenc Fehér and Agnes Heller, *Hungary 1956 Revisited: The Message of a Revolution a Quarter of a Century After* (London: Allen and Unwin, 1982).

8 See for example William Henry Chamberlin, 'The Munich called Yalta', in Fenno, *Yalta Conference*.

9 The widespread existence of the Yalta myths is due in part to the initial secrecy with which the negotiations in 1945 were conducted, and in which their actual contents were later enveloped. The spreading of such myths was in this sense encouraged by Kissinger's diplomacy, whose excessive secretiveness and outright perfidy seemed to be, and to a large extent still was, the direct continuation of Yalta. Time and time again events surfaced which seemed to corroborate the most venomous of the Yalta myths. We know from the book of Zdeněk Mlynář, *Night Frost in Prague* (London: C. Hurst, 1980), p. 241, that during the 'negotiations' between Brezhnev and the abducted Dubček leadership, the former presented a letter to the Czechoslovaks originating from the pen of President Johnson which had been written in reply to Brezhnev's own letter to the President prior to the invasion of Czechoslovakia. The President, who had been advised by the General Secretary about the Soviet intention of invading Czechoslovakia, assured Brezhnev that the United States was standing by the Yalta agreements concerning Czechoslovakia and Romania, whereas to the knowledge of all historians such agreements had never existed in the first place. Therefore either Brezhnev had bluffed or there had indeed been further secret agreements and deals between the superpowers about which the world was kept in the dark.

10 Timothy Garton Ash, 'From World War to Cold War', *New York Review of Books*, 34:10 (1987), p. 45.

11 But is an *arrangement* without institutions a *system*? No doubt, one of the two antecedents of Yalta, namely the Holy Alliance, was a very proper system with regular congresses, ceremonies, documents and functionaries. Versailles, for its part, had given rise to the League of Nations. However, if we consider Yalta not as a single event but rather as the symbol for a series of congresses, then the consecutive consultations and deliberations of the Big Three constitute a more or less systematic arrangement in which the will to a world government was gradually increasing.

12 A detailed description of the American design of this new world authority can be found in John L. Snell, ed., *The Meaning of Yalta* (Baton Rouge: Louisiana University Press, 1956), pp. 14–17.

13 The highlights of this not particularly engaging, at times sardonic, at times pompous tenor comes to full voice in Stettinius's extremely servile book, *Roosevelt and the Russians*. See for example page 112 where both Stalin's contemptuous remarks about Albania and Churchill's haughty metaphor about the eagle who allows the small birds to sing but 'cares not wherefor they sang' are recorded.

14 If someone finds the term 'imperialist' or 'colonial' to be exaggerated, one should bear in mind the following quotation from Hugh Thomas's book: 'The British might have preferred to run Germany indefinitely, on the model of India: sensible officials could have managed the Germans with firmness for a generation. After all, the Indian Empire would probably soon end and there would be administrators looking for work.' Hugh Thomas, *Armed Truce: The Beginnings of the Cold War, 1945–46* (New York: Atheneum, 1987), p. 342.

15 Kissinger's own hero Metternich, an obstinate enemy of the politics of the Enlightenment while at the same time a Voltairean-skeptical rationalist, was motivated by a similar kind of rationalist conception. Metternich regarded every actor who threatened to upset his masterpiece of European equilibrium as 'revolutionary', as a dangerous subversive – this included Alexander II as well as Napoleon. (And, it should be noted, the elements of the Enlightenment as well as those of the *ancien régime* could be found in an almost identical ratio in the concept 'equilibrium'.) See Henry A. Kissinger, *A World Restored: Metternich. Castlereagh and the Problems of Peace 1812–22* (Boston: Houghton Mifflin, 1957), especially the chapter 'Metternich and the definition of the political equilibrium'.

16 'Universalist' as a term of characterization for American political (above all foreign political) behavior derives from Arthur Schlesinger Jr., 'Origins of the Cold War', in Fenno, *Yalta Conference*. We find the term adequate and indeed illuminating, but we are applying it in a considerably modified form.

17 Naturally, the American efforts to establish a democratic world order can be theoretically reduced, even when they were consistent, to creating a mere hypocritical and apologetic facade in front of the rule of capital. This would be in perfect harmony with Marx's more than problematic way of interpreting democracy as a lie. And interpretations like this can indeed be found among the revisionist Yalta analyses; see Christopher Lasch, 'The Cold War, revisited and re-visioned', in Fenno, *Yalta Conference*. But this view reduces the whole world of politics to a one-dimensional marionette theater.

18 This contradictory trend already began at Yalta, most conspicuously in the debate on Iran. The American delegation raised the issue of restoring Iran's autonomy at the conference, with a view to protecting its independence from Soviet expansionism. At the same time there was no mistake about the American delegation pushing the interests of American oil monopolies in Iran; see Diane Shaver Clemens, *Yalta*, pp. 256–7.

19 Hannah Arendt, *On Revolution* (New York: Viking, 1963). For an analysis of Arendt's conception of the French revolution and of her comparison between the

American and French models, see Ferenc Fehér, 'Freedom and the "social question" – Hannah Arendt's theory of the French revolution', *Philosophy and Social Criticism*, 12:1 (1987).

20   See Martin Kitchen, *British Policy towards the Soviet Union during the Second World War* (New York: St Martin's, 1987), p. 217.

21   More recently, writers on the issue tend to underestimate the significance of the Churchill–Stalin bargaining in Moscow. As a rule, it is presented as an inconsequential manifestation of old-time, imperial instincts on the side of Churchill. The explanation for the historians' indifference towards the episode may first be located in the undeniable fact that Stalin, while being encouraged in his drive for East European sovietization by the conversation, never paid excessive attention to the figures. Secondly, no one really understands what the exact percentages stood for. Yet the fact remains that the American administration was in part worried, in part shocked by Churchill's policies; see Stettinius, *Roosevelt and the Russians*, pp. 10–12. The talks between Stalin and Churchill and the 'percentages agreement' had in fact accelerated the American preparations for Yalta.

22   See in detail Ferenc Fehér, Agnes Heller and G. Márkus, *Dictatorship over Needs* (Oxford: Blackwell, 1983).

23   See Stettinius, *Roosevelt and the Russians*, pp. 236–7.

24   In fact it is now well known and not just a matter of speculation that Stalin had no different motivation in 1945 than he had in 1921, while spreading the Bolshevik revolution into Poland with the bayonets of the Red Army, as can be garnered from his famous remarks to Djilas. There Stalin emphasized that this is a modern war and that armies spread their own social systems with their arms. Milovan Djilas, *Conversations with Stalin*, trans. Michael B. Petrovich (New York: Harcourt and Brace, 1962), p. 47.

25   The term 'revolution' in the context of Yalta is not meant to convey 'violent social change' (or it does so only occasionally); nor does it denote events and processes which are violent *per se*. What it does denote is the radical break with the 'Yalta system', a break which may or may not adopt the form of historical drama.

26   Whenever de Gaulle made statements about Yalta, he consistently emphasized two facts. First, the 'Anglo-Saxon' powers, as he was wont to call them, actively endorsed (and not just acquiesced in) the Soviet domination of Eastern Europe. Secondly, in exchange for this endorsement, the American administration controlled not just the policies, but also the territory of its allies via Nato. See for example Charles de Gaulle, *Memoirs of Hope: Renewal and Endeavor*, trans. Terence Kilmartin (New York: Simon and Schuster, 1971), pp. 199, 226.

27   See pp. 196–221 below.

28   Surprisingly, however, the destruction of the Polish underground army proved a tougher nut than had been expected. Jakob Berman, one of Stalin's most important and repulsive Polish gauleiters mentions outright civil war in describing the situation; see Teresa Toranska, *Them: Stalin's Polish Puppets* (New York: Harper and Row, 1987), p. 272. In a like manner we learn from Khrushchev's memoirs that the Red Army had been kept in a state of full alert in the Ukraine for two years after the war to fight the nationalists and other anti-Soviet partisans; see *Khrushchev Remembers* (Boston: Little Brown, 1971), p. 224.

29 George Schöpflin, 'A kommunista hatalomátvétel fázisai Kelet-Europában' (Phases of communist takeover of power in Eastern Europe), *Magyar Füzetek*, 13 (Paris, 1984), p. 93.

30 On the problem of 'Eastern Europe' see István Bibó, 'A kelet-európai kisállamok nyomorúsága' (The misery of the small states of Eastern Europe), in *Válogatott Tanulmányok 1945–1947* (Selected Papers) (Budapest: Magvetö, 1986).

31 Thomas, *Armed Truce*, p. 237.

32 Not even Mikořajczyk, an open partisan, can deny that the social reforms aimed at the modernization of a hopelessly antiquated Poland, which were on the forefront of the communist program, divided the supporters of his Peasant Party; *Rape of Poland*, pp. 195–200.

33 We find a thorough documentation of Gomułka's early 'national communist' leanings (from the interviews with Ochab and Berman) in Toranska, *Them*; and Gomułka represented a whole trend within Polish communism. While Rajik and the co-victims of his trial in Hungary were unjustly accused of national communism by the party leaders who sent them to the gallows as agents and spies, innocence of this kind cannot be so summarily asserted about certain key members of Dimitrov's group in the Bulgarian party. And as events would later demonstrate, both the Romanian and the Albanian communists alike favored a nationally-based dictatorship.

34 András Hegedűs is the epitome of this kind of *realpolitik*. He never ceased to emphasize that Hungary sealed its fate when her government left the Warsaw Pact; see for example Zoltán Zsille and András Hegedűs, *elet egy eszme árnyékában* (Life under the Shadow of an Idea) in Zsille's personally published edition (Vienna, 1986), p. 245.

35 For Nagy's intellectual experiments with neutrality prior to the revolution, see part II below, p 107.

36 All available pieces of evidence of this planned swap have been collected and discussed in part II below.

37 In Toranska, *Them*, pp. 70–1.

38 The removal of Chervenkov in Bulgaria and later of Rákosi in Hungary were clearly concessions of this kind made by Soviet leaders to placate Tito. In all probability, they would have acted against Hoxha in a similar fashion but they found an irremovable chieftain in the Albanian General Secretary.

39 The confidential messages of the American embassy in Budapest to the State Department during the Hungarian revolution of 1956, texts which were released 25 years later under the Freedom of Information Act, conclusively prove this total incapacity of American diplomatic observers to cope with the suddenness of the revolutionary drama. We have briefly analyzed these messages in part II, see pp. 71–2.

40 Ibid.

41 Mlynář, *Night Frost*, p. 241.

42 François Fejtö describes the beginning of Romanian separatism in *A History of the People's Democracies: Eastern Europe since Stalin* (New York: Praeger, 1971), pp. 228–34. See also Jacques Lévesque, *Le Conflit Sino-Soviétique et l'Europe de l'Est* (Montreal: Presses de l'Université de Montréal, 1970).

43   An excellent account of the seizure of power by the Afghan communists, of their rift and of the collapse of the 'Titoist' regime can be found in Beverly Male, *Revolutionary Afghanistan: A Reappraisal* (London: Croom-Helm, 1982).

44   See Ken Jowitt, 'Moscow "Centre"', *Eastern European Politics and Societies*, 1:3 (1987), pp. 333–5.

45   See once again pp. 000 ff. below.

46   Adam Michnik. 'On Resistance', in *Letters from Prison and other Essays* (Berkeley: University of California Press, 1985), pp. 56–7, emphasis added. We have also corrected the word 'civilian' to 'civil'. By contrast, the leading Hungarian dissident, Miklós Haraszti, continues the attacks on the Yalta system with a vocabulary which stems from an earlier period. His argument is that if observers describe the Hungarian situation in terms of progression, they compare the situation to that of 'Eastern Europe'. However, accepting the term Eastern Europe, a concept as heavily impregnated with the connotations of power, coercion and domination as only Foucault would have it, is tantamount to the acceptance of Yalta. See 'Les charmes fanés du modèle hongrois', *Le Monde*, June 19, 1987, p. 3.

47   Nor are the Polish anti-Yalta militants alone in their interpretation of Yalta. The following statement can be found in a report by Arthur Schlesinger, Jr., on a recent historians' conference on Yalta:

> The West European scholars unitedly absolved Yalta from having caused the division of Europe. They agree that Winston Churchill and Franklin Roosevelt as realists were well aware that the Red Army would decide Eastern Europe's future. In October 1944 Churchill had conceded much of Eastern Europe to Stalin as a Soviet sphere of influence. In January 1945, shortly before departing for Yalta, Roosevelt had told a group of senators that 'the occupying forces had the power where their arms were present'. Yet, despite their bargaining disadvantage, the western leaders did their best to impede and dilute total Soviet domination and to preserve the hope of an undivided Europe. They resisted in Poland, refusing to accept the puppet Lublin government and, in the Declaration on Poland, extracted Stalin's pledge to hold 'free and unfettered elections as soon as possible'. The Declaration on Liberated Europe extended the free-election pledge to the rest of Eastern Europe. The western objective was a 'moderate' Soviet sphere of influence comparable to the American sphere of influence in the Western Hemisphere and to the British in Southern Europe. ('West European scholars absolve Yalta', *Wall Street Journal*, June 16, 1987.)

There is more than one problem with this quick absolution of Yalta by the conclave of West European scholars. First, Schlesinger's reading of the texts of Yalta as constituting a non-recognition of the Lublin Committee is slightly dubious. Here we would rather have to concur with Diane Shaver Clemens, according to whom the text should be interpreted the way Stalin and Molotov had understood it. In this reading, the passage contained two steps: recognition of the existing government, instead of the stipulation of its immediate dissolution (and the existing government was the Lublin Committee); then the transformation of this existing, and *de jure* already recognized body into another, more extended one. The latter duly occurred when Stalin preserved his existing power structure and added a few Peasant Party ministers to it. If this reading is correct, Roosevelt and Churchill even made formal concessions to Stalin. The second problem is that it is difficult to understand how politicians who had, or ought to have had, some idea of the character of Stalin's regime could possibly believe that abandoning countries to Stalin's sphere of influence might ever mean anything else but the imposition of Stalin's methods on them, pledges notwithstanding. Thirdly, the term 'sphere of influence' which Schlesinger freely uses in connection with the American foreign policy, a term the universalist American diplomacy until Kissinger had always vehemently rejected, denotes the *de facto* transition from the universalist dream to an active and shared domination of the world which is, according to our reading, the underlying concept of 'Yalta'. If, therefore, Schlesinger's vocabulary is correct, the spirit of Yalta has won even if the system of Yalta has collapsed.

Part II

The First Assault:
Hungary, 1956

2

The Impact on the World

THE HUNGARIAN REVOLUTION AND SUPERPOWER POLITICS

The decade following the end of the Second World War – the classic era of the Cold War – was dominated by two apparently totally contradictory, but functionally almost equivalent, conceptions regarding the genesis, the character, and the prospects of longevity of the communist-ruled regimes of Eastern Europe. The first viewpoint stated with an air of doctrinaire superiority – and this was the dominant tone, particularly in the American press – that all East European and Asian communist systems were simply Soviet exports, and that if they did not enjoy Soviet military and secret police presence and support they would automatically collapse. Yet subsequent events of the most varied character and value content in Yugoslavia, China, Albania and other countries testified to an infinitely more complex situation.

Parallel to this theory, though diametrically opposite in content, there emerged an equally important, if less publicized, conception of the Cold War. This was the belief in the indestructibility of communist systems from within.

The Hungarian revolution of 1956 eliminated for ever this idea of the indestructibility of the Soviet regimes from within. This was the first consequence of the Hungarian revolution which can truly and without exaggeration be called world historical. It provided a number of important lessons – lessons all the more important because *both* theories outlined above coincided as far as their practical function was concerned. Both of them catered, even if from opposite angles, for the ideological and practical demands of the Cold War. Both political prejudices were firmly rooted in the *system of Yalta*. The 'meaning of Yalta' is still a hotly debated issue among historians. Our interpretation of the event and 'the system' appeared in part I.

It was against this general world constellation that the Hungary of 1956 revolted. There was some vague knowledge of the Yalta decisions within the politically unskilled elements of the population, but their full impact was not immediately visible in the peace treaties concluded between 1945 and 1947 for instance, in the Hungarian peace treaty of Paris, 1947). In addition, in the period prior to the communist takeover there existed in Eastern Europe a popular myth and a highly questionable and ambiguous attitude of the liberal parties of the region, and conjointly these two factors contributed to blurring the clear vision of large sections of the population. The popular myth consisted of the idea that the Western powers, now in an unassailable position of economic and military technological superiority, had only been 'temporarily outsmarted' by the Soviet leadership, and that very soon the balance of power would be restored to adequate and proper proportions. Yugoslavia in 1948 seemed to be bearing out this interpretation. Without thorough strategic studies the 'man in the street' thought that it was mostly (if not solely) the American nuclear umbrella which sheltered Yugoslavia from Stalin's invasion. (We would add that the determination of the Titoist leadership and its popular support should be regarded as being of nearly equal weight.) The ambiguity, if not outright cowardice, of the liberal parties in Eastern Europe lay in the fact that their professional strata were vaguely aware of the hidden dimensions of the Yalta–Potsdam iceberg, but remained silent and behaved as if everything happened according to parliamentary rules. In spite of a growing desperation, the popular myth of this equilibrium soon to be restored by the Western powers persisted, and was projected into the period subsequent to the communist takeover. Let us repeat: it was Hungary 1956 *alone* that debunked and annihilated it. The North Korean military adventure had undoubtedly questioned the general lines of division drawn by the victorious superpowers, but it did not question – indeed, it rather confirmed on both sides – the very rule of the superpowers. The riots in East Berlin in 1953 were a famine-inspired revolt that failed to reach the necessary level of self-articulation that would call into question anything of the existing system of world domination. The same can be said for Poznan in 1956. The Polish October presented a far more complex case; but given what seemed *then* to be an exceptional piece of historical luck – namely, that a reform communist leadership could successfully channel these forces – the movement remained primarily concerned with the inner structural tensions of Poland, and showed an increasing, though hostile, indifference towards world events. But, on October 23, Hungary exploded in the face of all those who in their boundless wisdom had created the Yalta system of superpower domination, and set a question mark next to it which has subsequently only increased in prominence and portent.

In a strange way, this explosion was achieved by the double character of the Hungarian revolution. It was a radical transformation eliminating overnight the seemingly immovable edifice of the Stalinist regime, *and* a collective offer of historical compromise by almost a whole nation. While this first aspect is generally known, and forms part of the popular mythology, nearly everyone except certain experts is ignorant of the second. It is therefore time to shed some light on the wisdom of this revolution.

At its heretical and 'counterrevolutionary' height, when the 'traitorous Nagy government' decided to leave the Warsaw Pact, Hungary had neutrality as its topmost demand. There was no political force worthy of the name in the havoc of those days which would have suggested that Hungary join Nato. This may be called 'counterrevolutionary cunning' by the official chroniclers of the East – a cunning which shrewdly took into account the limits of Soviet patience – but, even if this were so, the same shrewd calculation has been working perfectly well for 35 years in Finland, to the utmost satisfaction of that same Soviet leadership. And the content of the Hungarian compromise, from the perspective of foreign policy, was precisely the 'Finlandization' of Hungary. The offer of compromise has to be understood literally. Nagy's second government repeatedly and officially assured the Soviet leaders of its intention to remain outside all military pacts and to sustain peaceful and preferably friendly relations with the Soviet Union.

But of more importance than this was the strange event that took place in the early hours of November 4, the first day of the second (and final) Soviet invasion, in the Hungarian parliament – a building occupied by the Soviet army and abandoned by the ministers of the Nagy government, who were mostly seeking refuge, in vain, in the embassy of Yugoslavia. It was at this moment that István Bibó, a man unknown to all except the élite, joining Nagy's government only a day earlier, and perhaps the greatest postwar leftist (non-doctrinaire socialist) political theorist of Eastern Europe, formulated, in his capacity as state minister of the last Nagy government, a final statement as 'the sole representative of the only legitimate Hungarian government left in the parliamentary building'. Bibó states:

Hungary does not intend to follow an anti-Soviet policy. Moreover, it is her intention to coexist in a community of free East European nations whose objective is to establish their lives on the basis of the principles of freedom, justice, and a society free of exploitation. In front of the world I reject the slanderous statement that the glorious Hungarian revolution was a hotbed of fascist or anti-Semitic escapades; in the struggle, the entire populace participated without class or religious discriminations.

Moving and magnificent was the humane and wise attitude of a people in revolt – an attitude always capable of distinction, and which was turned alone against the oppressive foreign army and the squads of internal myrmidons . . . I appeal to the Hungarian people not to regard the occupying army or the puppet government eventually created by it as lawful authority, and to turn against it with all the means of a *passive* resistance . . . I am not in a position to order armed resistance. I joined the government only a day ago; I am not yet informed about the military situation. It would be utterly irresponsible on my part to dispose of the blood of the Hungarian youth. The people of Hungary have spilt enough blood to prove their dedication to the cause of justice and freedom for the world. *This time it is the turn of the world powers* to demonstrate the strength of the principles incorporated in the Declaration of the United Nations and the strength of the freedom-loving peoples of the world. I appeal to the great powers and to the United Nations for a courageous and wise decision on behalf of the freedom of my subjugated country . . . God save Hungary.[2]

This seemingly old-fashioned text, which must sound somewhat Risorgimento to the historically trained ear, was in fact a wise, circumspect, manifold and realistic document. It was by far one of the greatest constitutive acts of statesmanship in postwar Eastern Europe, and already contained all the elements of Bibó's 'Draft of a compromise solution of the Hungarian question' – this most important document written by him during the following five days and later smuggled out of the country. The 'Draft' presented a compromise to the Soviet Union of a type that would have resulted in a course far freer from uprisings and revolutions.[3]

The first three points of the 'Draft' provide a résumé of the immediate situation after November 4: the pretexts (of restoring order) given by the Soviet army to legitimise its intervention, and the obviously false promises of the Kádár government to 'negotiate' the immediate withdrawal of the Soviet army with the Soviet government as soon as order was restored (as if they had a mandate at all to negotiate with their masters). The fourth point, however, must be quoted in full:

It has become impossible to maintain socialism in Hungary *in the form of a one-party system* because the appeal to the Soviet army to intervene, in the first case made by the MDP [the pre-revolutionary name of the Communist Party] and in the second case by the Socialist Workers' Party [the name of the Kádárist organization], annihilated the reputation of both parties and any governments eventually relying on them. Without a genuine multi-party system, having real authority, Hungary cannot be governed, the less so as the only communist who has preserved his reputation before the Hungarian people, Imre Nagy, has also accepted the multi-party system.[4]

The fifth point comprehensively covers the Soviet fears of a Hungary that could become an obedient tool in the hands of Western power centers, but it solidly rejects the view that the new coalition government could not have eliminated such threats to Soviet security. The morally and politically crucial sixth and seventh points, which amount to a sublime self-defense before 'History' of a butchered and slandered revolution, read as follows:

A blocking of the road to an orthodox capitalist, anti-communist and arch-conservative restoration must not be a concern restricted to the Soviet Union and the communists, but it should also be a goal of the Hungarian youth, working class and army personnel who fought out the revolution, paid for it with their blood, and who in the main are not communist but overwhelmingly call themselves socialist. It would be morally inadmissible for the beneficiaries of a freedom won by the blood of revolutionaries to be forces of restoration placed in power by the votes of older generations. It ought to be considered as well that such a reactionary turn transforming Hungary – a nation located amongst communist countries – into a fifth column of the West would, on the one hand, become a constant stimulus to further aggressive plans and, on the other, a menacing sign for the freedom-loving communists of other people's democracies in planning the liberalization of their own regimes. By contrast, *a solution which combined socialist achievement with the guarantees provided by free institutions* would set an example which would stimulate imitation.[5]

What does Bibó mean, and what does he *not* mean, by 'compromise'? The text itself, with its moral pathos emphasizing the primogeniture of the socialist (even if not communist) younger generations, of the creators for a short while of Hungarian freedom, leaves no doubt at all that the maintenance of what by habit we now call 'democratic socialism' was not part of a formula dictated by compromise but a sincere conviction of Bibó's. Further, his broadly based considerations both take account of and try to promote the whole process of de-Stalinization sparked off by the Twentieth Congress of the Soviet Communist Party. It is precisely by virtue of such a broad political foundation that they could indeed become a draft for a *compromise* solution – something which the Soviet leadership could at least have considered (if it had wanted to) as a basis of negotiation. But, speaking from the Soviet point of view, these considerations meant more than just 'Finlandization': they went beyond what amounted to strict neutrality, and in effect meant governments whose existence would be endorsed by the Soviet Union, with certain mild restrictions on the press but an otherwise unlimited liberal market system and political pluralism. Bibó's principles called for an (actual or virtual) referendum creating an *explicit national consensus* on which the compromise could be based.

Bibó's first point makes it very clear that the basis of the new legitimacy is not the 1949 sham constitution – a Soviet and Rákosi dictation – but the day of the revolution: October 23, 1956. As a result, the last legitimate Hungarian government is Nagy's second cabinet. The second point, the settling of the international status of a future Hungary, is one of the most interesting parts of the whole document, and absolute and irrefutable proof of its realism and willingness to compromise.

2 (Alternative A): A solution of foreign policy would be that Hungary leaves the Warsaw Pact but remains part of the consultative agreement dealing with European peace and security, provided that Yugoslavia joins it under the same conditions.
   (Alternative B): A solution of foreign policy would be that Hungary leaves the Warsaw Pact and signs a bilateral agreement with the Soviet Union.[6]

Since we are chiefly concerned here with the impact of the Hungarian revolution on the general strategy of the West, and with the overall question of compromise, we shall only mention that points 3, 4 and 5 constitutionally guarantee the personal safety and career prospects of communists who would lose their power monopoly, and regulate the constitutional framework of a new Hungary, making it very explicit that the nationalization of the main 'forces of production' and the agrarian revolution of 1945–6 must not be repudiated, while at the same time, and *for the first time in any country's history*, making the self-managed direction of factories a constitutional stipulation.

This somewhat lengthy digression was introduced to prove that the Hungarian revolution was a revolt against a world constellation created by the Yalta agreement – a revolt which, with its readiness to compromise, offered one single and never recurring opportunity for the West to redesign its whole postwar strategy and to establish with honor a situation equally beneficial both for itself and for the nations of Eastern Europe.

Instead there obtained an ever widening and unbridgeable gap between the strident propaganda and the solemn promises made earlier to 'restore the freedom of Eastern Europe', and the absolute impotence – even reluctance – which followed the Hungarian revolution (apart from the later rhetorical exercises in the United Nations which did not even diminish the number of executions). The result was a major loss of face for the Western powers, a second moral Munich. Hammarskjöld performed endless maneuvers to block discussion of the appeal by the Nagy government and, with regard to the United States, Miklós Molnár convincingly states that 'no diplomatic measures, no pressure, no offer of mediation revealed any desire on the part of the Americans to support Nagy's Government; there was even a slight decrease of interest from the moment when Hungary declared its neutrality!'[7] And Britain, the offended partner, spelled out this feeling. Sir Anthony Eden, himself responsible for the ill-timed Suez action, wrote concerning the procrastination over the Hungarian question in the United Nations:

Five days passed without any further council meeting upon Hungary, despite repeated attempts by ourselves and others to bring one about. The United States representative was reluctant and voiced his suspicion that we were urging the *Hungarian Situation to direct attention from Suez*. The United States Government appeared in no hurry to move. Their attitude provided a damaging contrast to the alacrity they were showing in arraigning the French and ourselves![8]

But as the Hungarian (and later other East European) masses very quickly got the message – or, rather, the lack of any response – this corroborates what we have said earlier: that the Hungarian revolution was a revolt against *all* signatories of the Yalta agreement. Let us quote Bibó again, this time from his essay, 'The situation of Hungary and the international situation', written a few months later and only a few weeks before he was imprisoned for many years.

The situation of Hungary became a scandal of the world. *The Hungarian situation is a scandal, first of all, of the Western world.* For ten years now the Western world has cried: 'The East European countries have not by themselves chosen a form of government based on a one-party system, but have had it introduced through the interference of the Soviet Union, and they are not satisfied with it.' The Western countries have been so informing the population in the hope that sooner or later they will have to create a new form of government. They have not promised the East European nations that they will launch a nuclear war on their behalf, nor have they appealed to them to initiate inconsiderate uprisings. But so much has indeed been included in these assurances that – provided it becomes possible through the international constellation and the resolute attitude of these very nations – the Western world will deploy its whole economic, political and moral weight in order to put the cause of these nations on the agenda and resolve it in a way satisfactory for them. *The Hungarian revolution has created both the preconditions and the legitimacy of such a global bargaining* . . . If this is not enough, what else would be needed to impose a conference on the world powers which would bargain, together with guarantees satisfactory for the Soviet Union, for the independence and freedom of Hungary? Instead, what is happening is a theatrical debate on the Hungarian situation in front of the plenary session of the UNO, with solemn and ineffectual resolutions . . . even though everyone has always known and knows now that the UNO as an instrument of peace is only as valuable as the power and the determination of the great powers participating in it . . . But what fails here is not the UNO but the political responsibility and the moral mission of the great powers.[9]

What are the actual political facts that validate Bibó's view (as well as our thesis) that the Hungarian revolution really did create the conditions (and the justification) for a global renegotiation of the Yalta situation? First, the Soviet Union was in a deep power crisis after Stalin's death, and at the time of the Hungarian revolution this crisis had not been even temporarily solved. Indeed, the revolution intensified this internecine strife. No Western Philbys were needed to know this. Secondly, the United States was in an exceptionally good moral and political situation. America had not participated in that epilogue to French and British imperial escapades, the Suez campaign. Her prestige in Asia and Africa was therefore still very high, and she would have received, as a non-colonialist global power with a then unquestioned technological superiority, the support of a large number of non-aligned countries for her politics (a situation soon to change), had she tried to negotiate the proportions and, in particular, the methods of world government. Finally, whereas in the case of any intervention in German, Polish or other East European affairs, where the governments in question – governments still relying on raw power and with no real legitimacy at all – could have rejected a Western approach as 'interference with their internal affairs', this could not have been so with Hungary. Hungary, with a government as legitimate as any after the communist takeover, pleaded for an international collective negotiation. The American strategy has often been described as dilettantish. No repetition of the statement is needed. It will suffice to mention that in the late 1930s and early 1940s the United States had one ambassador in Moscow (Davies) who made reports to the President to the effect that Stalin's purges were fair trials of conspirators and possibly spies, and another in London (Kennedy) who in 1940 wrote off the British capacity for resistance and instead suggested direct talks with Hitler. It is more rewarding to scrutinize the aims and objectives of this policy.

To begin with, the American policy-makers regarded Britain as their future main competitor in the post-Hitler period. This attitude was a strange compound of naïve but candid liberal feelings and anti-colonialist pride – the self-assurance that the United States was destined for a worldwide mission. It also exhibited traditional anti-British resentment and an overwhelming amount of expansionist egoism. But, whatever the motivation, the selection of the main target was totally mistaken; and this misguided tack made the leading American policy-makers totally blind to the *real* power proportions. They systematically underestimated the strength of their real competition, Soviet and Chinese communism, and equally systematically overestimated the strength of their allies. The grossest example of their wishful thinking (about which Churchill expressly warned them) was their blind belief in Chiang Kai-shek's military and political reserves and future chances. They also suffered from the typical American disease: the pragmatic overestimation of technological superiority, which they partly believed unchallengeable (and had a very bitter snub in 1949 when the existence of the Soviet nuclear weapon became known to them), and to some extent viewed as a universal remedy for complex social situations. In this respect, the British with their century-old colonial experience were far more realistic. Finally, even if they boasted about not being *ideologues* or fanatics, but down-to-earth pragmatists of a good traditional homemade style, the creators of the American strategy introduced a misplaced 'Hegelian dialectic' into their plans. They believed that unfreedom can serve the purposes of freedom; that liberal democracies can be effectively defended (without being irreparably compromised) by the most illiberal tyrannies. It was this complex in its entirety that was called the 'free world'. The road leading to the Vietnam defeat started at the moment they decided upon sponsoring several cliques of corrupt and cruel officers as allegedly effective safeguards against communism.

To give a brief account of the pros and cons of this policy, in all fairness it must be said that for all its crucial and inherent weaknesses it was still a better Western strategy than the British produced, if for no other reason than that it did involve the nuclear deterrent (an absolute prerogative for some time), which the British strategy did not. As mentioned earlier, we have no doubt whatsoever that Stalin's surprising tolerance towards Yugoslav independence was mainly (even if not exclusively) due to the American nuclear umbrella. Though undoubtedly relying on powerful internal forces, it was American patronage that played a crucial role in the creation of the Japanese parliamentary/liberal system – a fundamental, new and positive development in Asia. If we add that this American competition thoroughly undermined the chances for survival of the British empire, then the nations of Asia do not finish with a totally negative balance in their transactions with the United States. The chief fault of these ideas was, of course, the misconceived and arrogant idea of *pax americana* – a policy with the explicit purpose of American world domination. This was both a reactionary strategy and one that, for a number of historical reasons, could not hope to produce the expected results anyway. The main loser in all this was Eastern Europe – a region where American propaganda daily promised 'freedom', in which it planted hopes, and for which it did not lift a finger.[10]

But the Hungarian revolution offered a real opportunity to eliminate certain structural weaknesses in the American strategy. Stalin, a man with whom fruitful negotiations were impossible after the war (whereas earlier – as his pact with Hitler demonstrates – he could be a flexible and even humble partner), was now dead. His heirs, deeply involved in infights, gave material proof of their limited readiness to talk. In 1955, after very long and loud propaganda to the contrary, they consented to the separate handling of Austrian neutrality, earlier bound up by them with the German peace treaty. As we have repeatedly mentioned, Hungary provided a legitimate excuse for the Americans to become negotiators of goodwill in this complex situation. This would have provided for them (and also for the world) the following benefits. First, at least one great power would have lived up to its word and its promises, and this by itself might have steadied an already very shaky United Nations. It would have presented the Americans as peacemakers, not as cold warriors, and would have undoubtedly eased the tension of the postwar decade. It might also have opened a new era in world government – an era that did not witness daily the threat of nuclear confrontation. Finally, the reunification of Germany could have been attempted.

THE SOVIET INTERNAL FIGHT AFTER STALIN AND THE HUNGARIAN REVOLUTION

The impact of the Hungarian revolution on the *Soviet Union* can only be understood if we consider, both logically and historically, the various strategies with which the Soviet leadership grappled between the time of Stalin's death and the actual outbreak of the Hungarian revolution.

The turning of the tide in Hungary was signalled by a swift, unexpected and dramatic event: the people learned overnight in June 1953 that the central committee of the party (in a session not even the resolution of which was published) had appointed Imre Nagy, the scarcely known Minister of Natural Taxation and former Minister of Agriculture, as Prime Minister. Nagy's parliamentary speech on 'new governmental policy' (to which we shall return shortly) revealed him as a leader rather than a second man, and when the frightened party apparatus hysterically demanded guidelines Rákosi addressed them a week later at a Budapest party organization meeting and gave an 'interpretation' of Nagy's speech that in plain Hungarian was equivalent to a counterprogram. This much is generally known, but the reasons for such a drastic leadership reshuffle are less clear, and an explanation is called for, given that Hungary was the only country where events led to such change. The Soviet trend was to the contrary, and was so marked that even Ulbricht, with his spectacular fiasco of the Berlin uprising only a week before Nagy was secretly appointed in Moscow, was able to save his head and his position.

In looking at the dramatic summoning to Moscow in June 1953 of Rákosi, Farkas, Gerő, and Dobi, who were all members of the Hungarian Political Bureau, and of Szalai (Rákosi's secretary) and Nagy (the unexpected companion who was *then not* part of this political body), the most plausible account of this event stems from *Nagy's Memoranda* collected in *On Communism* (1957). The story amounts to the following. There seemed to be a far-reaching consensus (with the exception of perhaps, Molotov and Kaganovich) between the otherwise warring factions of the Soviet Political Bureau regarding the necessity of implementing changes in Hungary, including a spectacular leadership reshuffle. The Soviet leadership was outraged by the Hungarian situation, and Khrushchev is quoted as saying that, without changes, Rákosi would be 'chased away with pitchforks from Hungary'.[11]

The same source mentions Beria's statement that Rákosi intended to be the first Jewish king in Hungary. Khrushchev seems also to have attacked the degree of power concentrated in Rákosi's hands (he was at that time both General Secretary and Prime Minister). If we finally add that Nagy's 'new policy speech' leaves no doubt about his (at least partially) 'Malenkovite' consumerist intentions, it is easy to imagine – an idea positively confirmed by Nagy in the *Memoranda* – that Malenkov was also instrumental in Nagy's promotion. The above remark by Khrushchev, which has a ring of plausibility, also gives some clue as to the reasons for the reshuffle. The 'pitchforks' indicate the danger of a peasant uprising, and Hungary was indeed on the brink of an agricultural collapse – a situation about which the Soviet leadership must have had some knowledge, considering that it was to the

Soviet Union (and to the Soviet Union alone) that the Hungarian leaders must have turned for immediate aid. It is also widely accepted that Nagy himself had kept one unidentified member of the Soviet presidium informed of the coming agrarian catastrophe. In the immediate aftermath of Berlin, and of the Pilzen riot, during which the portraits of Masaryk and Beneš had appeared in the ranks of the demonstrators, the last thing the Soviet leaders wanted was a further mutiny caused by famine. And so, reluctantly, they resolved upon the first fateful decision of their new collective rule.

However, the effects of this decision were beyond their immediate control, and raised totally unexpected problems for them. The 'new policy speech' was an event unprecedented in the history of communism. Here was a surprisingly sincere and outspoken statement condemning not single mistakes and occasional errors but the overall political strategy of an entire period. It was delivered by a man not responsible for the actions condemned therein (especially not for the crimes), and in effect became – without, of course, using Stalin's name – the first de-Stalinizing speech. It was not the usual Stalinist trick of making conciliatory gestures and false promises in order to defuse tension. It immediately opened up new social channels and provided opportunities for new lifestyles. Peasants could leave the kolkhozes (collective farms) they had been forced into (an unheard-of liberalization), an accelerated industrial strategy of producing elementary consumer goods was set in motion, and the occupants of internment camps were released. This final step evidenced an absolutely fundamental part of Nagy's policy: his determination to put an end to the rule of terror, the first show of which was the public admission of the existence of this very rule. Finally, certain 'nationalist' overtones indicated a receptiveness towards 'national communism'. In its entirety, the 'new policy speech' meant that the Hungarian genie was out of the bottle, and it had become a *Soviet* internal problem of the first order.

In February 1955, Malenkov was ousted from the post of prime minister, his politics of an accelerated growth of light industry (in order to produce certain essential consumer goods that were totally lacking) being branded as a rightist deviation; and somewhat more than a month later, during the March meeting of the Hungarian Central Committee, the same fate befell Imre Nagy. The connection between the two events was too obvious to escape anyone, but we have factual evidence from the same source – namely, from Imre Nagy, who had told the story to his closest friends – of the causes of the turn. 'Prior to the meeting of the Soviet Central Committee [which was to brand Malenkov's policy as Bukharinist] a Hungarian delegation had appeared before the Soviet presidium in Moscow. The date of this confrontation is in doubt, but appears to have been in the first half of January 1955.' Once again, just as in June 1953, heavy accusations were made, but this time not against Rákosi, but against Imre Nagy. Nagy was reproached first of all for the economic failures of the New Course: the setback in industrial production, the collapse of most of the agricultural collectives, chaos in foreign trade, and hopeless indebtedness. All these were fields where the Prime Minister had very little control; the accusations were addressed to the wrong person. *There were also accusations of a different kind, more general in nature: unrest in the country, formation of factions and cliques in the Party, open activity of the 'enemy', too many liberties permitted to anti-Party and counterrevolutionary elements.*[12]

In the main, the content of this dramatic encounter comes as no great surprise to either expert or layman. But one aspect of it sheds light on the fact that the 'Malenkovite' policy was not a one-way street. It not only came as a 'suggestion' from Moscow and found its adequate agent in Nagy, but things happened the other way round as well. The implementer of moderate changes turned out to be dangerously radical (this view is incorporated in the charges stressed by us), and his radicalism influenced negatively the position of his main supporter in Moscow. This is specifically stated by the chronicler.

Malenkov's star was already in decline; for this reason he now showed much accommodation towards the views of his colleagues, and was willing to pose as spokesman, on behalf of the Presidium, in denouncing the Hungarian Prime Minister. *Malenkov had also been accused of endangering, by his economic and foreign policy, the orderly development of the People's Democracies.* In attacking Nagy, he had the opportunity to correct his mistakes.[13]

In our view, this is an irrefutable corroboration (via the witness, Nagy himself) of what we have assumed from the outset: that both the events leading to the Hungarian revolution and its actual outbreak had decisively influenced the Soviet internal power struggle.

Nor were the Soviet leaders, slowly sizing up their chosen man, totally unfounded in their concerns. Unlike Malenkov, the Hungarian premier combined four elements in his policy: an acceleration in the production of consumer goods; the transformation of several traditional Soviet institutions (especially in the field of agriculture); a demand for the rehabilitation of all Stalinist victims (years before Khrushchev's 'secret speech'); and another totally unprecedented gesture – an open alliance with representatives of the 'thaw' and, first of all, with certain dissenting intellectuals. All this could be a more than instructive parable, as well as providing Malenkov's enemies with a basis for accusations about where this policy would lead.

From the end of 1955 onwards, Hungary in general, and the ever-strengthening Nagy group in particular, became direct challenges and an incessant problem for the whole system of Soviet societies. During 1956 it seemed that the Soviet leaders were fighting a losing battle, constantly arriving with fatal delays at the battle scene. Moreover, for the first time since Trotsky, a near-blatant factional activity had appeared in a communist country – a constant and quasi-public pressure on the leading organs of the party in the form of an alternative program. The Soviet leaders made consistently belated moves. They were resolved upon the 'secret speech' read by Khrushchev at the Twentieth Congress of the Soviet Communist Party (which in Hungary had lost all secrecy within two days), but immediately after it tried to save Rákosi, the one person who had been compromised up to his neck in the murders of the Stalinist era just condemned. When they finally sacrificed him, their choice of replacement fell on Gerő, a man hardly less responsible, and hardly more popular. To this, from Poznan onwards, not only the fact of the 'Polish thaw' had been added, but the interference of the Polish cause with the Hungarian – the increasing consciousness of *tua res agitur* on both sides.

Isaac Deutscher's analysis of the possible alternatives of Soviet development in his *Russia after Stalin*, made immediately after Stalin's death and apparently a spectacular example of successful political prediction, was, in our view, totally false. Deutscher trumped up three alternatives and tied them in with three names. The first was a return to Stalinism pure and simple, and the 'natural' candidate for this avenue was Beria; the second was military dictatorship or Bonapartism, perhaps with Marshal Zhukov at its head; and the third was reform, which at that time was naturally linked with the name of Malenkov, not Khrushchev. The very early coup in which the Political Bureau simply had its most dangerous colleague killed; later, Zhukov's somewhat increased, though very short-term, political role; and, finally, Khrushchev's reformism following Malenkov's elimination – a volte-face in which Khrushchev 'snatched', as it were, many elements of Malenkov's politics: all these seemed to support Deutscher totally. But this was only apparently so. The following objections can be made to Deutscher's tripartite division of future alternatives. First, we shall argue that a return to Stalinism pure and simple was only a logical possibility. It was in every way a social impossibility except in the imminent danger of war. Secondly, in our view (and here we can only state it, not argue it in detail), Bonapartism or a military dictatorship was then, with a fairly underdeveloped armaments production, not even a logical possibility. Thirdly, 'reform' is too vague a category to represent a concrete option. We have to specify what sorts of reforms (in the plural) are meant by it. The Hungarian revolution had to grapple with very different alternatives from those proposed by Deutscher.

In what follows we delineate four options between which Soviet policy vacillated for the three years between 1953 and 1956. It was obvious that something ought to be done, given the tensions of which the Soviet leaders were daily informed in confidential papers, but when it came to practical steps none of them wanted to admit the feasibility of the Hegelian dictum that, in order to *change* something, *something* must be changed. They frantically strove to defuse the tensions *and* keep everything as it had been, and it happened only in the confused infights between factions, the frequent volte-faces that introduced overnight brand-new political personalities to a surprised population, and particularly in the dialogue with a popular dissatisfaction imposed on them for the first time since the civil war that a politics of a *limited reform*, otherwise called Khrushchevism, was forged. It is not a view which is a result of our national bias, but, we believe, an objective historical assessment, that this Hungarian rebellion, which could be neither halted nor retarded by any type of trick, played a constant and crucial role in the 'education' of the Soviet leaders, both in a positive and in a negative sense.

The first option of an early détente, in complete contrast to Deutscher's assumption, and according to mounting evidence, can be connected with Beria. It consisted of quick and spectacular gestures of inner liberalization and/or 'Finlandization'. It seems to be a fact that the exposure of the 'Jewish doctors' plot' – the first public humiliation of the MVD, the Ministry of the Interior with its State Security police – was Beria's personal revenge on the functionaries of his former realm. During the last two years of Stalin's life, when Beria was already on the list of a new purge and virtually divorced from the organs of state security, these people had collected 'material' against him. We have seen him in his capacity as a supporter of Nagy against Rákosi, and the unsubstantiated rumor that he simply wished to 'sell out' the Soviet occupation zone of Germany to the Western powers had been persistently circulating in the well-informed areas of Eastern Europe.[14] But there were two problems with Beria, each of them sufficient to rule out his role as a 'redeemer'. He was, despite any temporary dissociation from the 'organs', the continuator of Yeshov's 'work', in both the popular and (what is more important) the official imagination. His roots in the secret police system were too deep to allow anyone to be convinced of his goodwill. But, secondly, and precisely for this reason, he 'overdid' what would have been immediately necessary for the apparatus. His sudden improvisations, lacking coherence and strategical conception, really did endanger the bases of domination of the Soviet apparatus. What he did perform during the short period of time that his other 'liberalizing' colleagues allowed him in fact contributed to the destabilization of a tyrannical system the stability of which he had worked at building up without the slightest hesitation at its human cost.

The second option was hallmarked by the name of Malenkov (whose program was partly snatched later, when he had already been overthrown, by Khrushchev), and consisted of very limited measures of an exclusively economic liberalization, mostly along the lines of favoring light industry (producing consumer goods) to heavy industry (the more accelerated development of which was an alleged 'law' of the 'construction of socialism').

However, for two reasons, Malenkov fought a losing battle from the beginning. The first was in part conditioned by accidental factors. This man, who in the days subsequent to Stalin's death had both the position of a (first) secretary of the central committee and that of prime minister, for reasons which are not yet satisfactorily clear let himself be maneuvered into the acceptance of the prime ministership alone, and from there tried to impose economic policy reforms on the party. An old-time apparatchik, he ought to have known better. In a Soviet society, where the party is indeed sovereign, this was no way to manage affairs. Malenkov's political fate was sealed.

Yet deeper still there was another factor, recognized by no one at the time. The social crisis pervading Stalin's system was so entrenched, and it had such severe effects on both the general social structure and international affairs, that it could in no way be solved with shallow consumerist measures. And to see what kind of a social reformer we have in Malenkov one fact will suffice. In early December 1956, Malenkov made a secret visit to Budapest, and the *next day* the Central Workers' Council, the brain and the headquarters of the workers' overwhelmingly socialist resistance to the Kádár government, was outlawed.[15]

The third option was the policy of the hardliners, the option described by Deutscher as that of returning to – in fact, rather upholding the continuity with – Stalinism 'pure and simple'. These people *apparently* had the strongest chance of success. To begin with, they had the great historical names. While a surprised world was still learning how to pronounce the name of the Ukrainian first secretary, Molotov, for instance, had already been Communist number two for decades internationally. They believed they could rely on the sympathy or, rather, what is the substitute for this in Byzantine power games, the interest of the majority of the apparatus, and their proposal seemed to be the safe way, the path that history endorsed.

However, even in Stalin's lifetime, immediately after the victory, the whole ideology of 'capitalist encirclement' – an ideology supplying an apparent legitimation and a psychological background to the terror – collapsed. Stalin's strategy of constant and self-repeating cycles of purges had outlived itself, and had lingered for some time because this type of regime can only be changed with the removal of its symbolic personal incarnation. And if a terrorist élite cannot even themselves be convinced of the absolute necessity of total suppression, or if they lose the conviction for it (and there are many signs that this was the case with the Soviet apparatus after the war), a policy of terror becomes historically dysfunctional. On top of this, there was no longer any 'social space' for Stalinism in the Soviet Union. By this we mean that Stalinism was roughly equal to the 'original accumulation' of industrial relations (to use Preobrazhensky's slipshod term, which simply means that costs, human or technical, did not count, only growth) *plus* a simple and forcible transfer of the necessary manpower from the villages. But for internal economic reasons there was no longer the rationale – and much less the opportunity – for these policies to be continued in the 1950s. Finally, it was obvious that the apparatus and, in a strange way, the Stalinist 'anti-party conspirators' – Molotov, Kaganovich et al. – too, were no longer prepared to live under a rule that meant constant self-decimation. In short, what appeared to be the strongest faction was in fact the weakest: a group without any kind of policy recommendation and without any response to new historical exigencies other than triumphant jubilation when one of the other factions failed or suffered a fiasco. Thriving on their colleagues' numerous blunders, when they themselves initiated concerted action they were soundly defeated, even if not purged.

The fourth option was the consolidation of a structure in crisis, conservative or liberal, but in both cases paternalistic. Here, three initial remarks are necessary. First, given the Soviet leaders' abhorrence of any actual change, this faction advocating consolidation (which meant, by implication, that they admitted the *fact* of the crisis) must have had great difficulty in finding its identity. Even when it did, it concealed it behind ideological double-talk about 'continuity in discontinuity' and the like. Secondly, there is quite a controversy in Western Soviet historiography on the matter of whether Khrushchev was a willing and, as it were, a hidden agent of such a reform, donning the necessary protective guise for quite some time; or whether, on the contrary, he was an aspirant to the role of a new Stalin, and that it was only the interplay of historical circumstances that forced him to play, when he did, the role of benefactor and liberator. There is no need for us to take a stand in this debate: it suffices to state that the mask grew to Khrushchev's face, basically through his being credited by the world with the authorship of the de-Stalinizing 'secret speech'. Thirdly, when we speak of consolidation, the concept simply covers the following. The majority of Stalin's heirs understood that for several reasons things could not go on as they had before: that, owing to a burgeoning publicity both inside and outside the Soviet bloc, 'something had to be done'; that such a personal rule could not be continued without a new personal dictatorship, and this they dreaded; and that even their proxies were becoming most adverse to being teleguided, as had become traditional and accepted under Stalin. Some of them were determined enough at least to grope in the dark for changes, and it is our firm belief that these people were (because they *had* to be) in constant dialogue with this Hungarian revolution-in-the-making, and drew many lessons from this process. A few changes which these proponents of consolidation introduced, with the constant intention of preserving the dictatorship system, can be mentioned. There was (after a short move to the contrary) a certain number of concessions made to the 'consumer' in the Soviet states. Khrushchev's famous 'goulash communism' had been baptised after the consumerist leanings of this new leader. The network of oppression has remained, both inside and outside (despite Khrushchev's boasting to the contrary, the system of concentration camps had been reintroduced, even if not on a Stalinist scale and with a Stalinist cruelty). But for the first time in Soviet history there was a tendency to make repressions limited in number and to an increasing extent goal-rational. This is the basic content of what was pompously called 'restoring the Leninist norms of socialist legality'. Furthermore, despite the reality of unresolvable inner tensions (one such tension being the structural impossibility of a normal regulation of succession in leading positions), the 'consolidators' had worked out a path of transition from personal rule to an oligarchy. Finally – and this will be analyzed in detail later – they also introduced at least some methods of interstate communication; methods which, though they could never prevent these inner tensions from erupting in the most violent way, at least made the relations between the Soviet center and its dependent countries functional, a situation that no longer held in Stalin's last years when these countries were increasingly run directly by the apparatus of the MVD.

The four options now having been outlined, it may be added that there was a fifth, but this was only ever logically present; it never had any socially influential representative. This option would have been a 'revolution from above', either with an option of opening up space for a self-awakening of democracy which would have returned the country to the state prior to the Bolshevik takeover (which had not yet made *utterly* impossible a resurfacing of political pluralism), or in an egalitarian form – in the form of Mao's cultural revolution. For the latter possibility there was no 'social space' in an industrialized Soviet Union, and for the former there existed no resolute and influential social actor. There can be hardly any doubt that the radicalism of the Hungarian revolution, which promoted the possibility of the fourth option, but weakened that of the fifth option just mentioned, contributed to the latter being discarded for a long time. But the process can be viewed the other way round as well. Had the Soviet leadership been resolved at least to consider seriously the various Hungarian proposals of compromise, all of which were aimed at preserving some form of socialism together with political pluralism, such an attitude could have become a point of departure for similar experiments in the Soviet Union. Learning from history can be a two-way process. Yet, when the Khrushchevite politburo had crushed all organs of the Hungarian resistance, instead of even trying to negotiate with them, and when, instead, it had unleashed a series of reprisals directed primarily against the representatives of political pluralism, it effectively sealed off an alternative for Soviet development as well.

The impact of the Hungarian revolution on the warring factions and their slowly crystallizing options, briefly summarized, is as follows. The option of 'Finlandization' had been thoroughly rejected. It did not seem to be a lucrative business: given the more theatrical, instead of down-to-earth and pragmatic bargaining, attitude of the West immediately subsequent to the Hungarian revolution, it simply proved to be a dead end anyway. The option of consolidation, in the form it eventually took, promoted paternalism but did not tolerate any trend of self-articulation from below. In the relation between the communist states its most important result was the 'underground' victory of the principle of 'national communism'. This latter aspect needs further analysis.

A first and obvious point is that 'national communism' was *not* a Hungarian but a Yugoslav invention. Its first official – though only partial – acceptance was indicated at the historic meeting between Khrushchev and Tito in Belgrade in 1955 during the first stages of the Soviet–Yugoslav reconciliation. Yet it became very clear in 1955–6 that the 'Yugoslav bid', albeit inevitable for any de-Stalinizing consolidating trend, was one of the least fruitful of Khrushchev's business ideas. Having undergone their rehabilitation as a socialist country and a communist party, the Yugoslavs became overnight not only an acceptable but also *the* natural model for all opposition elements who wished to remain within the framework of the Soviet system but who intended to change its structure and physiognomy. Since Khrushchev himself had admitted that the Yugoslavs had suffered much injustice, reparation had to be made, and up until the Hungarian revolution these people enjoyed an ever-increasing say in questions the decisions over which had previously been a jealously guarded Soviet privilege. For instance, all of politically minded Hungary knew that Rákosi's successor, Ernő Gerő, an exceptionally unlucky choice, had become accepted only when he 'accidentally' met Tito on a hunting party in the Soviet Union and had talks with him. The fact to which we shall return later – that the Yugoslavs themselves squandered their political capital – is another question. But, as matters stood in late 1955 to early 1956, the Belgrade deal sanctifying (or at least tolerating) 'national communism' seemed to be a bargain for the Yugoslavs alone, since they did not show the slightest inclination to join the Soviet sphere of influence (a step which in 1955 received official status with the agreement creating the Warsaw Pact), yet still influenced – and in Moscow's view to a dangerous extent – the countries depending on the Soviet Union. So 'national communism' very much needed the joint Polish–Hungarian push during the historic autumn of 1956 in order to become a *practically accepted* policy, while *officially* it had increasingly become anathema. After the death of Stalin, the only man whose authority the mini-Stalins begrudgingly accepted, 'national communism' was publicly and ideologically outlawed, and yet clandestinely practised in the form of 'consultations' between the leaderships of Warsaw Pact countries and the Soviet politburo. There can be hardly any doubt that Hungary became a turning point in respect of accepting and implementing this new policy.

After a quarter of a century, it is about time to take an objective view of national communism, once the pet object of both reformist communists and anti-communist liberalism. Apart from acting to defend the country's national independence so dearly bought during the war (something of value in itself), the 'national way to socialism' in Yugoslavia led to a real compromise between the leading political group and the population – a compromise entailing not sham but genuine concessions. Conversely, the most negative version is probably displayed by Albania, where the equally laudable aim of defending national independence has been perverted, and serves nearly exclusively the purpose of rationalizing a system of terror – a system sustained in perfect isolation for so long only because it also preserved the politically vacuous rural backwardness of the country.

Apart from governments that remained proxies pure and simple of the Soviet Union, such as the German Democratic Republic (still a formally occupied country), Bulgaria, or Husakist Czechoslovakia (countries that occasionally blackmail the Soviet leadership for more material goods, but generally remain supplicants), or countries that became dependent allies in the pursuit of building their own empire, like Vietnam, there has emerged since 1956 a region comprising limited national communist countries. These nations – Romania, Hungary and Poland – seem to be constantly desynchronized with each other. Consequently, though up until now they have represented only variations of the same limited formula, they have either been critical of each other (as with Poland and Hungary) or openly at loggerheads (very much the case with Hungary and Romania). Now, compared to the countries discussed heretofore, the motivations for limited national communism of the countries in this compound are totally different. In Gomulka's first period in Poland, and with Kádár from the mid-1960s onwards in Hungary, it was a lukewarm anti-Stalinism of the Khrushchevite brand that prevailed. In understanding the Romanian case, though, we have come to accept the assessment of a Romanian writer, Tismaneanu, according to whom the motive for Gheorghiu-Dej and Ceauşescu loosening the ties with Khrushchev's Soviet Union was the exact opposite of that operative in Poland and Hungary. These men were scared by the predictable gestures and rhythm of that form of de-Stalinization exhibited by the First Secretary, and in order to keep their arch-Stalinist system intact they made slow movements towards separation that inflamed Romanian chauvinism.[16]

The fruits of these different national communisms, whether they were powered with Stalinist or non-Stalinist ideas, turned out to be totally contrary to expectations. As is generally known, Poland experienced an unbroken series of crises and internal catastrophes, while the invariably repressive Romania was successful for quite a long period – at least, as far as its extensive (but very badly applied) industrialization policy was concerned.

But in what sense can these very different governments be equally labelled as *limited* national communisms? Well, all remain, though some only formally, some substantively, within the framework of the Warsaw Pact. Secondly, even if they have wholly different economic strategies, they have not left Comecon. Lastly, though they can be most disobedient on various foreign policy matters (as Romania has repeatedly been with regard to the Middle East or world conferences of communist parties), they have never experimented with deep internal social reforms, not even of the Yugoslav type.

In the final analysis, one can say that the process which both led to and ended in the Hungarian revolution, and which in our opinion directly influenced the options chosen by Soviet policy-making bodies, had two main results: it promoted and favored the option of *consolidation* in this gradual transition from a liberal to a conservative character, *plus*, subsequent to the Khrushchev period, that of a global expansionism. The reason for this path is clear when it is understood that those who implemented this policy were the same people who had crushed the most democratic result of all these social changes: Hungary 1956. It also resulted in the unofficial acceptance of national communism – a communism which sometimes could and at other times could not keep the nations concerned within the orbit of Soviet power.

THE HUNGARIAN REVOLUTION AND THE WESTERN LEFT

If we analyze first of all the impact of the Hungarian revolution on the *communist parties*, with a particular view to those which later became, for a shorter or longer period, either truly or only superficially 'Eurocommunist', at first sight the result is nearly totally negative. The communist parties seemed then (with such exceptions as the Larsen-led Danish Communist Party) to learn so little, if anything at all, from the Hungarian October; they were prepared to side so quickly with an occupying army forcibly suppressing the first postwar general strike of a working class in Europe that, as far as communism was concerned, the cynical dictum of Frederick the Great seemed then to reign supreme: that God always sides with the stronger battalion.

On the other hand, it would be unjust not to recognize a kind of bifurcation which partly took off and partly gathered momentum – in the process of preparation for and the actual events of the Hungarian revolution – between the communist parties wishing to remain loyal to the Leninist–Stalinist tradition as the only true source of inspiration and political strategy and those proposing to reconsider the whole problem of socialism. The most immediate touchstone was whether one supported the hardline policy of repression or, to the contrary, a policy that was not only more mild, but actually promoted de-Stalinizing policies. In this sense, the party leaders' different attitudes speak for themselves. Pálóczi-Horváth, in his book on Khrushchev, quite coherently argued that Thorez fought actively for the re-Stalinizing faction at the Twentieth Congress of the Communist Party of the Soviet Union (an action not at all surprising given his past and personality). Thorez became part of a movement aimed at halting the gathering momentum of de-Stalinization. On the other hand, it is equally well known what hysteria Togliatti provoked when, in his interview in *Nuovi argomenti* in 1956, he raised the question of whether the system of the Soviet Union had become 'distorted'. Despite his predictably negative answer, he received an unprecedented public rebuke via a Soviet central committee declaration. The hysteria is totally understandable. People with even the slightest recollection of the history of working-class movements immediately viewed it as the ironical revenge of history that Togliatti, one of the most ardent opponents of Trotskyism, reformulated, in the form of a question, Trotsky's thesis about the 'perverted workers' state'.[17] Once again we cannot support our thesis with actual documents, but given the fact that the Italian Socialist Party broke its alliance with the Italian Communist Party precisely because of the Hungarian revolution (which proves that the Hungarian situation *was* on the minds of communists) it is highly unlikely that the Hungarian October did not subsequently play a considerable role in both the theoretical and political considerations of the Italian communists – a state of affairs which made them the only critics of Khrushchevism from the position of democratic socialism within communism.

The end of the alliance between the Italian socialists and communists *as a direct result of the Hungarian revolution* gives good reason to term the events of October 1956 the death-knell of the Popular Front policy. The break was given even more emphasis because one important element of the package deal that Khrushchev presented as part of his de-Stalinizing program at the Twentieth Congress was precisely the endorsement by Soviet communism of the 'parliamentary road to socialism' – a direct return to Popular Front phraseology. The Popular Front was a direct continuation of the Trojan horse strategy formulated in the early 1920s (and spelled out as such by Dimitrov himself): a strategy based on a blueprint for the silent encirclement and liquidation of a closest ally.

In this respect Hungary provided quite specific lessons. First of all, in Nagy's second 'counterrevolutionary' government, the social democrats, who had allegedly been discarded by the working class itself, resurfaced. They were represented by Anna Kéthly, a woman with the unusual record of not yielding to the physical and moral pressure of the Stalinist prison, of not betraying her own cause under inhumane duress. She was certainly no great theoretical proponent of socialism, but these ideas did not entail a system of terror, and she added to them the force of an unbroken will and a moral determination. Equally important was the lesson ensuing from the fate of the so-called 'leftist' faction of Hungarian social democrats. These people, partly because of the belated fanaticism of their mythology of 'class unity', and partly – even mostly – because of weakness and ambition, helped Rákosi to eliminate their own party. But they were paid in kind. A truly lunatic system of police terror imprisoned even these weaklings: men rejected by social democracy and never really accepted by communism. This event, which was not generally known but which became a public scandal in all its disgusting aspects before the revolution, taught a great lesson to those still needing it. This lesson did not simply amount to the conclusion that 'socialists must not give credit to communist promises'. What became ultimately questionable through this unmasking of coercive East European fusion between the two workers' parties was the very slogan of 'one class – one party'. And it is exactly this slogan that comprised the cornerstone of the Popular Front policy.

One immediate consequence of the Hungarian revolution or, more precisely, of its suppression by the Soviet military was the mass exodus of the intelligentsia from practically all communist parties.[18] This, of course, had no impact on the electorate. It belongs to the unpolished view of the working class to know that wherever a considerable proportion of it voted communist (for instance, in France, where the Communist Party fulfilled to a great extent the role of an aggressive, nationalistic and, oddly enough, pro-Soviet Labour Party) they stuck to their party until the perfidy of a communist leadership, like the anti-Mitterand campaign in the late 1970s, affected them in their direct interests. But the effect of this gradual loss of intelligentsia – a process that seems to be irreversible – cannot really be measured in quantitative terms either. It had several byproducts, one of which was that for the first time in 30 years (with the exception of the Trotskyite movement) there came about, in the form of the New Left intelligentsia, a leftist theoretical challenge to communism. Even if several of them had abandoned Marxism, or whatever kind of leftist ideology for that matter, enough had remained to present a problem for the ossified communist ideological apparatuses. Actually, Hungary 1956 was also the final straw in this respect. For a long time a tacit revolt against the mummy of the theory of Soviet Marxism had been gestating – a revolt which now broke loose in several forms and which spread over many continents, primarily that of Europe. Also, as has been mentioned, the communist movement lost along with these defectors its bid for cultural hegemony. Of course, the concept in its deeper Gramscian meaning is more than a 'star list' which a certain party can present to a nationwide audience. Primarily, it means the capacity of a movement for generating the values and lifestyles which became paradigmatic for the overwhelming majority. But intellectuals, whether we like it or loathe it, are precisely the social agents who produce the blueprints (repeatedly revised and rewritten by practical movements) of such new values and lifestyles, and when they leave a party they both testify to and partly create an incapacity of that party to produce new social solutions. Thirdly, the personage of the fellow traveler practically disappeared. After Hungary 1956 this attitude gradually lost its fascination in the West, and people rather viewed it as something dangerously inconsistent, particularly when leftist movements of the most different persuasions were prepared openly to criticize the Soviet Union. The Hungarian people's consensus against a regime which called itself socialist; the brutality and cynicism with which the revolt had been quelled; and a government simply forced on to a rebellious nation: these events also shook the fellow traveler.

Finally, we must mention those representative intellectuals who in the radical left were practically alone in defending the cause of the Hungarian October. Foremost amongst these people was Sartre, and the Hungarian issue of *Les Temps modernes*. This journal, then at its height as far as its political influence and independent radicalism were concerned, made it very clear (something often now forgotten even in the liberal press) that October 1956 was not a mob uprising or a counterrevolutionary mutiny, but an event deeply rooted in the structure and the politics of the Stalinist years. Yet Sartre himself lived far too visibly under 'Stalin's shadow'. Even if he understood the reasons for this revolution he could not ultimately legitimate it via his philosophy of history, a philosophy for which the Soviet Union still remained the chief reference point, the moral datum line, the nucleus. Sartre, in effect, became the last towering example of the fellow traveler. He was particularly unjust and condescending towards the minuscule group of post-Trotskyites, the group of *Socialisme ou barbarie*. This band, whose most important members were Castoriadis and Lefort, is now at the center of post-Marxist radical discourse, and its great achievement was then the unhesitating defense of the revolutionary masses in action and the latter's spontaneous genius in creating adequate organs of self-government. But a then equally lonely and hardly known representative of non-Marxist radicalism, Hannah Arendt, joined them, first in a booklet immediately following the events and subsequently a few years later in a brief but magnificent analysis of the Hungarian workers' council movement. In this essay, 'The revolutionary tradition and its lost treasure', she cites Odysse Barrot concerning the revolution of 1871:

'En tant que révolution sociale, 1871 procède directement de 1793, qu'il continue et qu'il doît achever . . . En tant que révolution politique, au contraire, 1871 est réaction contre 1793 et un retour à 1789. Il a éffacé du programme les mots "une et indivisible" et rejètte l'idée autoritaire qui est une idée toute monarchique . . . pour se rallier à l'idée fédérative, qui est par excellence l'idée libérale et républicaine . . .'
In order to prove what Odysse Barrot felt to be true, we must turn to the February Revolution of 1917 in Russia and to the Hungarian Revolution in 1956, both of which lasted just long enough to show in bare outlines what a government would look like

and how a republic was likely to function if they were founded upon the principles of the council system. In both instances councils or *soviets* had sprung up everywhere, completely independent of one another; workers', soldiers', and peasants' councils in the case of Russia and the most disparate kinds of councils in the case of Hungary: neighborhood councils that emerged in all residential districts, so-called revolutionary councils that grew out of fighting together in the streets, councils of writers and artists, born in the coffee-houses of Budapest, students' and youths' councils at the universities, workers' councils in the factories, councils in the army, among the civil servants, and so on. The formation of a council in each of these disparate groups turned a more or less accidental proximity into a political institution . . . The common object as the foundation of a new body politic, a new type of republican government which would rest on 'elementary republics' in such a way that its own central power did not deprive the constituent bodies of their original power to constitute. The councils, in other words, jealous of their capacity to act and to form opinion, were bound to discover the divisibility of power as well as its most important consequence, the necessary separation of powers in government.[19]

THE EAST EUROPEAN CONTEXT

The summer and fall of 1956 were a unique phase in the history of Eastern Europe: a period unparalleled since the seventeenth century and Jan Sobieski, when the Catholic nobility of Poland and the Catholic and Protestant nobility of Hungary united to defend Christian Europe against the Muslim Turkish invasion. It was a brief but *synchronized* action in a generally desynchronized era. The traditional superpowers of the region – the Ottoman empire, the Habsburg monarchy, and Russia, countries later joined by Bismarck's Germany – had experienced easy success with their politics of 'divide and rule'. The nations or national groups of the region had so divided themselves as to fall victim to any expansionism, and this was not otherwise after 1945. It couldn't be otherwise since in Eastern Europe the whole irrationality of the 1918–19 Paris-Versailles peace treaty system (a system condemned *then* by Soviet Russia and the Comintern) had been repeated once again, this time under the aegis of the 'superior wisdom' of the 'Yalta system'. It will suffice if we simply list the most detrimental factors influencing political life in this region to date. The first was the usual phony moralizing of the victorious powers: the decisions as to which nations were 'guilty' and which deserved citations and rewards – a very questionable method in an international politics already laced with strong doses of Machiavellian cunning. Thus Romania, the only country not simply Hitler's ally, but under Marshall Antonescu having her own 'national way to the final solution', her own annihilation camps, was declared not guilty. Indeed, for what were judged as her merits – amounting to nothing more than the shrewdness of her utterly corrupt and brutal ruling classes in deserting Hitler at the very last moment, a shrewdness and efficacy the equally brutal and corrupt Hungarian ruling classes did not display – Romania was given Northern Transylvania, a region overwhelmingly populated by Hungarians, and which since that time has been unceasingly a source of tension between the two countries. Though it has no bearing on the evaluation of this moralizing injustice, it should be mentioned, for the sake of impartiality, that the democratic Hungarians must themselves bear a responsibility for not creating a resistance movement at least strong enough to tear *their* country away from Hitler's defeated cause (in a similar manner) at the very last moment. Even in the cases where it was debatable whether territorial changes were to the advantage or the disadvantage of a particular nation (as with Poland, where the argument is that the regions gained from Germany in exchange for those 'reunited' with the Ukraine were economically far more valuable), the changes themselves took place without a referendum, without even formally inviting the nation concerned to the polls. Poland, a valiant ally against Hitler and legally one of the victorious nations, was a chief victim of this process. Secondly, an inhumane policy of mutual and coercive population transfer was encouraged by the victors (mostly by the Soviet Union). Public knowledge of this policy was suppressed. The Soviet press never wrote of it, and the East European press, working under Soviet military supervision, scarcely mentioned it either, even during the brief quasi-democratic period of 1945–8. The expulsion of the German minorities from Poland, Czechoslovakia, and even from Hungary (Hitler's last ally) was an utterly hypocritical act exacting hundreds of thousands of victims from a national group literally driven out of their homes without the most elementary means of survival; and this act, together with the equally inhumane forced exodus of the Hungarians from Slovakia, was a policy of brutal and stupid injustice matched – rather surpassed – only by the Soviet postwar mass deportation of parts of the population of the Baltic republics (or people such as the Crimean Tartars). Thirdly, Yugoslavia seems to be the only exception to the far from golden rule that it counted as 'pernicious nationalism' whenever minority national groups (Slovakians, Hungarians in Romania or in Czechoslovakia, and the vestiges of minority Germans in Poland and in Romania) tried to publicize either their sufferings or the discrimination directed against them, while it was 'progressive patriotism' when the leading nation, the 'nucleus', asserted its primogeniture and prerogatives over them. (This is said without the slightest intention of embellishing the Yugoslav situation, which deserves severe criticism in many respects, including the national question.) Finally, this whole system of moralizing injustice, of brutality on a massive scale, and of apparent irrationality had at least one instrumentally rational principle behind it, the only one that in the long run proved to be productive for the main victor, the Soviet Union: it divided these nations, in which new elements of disaffection have been added to traditional hatreds.

A moment of accord was brought into this complex web of reciprocal mistrust, disaffection, and suppressed but unmistakable hostility by the unformalized but palpable alliance between Polish and Hungarian social forces in the autumn of 1956. This alliance can account for the fact that, having their hands full with Hungary, the Soviets decided to give Gomulka's team a go; and, whatever the lamentable outcome of this regime, it was still a better solution than a bloodbath. In this sense Hungary saved Poland. Bibó formulates this aspect of Hungary 1956 in the following way:

It is now fashionable, both on the right and on the left, to regret the unreasonable momentum of the Hungarian revolution outrunning the self-imposed limits of the Polish action. Such a regretful reprimand does not make much sense, first of all for the reason that the Hungarian and the Polish movements were interdependent, and it was precisely this being nonplussed by the Hungarian events that made it possible for the Polish movement to stop where it did.[20]

Adam Michnik corroborates this statement word by word, a quarter of a century later:

Of course, we have to keep in mind that at that time [October 1956] the burning Budapest testified that there is a very narrow range of possible changes, that the most important rules of the game are fixed by Soviet presence and they are not being vetoed even by the West. Imre Nagy's appeal for aid and the silence of the Western governments were much too clear a signal of *the substantial validity of the Yalta agreements* and of the fact that no one will help us if we do not help ourselves.[21]

On the other hand, the radicalism of the revolution, which to date has comprised a regulative idea but not a blueprint to copy, together with its equally radical defeat, disbarred from that point onwards all synchronized action and alliance in Eastern Europe. Never again (except perhaps for the protest actions of a few Polish, East German and Hungarian intellectuals) has this spirit of alliance, this happy moment, returned, and certainly not in the form of an influential political factor.

The main loser (after Hungary, of course) was Yugoslavia, but the Yugoslav leaders were far from innocent in missing this historical moment for themselves and for other countries. Tito had a unique opportunity in 1955–6. It is difficult to match the degree of self-humiliation to which the Soviet leaders exposed themselves when at Belgrade airport they publicly admitted that their policy was mistaken, though childishly blaming it on 'Beria and Abakumov'. Carried out by people accustomed to sending millions to the Gulag and to regularly purging their friends of yesterday, this was not an act powered by qualms of conscience. But if they wanted some sort of a change, a state of affairs which differed at least to some extent from that under Stalin – and they certainly did – then they had to settle the biggest public blunder of Stalin, the criminalization of Yugoslavia by the Cominform. (They also realized that, as long as she remained penalized by her 'revisionism', Yugoslavia would remain a natural focal point of all elements of dissatisfaction.)

But this involved the immediate 'undoing' of the show trials, where the chief and collective accusation against those charged was, nearly without exception, their criminal conspiracy with the Yugoslav Gestapo agent, Tito. In addition, it involved almost all first secretaries of the area, and first of all Rákosi, this busybody of the anti-Yugoslav witchhunt, and naturally Chervenkov, too, the Bulgarian Rákosi, whom Tito had received as a 'first gift' of the Soviet leadership. There were matters to settle in Poland and Czechoslovakia also, even though Bierut died (or committed suicide) right after the Twentieth Congress, and even if Gottwald was no longer alive, and the Czech show trials had more than just anti-Yugoslav ideological foundations (for instance, anti-Semitic/anti-Zionist overtones). But the latter was still a file to be urgently opened. As to Gheorghiu-Dej, Stalin's main minion in Yugoslav affairs, he made the famous report in the name of the Cominform against Yugoslavia. Hoxha's murderous trials were equally directly aimed against Yugoslavia. Consequently, the Yugoslav leaders had totally legitimate reasons for setting as a condition of normalization the exposure of all these Stalinist manipulations, the immediate dismissal of the main culprits, and the rehabilitation of the victims. Whether successful or not, such a resolute (and preferably public) demand would have made them the natural focal point of all the forces that were demanding changes in Eastern Europe and, without exploiting journalistic pathos, true champions of liberty in the region. There are many details we are unacquainted with, but there is no evidence, and not even any rumours, as to any resolute Yugoslav determination on this question, except perhaps for the cases of Rákosi and Chervenkov, regarding whom the Yugoslav leaders gradually gained ground with the Soviets, and Hoxha, in whose case they didn't because Hoxha was out of Soviet reach to the same extent that Yugoslavia itself was in 1948. This opportunity was missed, and it never returned. It is even possible that this apparent anomaly on the part of the Yugoslav leadership is connected with the fact that the Soviet politburo was demanding too high a price for concessions, perhaps even the price of Yugoslavia's joining the Warsaw Pact, in exchange for the dismissal of all anti-Tito leaders and a partial liberalization. If this was the price to pay, then the Yugoslavs had a strong case for declining to do business, and instead remaining distant observers of the events.

But, if there were mitigating circumstances in the assessment of the political line taken by the Yugoslav leadership *prior* to the outbreak of the

Hungarian revolution, nothing can defend its perfidy and narrow-mindedness *during* and *after* it: a deplorable approach of which then only the tip of the iceberg was visible to the layman, but about which more and more painful details have been revealed ever since. The two-edged character of the situation is best illustrated by Tito's famous speech in Pula, on November 11, 1956, which was tantamount to the formal acceptance of the Soviet intervention and the Kádár government. This was the first official statement that left no doubts regarding just where the earlier 'radical' Yugoslav now stood. On the other hand, it was formulated in Tito's usual outspoken manner – something that did not detract at all from its most negative content, but which a Hungarian leadership hastily reverting to its original Muscovite style was most reluctant to publish. And when the *Népszabadság*, the Kádárist party's daily, published the speech, the official outrage at the top was so vehement that the editor-in-chief was immediately demoted. Even so, this report made publicly available the essential message – never forgotten – that one should not be deluded into relying on the political aid of Yugoslavia. Since then more important details have been printed, stemming from very different quarters but corroborating each other. From one angle Khrushchev, in his memoirs smuggled out to the West (containing, as expected, a pack of self-apologetic lies, but the ultimate reliability of which, to our knowledge, is not questioned by the experts), and from another angle Micunović give a coherent story which we shall sum up with the words of Micunović. The secret negotiations between the Yugoslav delegation (Tito, Ranković, Kardelj and Micunović) and the Soviet delegation (consisting of Khrushchev and Malenkov alone) took place from seven o'clock in the evening of November 2 to five o'clock the following morning. Khrushchev first informed the Yugoslavs that they were actually the last to be consulted regarding the Soviet plans for Hungary, to which all countries gave their consent, except for certain objections on the part of Gomufka. Then Khrushchev, who in later talks with the Yugoslavs in 1957 showed surprising and coldblooded indifference about the fate of Yugoslav communists then recently murdered by Hoxha, obviously regarding such acts as a party prerogative, started off emotionally without giving any serious analysis of the course of events, saying that communists in Hungary were being murdered, butchered and hanged. He mentioned Imre Nagy's appeal to the United Nations and the four powers, and the withdrawal from the Warsaw Pact. It was a question of whether capitalism was restored in Hungary. Whether Nagy was just a tool or had himself long been an agent of imperialism was not clear at the moment.

'What is there left for us to do?' Khrushchev asked, meaning the Soviet Union. 'If we let things take their course, the West would say we are either stupid or weak, and that's one and the same thing. We cannot possibly permit it, either as Communists and internationalists or as the Soviet state.' He said they had assembled sufficient troops and that they had decided to put a stop to what was going on in Hungary. Khrushchev turned again to the question of intervention by the Soviet Army. He said that there were also internal reasons in the Soviet Union why they could not permit the restoration of capitalism in Hungary. There were people in the Soviet Union who would say that as long as Stalin was in command everybody obeyed and there were no big shocks, but that now, ever since *they* had come to power . . . Russia had suffered the defeat and loss of Hungary. And this was happening at a time when the present Soviet leaders were condemning Stalin . . . Malenkov let it be known that everything in the Soviet Union was ready for the second military intervention against the Nagy government to start right away. It is clear that the Russians are going to intervene frontally and with great force, because they are completely isolated from the Hungarian people . . . We explained that we were also concerned at the swing of events to the right, toward counterrevolution, when we saw the Nagy government allowing Communists to be murdered and hanged. There would have to be intervention if there was a counterrevolution in Hungary, but it should not be based exclusively on the weapons of the Soviet Army. There would be bloodshed, with the people of Hungary fighting against Soviet troops, because the Communist party of Hungary, as a result of what had happened in the past, had disintegrated, and no longer existed. We suggested that in the present situation there should be some political preparation, an effort to save what could be saved, and to set up something like a revolutionary government composed of Hungarians who could give the people some kind of political lead. A short discussion of the possible leaders followed, in which the Soviet delegates supported Münnich, the Yugoslav leaders Kádár. The Russians are obviously in favour of Münnich but are not against accepting our proposal. We pointed out that much depended on what the policy of the new government would be. Some of us suggested that the new government should condemn sharply and categorically the policy of Rákosi and Gerő as well as everything in the past which led to this situation: Khrushchev and Malenkov reluctantly agreed. Once again the debate about the First Man had been resumed, but when Micunović pointed out to Khrushchev that Münnich had been somewhat compromised by being Rákosi's Moscow Ambassador in the anti-Tito times, Khrushchev gave his agreement to the Yugoslav request.[22]

With regard to the subsequent fate of Nagy, who was simply abducted together with his group, taken first to Romania and later executed, and the role of the Yugoslav leadership in it, Micunović very valiantly (and more or less convincingly) defends his government's twofold aim: to protect the lives of his group while excluding them from political life for good. But on this issue it is very typical how Micunović protests to Khrushchev on June 19, 1958:

I raised the question of Nagy's execution. I told him that the whole world was shocked, and that an irreparable mistake had been made, and that it would be difficult for anyone to conceive anything worse for the Soviet Union and Hungary. *Nagy had meant less and less politically in Hungary, but they had now liquidated him physically but had resurrected him politically.* It was obviously a disagreeable subject for Khrushchev. He said it was Hungary's affair, and not the Soviet Union's [about which Micunović, and rightly so, does not believe a word] but that he personally approved what the Hungarians had done and would have done the same himself. He reproached me as a Communist for referring to world public opinion, saying that Communists have other, class criteria in such matters.[23]

It is here most appropriate to quote the unfortunately evergreen Talleyrand: 'C'est plus qu'un crime, c'est une faute.' For, on the one hand, the Yugoslav perfidy did not pay them in terms of influence. In fact, just the opposite occurred. The last moment that top Soviet delegations discussed the political fate of Eastern Europe with Yugoslavia, or asked the Yugoslav leaders for any kind of advice, was precisely this fateful November 2, 1956. It would be a cavalier statement without foundation if we were to say that, had Tito and his colleagues vetoed the Soviet decision, a second intervention would not have taken place. We have seen that, in all probability, they never had that much influence over Soviet decisions. But a veto could have constituted a serious obstacle to the course of intervention. Not only would the Yugoslav attitude have then become unpredictable (Yugoslavia could even have served as a basis for protracted Hungarian resistance), but it could also have influenced the attitude of the West, whose ominous silence (except for propaganda exercises) not only did not escape Yugoslav attention but in all probability also had a crucial impact on the Yugoslav leaders. Yet the result, whatever the underlying strategic or tactical considerations, was that Yugoslavia remained anathema for all East European countries – practically just as suspect as in the good old Cominform days, though minus the unnecessary and compromising verbal acrobatics.

On the other hand, the motives behind the Yugoslav decision were most likely narrowminded. It is obvious that for them leaving the Warsaw Pact could not qualify as a counterrevolutionary action. And in whatever light the character of the Hungarian events might have appeared to the Yugoslav leaders, and even if they regarded them as a genuine counterrevolution, nothing sanctified, in terms of *their own politics*, their offer of political support to the intervention in order to suppress the revolt. Ever since their break with the 'socialist camp' in 1948, the Yugoslav leaders had had to learn to coexist with capitalist countries, and sometimes with those that were least liberal; and, if the worst came to the worst, Hungary would have been only one more on the list. At the same time, offering to help intervene in another nation's affairs on *ideological grounds* set up a very dangerous precedent regarding future prospects for Yugoslav independence. The only reasonable explanation is that the 'Djilas complex' of Tito and his associates had gained the upper hand. The moment Hungary returned to political pluralism, even if only for a few days, they felt the ghost of Djilas's program knocking on their door. But as usual, fear inspires bad solutions.

A far more clandestine but equally tortuous story is that of the *Romanian* reaction to the Hungarian revolution. It is first of all remarkable that the Imre Nagy group had been deported to Romania, which was far from being the appropriate place. Why not the Soviet Union? Why not the reliably arch-Stalinist Czechoslovakia, which showed eagerness to support the invasion and Kádár's regime? The selection of Romania suggests that the Romanian leadership *volunteered* for this honor; that they were personally and directly involved in the speedy and obviously repressive solution to the Hungarian crisis. We know definitely from Lukács that, apart from Soviet and Hungarian emissaries, the Romanian 'supervisors' – the usual mixture of highly placed policemen and ideological inquisitors – played some role in the attempts at 'convincing' the Nagy group to give up its ideology, betray its promises and join the Kádár leadership. Gheorghiu-Dej and his Political Bureau very soon had reasons for having fears about Hungary 1956: for the first time since the war there were signs of pro-Hungarian political activity (at the universities of Cluj and Bucureşti), and this, even more ominously, could not simply be passed off as the predictable nationalist reaction of the Hungarian minority, for the swift wave of reprisals (arrests and rash sentences) hit young Romanian intellectuals, too. But the events of the Hungarian revolution instilled even deeper anxieties in the Romanian leaders. Not wishing to risk their rule with Khrushchevite escapades, they pulled out of the Hungarian conflagration as swiftly as possible, afterwards going their own national (and rather chauvinistic) way of relentless internal repression.

Ulbricht did not hesitate to regard the events as constituting a counter-revolution, and when, following the uprising (and probably even stimulated by it), Wolfgang Harich's ill-fated 'loyalist' opposition appealed against him to the Khrushchevite leadership he cracked down on the 'conspirators' without hesitation. In a way, Hungary 1956 was a final victory for Ulbricht. It confirmed his misgivings and warnings. Even though he had survived it, he had never really felt safe in his seat after the 1953 fiasco of provoking the first workers' revolt against the 'workers' state'. Shrewd politician that he was, he now understood that the Western impotence or unwillingness for the post-revolution talks that may well have resulted in the politics of détente (a politics the consequences of which might be very grave for him) would ensure the existence of his 'socialist East German nation'.

In Czechoslovakia, the only reaction was a secret resolution on the part of Novotny's leadership (and arrived at, of course, without any great moral qualms) *not* to launch an investigation into the show trials, and not to instigate any kind of public rehabilitation (the memory of Rajk's funeral on October 6, 1956 in Budapest, the first mass gathering that demonstrated the visible and increasing rage even of those who desired only the reform of the regime, was still very fresh in the minds of all observers). It was even decided to delay secret or unpublished acts of rehabilitation for as long as possible. In other countries, various courses of action were taken. Bulgaria played no part in this piece of history other than its usual automatic endorsement of Moscow's decision. Albania, on the other hand, was already in increasingly open revolt against the 'Khrushchevite treason' of the policy of the Twentieth Congress.

The Hungarian revolution very quickly became taboo in the Eastern bloc. It was never mentioned with any positive connotation, and was generally expunged from the records, pushed into total oblivion. To begin with, everyone had to pay tribute to the Soviet Union's intervention in the name of 'proletarian internationalism and solidarity'. Even Gomułka joined the chorus, and there is no reason to believe that he did so under duress. But after this an information blackout set in, and only so-called 'theoretical' documents analyzed the 'lessons' to be drawn from Hungarian 'counter-revolution' – lessons that, of course, were never identical with those actually drawn by the leaderships involved. One important and real lesson was that of stepping up the 'divide and rule' policy. Moreover, the Hungarian revolution, an overwhelmingly *social* event, was translated by communist apparatuses into the language of anti-Hungarian chauvinism, mostly in Czechoslovakia and in Romania, but also in the Soviet Union (already Khrushchev had pointed out to Micunović the bitter feeling of the Russian citizen towards the Hungarians who 'had fought against us' in two wars). In Romania, a decade of shameful cultural oppression of the Hungarian national minority was rationalized as 'justified suspicion' of these 'counterrevolutionary Hungarians'.

All of this, it should be understood, was only part of a wider setting, a setting to which Hungary herself, with her almost publicly pursued policy of anti-Romanian nationalism, was no exception. Similar symptoms could also be observed in the Czech–Polish relations, which had never been all that warm. Equally, there had never been any effective obstacle to giving (not too public) vent to the expression of 'anti-Yugoslav' feelings, which were actually nothing more than revamped centennial hates and aversions. And one historical moment did arrive when the Soviet leadership could test the success of its desynchronizing policy via inciting (or at least tolerating) mutual national hatreds: in August 1968. In 1956, they failed to mobilize the Warsaw Pact forces against a rebellious Hungary, and had to do the job alone. Obviously, this was not a military problem for the army that defeated Hitler's Wehrmacht, but a political matter of implicating others in the deed. We know from Pálóczi-Horváth's account that it was precisely Rokossowski's report to Khrushchev on the night of October 19 about the total unreliability of the Polish army which caused the First Secretary's abrupt volte-face the next day, a reversal that effectively endorsed the installation of the Gomułka group: so the Polish army could not be used. If anything, a Romanian presence in the military action could have given rise to a peasant *guerrilla* feeding on a deeply rooted nationalistic hatred. Similar considerations applied to the Czechoslovakian military presence. As far as the armed forces of the East German regime were concerned, even their symbolic presence (and Ulbricht's government could not, in all likelihood, provide anything more at the time) would have been a danger. A *German* occupying army, *anywhere* in the world, under *any* banner, little more than ten years after the war, might have raised grave considerations within the Russian population as well. But owing to a carefully administered desynchronization and division between the East European states these obstacles no longer required consideration by the Soviet leadership in 1968, and the privilege was granted to all the governments of Eastern Europe to soil their hands with the collective oppression of Czechoslovakian liberalization.

It is against this background that we can formulate the only norm that Hungary 1956 provides for the *whole* of Eastern Europe. This is *not* the norm of a political revolution. Though it is perhaps too rigid a formulation when Michnik rules out any future relevance of the Hungarian experience, it will certainly be decided from nation to nation by the social actors themselves as to what form, if any, their emancipation will take. But, should Eastern Europe achieve any emancipation at all, it cannot afford again the total desynchronization which it experienced for two decades. The need for collaboration in such emancipatory efforts had already been given expression by Imre Nagy in 1955, in a strange, but perhaps not accidental, stylistic and substantive resemblance to Bibó:

Hungary has found herself for centuries to be the battleground of hostile forces, the target of adversaries, and she could not find her place among nations. The consequence of this was a series of national catastrophes. The great, but belated, historical conclusion had been formulated, after the defeat of our glorious war of independence [the revolution and war of independence of 1848–9], by Lajos Kossuth, by our national hero, and it was he who showed the way to follow. In order to ensure the independent, sovereign and free existence of the Hungarian people, Kossuth did not have in mind any kind of alliance with a great power or with a group of great powers, but a close co-operation between neighbour countries, in the framework of a federation of free nations enjoying equal rights. It is exactly these ideas that we have to return to.[24]

1956-81

NOTES

1 In what follows we shall quote from this and other statements by István Bibó from the Hungarian emigrant journal *Magyar Füzetek*, 4 (Paris, 1979). All our translation and italics.

2 Bibó, 'Statement of the Imre Nagy government', quoted in ibid., pp. 9–10.
3 Bibó, 'Draft of a compromise solution of the Hungarian question' (1957), in *Magyar Füzetek*, 4, p. 138.
4 Bibó, 'Draft', p. 139.
5 Ibid., p. 140.
6 Ibid.
7 M. Molnár, *Budapest, 1956* (London: Allen and Unwin, 1971), p. 220.
8 Quoted in F. A. Váli, *Rift and Revolt in Hungary* (Cambridge, Mass.: Harvard University Press, 1961), p. 355.
9 Bibó, 'The situation of Hungary and the international situation' (1957), in *Magyar Füzetek*, 4, p. 144. Once again, this department can be called the just historical punishment of empty illusions. But we think that the Hungarian 'testing' of the trustworthiness of international institutions was a more democratic and more radical attitude than their sterile rejection *a limine*. Bibó's efforts to contact President Eisenhower directly in the early hours of November 4 when the second and final Soviet intervention had already been launched have to be added to these attempts at 'testing'. Recently Andor C. Clay (Sziklay Andor), American diplomat and intelligence adviser of Hungarian extraction, active between 1945 and 1972, published as parts of an analytical essay certain documents released by the 1966 Freedom of Information Act which included telex conversations between the American embassy in Budapest and the State Department in Washington, dated October 25 and November 4. In the second text the representative of the American embassy reads the text of a statement handed over by Bibó personally during the telex conversation. The text had apparently been worded by Bibó and Zoltán Tildy (another non-Marxist, non-socialist minister of state without portfolio of the second Nagy government, ex-President of the Hungarian republic). For substantive reasons which have been shown and which will become clear for the reader, we believe that the text was, in the main, the work of Bibó. (Our translation into English.)

In the present emergency situation Hungary turns with exceptional trust in the direction of the peaceloving policy, wisdom and courage which have been given voice by the President so often and so emphatically. Even if the Hungarian populace resists the attack with an ultimate resoluteness, there can hardly be any doubt that it will be defeated in this struggle against overwhelming odds, unless it gets support. At the moment, the most urgent support is political, not military, in nature. It is obvious that this new phase of Soviet plans stands in close relation to the British intervention in Egypt.

The occupation of Hungary would not only mean a renewal of oppression in this area; it would also put an end to the trend of self-liberation that had been commenced in other East European countries in a way inspiring so much hope. It would undermine as well the American policy of liberation that has been practised with so much vigor and wisdom. It would also shatter the confidence in the United States of all East European nations; on the other hand, it would involve, under the adverse impact of the intervention in Egypt, a process of isolation of a kind that could only conclude in catastrophe. We are at the historical juncture that has often been alluded to by President Eisenhower and the Secretary of State, Dulles, when they have stated in their speeches that it is only through risking a world war that the road leading to a new world war can be blocked. Without the intention of advising the President, we have to call to his attention the possibility that, taking into consideration the mandatory necessity of avoiding the gravest consequences, he could, on the one hand, put an end to the intervention of Western powers in Egypt; on the other, he could appeal to the Soviet Union to withdraw its troops rapidly from Hungary. We are fully aware of the moral weight, as well as the practical difficulties, of such a double decision. (*Irodalmi Ujság* (Literary Gazette), XXXII (July–October 1981), special supplement, London, p. M10)

10 As a general characterization of the American policy-makers we can safely accept as objective the words of Tibor Méray, author of *Thirteen Days that Shook the Kremlin* (New York: Praeger, 1959), the first significant chronicle of the revolution, a convinced liberal conservative who cannot be accused of leftist antipathy to America: 'it has never occurred, not for a single moment, to the leaders of the United States to do anything tangible in support of or to rescue the Hungarian revolution. They have undeniably felt sympathy to it, but this sympathy never went beyond a few humanitarian gestures or statements. They had neither plans nor intentions to lend effective aid or to bind the hands of the Soviet Union' (*Irodalmi Ujság*, XXXII, p. M2). More particularly, the analytical article by A. C. Clay, and the documents collected and first published in it, allow for the following conclusions. First, both in their exoteric and semi-exoteric considerations, the chief American policy-makers – President Eisenhower; Secretary of State J. F. Dulles; R. D. Murphy, Political Secretary of the State Department; Bohlen, the American ambassador in Moscow; Henry Cabot Lodge, United Nations chief delegate of the United States – considered, if anything beyond general and non-binding statements, only the military action and immediately came to the same conclusions to which Joe Citizen would have instinctively come: namely, that (a) it was too dangerous and (b) they would have to contact the Hungarian insurgents through impenetrable channels, countries which were either Warsaw Pact members or communist or non-communist neutral states (Yugoslavia and Austria). In other words, they realised that access was, in a simple geographical sense, denied to the American armed forces. Unfortunately, and taking into consideration both Eisenhower's main consideration of his re-election on November 4, 1956, and the departmental and personal infights so amply documented even in these days, the satirical tone of the above sentence is not a piece of cheap and frivolous anti-American propaganda but a relatively restrained description of a very sad state of affairs. The only option beyond the military, which, however, hardly deserves the denomination 'political', has been reported by Bohlen (in the same article by Clay, ibid., p. M13): '[On October 29] I received a cable from Dulles instructing me to forward an urgent message to the Soviet leadership to the effect that the United States do not regard Hungary, or for that matter, any member of the Soviet bloc, as their potential military ally . . . The same afternoon I had an opportunity to forward the message to Khrushchev, Bulganin and Zhukov; but the American guarantee had no impact on the Soviet leaders; they had already made their decision: the revolution had to be crushed.' Now, this is a serious moment worthy of analysis in some detail. We know almost certainly – and we shall come back to this at a later stage of the analysis – that October 29 was *not yet* the moment when the final decision was taken. As a result, American foreign policy still had a chance. In

addition, we need not have a pro-Soviet bias to see why Dulles's suggestion was unacceptable, even unfit for serious consideration on behalf of the Soviet leaders. For Stalin's heirs it was small consolation indeed if the American Secretary of State assured them that he did not intend to include *their* East European vassals in the Western military alliance. If the Soviet Political Bureau was ready to negotiate at all (which is questionable), its members wanted something incomparably more substantial as a first step. No single suggestion, only a *package deal*, could have helped, and it will become immediately clear to the reader that Dulles did not even mention Egypt; in other words, he did not even suggest a share in world government for the Soviet leadership, and *less* was simply not satisfactory for them. It is very difficult, however, to believe that this idea simply had not occurred to Dulles. It is incomparably more likely that the whole Bohlen message was an empty gesture for posterity.

But, secondly, a dominant weakness of American diplomacy comes to the fore in these documents, a weakness for which the political élite of the United States has repeatedly (most recently in Iran) paid such a heavy price; American experts simply cannot read the accelerated events of a revolution. The result is that a habitual attitude of 'take your time' prevails in a situation where usually there is no time at all, except for a few minutes the potential of which never returns. Let us quote an interesting passage from the telex conversation between the American embassy in Budapest and the State Department on October 25. The actual impact of the hesitation so characteristic was nil, precisely because of the predetermination, analysed above, not to take any step at all, except gestures of a mere propaganda value. But had the proper authorities of the United States intended to act they could not have relied on their main source of local information, their political assessors in the embassy. Here is how they sized up the situation in a crucial hour:

It is impossible to predict developments. Yesterday we had the impression that he [Imre Nagy] would be blamed for the appeal to the Soviet Army and he would lose his popularity enormously. Today we don't know where he stands and how the population will judge upon the line of demarcation between Nagy and Kádár . . . I repeat, we do not know but we assume that Nagy is in fact Prime Minister. Should the blame for the appeal to the Soviet Army be put on Gerő, and should he become the scapegoat for all what happens now, and should Nagy make further concessions, he could yet have a chance. But we don't have enough knowledge for stating anything with an air of certainty.' (*Irodalmi Ujság*, XXXII, special supplement, p. M10).

Now, this is a conscientious dissertation cataloging all logical alternatives but definitely not a political document which simply *must* run the risk of making policy recommendations then and there. We have already seen, and will see later, that the situation was, in fact, difficult and hardly scrutable; equally, that the American leadership did not intend to act. But, with all this, 'no recommendation' suits only the purposes of a 'no-win policy'.

11   All accounts – those of Méray, *Thirteen Days*; Miklós Molnár and László Nagy, *Imre Nagy: réformateur ou révolutionnaire?* (Geneva/Paris: Librairie E. Droz/ Librairie Minard, 1959), G. Pálóczi-Horváth;, *Khrushchev: The Road to Power* (London: Secker and Warburg, 1960), and the book by Váli mentioned above on

which we here rely – take their information from Imre Nagy, *On Communism: In Defense of the New Course* (New York and London: Thames and Hudson, 1957), which contains various memoranda that Nagy had circulated in Hungary during 1955 and 1956. The most laconic summary of the general atmosphere of the meeting is given in the following words: 'The shocking situation was described by the key members of the Soviet Communist Party, who declared that the mistakes and crimes of the four-member Party leadership in Hungary, headed by Rákosi, had driven the country to the verge of a catastrophe, shaking the People's Democratic system to its foundations, and that, unless prompt and effective measures were taken to bring about a change, the people would turn against them and, to quote Khrushchev, "we would have been booted out summarily" ' (Váli, *Rift and Revolt*, p. 4).

12   Váli, *Rift and Revolt* pp. 156–7 (emphasis added).
13   Ibid. (emphasis added).
14   Selling out Germany was, perhaps, too farfetched an idea even on the part of such an uninhibited adventurer as Beria. But it was at least partly corroborated by the fact that Zaisser, the Minister of State Security in East Germany, who was 'apparently backed by Malenkov and Beria in Moscow', who 'was an unlikely security chief, a secret policeman with mild manners who believed in *a united and neutral Germany*' (as J. Steele characterizes him in his *Socialism with a German Face: The State That Came in from the Cold* (London: Cape, 1977), pp. 86, 97), belonged to the forefront of the anti-Ulbricht opposition in the Political Bureau. Both before and immediately after the Berlin uprising he blamed all ills on Ulbricht's policy. Vague as this reference is about his being backed by Beria, and despite the fact that the latter in the last years of Stalin had only formal contact with the security organs, if we consider that his lines of *personal* connections had been kept constantly alive, then Zaisser, a Minister of State Security, with views of German unity and neutrality, *could* have been the spokesman of Beria's shortlived policy.

Yet there is still further documentation of a possible deal with the Western Powers aimed at the exchange of Ulbricht's East German state, perhaps for an early version of détente, and allegedly initiated by Beria, stemming from the Italian communist leader, Pietro Secchia. Pietro Secchia's personality and political role could be compared to that of André Marty in the French Communist party. Constantly a man of action, preferably of armed action, a potential challenger to the authority of the leader, for a long time, the repository of Moscow's confidence, he got into a conflict with Togliatti and was forced out of the leadership. When in retirement, he published some of his notes, in *Annali* (Feltrinelli), *Archivio Secchia*, where narrating an almost daily schedule of the year of 1953, he states that on July 9 he was sent by Togliatti to Moscow. Togliatti told him that a confidential invitation had arrived from the Soviet leaders who wanted to disclose some particularly important information. He arrived in Moscow on the same day and read of Beria's arrest (which was reported by *L'Unita* a few days later). He was driven from the airport to the Kremlin where a 'meeting' took place (about the character of which he says only that Malenkov, Molotov and Khrushchev were present, and that Molotov presided over the meeting). His *Notes* containing the agenda, the accusations against Beria, were later published by his secretary, Seniga, when the latter quit the Communist party, in his book *Togliatti e Stalin* (Milan: Sugarco, 1961, new edn 1978). In point 6 of the detailed list of accusations, in all probability a collective document of the politburo which deals with Beria's 'crimes' in the field of the national question where he allegedly tried to undermine the 'friendship among the nations of the USSR' we read the following:

Beria's hostile political turn appeared in sharp relief on the occasion of an examination of the German problem *at the end of May of this year* [emphasis added]. Beria's suggestions regarding this question can be summed up as the abandonment of the course of socialist construction in the GDR and as the adoption of the course of transforming the GDR into a bourgeois state which would have meant capitulation pure and simple in front of the imperialist forces. At the same time, Beria has gone so far in more recent times, that, under the pretext of a struggle against the weaknesses and exaggerated measures in kolkhoz-building in the countries of the people's democracy and in the GDR, the anti-kolkhoz concessions started to manifest themselves in him to the point where he simply suggested the dismantling of the kolkhozes in these countries.

The point of time and the problem of cooperatives which played a major role in the Hungarian crisis of 1953 (in which we know that Beria supported Imre Nagy against Rákosi) authenticates fully Secchia's notes as published by Seniga. This new document turns something which had only existed as gossip into a historical fact: now we know that Beria did suggest to the Soviet Political Bureau the abandonment of the GDR obviously in the wider context of bargaining with the West. Of course, we repeat, we do not know whether such an offer ever reached Western ears.

15   [The best description and analysis of Kádárist 'normalization', including the commanding role of Soviet leaders in it, can be found in János Kis, 'Kádárist normalization, 1956–57', MS.]

16   [See Vladimir Tismaneanu, 'The Tragi-comedy of Romanian communism', in F. Fehér and A. Arato, eds, *Crisis and Reform in Eastern Europe* (New Brunswick: Transaction, forthcoming, 1990).]

17   A word about the attitude of 'genuine' Trotskyism to the Hungarian revolution is appropriate here. One need not accept Castoriadis's characterization of Trotsky-ism as a faction of the Stalinist bureaucracy in exile – at least, not as an all-embracing description of all shades of Trotskyism – in order to admire the quotation by Mandel (in *Quatrième Internationale*, December 1956):

Socialist democracy will still have to engage in more battles in Poland. But the main battle which allowed millions of proletarians to once again identify with the Worker's State, is already won . . . The political revolution which, for a month now, shakes up Hungary, has shown a more spasmodic and unequal development than the political revolution in Poland. It did not, like the latter, fly from victory to victory . . . This is because, contrary to the situation in Poland, the Hungarian Revolution was an elementary and spontaneous explosion. The subtle interaction between objective and subjective factors, between the initiative of the masses and the building of a new leadership, between pressure from below and the crystallization of an opposition faction above, at the summit of the Communist

Party, an interaction which made possible the Polish victory, has been missing in Hungary. (Quoted in Castoriadis, 'The Hungarian source', *Telos*, 29 (St Louis, Miss., 1979), p. 6)

What is really depressing here, is not the caricature of prediction. Everyone can make false predictions. It is the value choice that counts. For Mandel, a compromise that is solidly supported by Soviet armor is automatically more valuable than the self-organization of a people, which shows the apologetic function of the theory of the 'perverted workers' state'. It is also very strange that Mandel's memory so characteristically fails: the interaction between an opposition faction and 'the initiative of the masses' was *not* missing from the Hungarian revolution; with many difficulties, it finally came about. But the opposition was abducted, and the mass initiative crushed by a more powerful 'perverted workers' state'. In order to document further the total failure of Trotskyism in the face of the radical action of the masses we will briefly return later to Isaac Deutscher's analysis of Hungary in 1956 – this major disgrace of such a great historian.

18 We do not have any statistical survey tabling the proportions of these 'defectors': it is therefore our *impression* that the largest outflow took place in the French Communist Party, in the party *sui generis* of representative intellectuals, and that the smallest exodus hit the Italian communists. But, even if our assessment is not correct, the fact of the intellectual mass exodus is.

19 Hannah Arendt, *On Revolution* (New York: Viking, 1963), pp. 270–1.

20 Bibó, 'Situation of Hungary', p. 183.

21 Adam Michnik, 'What we will and what we can', address to the oppositional Free University in Warsaw, November 14 1980, in *Magyar Füzetek*, 8 (Paris, 1981), p. 16 (emphasis added).

22 Veljko Micunović, *Moscow Diary* (Garden City, NY: Doubleday, 1980), pp. 133–44. This is a straightforward story, but a couple of additional commentaries are still needed here. First of all, from the whole course of negotiations it became clear that the Soviet leadership was genuinely scared of a possible Western intervention, which shows that they were not contacted by the United States for serious negotiations and which corroborates our earlier point about the fatal mistakes of the West. Secondly, and even if we disregard the phony commiseration of people for their 'comrades' who had had a thousand times as many communists murdered in their own time as were lynched by Hungarian insurgents, at least some of the real reasons become visible. There were, in the main, two considerations inducing the post-Stalin Soviet leaders to the final decision – neither of them, of course, involving ideological double-talk about the restoration of capitalism. The first was the fear of their own apparatus, which anyway was scrutinizing the de-Stalinizers suspiciously; the second was the fear of the crippled reputation of the Soviet state. Finally, it becomes clear from the chronicle that even the initial formula of Kádárism, that is to say, distancing the leadership equally from the 'mistakes of the past' and the 'treason of those supporting the counterrevolution', was in the main a Yugoslav invention. The Soviet leaders simply wanted 'order restored' and reprisals.

23 Ibid., p. 396 (emphasis added). There are two important features of the Yugoslav attitude worth mentioning. The first is that only then had it started to dawn upon

them that their attitude in the Hungarian question just did not pay in terms of pragmatic policy, either. On page 395, Micunović remarks: 'Some of the charges which are laid against Nagy can apply to us: His appeal for the "liquidation of military blocs" and his support for "national communism", as the West used to describe the internal system of Yugoslavia.' Many Hungarians could have suggested to the Yugoslav leaders in time that, should they yield and deviate from their self-professed principles in the Hungarian question, they would find themselves on the same bank of accused as the victims of the Hungarian revolution. The second remarkable feature of this most remarkable conversation is that Micunović uses Khrushchev's cynical argument against Stalin, this time against Khrushchev. As Khrushchev stated in the 'secret speech' that, for instance, Bukharin's execution was 'superfluous' since he no longer represented political power, Micunović now stated that Nagy's execution was superfluous for the same reason. This means by implication that the Yugoslav still felt it legitimate to murder one's political enemies in a 'legal' way if this was deemed necessary by a certain authority possessing superior wisdom; and also, by implication, that the principle of dictatorship and goal-rationalist/Leninist (instead of increasingly irrational Stalinist) terror had remained valid for the Yugoslav leadership.

24   Quoted in Molnár and Nagy, *Imre Nagy*, pp. 51–2.

3

The Impact on Hungary

THE HUNGARIAN REVOLUTION: A 'SIMPLE MATTER'?

There is a tendency among professional and non-professional interpreters of the Hungarian revolution to simplify matters with regard to its meaning. Some call it a 'simple matter' of restoring national freedom, a 'national revolution'; others an equally 'simple matter' of restoring political liberties, a 'liberal revolution'. But the two concepts are not, and never have been, coextensive, and this 'simple matter' is somewhat more involved.

In judging the arguments for and against the thesis that characterizes October 1956 as a 'national revolution', we must set aside any formal definition of the term 'revolution' (as against 'rebellion', 'revolt', 'uprising'), as well as the verbal pyrotechnics distinguishing wars of national independence and social revolutions: these are grossly sterile enterprises. It is beyond all doubt that the *fight for national independence* stood at the pinnacle of those celebrated thirteen days for the very simple reason that every change had to be fought for against the military presence and oppressive role of the Soviet army. At this point it must be understood as absolute fact (this issue was much debated in the assessment of Imre Nagy's political character) that the Soviet army intervened *prior* to any Hungarian appeal that it received, and particularly *prior* to any consent to intervention given by Nagy (to put his name to the appeal), and that the Soviet presidium and their Hungarian emissary, Andropov, were already the real repositories of power on the night of October 23.[1] Apart from a few murderous attacks of the hated 'Blues' (the AVH commandos, the state security police) on peaceful demonstrators, which left far more victims than the number of 'Blues' later lynched by infuriated crowds, the Hungarian armed insurgents nearly always fought against Soviet armed forces, and hardly ever against Hungarian units. (Miklós Molnár, in his *Budapest, 1956*, amply verifies that the attitude of the Hungarian army covered the whole range from passive non-interference to active support – the latter less frequently – with sporadic instances of hostility against the masses.) Apart from the wider sociopolitical setting, this fact naturally made the revolt prima facie a national issue.

But the 'wider sociopolitical setting' was very much present, and not only objectively, but also subjectively – in the consciousness of an insurgent people.[2] Unaware as the (mostly young) insurgents had actually been of the unassailable strength of the pact agreed upon between the great powers, they were to some extent even propelled onwards by their naïveté. Millions of Hungarians daily generating revolution still had good reason to believe that their national separation from the Soviet bloc, provided it was successful, would be most welcome to the West. After an eventual victory, Hungary, as a nation, would receive the consideration and understanding from the West that it so painfully missed in the peace treaties of 1918–19 and 1947; the first treating Austria, the kernel of the Habsburg empire, much more kindly than the mutilated Hungary; the second giving considerable territorial priority (after the real victims of Nazism such as Yugoslavia and Czechoslovakia) to Nazi allies such as Romania, and even to Austria over Hungary. Indeed, this was not an exaggerated optimism, if the Hungarians believed that a victorious anti-Soviet revolution would incline the West favorably towards them for the first time in a century. And it is this unvoiced expectation alone in regard to which the 'conspiracy theory' applied to the Hungarian revolution holds water. This insurgent nation in its entirety – or, at least, nearly all its adult citizens – understood perfectly well (and this is widely corroborated by our personal and casual conversations on the streets of revolutionary Budapest) that even the slightest public mention of a revision of the peace treaties would be fatally counterproductive to the Hungarian case. But the same people expected, in an often undefined and generally unarticulated manner, that after victory the 'era of injustice' would be abolished. In our estimation, it must have been a very insignificant and foolish minority that seriously considered borderline revisions; and it very rarely happens that nations are *that* ignorant of general trends. The majority of Hungarians thought in terms of material-financial compensation for the injustices suffered at the hands of a biased world; they thought in terms of concrete rewards for the valiant deeds of national revolution.

Here we come to the third major point of our further analysis: that is, to the language, the symbols and the atmosphere of an almost compelling but certainly very imposing national consensus which predominated as the most immediately visible symptom of those thirteen days. The unceasing singing of the national anthem; the continuous emphasis on the presence of the national tricolor and the traditional Kossuth blazon on all public buildings, in lieu of the symbols created by the communist regime (which represented for the population Soviet occupation *tout court*); and the endless repetition and recital by the masses that 'we all are Hungarian': all this was a display of gestures which often seemed either quite infantile or plainly obsolete to Western visitors, for whom the question of a people's national existence, despite the Nazi intermezzo, seemed to be a matter settled a very long time ago. For us, reformist socialists who had been brought up with a traditional – and far from unfounded – suspicion of Hungarian nationalism, this was an irritating symptom, and even a dangerous signal. Of course, in the moments of a nationwide crisis of the type where both those at the top and those at the bottom try to bridge a most dangerous gap and avoid a civil war, the national community seems to be the most expedient common denominator for unifying the warring social forces. Yet, although all these actions had a directly political function, where national consensus did emerge in the Hungarian revolution (primarily on the part of certain followers of Imre Nagy) this was not its prime feature. Rather, this national consensus served as a defensive shield for a nation that – apparently pathologically, but in fact with very good reason – distrusted everyone who had the slightest connection with a dictatorship being toppled by a process of stubborn demonstrations and street fights, whatever the newly acquired political physiognomy of the latter may have been. Even Imre Nagy, as a result of allowing the addition of his name to the appeal to the Soviet army (a gesture we shall discuss later), seemed to have lost popular sympathy for a short time. And if one considers the strange course of events during which Kádár gave a radical speech on November 1, and was then mentioned little more than a day later by Khrushchev and Malenkov as the possible chief representative of an authority overseeing Soviet military administration, one perhaps will not regard this general mistrust as all that paranoid. A nation constantly misused and betrayed, a nation accustomed to the fact that the more radical its left, the less sympathy it feels for its *grievances as a nation* – this nation wanted to implicate everyone in the common cause by employing the forceful gestures of a national consensus.

All of the foregoing seems clearly to support one 'simple' solution: that the Hungarian revolution was 'simply' national. But such a statement, especially considering the very marked presence of an aggressive impetus for national consensus, raises immediate explanatory problems with regard to the other, equally 'simple', principle of explanation: the liberal one. Eastern Europe hardly ever witnessed the generally happy marriage of early nineteenth-century liberalism and nationalism. The Czech example, where an overwhelmingly tolerant liberalism led the nationalist struggle, was the exception rather than the rule. In early twentieth-century Hungary, nationalism, as far as the majority of its representative types was concerned, was illiberal and parochial, with strong authoritarian leanings. Later, a more plebeian version of nationalism appeared (in the movement of the populists in the late 1920s and early 1930s) which, although it displayed enduring merit in shaping a radical collective consciousness, especially regarding the peasants' lot in a 'country of three million beggars', was from the start outrightly sceptical towards – if not a total rejection of – liberalism. Liberalism, on the other hand, was leaning towards the compromise with the Habsburg empire, the famous *Ausgleich*, in the nineteenth century, and not as to the 'lesser evil', but as to the proper order of things. In other words, it was Jewish/ cosmopolitan, or it was confederalist, and time and time again it undertook intellectual experiments with the dream of Kossuth's old days, the Danubian confederation. Even if remarkable mediators between the two poles can be discerned (the most representative of whom was László Németh, by far the best intellect of the populist movement), the opposing extremes were not limited to the intellectual life and the intelligentsia. Consequently these two apparently 'simple' solutions are both relevant to an extent, since elements of both were present in the events, but they are mutually incompatible if either of them is used as an exclusive explanatory model. And there is a particular reason for their mutual incompatibility. Liberalism is by definition a contractual arrangement of the state of social affairs, whereas nationalism (mostly) in the case of nations experiencing a dangerously and coercively delayed national existence is, for historical reasons, an organic arrangement of the state of social affairs.

There is no need to raise the centennial debate about the character of social contract to understand this basic difference between these two conceptions. Whatever form the contract should assume (it may be, in exceptional cases, a preceding one creating a total national *tabula rasa*, as with the United States of America; it may also be, and mostly is, partial and tacit consensus by the act of not questioning the rules of the game, and the like), in all cases it ideally turns to the individual to gain his or her consent to the politics pursued by the government – a government whose (equally ideal) objective is the common weal. This structure assumes the right of – even if it does not necessarily produce the preconditions and the guarantees of – changing policy objectives on the part of the citizenry, and also of leaving the framework of the contract, of substituting one nation-state for another one. Organic nationalism is by its very nature intolerant toward the idea of choice, elective affinities, contract, and especially toward the cancelling of contracts. It considers the fact that one is born into a nation, which is viewed, to use Tőnnies' categories, as a *Gemeinschaft*, and not as a *Gesellschaft*; as destiny and moral duty, a *Gemeinschaft* in which all rights are invested with the impersonal entity called 'nation', to which the individual really is only morally bound *accidentia*. A line of a famous Hungarian national poem, 'You must live and die here', expresses unequivocally this organic-irrational intolerance which can lend cohesive force to a group of otherwise egoistic individuals in emergency situations but which necessarily generates the intolerance of the general against the particular. Now, the drive to national consensus that surfaced in the Hungarian revolution was unambiguously organic in nature, which very strongly contradicts its interpretations as a 'liberal revolution'. But it has to be mentioned that one of the main protagonists of the revolution who has repeatedly appeared in our analysis,

Bibó, was at the same time the principal theorist of transforming intolerant-irrational organic nationalism into a kind of contractual patriotism. He certainly was not a cosmopolitan, and he bore a special responsibility for, and displayed an unusually strong emotional attachment to, his nation, but it was one of the prime objectives of his theoretical efforts to eliminate all elements of (national or racialist) discrimination and irrational-coercive obligation.

This tension between the two tendencies holds true in spite of the fact that the trend which we called the 'aggressive drive to national consensus' had never reached the truly tyrannical level of fundamentalism. Of course, all considerations regarding a revolution and a social upheaval which lasted for thirteen days have to be very cautious with far-reaching generalizations. Nevertheless, we think that there is a straightforward explanation of the non-fundamentalist character of this constellation: in contrast to Irish and Polish nationalist movements, the Hungarian movement *was not religious*. Of course, we do not mean to say that there are no religious people in Hungary, and not even that a majority of the population were not religious. In all probability the majority were, and still are; and if there obtained a full, and not a restricted, religious freedom in Hungary, people would profess their religious creeds publicly and in great numbers. But the thesis according to which the church has a far greater cohesive force and therefore progressive role in Poland than elsewhere because it had been for centuries the only substitute for a national independence and a separate cultural existence – such a thesis was never characteristic of Hungarian historical development. True, Transylvanian Protestantism caught between two world powers, the Ottoman and the Habsburg, became a bastion of what we call now, with a considerable amount of arbitrary modernization, 'genuine Hungarian substance'; and, equally true, Hungarian Protestantism, under constant duress, developed an ethic of bearing vicissitudes with manly dignity. It helps to explain matters when we see that both Bibó and Nagy came from families with such a Protestant background. But this 'genuine substance' and this ethic of 'dignified endurance' became a national pattern with an ever-declining (or perhaps totally lost) religious coloring. Further, and more important, in the storms of Hungarian history there had occurred a dramatic break between ethics of a religious origin and the actual religious institutions. Whereas in the seventeenth century it was relatively easy to locate where the Hungarian Catholic Church stood (it sided unhesitatingly with the Habsburgs), just as it was with the various Protestant churches, which were so many hotbeds of constantly fomenting Hungarian rebellions, one of the great deeds of the Hungarian war of national independence of 1848 consisted of an amalgamation of Hungarians of all religious persuasions (including the Jews emancipated by the revolution, who in great disproportion participated in the Hungarian insurgent army) in one nationalist enthusiasm. From this time onwards it became very difficult – if not impossible – to identify one or the other church fully with the cause of Hungarian nationalism, or, conversely, to separate fully any church from this cause. The positive result of this situation was the fairly widespread separation of nationalism and religiosity. Individual nationalists could be, and eventually in their majority perhaps were, religiously inclined, but their actions were not motivated by religious considerations and they were certainly not guided by religious institutions. In modern Hungarian history it happened rather the other way round. And to show just how many people are blatantly ignorant of this Hungarian past and present who should not be so ignorant we need only quote the following paragraph of Isaac Deutscher's personal version of the Hungarian revolution (from L'Espresso, November 25, 1956):

a religious peasantry had risen and thrown its weight behind the anticommunists . . . The ascendancy of anticommunism found its spectacular climax with Cardinal Mindszenty's triumphal entry into Budapest to the accompaniment of the bells of all the churches of the city broadcast for the whole world to hear. The Cardinal became the spiritual head of the insurrection.[3]

This historical picture of the 'white' Cardinal entering the capital to the accompaniment of bells is not only part of an unacceptable analysis of the Hungarian revolution, but is, without any doubt at all, fatally ignorant of Hungarian realities. Since Pázmány in the seventeenth century, no Hungarian cardinal has played a central – or even important – role in Hungarian politics. For, since that time, there has not existed the foundations for (any) Hungarian fundamentalism that would enable him to do so.[4]

There are a number of symptoms, a series of social problems, which in fact constituted the main concern of the shortlived Hungarian revolution, and which cannot be accounted for either by nationalism or by liberalism, and not even by their simple combination. It is this complexity that makes such an apparently simple revolution one of the truly radical and most complex social occurrences of this century. And there are many lessons still to be drawn from it. In what follows, we shall point out the phenomena that cannot be explained by a purely liberal account.

The primary obstacle to a fullblooded and orthodox liberal transformation of Hungarian society consisted in the circumstance that, in arranging the complex affairs of the Hungarian agenda, the formal and substantive aspects of freedom simply could not be separated. Liberalism, traditionally and formally, is concerned about, on the one hand, the constitutional guarantees of individual freedom and, on the other, the duties which follow from and are collateral to such civic liberties. The primary concerns of any consistent liberalism are the freedom of property (in a preferably unspecified way) and the form of government that has the duty to implement and safeguard civic liberties. It is precisely this which comprises the formal system of liberties:

formal in the sense that the more sound a liberal constitution is, the less explicit it remains regarding any particular substantive organization of the socioeconomic order of the given society, as long as any such order guarantees constitutional freedoms, including that of pluralism. Now, in the post-revolutionary and, as it seemed at the time, post-communist Hungary, no liberal arrangement of social affairs was possible, because the fundamental document, the constitution, or any draft of a constitution, had to be explicit and unambiguous regarding the crucial point – namely, how it interpreted the freedom of property. And we saw earlier when briefly analysing Bibó's 'Draft' that his solution was specifically and explicitly democratic socialist in this respect, while there is good reason for interpreting Cardinal Mindszenty's speech as an appeal to an offensive against all expropriated forms of property. We shall come back to the fundamental problem of property later, but it should be remarked here that, while there was a general discontent with the form of property that the communist regime introduced, no objective observer of the events can state that the popular majority wished to return to the pre-1945 situation. This certainly was true concerning the outcome of the agrarian revolution. Ferenc Donáth, the leading Hungarian communist expert on agrarian problems, who was the victim of a show trial during Rákosi's period, and later a victim of a not more 'legal' trial of the leading members of the Nagy group (he received 12 years' imprisonment for his role as a state minister without portfolio of the second Nagy government), proves beyond any doubt, in his brilliant book on the 1945 land partitioning process, *Reform és forradalom: a magyar mezőgazdaság strukturális átalakulása, 1945–1975* (Reform and Revolution: The Structural Transformation of Hungarian Agriculture, 1945–1975),[5] that this had been a genuine revolution. This partitioning had been implemented by spontaneously created peasant committees (who professed several different political creeds but whose members were equally revolutionary-minded), and mostly happened not with the help of but *in spite of* the coalition parties, all of whom of course had different attitudes to it, but who all agreed that it was a matter for 'experts' and had to be taken out of the hands of 'ignorant laymen'. In industry, the dissatisfaction of the workers with the prevailing state of affairs and the existing forms of expropriation in 1956 was aggressively overt and explicit. Nevertheless, the goal of new forms of socialization remained a postulate, as did important parts of the goal of workers' control. Early forms of the latter, in the triad of owner, trade union and factory committee (more or less freely elected), were achievements of the 1945–8 period which the majority of the working class were not at all ready to relinquish. These were all matters far beyond the conceptual framework and the solutions characteristic of any orthodox liberalism, but were precisely the matters which had to be deliberated upon and resolved before a new Hungarian constitution could be drafted.

In addition to the formal-substantive issue, all liberal arrangements of future social affairs raised a question which no honest liberalism can avoid: what will be the basis of legitimation for the new, allegedly liberal, social order? Viewed from this aspect, there were only two straightforward answers to the question during the revolution, *neither of them liberal.* The first had been provided by Cardinal Mindszenty. His insistence on calling the events a war of independence, instead of a revolution, was more than just terminological hairsplitting. The implication was that the independent (that is, pre-1945) Hungary had its accepted traditions, values, historically legitimized social order, and that all revolutions are necessarily directed against this order. For the Cardinal, Hungary had her unbroken tradition, and the catastrophe had quite obviously only been caused by her losing her independence. Once this was restored, no new social considerations or reforms would be necessary. Despite certain references to rights and liberties, this was the undiluted lingo of *conservatism,* and one accompanied by very little liberalism, if any, as the adult population of Hungary could still very well remember from its youth. But this stance had one technical advantage over its competitors: it did not entail headaches about 'tradition'. It enjoyed the backing of the 'millennial' tradition of the Hungarian 'historical' classes.

The second answer to the question of a liberalist legitimation can be found in Bibó's 'Draft' which was *more than liberal,* because in it Bibó combined his Cartesian-liberal convictions with a non-doctrinaire socialism. As a consequence, his solution also escaped the technical problems unavoidable with any genuine liberal attempt that lacked a continuity with the existing Hungarian liberal traditions. For Bibó, October 23 saw the birth of a new revolutionary legitimacy, which he interpreted as a historical act putting a final end to the Hungary of both communist and conservative dictatorships; as the day of the first victorious *radical-democratic* Hungarian revolution. There is a fundamental paragraph in his 'Draft' which we quote in full:

The compensation for all the economic and moral injustices, infringements of rights, and property expropriations must under no conditions be implemented on the basis of the restitution of the *status quo ante;* all compensations have to be effected whilst observing the ban on exploitative situations, and *not according to the measure* of the economic power position, but to that of destroyed homes, annihilated careers, the confiscated yield of personal fortune acquired by work.[6]

In short, then, we regard the Hungarian revolution as neither exclusively national nor exclusively liberal, but as a far more complex scenario. In the main, we subscribe to Bibó's conception: that it was the first radical-democratic revolution of Hungarian history.

WAS THE REVOLUTION NECESSARY?

This question, so often asked about the Hungarian October, loses much of its sense on closer semantic scrutiny. For such a question, if it is properly asked, is addressed to the subject *sensu stricto* of the action, and can be reformulated in the following manner: 'Was it reasonable on your part to act so?' or, alternatively, 'Were you compelled, either by internal or external, motives, drives or "urges", to make a revolution?' And to all questions about 'making a revolution' Hannah Arendt's answer inappellably applies:

Textbook instructions on 'how to make a revolution', in a step-by-step progression from dissent to conspiracy, from resistance to armed uprising are all based on the mistaken notion that revolutions are 'made'. In a contest of violence against violence the superiority of the government has always been absolute; but this superiority lasts only as long as the power structure of the government is intact – that is, as long as commands are obeyed and the army or police forces are prepared to use their weapons. When this is no longer the case, the situation changes abruptly. Not only is the rebellion not put down, but the arms themselves change hands – sometimes, as in the Hungarian Revolution, within a few hours . . . Only after this has happened, when the disintegration of the government in power has permitted the rebels to arm themselves, can one speak of 'armed uprising', *which often does not take place at all or occurs when it is no longer necessary.* When commands are no longer obeyed, the means of violence are of no use; and the question of this obedience is not decided by the command-obedience relation but by opinion, and, of course, by the number of those who share it. Everything depends on the power behind the violence. The sudden dramatic breakdown of power that ushers in revolutions reveals in a flash how civil obedience – to laws, to rulers, to institutions – is but the outward manifestation of support and consent.[7]

A short study of the manifest forms of the Hungarian revolution will immediately testify to the veracity of Arendt's claim that this revolution had not been made, but had indeed 'continuously made itself'. First of all, the myth that the Hungarian revolution had been a primarily military action must be debunked. Its unstoppable momentum, augmented by at best only a few thousand armed insurgents,[8] made obsolete many a sterile discussion of nineteenth-century socialists (primarily of Engels, who liked the role of a revolutionary general) as to whether and to what extent armed actions are still conceivable in the era of 'modern weapons', especially heavy artillery. Arendt's statement about the armed uprising that 'often does not take place at all or occurs when it is no longer necessary' was in fact a straight translation into words of events. It was not a mythical military counterpower, but the faltering spirit of discipline of the army and the police forces, and including that of the commanding officers (systematically eroded for years by the moral and political propaganda of rebellious – and mostly, though not exclusively – communist writers and journalists against the incurable Stalinism of the regime), that made an armed uprising totally superfluous and, where it did occur, an event *ex post facto*. But another factor must be immediately added as well. The spirit of national consensus (which we have already analyzed) suddenly appeared here and wrought a powerful effect on the social actors. Whether one believed or only pretended to believe that 'all Hungarians are brethren', armed action on the part of Hungarian military personnel (except, again, the AVH forces) became in most cases a paralyzing moral impossibility.

In order to understand the 'non-made' but 'self-making' character of the revolution, it is necessary to deflate yet another legend. It had been a Hungarian joke for many years that the Hungarian people examined too diligently the Soviet films about the October revolution, and thus memorized (and then imitated) how revolutionaries took over the power centers (telegraph, railroad stations, barracks, etc.) of Petrograd, paralyzing the Provisionary Government. This will do for a joke but it is a false description of the events. There were hardly any public buildings taken over by particular groups of the Hungarian masses participating in the revolution. The siege of the radio building at about 9 p.m. on October 23, which provoked the first salvos of the 'Blues' and which touched off the actual uprising, was rather an angry reaction to the stubbornness of the authorities in refusing to allow the people to broadcast their petitions. In fact the broadcasting services were simply switched off and the government announcements were broadcast from that evening onwards from the parliament building: the power stations themselves, located outside the cities, were mostly guarded by Soviet units, and even when they were not, there were no attempts at cutting them off. And the people were not stupid enough to believe that an impromptu siege of the radio building would destroy the Hungarian government's broadcasting capacity. Of course, certain public buildings had in fact been occupied: first of all the prisons, still full of political prisoners,[9] and the printing houses, in order to print and distribute all sorts of revolutionary appeals, newspapers, manifestos and documents. In a word, one can say that, while the Hungarian revolutionaries had not occupied the Winter Palace, they did lay siege to the Bastille.

What were the actual methods and manifest forms of the Hungarian revolution? First of all, the *general strike*, which later (after the second intervention and when the workers' council already had a headquarters in the form of the Budapest Workers' Council) became a concerted action, had in fact started – spontaneously and sporadically but always gaining momentum – immediately after the morning of October 24. This was partly due simply to the impact of the chaos following the first intervention (it is difficult to sustain normal industrial activity when a city is full of hostile and nervous soldiers who can't understand the language but are ready to shoot at the first sign), and partly occurred as a spontaneous and angry reaction to the flood of government communiqués between October 24 and 26, which poured slander and abuse on the working class (in whose name they supposedly ruled the country). But the unorganized nature of the general strike meant that at least some, and occasionally most, of the workers still went to the workplace, and this provided an opportunity (the first in practically ten years) for workers to meet and discuss freely the state of affairs. It was from these casual meetings that the new historical institutions, the workers' councils, gradually took shape.

Secondly, the unstoppable cycle of peaceful but passionate *mass demonstrations*, in Budapest and in the countryside alike, carried the slogans and the message of the revolution farther than any 'central command' could have done. In fact, the demonstrations were reminiscent of ancient choruses, in which the slogans, responding to and interacting with one another, educated the participants. And this really was a process of self-education. We remember quite well how surprising (and almost unbelievable) it was for us, as then reformist socialists, when the slogan 'Imre Nagy into the government!' had turned within an hour among 300,000 people demonstrating on the streets on October 23 into another, creating total *tabula rasa:* 'Free elections!' 'Self-education of the masses in the revolutionary process' – this dry slogan of party seminars had become a vivid reality, and the constant demonstrations which had as their sole function this self-manifesting and educating goal became irresistible.

Thirdly, the whole country had been transformed into *one collective moment of civil disobedience.* The world soon realized this because the government broadcasts had alternately pleaded with and intimidated the population, one minute threatening them with immediate extermination via martial law, the next minute appealing to their 'better feelings'. This somewhat surprising vacillation between paternal rigor and tender maternal affection was a result of the simple reality that people no longer obeyed one single government decree, much less the political decrees, and not even the unpolitical (civilian) ones. Even the streetcars followed, whenever they could, a 'self-managed' schedule. Sometimes this stubborn disobedience seemed to be, and indeed often was, a goal in itself, and it produced enormous chaos (and the government, sending a whole nation, after a well-organized system of terror, into complete disarray with its own obdurateness and indecision, later banked on this chaos for its propaganda). This single-minded disobedience revealed the main characteristic of this rebellious subject: its undomesticable anti-authoritarianism.

Finally, and without much ado, people had simply brought about the *freedom of the press* without waiting for any permission or encouragement. Those who earlier liked to portray in their propaganda films an unperturbed

Lenin in full equanimity in the midst of total revolutionary havoc later were scandalized by the 'disorderly way' in which the Hungarian revolutionary press was produced, printed and distributed. But in fact it was a very encouraging sign and a display of the general integrity of the revolutionaries, that after the Dudás group (one of the most adventurous) had taken over the printing house of the party press they did not veto the simultaneous publication of any (perhaps antagonistic) journal. There was only one publication that the printers refused to put out: the *Virradat* (Dawn), the journal of the Arrow Cross movement, the Hungarian Nazis.

The voice of *realpolitik* will certainly make the following objection. The Hungarian nation ought to have known, both by virtue of her lengthy past experiences with great powers from the Ottoman empire to the empire of the Romanovs, and her experience of Soviet communism, that such a challenge by a small nation would not remain unpunished. It ought to have been realized in advance that such occurrences as thousands killed in police action, hundreds afterwards executed, and tens of thousands imprisoned for many years, along with a social and cultural life the dynamics of which lie suspended for many years – that these things would very likely happen. In fact, they were rather lucky to escape the series of Katyns and mass deportations that many of the 'martyr nations' of the Soviet Union experienced. Also, luckily, they had a 'leader' imposed upon them (in an agreement between two foreign governments, the Soviet and the Yugoslav) who turned out to be a remarkably lucid Machiavellian realist. What they have finally achieved could have been achieved with a much more moderate movement, or rather, it could have been achieved only by a more moderate movement. This is an argument which cannot simply be dismissed. It has to be answered point by point.

Bibó, in the first sentences of his 'Draft', also refers to the charge of a 'lack of realism', and angrily answers it: 'In so far as it [the Hungarian revolution] was declared a posteriori to be without a deliberated perspective from the beginning, it was made and it unfolded unaccompanied by such a perspective not because of its own insensible attitude but because of its being abandoned to its fate.'[10] But of course the moot point here is not the perfidy and shortsightedness of Western governments, more than sufficiently proven, but, rather, the attitude of the other side. Was the Soviet leadership ready, even for a historic moment, to consider realistically the alternatives presented by the Hungarian revolution, or had it worked always with one alternative? Molnár writes the following:

Whatever the Soviet attitude was in reality, all the decisions made by Nagy between October 27th and 31st seemed to have been ratified by Moscow, *including the re-establishment of former political parties and the withdrawal of troops.* If one may believe Western observers, Khrushchev, on being questioned on October 29 at a reception at the Turkish Embassy in Moscow, even went so far as to envisage a neutral status for Hungary similar to that of Finland [which, by definition, would have included the abrogation of the Warsaw Pact membership on the part of Hungary]. *Pravda* announced on October 30: 'Budapest returns to normal life.' The following day the famous declaration of the Soviet Government was published, which admitted that faults and errors had been committed by Moscow with regard to the People's Democracies, in that they had reduced 'the significance of the principles of equality of rights in relations with the Socialist states.' It is a declaration of principle, but also an announcement of a major decision, worded: '. . . the Soviet Government is ready to take part in negotiations with the Government of the People's Republic of Hungary, and with other signatories of the Warsaw Pact, concerning the question of the presence of Soviet troops on Hungarian territory . . .'[11]

Even if Khrushchev's remark about the possibility of Hungary's 'Finnish status' was an unashamed lie, the fact remains that the type of lie that a politician can afford is not a matter of random choice. Can one imagine a Soviet politican then, who would *lie* that the politburo is considering the possibility of Ukrainian independence and neutrality, or the possibility of the restoration of the multi-party system in the Soviet Union? Accordingly, it is reasonable to assume (and we do) that during the crucial days of October 27 to November 1 there were at least earnest and influential factions in the Chinese and Soviet leaderships (then in constant communication) that were not dogmatically resolved upon the second intervention.[12] This is also evidenced by the fact (already mentioned) that on November 1 Kádár made his speech in the name of the 'new' (that is, reorganised) party declaring October 23 the day of a glorious uprising restoring Hungarian freedom and national independence. Kádár, one of the most suspicious minds ever involved in Hungarian political life, who, as a prisoner for many years, had learned the Russian lesson the hard way, was hardly the man to be lured into such a gravely incriminating statement without both prior consultations with Andropov and the belief that there was at least a chance of the 'Finlandization' of Hungary (in which case, of course, he did not want to find himself totally out of power). To our mind, all of this confirms that the Hungarian *revolution* did have a chance of lasting success, provided that three factors were simultaneously present: a collective-national Hungarian readiness for a measure of compromise (particularly in matters regarding Soviet strategic interests, and readiness in this respect has been amply proved by us); a convincing signal on the part of the Western, and in particular of the American, governments that détente would be initiated forthwith (and its absence has equally amply been proved by us); plus the combined pressure on the part of Chinese, Yugoslav, Italian and French communists on the Soviet government to come to terms with the Hungarian defeat. We know where we stand as far as the third prerequisite is concerned.

Bibó makes the following short statement on the *cause* of the events becoming revolutionary:

But, anyhow, the fact that the Hungarian revolution gained momentum was not a result of its own insensibility but of the foolhardiness and bloodshed provoked by the leadership and the secret police forces; and the revolution, despite its being unprepared and unorganized, when seen as a response to bloodshed, was remarkably sober, humane and moderate.[13]

Though this much is undoubtedly correct, a full understanding requires a much longer and more complex explanation. First, the long period between June 1953 and March 1955, with its alternations between verbal renewals of the promises contained in Nagy's 'new policy speech' and their subsequent and constant miscarriage caused by a shrewd sabotage of the Rákosist leadership (including even – except for certain leftists – the decelerated release and rehabilitation of political prisoners), had made an already mistrustful population hostilely skeptical towards *any* promise coming from communist governments. The miracle was rather that the explosion came so late, not that it came. Secondly, and on the other hand, the practically open factionist activity between March 1953 and October 1956 of mostly, though not exclusively, communist intellectuals – put another way, the activity of a 'pressure group', an activity which was later 'legally' declared high treason, and something which at any rate had happened for the first time in communist countries for 30 years – this activity was double-edged. In part, it undermined the moral stamina of many Stalinist or ex-Stalinist key functionaries. The classic case is that of Sándor Kopácsi (later condemned to life imprisonment), the police commissioner of Budapest, who was gradually convinced by the literary propaganda that shooting at his own people was a crime, and not a duty. But even those who still remained loyal to old-time Stalinist convictions had at least become uncertain about the 'best' way of acting, and reluctance in a critical situation is fatal from the standpoint of tyrannical governments.

As interpreters of the events we simply find it unfair when the present party chroniclers blame everything on the 'indecision' of the 'compromised' Gerő leadership. Gerő was anything but unprepared for the role of a mini-Stalin. A communist with a long and heroic record, his behavior under the torture of the Horthy police in 1923 was a model case of Bolshevik standards. He had been a trained Comintern functionary, learning in France how to manipulate political parties, learning in Spain how to manipulate a mass revolution; he was a colonel of the Soviet army, a perfectly coldblooded man, and a person of remarkable intelligence. A full capacity for decisive action, for cracking down on the opposition (and on a whole people, if necessary) was present in him; it could even be said to be his natural inclination. *But to act on his own was both against his convictions and the functions assigned to him by the Soviet leadership,* and the directives – which later became merely 'signals' – that he received from Moscow were contradictory, confusing, and changed by the week. It was somewhat cavalier on the part of Khrushchev to call both Rákosi and Gerő 'idiots' in front of Micunović. The constant inner struggles of an as yet unconsolidated Soviet leadership made their puppets incapable of action, and this incapacity reached its peak in the evening and during the night of October 23 – a deficiency characterized by Lukács via the cynical wisdom, 'Nothing is worse than a weak-handed tyranny!'

In fact, during this memorable afternoon, evening and night, this leadership did everything and yet nothing; they did too much and yet not enough. First they banned the mass demonstration, and then later changed their mind and gave public consent to it, which was no sign of liberalism but of indecision. During the demonstration none of the leaders was visible; nor, for that matter, were they visible at any time during the revolution, the sole exception being Imre Nagy, whom they implored to 'appease' the masses, but who did not receive any official capacity or bargaining power to enable him to do so. As it seemed then, the only result of this undertaking, doomed from the outset, was to kill the reputation of a rival before the masses. Gerő, in a speech broadcast by Hungarian radio at 8 p.m., insulted the entire population in a typically arrogant manner,[14] and it was a natural reaction that a nervous – even hysterical – and ever-increasing crowd would want to enter the radio building and have their various manifestos broadcast. This situation can be properly dealt with by a government in two ways and only two ways: either its proper authorities are armed and then deployed to defend to the utmost the (symbolically crucial) radio building (which – as we shall show later – without negotiations is a plain 'declaration of war' on the populace), or it can attempt negotiations, having at least certain documents broadcast in the hope that next day the atmosphere will calm, and the protagonists will be more amenable to productive discussion. But the Gerő leadership invented a third answer: the numerically weak AVH unit defending the radio building was authorized to shoot salvos at the crowd, and in the intensive barricade struggle that ensued it was annihilated by a crowd that produced arms from all directions. On the lighter side, the armored military unit sent to support did not even have ammunition; this was obviously in order to avoid serious bloodshed. The leaders immediately went into a central committee session, which, after an all-night debate, brought Nagy personally, as Prime Minister, into the leading body of the party (without even consulting him about this decision: he was waiting in the lobby), yet this was done without bringing any of his allies into similar central positions; all the hated names were left in the leadership. Moreover, this meeting had at least endorsed, even if in all probability it did not initiate, the first Soviet invasion. This was, indeed, everything and yet nothing. It was more than sufficient to inflame a rebellion. In fact, the communist leaders had left their people with no other choice but that of a total revolt against them.

THE NEW REPUBLIC

In delineating the great *constructive* act of the Hungarian revolution, we would be with the spirit of Arendt if we raise first of all the question of *legitimation*. Arendt was firmly convinced, and in our view correctly so, that without forging a new consensus and opposing it to the traditional one there is no body politic deserving to be termed radical. Without such a new consensus only a further despotism can come about. In this respect, the political leaders (if such a description fits at all the identifiable protagonists of this eminently anti-authoritarian revolution) had been confronted with a serious problem, and one that escalated as the revolution swept ahead. With some cynicism, it could be said that it was only for two extremists that the situation presented no difficulties: for Gerő and for Mindszenty. For the First Secretary, legitimation (if he was concerned with such 'bourgeois' formalities at all) began with the 1948 takeover – an event formalized into some sort of a constitution in 1949, all deviation from which was illegitimate. For the Primate, in an equally simple way, everything from 1948 – perhaps even from March 1944 – onward (the latter being the date of the German occupation of Hungary) was illegitimate. But what could a genuinely reformist communist like Imre Nagy, or a non-communist radical representative of a nation in revolt, such as Bibó, accept as a real, democratic and radical basis of consensus? There was no easy way to answer this question. Up until October 23, it was the intellectuals (and, of them, mostly the communists or ex-communists) who acted demonstratively in the forefront of a tacit public opinion, but this could not be accepted as a substitute for the public opinion proper.[15]

Consequently, if the new political actors intended to act honestly, and they certainly did, they could not refer to any preforged and expressed consensus. It was equally impossible to legitimize the new and still emerging social order either by the existing laws or by any tradition: by the existing laws, for the simple reason that a pluralistic democracy (already demanded during the October 23 demonstration, a demand growing into a general slogan during the days between October 24 and 30) was incompatible with any existing law in Hungary, however flexible the decrees of the regime; by tradition, because in Hungary history could not provide the necessary guidelines, as, for instance, it could in Czechoslovakia. If we only look back at the example of the Pilzen demonstration, during which the portraits of Masaryk and Beneš had suddenly materialized, we can at least *assume* that the tradition of the liberal–pluralistic republic was still alive in Czech political memory. But in the case of Hungary even this shaky ground for a new legitimation could not be trumped up out of the depths of history. For the majority of Hungarians, we do not have the slightest doubt, the tradition of prewar Hungary had vanished, and this was a good thing, too. But the laws and decrees of the coalition days (1945–8) would no longer have been adequate, either, and realistic observers of the events (some of them on the liberal side) had admitted as much.[16]

It is by way of this 'legitimation gap', and not via a lack of either courage or resolution, that we can explain the drawn-out process of a final decision on the part of many protagonists. Imre Nagy was appointed Prime Minister in the early hours of October 24 by István Dobi, the 'President of the Presidential Council'. At one time Dobi had been an honest organizer of landless peasants in their fight against the landowners, but had then become an alcoholic and a political weakling; a man who begged his ex-Smallholders mates during the revolution for admittance, but who would have appointed Andropov as Hungarian prime minister on the spot had he been ordered to do so with sufficient firmness. The problem for Nagy, in his later attempts to extricate himself, was obviously the concern with the Robespierrian question – the problem of 'in the name of what' could he start everything anew, and what would be the generally acceptable form of this new beginning. Similarly, the procrastination of Béla Kovács concerning his joining the second Nagy government (or of coming to Budapest at all to participate in political life), or that of Bibó who, as we have seen, became a political actor only in the last two days of the revolution, was very closely connected with the problem of legitimacy – a problem that for both of them was very important, as both had been brought up in a legalistic spirit.

These different but equally representative protagonists of the revolution had obviously grappled with different problems regarding legitimation. It was after a long struggle with his Bolshevik conscience that Nagy had come finally to accept the multi-party system.[17] But from the start it seems that he was determined *not* to enforce to any great degree his so-called 'legitimate duties'; these would inevitably have bound him to massacre many thousands of his compatriots. Here is a decisive statement of Nagy's from his trial – an act by which he knowingly tightened the rope around his neck. Nagy maintained even at the trial, when his approval of this decree (of martial law decided by the central committee session during the night of October 23–4 against 'counterrevolutionary elements' – in other words, against the insurgents) would have been in his favor, that he had interpreted it as a measure affecting 'only common criminals against the common law' (Hungarian Government White Book, p. 73). When asked in court whether he intended it to be applied to the rebels, Nagy replied: *'No, I did not want the law applied against them.'*[18] This and similar acts during the days October 24–7, after which he set himself free and transferred his headquarters to the parliament building, were already punctures made by him in the 1949 constitution – a document the legitimacy of which was sham, and which was imposed on a people who now, in their revolutionary spirit, wanted to rid themselves of it. In so far as his 'legal' executioners state this of Nagy, they appraise his personality and convictions with relative correctness (though we shall see whether this gave any legal entitlements to try him). As time went on, Nagy must have increasingly realized that he had to choose between this sham legality and the explicit wishes of the people. And among these wishes there was one certainty: the people wanted a multi-party system and genuinely free elections. Upon finally deciding to side with the masses *and remain in office* (and at least *for this man* we are justified in attributing unselfish motives for this), he had to search for a new principle of legitimation that had nothing to do with Dobi and his associates.

This was the principle embodied in the draft programme of his second government. As stated in Kádár's speech on November 1, it accepted: first, October 23 as the basis of the new situation; secondly, the multi-party system, which the government in fact represented, though with the proviso that only the 1945 coalition parties could participate in it; and, thirdly, the neutrality of Hungary. In the light of this short, compact and dramatic statement, it is more than a heroic gesture that Imre Nagy, when asked about his 'civilian status' during his trial, gave his position as the 'President of the Council'. When, after the furore that this gesture caused among the 'judges' had subsided, he was corrected by the president of the tribunal ('You are the ex-President of the Council'), he answered: 'I do not think so. My appointment dates back to October 24, 1956. No legal authority has questioned this appointment.'[19] Nagy must have known that Dobi had signed his demotion (and Kádár's appointment) on November 4 or 5, and had done so without any hesitation whatsoever. But this, together with the fact that he declined to appeal for clemency, was *more* than an act of courage or staunch dignity in the face of death: it was a last act of abrogation of the legitimation of the ruling power in the name of another legitimation created by the revolution of October 23. We have seen from Kővágó's book that Béla Kovács had reservations quite contrary in character. Similar – even though differently motivated – suspicions are manifest in the attitude of Anna Kéthly, the leader of the social democrats. First, she wanted to obtain the consent of the Second International (a body which later, in a most disgraceful way, and as a gesture of *Ostpolitik*, made a motion to expel their comrades in exile in order to mollify Suslov and company – a strategy which was, of course, not in the least successful). This was not only a moral, but also a logical step. The Nagy government could have been a kind of continuation of a Popular Front government, and that would no longer have been consistent with social democratic policy. Consent was therefore necessary. In his 'Draft', Bibó seems to have found the happy synthesis between these two poles, even if this remained for at least a quarter of a century a purely theoretical gesture hidden from the majority of his nation. The phrase from point 1 of the positive part of his 'Draft' – 'The government deduces its legitimacy from the Hungarian revolution of October 23 and not from the Rákosi Constitution of 1949'[20] – combined with further clauses which have already been quoted and/or analyzed, produces this synthesis or reconciliation. On the one hand, these points provided constitutional guarantees of all human and civic freedoms, including free elections with the participation of non-socialist (liberal or liberal–democratic) parties. On the other hand, they provided equal constitutional guarantees for all the structural changes which had been implemented after 1945 (agrarian reform, property expropriation), though without perpetuating the then tyrannical forms of the latter, but, rather, partly leaving open the door for new forms of ownership, partly legislatively ushering in self-management. This new basis of legitimation was based on a concept that we may call 'consensus in the making'.[21]

Nevertheless, after consideration, does not the new draft constitution, based on this 'consensus in the making', turn out to be a conflict model containing necessarily colliding elements between the formal and the substantive aspects of freedom? This objection has been repeatedly raised against all interpretations of the Hungarian revolution that candidly took into account two of its apparently diverging and yet fundamental aspects: the visible quest of the population for new democratic forms of *socialized* property, and the equally visible and irresistible demand of a free multi-party system. Let us also note that while Bibó's draft constitution seems to be a genuine synthesis of the main tendencies of the revolution, and while at least in the political sphere it does contain restrictions of a substantive nature (no reappropriation of the land confiscated and partitioned during the agrarian revolution, or of any other major 'force of production', such as factories and big enterprises; and limitations on the size of privately owned land, while, of course, guaranteeing the freedom of all sorts of small property such as the peasant's land, the merchant's shop and the like), it does *not* contain any limitation regarding the formal aspects of civic liberties, especially the rights of any party to enter the electoral campaign. (Obviously there was a tacit agreement, which was otherwise imposed on Hungary by the peace treaty by all victorious powers, to ban all fascist parties.) Now, are not these two tendencies conflicting ones? What happens if a party with a programme of general reappropriation of socialized property appears on the political scene? Was not Bibó's draft constitution a deeply inconsistent document revealing the inner and unresolvable contradictions of the Hungarian revolution; a document that aimed at complete freedom, and which intended to retain, *after substantial social changes*, what could appropriately be called a 'socialist system of property'. Bibó, here again, displayed his theoretical greatness both as a statesman and a lawgiver to his nation when he simply considered that a democratic constitution is not an abstract expression of liberties, rights and duties, but *their expression based on the particular type of consensus which preceded and brought it into being.* The rules of the game are set according to the consensus founding the body politic, and Bibó, in our view correctly, had assumed that the rules prescribed by the 'consensus in the making' were basically socialist ones in so far as they wished to retain in an *essentially modified* form the expropriated property relations and, by democratization, even emphasize their socialist character. Therefore the substantive limitations and the unlimited formal liberties are in complete harmony in his document.

But the Hungarian 'men in the street' very clearly understood one important lesson of history: that without an adequate and imposing social force all constitutions, even the best ones, are exposed to the dangers of Weimar; to being overthrown either by Stalinist or by ultra-rightist conservatives. The general slogan of the revolution, 'We do not return either land or factory' (a slogan which cannot even be denied by the official 'history' of the events, though it is called a 'shrewd trick' of the 'revisionists'), was directed against both. Departing from this and other needs, the Hungarian revolution created its own and totally original *dual system*: a model form of the 'New Republic', which consisted in the combination of councils and traditional political parties in a unified system. We have to distinguish it from what is called, wrongly in our view, 'dual power', in imitation of Russian political history between February and October 1917. The coexistence of Soviets and traditional political parties was transitory, imposed on both sides by extraordinary historical situations, and not meant as a lasting solution by either of them. With the exception of the Menshevik and SR parties, and, as it seemed then (but only then), the Bolsheviks, the traditional political parties wanted liberalism (in the form of the republic or the constitutional monarchy), but they loathed the interference of the masses in 'their business' of policy making. The masses of soldiers, peasants and factory workers were mistrustful of professional politicians, and with good reason. The former had a socially more radical (even if vaguely formulated) program, but since they had not then experienced the beauties of a one-party system, and had, through the dark centuries of Russian political history, undergone something less than a general democratic education, they were quite careless about constitutional guarantees of a political pluralism. Not so the people in Hungary in 1956, after eight years of an exceptionally brutal and murderous one-party dictatorship. The thrust of constitutional guarantees – guarantees expressed by and consolidated in a free multi-party system – was irresistible. But since the Hungarian masses had lived under a system of 'dictatorship over needs' two overwhelming character traits of the *subject* (not the *citizen*) of these sytems, generally overlooked or only negatively treated, came equally and irresistibly to the fore in the moment of social explosion: a general distrust (sometimes heightened to hysteria, and often driven to its other extreme: uncritical and dangerous credulity), and indomesticable anti-authoritarianism. The latter is not necessarily identical with a total lack of social discipline, though it involves the acceptance of self-imposed discipline alone. It was from these two needs that the political initiative of creating councils (of the most varied sort) had sprung. Coming immediately to the functions and the character of these councils, it will suffice to emphasize that, in Hungary 1956, the famous 'crowd in the revolution' did want political parties. It felt stronger sympathies for certain of them, barely tolerated others, and all in all deemed their permanent (and not merely temporary) existence as a necessary feature of the state of affairs, *yet did not for one instant consider abandoning itself to any one or more of them*. The people knew that sooner or later they would have to return to work; that they would have to go back to their factories, enterprises and land (even if not under conditions imposed on them by the 'People State', which they were no longer ready to tolerate), and would consequently need the relative independence of the political class, plus its expertise. Yet they were adamant that social and political matters would not slip out of their fingers again, even though the melodies of campaign speeches might be ever so sweet, and their lyrics enticingly nationalist and freedom loving. The *coexistence of political parties and councils* (with certain exceptions discussed below) was an express and general wish of the 'crowd in the revolution': the system was *not* identical with the Russian 'dual power'.

The political role and composition of the workers' councils was an important factor in the events of the Hungarian revolution, and a short summary of their genesis, objectives and functions is now called for. We will base this on the work of Molnár and especially Lomax, the two historians who did the most for the objective and sympathetic portrayal of these genuinely revolutionary institutions. Molnár begins his chronicle on October 26:

In the space of forty-eight hours all the factories in the country had their elected councils, and at the moment of the cease-fire several central councils, representing the workers of a whole town or department, were formed, in particular at Miskolc, Győr, Magyaróvár, and in certain suburbs of Budapest.[22]

To this, Lomax adds the important example of a small but industrially all-important town, Salgótarján, in which the steel foundry and its workers' council became the centrepoint of the workers' resistance to all Stalinist manipulations and threats.[23] Molnár further characterizes these councils in a manner that we do not wholly agree with.

In short, instead of imitating the Yugoslav model, which was little known, they followed the Soviet models of 1905 and 1917, exactly as they had been taught in Marxist courses, and intended to apply them according to their own inspiration. The first concern of the councils, moreover, was not production but strikes; political strikes, which soon became general and were used to support the armed uprising and impose the people's claims on the Government.[24]

Even if Molnár emphasizes the enormous political service that the councils had rendered for the revolution ('But without the councils the rebels would not have been able to impose on the Government their conditions for the cease-fire'), it is still important to turn to Lomax's analysis to see the full implications of the statesmanship of the workers' councils:

Finally, on 31 October, a Parliament of Workers' Councils was convened for the whole of Budapest, at which delegates from some two dozen of the city's largest factories were present. The meeting drew up a statement of the basic rights and duties of the workers' councils, which were formulated in the following nine points: '1. *The factory belongs to the workers.* The latter should pay to the state a levy calculated on the basis of the output and a portion of the profits. 2. The supreme controlling body of the factory is the Workers' Council, democratically elected by the workers. 3. The Workers' Council elects its own executive committee, composed of between three and nine members which acts as the executive body of the Workers' Council, carrying out the decisions and tasks laid down by it. 4. The director is employed by the factory. The director and the highest employees are to be elected by the Workers' Council. This election will take place after a public general meeting called by the executive committee. 5. The director is responsible to the Workers' Council in every matter which concerns the factory. 6. The Workers' Council itself reserves all rights to: (a) Approve and ratify all matters concerning the enterprise; (b) Decide basic wage levels and the methods by which these are to be assessed; (c) Decide on all matters concerning foreign contracts. 7. In the same way, *the Workers' Council resolves any conflicts concerning the hiring and firing of all workers employed in the enterprise.* 8. The Workers' Council has the right to examine the balance sheets and to decide on the use to which the profits are to be put. 9. The Workers' Council handles all social questions in the enterprise.'[25]

Whereas it is clear from this and similar documents that the working class (and generally, the 'state wage-earners') of Hungary had radically raised and equally radically solved the problem of ownership in a socialist way, it is yet equally true that views had, then and after the second intervention, diverged as regards the extrafactory, directly political and governmental functions of the councils. On the one hand, Molnár quotes a very interesting (though in all probability a minor) example of an attempt at organized, universal and direct workers' (or producers') democracy – 'The delegation from the Borsod workers' council "*resolutely condemns the organization of political parties*" '[26] – and Lomax analyzes in detail how after the second intervention, under crippling political conditions in which the working class had resolutely fought for a long time against the intervening foreign army and its Hungarian agencies, the ideas of a National Workers' Council (a kind of council-government) had arisen. But, in the main, one seems to be entitled to say that the state wage-earners had clung firmly to their property, the units of production, resocialized in the form of a direct democracy, but had accepted the existence of a pluralistic political 'upper structure', the multi-party system, and free elections. And it is precisely the workers' councils as *collective proprietors* wherein we must look for both the social guarantee and the basis of the 'consensus in the making' which induced Bibó to introduce substantive restrictions into his draft constitution. And it was not mere guesswork on this theorist's part when he asserted the existence of such a 'consensus in the making'. He could, and he did, avail himself of two objective forms of evidence: of documents, and of the manifestation of a will of all (or nearly all).

The points we have italicized in the long quotation from Lomax raise two important problems. The first relates to the ultimate authority of ownership and reveals the single inconsistency of Bibó's theoretical masterpiece, the 'Draft of a compromise solution of the Hungarian question'. As we re-member, the October 31 resolution stated that 'the factory belongs to the workers', and it is this that decides the question of property in favor of collective ownership of productive units (or units of production) by workers' committees. Subpoints (bb) and (cc) of point (c) in the draft constitution assume (in bb) 'the retaining of the *nationalization* of mines, banks and heavy industry', and (in point cc) 'the *communal ownership* of existing factories based on the workers' management, and the workers' shareholding or participation in the profit'.[27] These are undoubtedly two distinct program-mes that in their contradiction circumscribe the first major task that this new Hungary born of a revolution ought to have decided upon, had the army 'rendering internationalist support' allowed time for such deliberations.

The issue of the workers' councils' explicit wish to reserve for themselves all rights of hiring and firing the personnel of the factory is somewhat more complex. Such a proviso must sound strange to Western workers, so accustomed to the existence of trade unions and the guarantees provided by them precisely against standdowns, firing, and the like. This is doubly strange if one first considers the fact that the only important and relatively free sections of the Hungarian working-class movement between the world wars were the so-called 'organized workers' (in other words, the trade union members), and so unionism had been an important Hungarian tradition; and secondly, if we think of the Polish breakthrough via Solidarity. There are also important theoretical considerations against such a solution, because there is wisdom in the duplication of the individual into both *direct proprietor* (in his or her factory, enterprise, office) and member of a *direct municipal democracy* (a *citizen*) participating in a pluralism of political parties, however much these two distinct roles can, under specific circumstances, run counter to one another. And, equally, there is wisdom in tridimensionality, the third function being that of the trade union member. There are certain functions (such as sustaining the regional or branch wage level, the level of unemployment and the like) which cannot be invested with a unit of production necessarily preoccupied with its own level of profitability and social security problems but not directly involved in similar problems of other units or the industrial branch. These functions can, of course, be invested with the state exclusively, but only at the price of dangerously increasing its power. Thus a really free trade union becomes a necessary addition to the new system of socialization, and it was the single major flaw of the state wage-earners' radicalism that they practically denied the trade unions any social role. At the same time, it is also an understandable flaw. The general anti-authoritarianism, this leading feature of the Hungarian revolution, turned strongly against the parodies of workers' agencies, the trade unions as they existed under a Leninist dictatorship. And while the workers (most realistically) did not deny the necessity of the *relative* separation of the state agencies (this occurring, of course, under close supervision) they believed that every matter concerning the workers' lot should be dealt with as close to the shop floor as possible. In their way of thinking, the trade union organization seemed to be too far removed, too abstract a milieu.

The surprising radicalism in the practical arrangements of social affairs on the part of the Hungarian masses was due to two factors, one 'necessary', the other 'accidental'. The first has been described sufficiently and need not be repeated here again in detail: that the subject of the system of dictatorship over needs is distrustful and anti-authoritarian, and therefore, if it is let loose, it only accepts social solutions which guarantee maximum liberty; and, whereas it is not by necessity undisciplined, it must be a self-imposed discipline alone that this subject will accept. It is exactly the type of institution that springs from such an attitude that we have described above. On the other side the 'accidental', or in a somewhat more accurate terminology, historically conditioned factor was the total social vacuum that the average Hungarian was confronted with the moment that the communist dictatorship clamorously collapsed. Prewar Hungary had proved bankrupt and criminal. No significant party or political and social force had a legitimate claim to the task of restoring its prewar social order. (And none made such a claim, for that matter.) But the coalition times of 1945–7 were not a tradition to return to, either. For a start, those years were not all that free. Already in 1946, the so-called 'Military Political Section' – in other words, the Hungarian military counter-intelligence, the head of which was General Pálffy (later executed with Rajk) – reintroduced the whole horrendous system of physical torture to obtain false confessions. The freedom of the press was extensively curtailed. The non-communist or anti-communist majority parties (or their coalition in the conglomerate called the Smallholders' Party) behaved with remarkable cowardice. They either remained silent as one disobedient MP after the other disappeared as a 'conspirator', or even contributed to their self-humiliation, which eventually became their self-liquidation. Most important, they could not produce – once again with the sole exception of Bibó, who wrote an extensive and constructive study of the 'crisis of democracy' – any counter-suggestion or alternative programme. There was no reason for either the young or the more mature to yearn for those years, even if people resurrected, in want of a better social imagination, the parties of the coalition times. Finally, and in sharp contrast to Poland, the Hungarian churches were obedient tools and suffering victims in the hands of the communist apparatus. They could not offer either a generally compelling and inspiring ethic or any social program, and at best (and very rarely) they lashed out against violations of religious freedoms. A people who, luckily, had found themselves in the first moment of their liberation in a total social vacuum, and who did not wish to accept any conservative authority, were left to themselves to invent new social solutions. And they did.

IMRE NAGY: A 'KERENSKY IN REVERSE', AN INCONSISTENT BOLSHEVIK, OR A NEW TYPE OF SOCIALIST RADICAL?

The Hungarian premier, murdered 'legally' in Soviet-Hungarian collaboration, on June 16 1958, almost two years after the revolution, presented a complex case of martyrdom and heritage for the democratic left.[28] Nagy's execution was greeted jubilantly by a part of the communist press, with silence by the other, and with indignation by socialists and non-party radicals and democrats, an indignation echoed by the Western world about the 'murdered great Hungarian patriot' – this from a world whose political representatives found him too 'red' to have negotiations with, and generated regular propaganda against him through Radio Free Europe. But after the eruption of protest, when (as Simone de Beauvoir describes) the circle of *Les Temps Modernes* was in utter despair at the news of the execution, and when Camus wrote a preface to a volume dedicated to his memory, Nagy no longer seemed to be held in high respect, even if still regarded as a champion of the Hungarian cause.

This great politician's public persona needs, therefore, a reappraisal. Nagy had two specific political–personal weaknesses. First, and most surprisingly for a Bolshevik of 35 years' standing, of all the situations he had been confronted with, it was a revolutionary explosion in which he felt most embarrassed, and at first completely paralysed. He needed to *distance* himself in time and space to consider the object and analyze the situation; and, failing this, he made only wrong moves. The monumental example of this was his impromptu appearance (under pressure from his friends) before a furious crowd during the evening of October 23, without a plan for any immediate action and, in particular, without *any* official authority to say anything. The outcome was predictable: the temporary self-destruction of his popularity. Equally surprisingly for a veteran apparatchik, he was heavyhanded and unskillful in intrigues and apparatus infights, almost unerringly choosing the wrong men for allies. When politicking in a Machiavellian spirit he had always fallen prey to the genuine Machiavellians.[29] But, strangely enough, both weaknesses, preventing the Prime Minister from acting at times as efficiently as was needed, but never decisively influencing the outcome of events, already suggested a new type of socialist radical. The Hungarian crisis between 1953 and 1956 became a representative drama of the inner disintegration of Bolshevism, and it produced, with many transitory types, three representative figures. The first was Kádár, the model type of the Khrushchevite, with his 'Khrushchevite Hungary' of the 1960s. The second was Lukács, the inconsistent Bolshevik; the man with the sincere conviction of being 'the authentic Bolshevik', and who, precisely because of this inconsistency, could become the defender of the revolution of 1956 – an indefensible cause when viewed from strictly Bolshevik premises. Moreover, Lukács was a constant critic of the halfheartedness of Khrushchevite promises to take a self-critical look at socialism – a halfheartedness which he himself shared in many respects, philosophical as well as political. The third figure was Nagy. This man, through his inner torments, transcended Bolshevism.

The first dimension of Nagy's historical role is that he was the first Eurocommunist, or rather, 'Eurosocialist'. In fact, he was anti-Khrushchevism personified. Nagy had taken the moral and political responsibility of Bolshevized socialism for the degeneration of an originally emancipatory cause so seriously that it had literally become for him a matter of life and death. His presence at the head of a government that sanctified the social and national self-liberation of a nation was the symbolic act of returning the power usurped by Bolshevism to those who alone could be both its source and its daily implementers; the 'masses', often respectfully alluded to in myth, always mishandled and oppressed in practice. Let us add, that all of this happened without 'liberal illusions' – at least, in the case of the Prime Minister, who himself had very specific provisos for his remaining in office, provisos that amounted basically to the exclusion from the cabinet of all parties that had not been registered in the immediate postwar situation, when the general trend pointed not to communism, but at least towards the left. But, one could remark, honorable as such a role of being a proto-Eurosocialist is, it is also a closed chapter in socialist history, and is generally so in history. All those who wanted to, have learned the lessons. And even if Imre Nagy was indeed, as we assume, the first Eurosocialist, this is at best a historical question.

And, indeed, the features that make Imre Nagy's honest life and stoic demise more than a tragic and sublime chapter of revolutionary history, and which resurrect him as a protagonist of the present, can only be gained by a sketchy reconstruction and a reinterpretation of the stages of this development. In doing this, we rely mostly on the book by Miklós Molnár and László Nagy.

To begin, it is important to know that (after the formative experience of his arrest and court sentence in the 1920s, during which trial he behaved in a courageous way that foreshadowed much of what was to come more than 30 years later) he became a 'deviationist in the agrarian question', an advocate of the democratic land reform and partitioning – not nationalizing – of the huge estates. This is important not only because he constantly preserved his heretic views in agrarian problems, making him the obvious choice of the Soviet leaders, and not only because he became acquainted and intimately worked together with Bukharin, but also because there was, right from the start, a visible element in all his agricultural heresies which grew into a central factor in his later political strategy. This was the demand for a political strategy *based on confidence*, without which a reasonable agricultural strategy is not conceivable.[30] This is the first appearance of the principle of consensus in his strategy.

We have mentioned (to the extent necessary within this framework) Nagy's 1953 'new policy speech', and also (very briefly) his fight with the Rákosist apparatus, which he finally lost, with the result that in March 1955 he was ousted from the leading body of the party, and later from the party itself. Here we only have to list the features that indicate this gradual transition. On the surface, Imre Nagy appears to be nothing more than the most resolute Khrushchevite politician in a period when Khrushchevism had not yet existed.[31] Substantively speaking – that is to say, taking a sociological inventory of the elements contained in it – his speech could easily be published in Kádárist Hungary (minus the name of the author); it would even appear *démodé*. In itself, not even his insistence on the rehabilitations is wholly his invention. Nagy himself remarks in his *Memoranda* that Khrushchev, in a conversation with him on January 1, 1954, urged the accelerated process of rehabilitations and blamed its slowness on Rákosi.[32] At that time there was a fair chance that he might have become what Kádár had in fact become: the model Khrushchevite. Even so, three elements discernible in his attitude in this period do in retrospect suggest something above and beyond a model Khrushchevite. The first is his persistence in a consistent policy objective of grasping the whole of social life in a given period. The incoherence of the speeches of Khrushchev and his mates was not only – and not even primarily – the result of an incapacity for clear thinking. Kádár, for instance, according to all fair reports, is a remarkably lucid and coherent man. But, first, no Khrushchevite speech is supposed to contain the condemnation of the *entire* preceding period, since even then, even amidst the most horrible crimes, the 'construction of socialism' went on without disruptions: continuity is emphasized through all minor discontinuities. Secondly, the more incoherent a speech is, the greater the room it provides for totally opportunistic tactical maneuvering. Kádár is a master of these deliberate incoherences.[33] Nagy put an end to these tactically useful ambiguities, and his main ambition was to work out as consistent a theory of a new phase of socialism (or a new approach to the problems of socialism) as possible. Further, he tacitly shifted the locus of decisions affecting a nation's life to the nation itself, instead of waiting for decisions from Moscow. Undoubtedly, he tried to keep as good a contact with Moscow as was possible (and lost in that competition against Rákosi). But we have suggested that his 'new policy speech' was something more than just a smooth tactical change in line with directions from Moscow; and in March 1955 he resolutely brushed away all attempts at mediation on the part of Suslov, even though he must have known from the Moscow confrontation that de-liberalization was, at least for the time being, the prevailing opinion in Moscow. This was in fact the first time that he had questioned Moscow's authority. Finally, in harmony with this, a tone appeared in his speeches that was regarded by the average (and sometimes even by the oppositional) communist as nationalistic, but which was simply a language comprehensible to those brought up via a Hungarian – religious and lay – literature, instead of being a shabby replica of party reports from the Soviet Union.

In the period between March 1955 and October 23 1956, Nagy was to question much more. He started to question the prerogative of the dictatorship to initiate and suppress all social movements from above. In other words, his attitude contained the demand of at least a degree of *political pluralism*. Obviously, we are speaking about the existence and activity of the so-called Imre Nagy group, later an important factor in his 'legal' murder. Here we have to follow closely the valuable analyses of Miklós Molnár and László Nagy, who established to begin with that it would be superficial to consider Nagy as the 'Hungarian Gomułka'. The Polish politician intrigued and won in the upper reaches of the party alone, while the Hungarian opposition centered around Nagy 'attacked the established power from the outside, as it were; at its basis', and not only in 1956 but earlier on, in 1955.[34] Further, these two authors meticulously characterize the composition of the Imre Nagy group, which consisted of the following subgroups: (a) his immediate entourage, personal friends and collaborators; (b) a representative group of writers and scholars that spoke for at least the higher-level communist intelligentsia, and which gave voice increasingly, and more and more irresistibly, to the general popular dissatisfaction; (c) a group made up of a certain type of party functionary – in part, economists, and particularly experts of agrarian questions, and, in part, the dissatisfied elements of the ideological apparatus; (d) the so-called 'Rajkists', some of whom were members of the International Brigades, and were exposed more than others to the barrage of the Soviet secret police in 1949–50.[35] But the term 'attacked the established power from the outside' needs some further qualification, especially taking into consideration what purposes it later served in court. Miklós Molnár and László Nagy made it clear that this term has to be understood between two extremes. On the one hand, the Nagy group had never been a secret conspiratorial centre (no amount of effort on the part of the Soviet–Hungarian 'investigating team' could conjure up *any* evidence to that effect); nor was it, on the other hand, 'His Majesty's opposition', a kind of clamorous busybodying of offended or neglected functionaries vying for what was up for grabs. It was of course no longer a Bolshevik type of action; it was a *pressure group*. The pressure group moves within two borderlines. On the one hand, it proceeds towards creating a public sphere broader and freer than that officially allowed, and takes certain risks by doing so. On the other hand, it is not at all the aim of the pressure group to overthrow the existing power. It does not declare the authority of this power to be non-binding, for it wants to exert pressure *on* it, not *against* it. That the latter was characteristic of the Nagy group and of Nagy himself is detectable from the fact that he simply sent his *Memoranda* both to the central committee and even to Andropov himself. This gesture was sometimes regarded as naïve, even though it was most consistent with the method of functioning of a pressure group. It is important to emphasize here that any secret conspiratorial activity is in flagrant contradiction to the very essence of a pressure group.[36]

What was the content of these famous *Memoranda*, which the author sent only to official authorities but which, as the main document of the pressure group, were circulating in Budapest, certainly not on the initiative of Nagy but equally certainly not against his will? Here he went a significant step farther than in the question of organization, which is a typical inner contradiction with committed Bolsheviks. Very characteristically, in his conception the initial step should be – and here we must closely follow the highly unusual terminology – the liquidation of the 'Bonapartist dictatorship' of the Stalinists 'which had crushed with one blow both reaction and the young Hungarian democracy . . . by destroying the democratic allies of socialism'.[37] The term 'Bonapartist' needs some explanation. In all probability, this was a substitute for the 'Thermidorian' characterization of the Stalinist regime, well known for its Trotskyite connotations to everyone with a party schooling, but it basically meant that overnight the Khrushchevite prime minister proceeded to elaborate a theory of the universal degeneration of a power which called itself socialist.

There are other generally important features of the position contained in the *Memoranda*, for example, the following:

The members of the party and the Hungarian people as a whole do not desire a return to capitalism. They desire a regime of popular democracy which would be the incarnation of the socialist theory, a regime which would take account of working-class ideals, *in which public life would rest on ethical foundations*, which would not be governed by a degenerate Bonapartist power *and dictatorship*, but by the working people itself in respect of law and order. The people would be master of the country, and would control their own destiny in a native land in which the life of the state and of society would develop under the emblem of love and humanism.[38]

Our italics here serve two purposes. First, we want to show that, whether wittingly or unwittingly, Nagy had introduced a *language* (for instance, rejecting the dictatorship *tout court*) which made him and his way of thinking no longer compatible with any kind of Bolshevism, including a reformist one. Secondly, the above is proof of Nagy's recognition: political activity, especially radical democratic or socialist political activity, must have some moral principles, otherwise it will degenerate into a system of tyranny. Nagy could be naïve (as indeed he was in the theoretical questions of morality) but the fact that he had sensed the need for such moral maxims spoke for the breadth of his perspectives.

In all probability, Molnár is right in stating: 'Nagy's comments do not imply that he had any intention of re-establishing the former coalition parties in reparation for the wrong done to them by the installation of a communist dictatorship. Until the revolution Nagy wanted the Popular Front to be the medium for his ideas.'[39] But his Stalinist adversaries showed themselves to be better judges of tendencies than he was when they sensed the threat in his 'Four Principles' elaborated in 1955, which are as follows:

1   the separation of state and party powers;
2   the reorganization of state administration so that the communities and the departments would not be under the authority of the Ministry of Interior;
3   the reinforcement of the role of the parliament and of the government (to the disadvantage of the party's power); and
4   the reorganization of the Popular Front.[40]

Obviously, this was an inconsistent program or, rather, one that had not been thought through, for if all these changes had been seriously intended, as they were in Nagy's case, they would have turned out, sooner rather than later, to be incompatible with the prerogatives of any single ruling party. But even in these halfhearted and internally contradictory suggestions the dominant question had been touched upon: *the source of legitimation.* If there can be such a thing as a 'cult of the party', if it is not a concession but a *right* (of the parliament, the government, the Popular Front) to be at least relatively independent, then the party as the sole and absolute source of legitimation is shaken in its position. This is clearly no longer identical with any theory of the 'dictatorship of the proletariat'.

Finally, the passages dealing with foreign policy principles are most telling, and foreshadow the drama of the revolution. The relevant quotation is the following: *'Our country must avoid participating actively in the conflict of the blocs,* must avoid allowing itself to be dragged into a war or used as the field for battles and manoeuvres. In all these questions one must allow a nation the right to decide for herself, beyond any possibility of argument.'[41] The comment on the possible shade of meaning is correct as well: 'He demanded a new federation of Danubian states strong enough to handle its own destiny . . . which would maintain close relations with the USSR, but would be able to set up its own socialist society in conformity with the requirements of its own situation, and would remain in every way outside the power blocs.'[42] After all this, the later abrogation of the Warsaw Pact should no longer greatly surprise the reader.

The next phase of Nagy's political activity (the second to last one) was that between October 24 and 28 (or perhaps 30) – one of the most criticized (and slandered), from several directions. On the one hand, there was quite a strong disillusionment on the part of many of the 'men in the street' who had earlier lionized Nagy. He let his name be adduced to the appeal to the Soviet army, and he did let a speech be broadcast that, even if it was in marked contrast to the aggressive threats of Gerő, and later the hardly less threatening talk by Kádár, the new First Secretary, was still one in which he called the tragic events 'counterrevolutionary' in character. It took a great amount of determination and the convincing talent of a genuine statesman on the part of the Prime Minister to regain his fading popularity. Nor should we believe that the first and confused gestures were all camouflage. Even if he had already transcended the boundaries of Bolshevism, there remained in Imre Nagy (as in all reformist communists) vestiges of the old instinct first to condemn (or at least distrust) the people for seizing arms, and then to think afterwards. The second type of criticism is straightforward, but, as Miklós Molnár correctly puts it, romantic: that when it turned out that his name was put to the appeal to the Soviet army Nagy should have left the central committee building on October 24 and identified publicly with the insurgents. Such an act would have resulted in a butchery ten times the size of that which finally took place, and would have put an end to any chance of the revolution articulating its demands. The third 'criticism' is the chapter written on these days in *The History of the Hungarian Revolutionary Working-Class Movement:* a chapter which displays Serovian moral principles and a logic unfit for a grammar-school essay, but which, precisely because of its undisguised hatred and bias, contains certain important admissions of his enemies.

In fact, after having committed the double mistake of allowing himself to be pushed into a politically suicidal speech before the parliament late in the evening of October 23, and then accepting next day the position of prime minister, without having a strong group of his own in power positions (which left him isolated between hysterical or resolute political enemies), Nagy had only three courses open. The first would have been Kádár's future option: putting down the uprising and the general strike with false promises of a future 'democratization', and then increasing the rule of terror. That would have been a straightforward course, but it is a source of certain types of greatness in history (for which nations feel longlasting gratitude) that some people do not readily admit that the shortest distance between two points is a straight line. The second course would have been resignation, and leaving the political scene for good. In all probability such a gesture would have saved his life, but equally certainly it would have left a nation exposed to its enemies, alone and without any leadership (since no other of his group had anywhere near his degree of authority). It would also have meant the betrayal of his earlier policy urging action. The third course, and that actually taken by Nagy, was the politics of paralysing the Stalinist action, which simply wished to crush the uprising – and all types of resistance, if need be – through carnage. He relayed the popular demands to the members of the central apparatus who were ready to understand the democratic and radical meaning of the message, and led constant talks with the Soviet leaders (from the 25th onwards, Andropov's political authority was supplemented by the presence of Mikoyan and Suslov, who carried the weight of the presidium with them) in order to attain evacuation. This was the *only* political course that could save the shortlived Hungarian revolution, provide it with the possibility of self-expression, and pass on its message and political legacy to posterity. We can only be grateful to the 'chroniclers' who in their blind hatred have erected a statue of the prime minister in the education of future generations by confirming his role of paralysing the impatient executioners of the Hungarian revolution.[43]

This reconstruction of the phases of Nagy's oppositional career (except the last) provides some features for us to begin to sketch his portrait. First of all, he was one of the most remarkable specimens of a novel type in political activity: the *post-Machiavellian* politician. This century has seen various sorts of 'politics of ultimate ends' at their most horrendous: a fanatical zeal filling the world with terror apparatuses and annihilation camps, losing in the process all their fanaticism and principles, and leaving behind them the sheer brutality of power alone. The reaction was predictable: an enormous increase, both on the left and on the right, of a self-conscious and even conceited pragmatism (with a Machiavellian twist) as an alleged safeguard against the horrors of ideological and moralizing politics. But, in this world of superpowers and nuclear stalemates – a world which survives only with the greatest difficulty – a post-Machiavellian politics is needed: a politics which would not deduce its legitimation from Rousseau's 'general will' (neglecting and violating the 'merely empirical' will of all), which would not combine 'virtue' and 'terror' in a new edition of Jacobinism, and which would not pompously believe in the omniscience of those purely pragmatic and short-term moves that would inevitably lead the world to the brink of self-destruction, and perhaps even push it into the abyss. In a long process of self-education in which he had been stripped of both the vestiges of Bolshevik zeal and the religious belief in the mystical 'general will' (whose representative is the party), in a development the result of which was not a new political doctrine deduced from moral principles but an absolute and unconditional belief in a politics having moral maxims, Imre Nagy stands before History as one of the first great representatives of the post-Machiavellian politician.

In addition to this, Nagy exhibited a further quality: he was the type of political personality the *anti-authoritarian revolution needed and will always need*, whenever and wherever it occurs. That he had temporarily lost his popularity is more often emphasized than the obverse: the incomparably more surprising fact that the crowd clung to him, despite false appearances and certain moves which were wrong (but never treacherous). He emanated an air of confidence, and after he had made certain decisive gestures, he was generally trusted. But it was far more than personal confidence that underlay his political appeal; that made him indispensable to this anti-authoritarian revolution. In contrast to popular misconceptions, such a revolution neither needs – nor does it tolerate – charismatic leaders. This is so for the perfectly simple reason that charisma by definition means the transfer of legitimation into the leader's will and personality, and this contradicts the principle of a democratically created consensus. Nor would a commanding man of conservative authority, such as the Cardinal Mindszenty, have been acceptable to the rebellious subject on the streets of Budapest. But Nagy was neither charismatic nor conservative-authoritarian. He behaved as a democratically appointed (and daily reappointed) *arbiter* who gladly took on his shoulders (for he felt it to be a moral duty) the nuisances of this 'chaos' and daily reappointment; who incessantly negotiated with often-colliding interest groups; who tried to forge, make and remake the new consensus. In this he was inexhaustible, imperturbable and determined. From the impact of events and the advice of his friends, he was always ready to learn; but people who regard him as a political pushover, a man receptive to each and every demand of any random group, simply misread the *gradual* maturation of his ideas.

Finally, but not at all of least importance, Nagy restored the *national dimension* of radical socialist politics. This century has, on the one hand, prostituted the idea of internationalism, has perverted it into an expansionism of secret travelling envoys and emissaries who have introduced to various countries Stalin's methods of government, often without even bothering to learn the language; and has, on the other hand – and as a reaction – given rebirth to the most vulgar 'socialist' chauvinism: a politics incompatible with any kind of democracy, let alone the radical type. Nagy's plan of a Danubian confederation was a polemic against both these political styles. He rejected the transfer of national legitimacy from one nation into the other, the 'fatherland of all workers', and had abrogated thereby a basic Leninist (and not only Stalinist) principle.

If it is true (and we believe in Jorge Semprun's maxim) that everyone should die his or her own death, then Stalin succeeded in robbing a generation of revolutionaries not only of their life, the meaning of their life, but also of their death. But the Nagy 'trial' was a reversal of this truly infernal trend. Not only did he die with simple grandeur and in full awareness of the burdens that both dignity and his self-professed moral–political maxims imposed on him, but his death, just as the last phase of his life, transcended the bounds of the purely individual. With a measure of Hegelianism, we could say that Hungary needed some good examples to be set on the part of the leaders of her systematically fallen revolutions – men who constantly provoked destiny but then abandoned their followers to their fate.[44]

In Hungary's long and mostly tragic history, the leaders of fallen revolutions and wars of independence behaved after defeat with an at least questionable sublimity. The best of these were the aristocrats. There was the Prince Rákóczy, who after a long anti-Habsburg war of independence in the early eighteenth century, became, first at the French court, later in the Ottoman empire, a recluse from politics and a mystical semi-Jansenist. There was the Count Károlyi, the great Hungarian democrat who left Hungary after the fall of the first shortlived democratic republic, doing this as a sign of separation from the communist rule but, even more emphatically, as a pre-warning against the restoration of the conservative forces of the past that he predicted and feared. He later became a fellow traveller, and one with many illusions, but he never became a tool in the hands of the Stalinist masters, and when the show trials started he broke off, with a symbolic gesture, relations with the 'socialist' Hungary. And there was Kossuth, who, after 1849, after a republican adventure which many skeptics predicted (and correctly so) would be shortlived, had an émigré career ennobled only by his last long years in Turin exile, where he actually formulated (in the self-criticism of an aggressive and foolhardy nationalism) the idea of the Danubian confederation which stimulated Imre Nagy. The worst and most self-humiliating example of behavior after defeat was the communist retreat in 1919, a retreat that took place after a short, unnecessarily violent, and inconsiderately administered rule in which this internally weak but provocative dictatorship succeeded in betraying the earlier hopes of the Hungarian workers for a rule by councils. In his abdication speech Kun declared the Hungarian working class unworthy of being ruled by the communists but he suggested that under the whiphand of the white terror they would learn the proper lessons. Moreover, he not only left behind him in Budapest certain of his political enemies from the party (to name them, Lukács and Korvin, with the cynical dictum – as communicated to us by Lukács – that they should try to become martyrs if they had such an irresistible inclination for it), but he then also evicted Szamuelly, his former ally, the man of terror, and a person not at all acceptable to the Austrian social democrats, from the train carrying the escaping government. He did not, however, forget to take with him a good portion (and perhaps the whole) of the Hungarian national gold reserve, which he and his emissaries later used to corrupt members of the Landler faction, a group with which he was in constant internecine strife.

After such a history as this, Hungary needed a person who would ultimately live up to his promise. Subjected to a tortuous process of legal murder, Imre Nagy lived up to the promises he had made to his nation and to his socialist cause. But since we have often used here the term 'legal murder' we owe some explanation.[45]

In the main, the document presented by the public prosecutor (as we can see from the Hungarian Government White Book, from Kopácsi's book, and from the various official descriptions of the 'Nagy case') contained three elements, each in itself amounting to high treason: conspiracy in the period prior to the 'counterrevolution' (actively preparing the way for an armed uprising); the premeditated disorganization of the centers of political power, and thereby complicity in 'counterrevolutionary crimes'; and the abrogation of the Warsaw Pact, *lèse-majesté*. All else is either verbal pyrotechnics or additional character defamation. Nagy chose for himself (and in our view correctly) a *double* technique of defence.[46] On the one hand, he used the technique that Trotsky had employed in his trial after the 1905 revolution, when the latter constantly referred to the fact that it was not he but the Tsarist government who had acted unconstitutionally. As a result, all leaders of the Petrograd Soviet fought for the *restoration* of an *infringed* legality and legitimacy. This was very clearly the case with regard to the third point of the charge, the abrogation of the Warsaw Pact. Disregarding now the issue of to what extent such an act can be declared at all a criminal offense, and even if we allow that Nagy could not have acted without the consent of the Hungarian parliament and the previous consultation with other Warsaw Pact countries (both are debatable points but neither would justify the death penalty), it is still undeniable that the Soviet government broke the promises formally confirmed by the declaration of October 30 about the inviolability of national territories of 'the socialist countries', and it was only *after* the unmistakable signs of a new invasion and a warning note to Andropov that the Hungarian government nullified the pact.[47]

Of the three points above, the theoretically more important are the first two, in respect of which Trotsky's technique could not be used. The dilemma boils down to simply this: can or cannot the activity of a pressure group (and we have seen that the Nagy group was a pressure group and nothing else, and no Serovian technique could produce evidence to the contrary) be declared conspiratorial? And further: can or cannot a political activity occurring *within* a leading political body, and aimed at changing the policy of this body (and this in fact was what the 'Nagy-Losonczy group' did) without using violence or threats against it, be declared destructive of the power centers? All citizens of a liberal-legal state will unhesitatingly answer in the negative. (One should strongly bear in mind that in the case of this being answered in the affirmative, then it follows that General de Gaulle ought to have been executed for his deliberately organized transformation of the Fourth Republic into the Fifth, and Nagy did considerably *less* than this.) But all Leninists (Khrushchevite or non-Khrushchevite), for whom the supreme value, the guarantor of the desired state of affairs, and the exclusive and inappellable source of all 'rights' (or rather concessions) is the political power, the executive, the judiciary, and the legislator in one person, will answer it thus: if such an activity leads even indirectly to the weakening of the 'socialist state', let alone a questioning of its authority from below, it is counterrevolutionary activity and has to be dealt with accordingly. And it is here that we can see why all the Khrushchevite propaganda about the 'restoration of the Leninist norms of socialist legality' was only ideological window-dressing serving to cover and uphold a *reduced* and *rationalized* system of terror; a system which can be – and actually is – incomparably more tolerable than the Stalinist (or even the Leninist) system was, but which still has nothing whatsoever to do with *legal order*. Any legal system deserving its name presupposes: (a) some sort of preliminary consensus (in whatever form it may be expressed) regarding its general principles; (b) a certain number of individual and collective rights that are not dependent on any policy objectives of any given executive power; and (c) certain formal and theoretical guarantees of such rights, and at least the formal possibility of renegotiating the basic principles of the legal system in question. Khrushchevism, in the rare moments when it spoke frankly, specifically denied all three preconditions. Consequently, its 'restored socialist legality' had only one means of dealing with people like Nagy and his group: murdering them under somewhat formalized conditions.

In a way, the entire Nagy affair – the negotiations made with him (obviously involving duress) in Romania, the final decision to finish him off, and the trial – had increasingly become a test of the Khrushchevite claim to the 'restoration of the norms of socialist legality', a test which revealed that the claim was false from the start or, rather, an ideological concomitant of a rationalized system of terror. That it is such a rationalized system, and no longer simply the cumulation of uncontrollable Stalinist purges (which hit the society like natural catastrophes, sometimes threatening the demographic equilibrium itself), is beyond doubt. But it had remained a system of formalized terror, and not a legalistic structure. Nothing shows this more clearly than the fact that Nagy was offered – publicly by Kádár, and privately by various confidential emissaries – not only impunity but also the possibility of participation in the Kádár government, an act which in itself is incompatible with any kind of legality. Either Nagy was guilty of counterrevolutionary crimes, in which case he had to face trial (and not ministerial promotion), or he was not. For the law, there is no third alternative. And this allegedly 'higher principle of socialist law', which is nothing else but an arbitrary and tyrannical principle of terror, has the effect that it can relapse at any time into plain 'Leninist' terror. Nagy's technique of being prepared to engage in a dialogue with the adjudicating terrorists served just that purpose of unmasking the Khrushchevite lie about restoring any kind of legality deserving the name, and exposing it as a somewhat up-graded form of terror.[48]

But what was the *function* of the trial, particularly at such a belated date, when Hungary had long been 'consolidated' (in other words, forced into a general state of silence and fear)? The 'Yugoslav explanation', that is to say, the reference to the fact that in 1958 Soviet–Yugoslav relations were again at a low, explains at best the choice of date of the trial. It does not explain its course, and even less its intended function. They could have murdered the members of the group without a legal rigmarole (just as they did in Losonczy's case), and 'informed' the population some ten to fifteen years later that they had died in the process of investigation; they could have deported them to the Soviet Union without any explanation; they could even have tried and either executed or pardoned them without any official statement. But they went out of their way to make the legal murder known, to publicize it as an act of 'higher justice', and to make a whole nation their accomplice via a forced silence. Our belief is that this was a trial of *communist disobedience*, inside and outside the Warsaw bloc. One should not forget that *all* the executed members of the group (or those murdered without formality) were known either in Hungary or abroad as communists: Nagy in particular, and also Losonczy, and Szilágyi and Gimes only in Hungary; and it was known even of Maléter, a soldier appearing on the Hungarian political scene only during the days of the revolution, a Soviet partisan and a sentimental communist (which he remained until his last moment). There is a particularly interesting and convincing documentation to the effect that the trial was designed as a warning to the adherents of a too determined national communism, or to those carrying the seeds of what has later, and for a very short period of time, been called 'Eurocommunism'. Kopácsi describes a significant moment of the trial, during which Nagy's lawyer, who in a spirit most contrary to the 'higher socialist legality' decided to be a counsellor for the defendant and not an aid to the prosecution, referred, in defense of certain of Nagy's statements, to opinions expressed by representative communists.

He keeps quoting certain opinions expressed by leading personalities of the international communist movement on the events of 1956 in Hungary. He quotes Togliatti, the first secretary of the Italian Communist Party and Ernst Fischer, the member of the Political Bureau of the Austrian Communist Party. The presiding judge interrupts him, yelling obsessively: 'You are not quoting the "international communist movement" but shrewd revisionists who deviate from the correct line!'[49]

From this episode it is very clear who were regarded as Nagy's accomplices in his 'counterrevolutionary crimes'; people who, because of technical obstacles, could not be put in the dock with the accused.

This prime minister, who believed himself to be a minister in the literal sense, who believed that he was empowered by his nation, carried out his final duty, discharged his final obligation. His death stripped his murderers of the legitimacy that is invested in, exists for, is constituted by, *the people and the people alone:* a nation that these murderers oppress, *never represent.*[50]

EPILOGUE: THE BALANCE SHEET OF A REVOLUTION

Nations, these anonymous-collective entities (or, less mystically, the subjects who constitute them) are utilitarian in the sense that they constantly measure gains against losses. In terms of such a calculation, was the Hungarian revolution a gain or, rather, a loss for the nation? The answer to this will not be simple. If we only think of the many hundreds of lives extinguished in the years of terror, if we operate with this absolute yardstick, the balance cannot but be negative.[51] We have to add to this not only the tens of thousands who had spent many years in prisons, but all those who have constantly had to live under unceasing police surveillance, who have silently suffered social disfavor, who are forcibly underemployed (unless they perform 'favors' for the regime). To be a '56-er' is still a very heavy burden in Hungary. This is an indicator which surely shows a *negative* balance.

Miklós Molnár, a loyal chronicler and defender of 1956, even declared the revolution to be a 'monumental mistake'. Precisely because we know that Molnár does not have *gains* but *meanings and patterns* in social action in mind, we have to object to his argument with the following: if they wish to state that Hungary 1956 has become obsolete, has become discarded by historical 'progress', then their statements are simply misleading. *For the first time in Hungarian history*, a revolution was so radical that none of its main objectives has been discarded by a subsequent development, as was the case with at least a good portion of the demands of 1848 during the period of the 1867 *Ausgleich*. What were the radical demands of the Hungarian revolution which have never even come close to being realized? First, the restitution of total national sovereignty. Secondly, the democratization of the work of socialization by a system of direct management, which would have put an end to the dictatorship over needs and which, at the same time, could have prevented a return to the previous system. Thirdly, people have learned from the early naïveté of attempts at creating a system of councils. Such a social experiment, if unaided by reliable political agents in the political sphere, may easily be betrayed, misused, and made totally empty; fit only for throwing away. Because of this, the crowd in the Hungarian revolution not only demanded a full restoration of general civic liberties (of religious confession, of a free press, and the like), but also specifically demanded a system of political pluralism – though, of course, one that would be closely watched by an attentive populace instructed by earlier experiences. A final addition to this is a document of the utmost importance, Bibó's 'Draft of a compromise solution of the Hungarian question' – a combination of substantive restrictions and a formally unrestricted system of liberties. In their entirety, these features reveal a new experience in the modern history of political revolutions, constituted by direct mass action, irrespective of the ideologies actually expressed and manifested by those crowds. One cannot say that any of these radical demands has even partially been realized. Consequently, the Hungarian revolution and its program remain on the *general East European* agenda, even if only as a *regulative idea*.

By the gesture of not appealing for clemency, a gesture which reached us after a very long delay, Imre Nagy, forger, arbiter, martyr and symbol of a murdered revolution, rejected the lamentable offer of being rehabilitated by those who were going to murder him, and did murder him. His will must be honored by all those who have respect for humanity, and especially by those who understand both his work and the greatness of the Hungarian revolution.

But in the end, after all of this, who will predict with certainty that there will be no public funeral for Imre Nagy in Budapest? And if there is, and this prime minister finally retires to his pantheon, then there can be very little doubt about the demands written on the posters of the mourners who would accompany him, and his companion-in-arms, to their symbolic grave.

1981

NOTES

1   It is proved beyond any reasonable doubt by F. A. Váli, in *Rift and Revolt in Hungary* (Cambridge, Mass.: Harvard University Press, 1961), and particularly by Miklós Molnár, in *Budapest, 1956: A History of the Hungarian Revolution* (London: Allen and Unwin, 1971), that the Soviet armored divisions were deployed at about 2 a.m. on October 24, at a time when the Hungarian central committee was still having its stormy meeting and when Imre Nagy was still waiting in the lobby for his comrades to make a decision. But the decision did not come from the Hungarian authorities; they could only give their a posteriori sanction to it.

2   We have a most interesting documentation of the fact that such a conclusion had been drawn up, not only by an outstanding theorist such as Bibó, but also by others and people who were not at all necessarily on the left. The evidence is in J. Kővágó, *You Are All Alone* (New York: Praeger, 1959), a document of suffering and exceptional courage, and one which contains a more than acceptable amount of naïve and narrowminded confidence in the Western democracies. Kővágó was one of the very few resistance fighters against the Nazis in Hungary. After 1945, as a young hero of the liberal–conservative Smallholders' Party, and by virtue of his immaculate anti-fascist record, he was elected mayor of Budapest – a very young person to be in such a job. It was easily predictable that he would be arrested after the communist takeover. He spent five terrible years in prisons no better than those of the Gestapo, run by men with unmistakable Gestapo-like mentalities. During this period he stuck to two fundamental principles: his passionate anti-communism and his unshakeable belief that the Western democracies, at the first available historical opportunity, would liberate Eastern Europe. He at least has the self-irony to describe in detail the foolish assessment of the actual situation to which his doctrinaire belief in the Western redeemers has led him. The *pointe* and the only elegantly written part of a weak book (but a very valuable document) is its conclusion. Kővágó, as the representative in exile of Hungary, spoke on behalf of his 'enslaved nation' in the United Nations. He was so excited during the first sentences (full of nineteenth-century pathos) that he did not realise what was going on in the hall. When, regaining calm and self-presence, he looked around, he realised that the hall was empty: the delegates had left to watch the arrival of an Oriental celebrity. The sentence which became the title of the book, 'Oh, my country! You are all alone!', burst out of him at precisely this moment. This is the feeling which we call the general, even if a posteriori, realization of the fact that the Hungarian revolution fought against the *whole* of the Yalta–Potsdam edifice.

3   Isaac Deutscher, *Russia, China and the West: 1953–1966* (Harmondsworth: Penguin, 1970), pp. 88–9.

4   It is a strange position indeed for us to defend Mindszenty. But ever since David Irving, who has 'scientifically proved' that Hitler was unaware of the 'final solution', and who has lately turned full circle, and has written a pamphlet against Hungary 1956, characterizing it as an anti-Semitic mob uprising, and in

which he accuses Cardinal Mindszenty of complicity in fascist politics – after all of this we have to say very clearly that Mr Irving simply and uncritically echoes clichés of Soviet propaganda. Mindszenty was undoubtedly a political advocate of a capitalism. But his 'crimes against the people', the basis of his so-called trial, consisted in a rightist *conviction*, occasionally a rightist propaganda, and in no conspiracy against a government whose legality was, to say the very least, itself questionable.

5   Published in Budapest by Akadémiai Kiadó, 1977.

6   István Bibó, 'Draft of a compromise solution of the Hungarian question', *Magyar Füzetek*, 4 (Paris, 1979), p. 140 (emphasis added). In our view, this is sufficient proof that this project went *beyond* liberalism. There is one point at which Bibó (who clearly wished to avoid confrontation with the Primate) explicitly rejects Mindszenty's position. There is no need, his 'Draft' further states, for any kind of United Nations army or police force to ensure the order or freedom of future elections. The latter is guaranteed by the fact of the revolution; the former by the unprecedented moral discipline of the nation. There is, however, one implicit limitation of liberal principles in all realistic attempts at formulating the future framework of parliamentary democracy in Hungary. It is not mentioned in Bibó's 'Draft', but the problem repeatedly appears in Kővágó's book mentioned above, in the chapters describing the wild conjectures and the somewhat more down-to-earth negotiations in the circles recognizing the Smallholders' Party. The problem consists in the following: Can any number of parties, without limitations, be legally registered, and therefore allowed to compete in the electoral campaign, or would there be certain limitations? The position of Nagy – a man who had, after the honest self-laceration of a Bolshevik career lasting more than 30 years, accepted the multi-party system and the pluralist principle that were both so alien to him, but did so consistently and without tactical considerations – was that he could only cooperate with the coalition parties legalized after 1945. (Tildy, the ex-president of Hungary and himself a member of the Smallholders' Party and a state minister without portfolio, mentioned this to Kővágó in the last days of the revolution.) This was not a tactically motivated decision, either, but simply the result of the conviction that these parties, and they alone, remained intact from being compromised by an alliance with either Hitler or an internal, homemade Hungarian fascism. The Smallholders' leaders had come, after much reluctance, to the same conclusion; they were, however, led by the tactical consideration that perhaps the Soviet leaders would be ready to accept the 1945 situation enjoying their endorsement, but certainly not anything beyond that. In rough outline this is in harmony with the 'Finlandization' of Hungary, and it means a (not constitutionally stipulated) restriction.

7   Hannah Arendt, *Crises of the Republic* (Harmondsworth: Penguin, 1973), pp. 116–17 (emphasis added).

8   Miklós Molnár's estimate (in *Budapest, 1956*, p. 134) of the number of armed insurgents (of course, *before* the second intervention) is as follows:

According to the Hungarian Government white paper, the Buda groups on the right bank totalled 1,200; a figure which included groups like that of Dudás, whose activities were political rather than military. At Pest, the Corvin Passage, Tüzoltó Street, and Kilián

Barracks groups, during the early part of the uprising, numbered 600–1,000, including the sub-groups and advance posts. In all there were 1,200–1,800 people in the central organised groups, who were later to form themselves into the revolutionary council of the armed forces. There were, however, many others whom we cannot include in this analysis owing to the lack of data and their extreme mobility.

After the second and final intervention the number of those putting up armed resistance seems to have been considerably larger for a short time, but it is fanciful to describe the Hungarian story as a *war* of independence. On the part of the Soviet army, it was rather a swift and brutal police action, and Khrushchev mentioned with satisfaction to Micunović within a few days that the results 'were far better and much quicker than they had expected'.

9 *The History of the Hungarian Revolutionary Working-Class Movement*, the official party version of the history of the working-class movements, claims that 3,000 (!) political prisoners were released by the 'counterrevolutionaries'. If we consider that the authors' data must be a diminution of the actual numbers, and that this alleged 3,000 comprised the number of political prisoners after a series of amnesties, this is a figure which in itself characterizes the prevailing situation under a 'Gerő liberalism'. *A Magyar Forradalmi Munkásmozgalom Története*, ed. the Institute of the Party History of the Hungarian Socialist Workers' Party (Budapest: Kossuth, 1979), p. 578.

10 Bibó, 'Draft', p. 143.

11 Molnár, *Budapest, 1956*, pp. 159–60 (emphasis added).

12 The autobiography *Khrushchev Remembers*, provides unexpected and, on the whole, irrefutable proof of the fact that such a historical moment did exist, although it is not entirely clear during which days. (In all probability, it was between October 25 and 31.) Of course, there are only indirect indications to that effect in the text. Soviet deliberation, Khrushchev wrote, took place when they pulled their troops out of Budapest. In the meantime – and this is brand-new information – Mikoyan and Suslov remained on the field of operations as emissaries or plenipotentiaries. They did not return home, as was generally assumed by both participants in the events and later chroniclers, but rather remained at Vecsés military airport, near Budapest, which was under exclusive Soviet administration and which became the improvized headquarters of all Soviet operations in Hungary. This gives us as the latest possible days of decision October 30–November 1, as we know now that, on November 2, Khrushchev and Malenkov were already in Yugoslavia for secret negotiations with Tito during which they informed the Yugoslav leaders about certain decisions – we shall describe them in what follows – that had been made in the previous days. We are simply going to quote the narrative of the crucial negotiations between the Soviet and the Chinese communist parties with a few abbreviations. Even if we have to take Khrushchev's statements with a grain of salt – particularly so at this point, where other information (for instance, that coming from Yugoslav sources and reaching the State Department) stated a much greater reluctance on the part of the Chinese than portrayed by Khrushchev – two features of the events stand out quite poignantly. The first is that, although the stronger Soviet option was undeniably intervention by force, the options of the leaders were, up

to a certain point, far from being closed, and in principle they could have been convinced against taking the fatal step. Secondly, whatever the Chinese boasting a posteriori about their 'major corrective role' was in regard to 'revisionist' Soviet policies, the Chinese were apparently subservient and irresolute – only, we repeat, less enthusiastic than the Russians would have them – at a moment when they in fact could have influenced Soviet development at a crucial juncture.

This was a historic moment. We were faced with a crucial choice . . . To make sure that all countries understood us correctly on this point, we decided to consult with the other Socialist countries – first and foremost with the fraternal Communist Party of China. We asked Mao Tse-tung to send a representative to consult with us about the events in Hungary. The Chinese responded quickly. A delegation led by Liu Shao-chi flew in. Liu was a man of great experience and prestige, much respected by us . . . We stayed up the whole night, weighing the pros and cons of whether or not we should apply armed force to Hungary. First Liu Shao-chi said it wasn't necessary: we should get out of Hungary, he said, and let the working class build itself up and deal with the counterrevolution on its own. We agreed. But then, after reaching this agreement, we started discussing the situation again, and someone warned of the danger that *the working class might take a fancy to the counterrevolution. The youth in Hungary was especially susceptible.* I don't know how many times we changed our minds back and forth. Every time we thought we'd made up our minds about what to do, Liu Shao-chi would consult with Mao Tse-tung . . . Mao always approved whatever Liu recommended. *We finally finished this all-night session with a decision not to apply military force in Hungary* . . . Later in the morning the Presidium of the Central Committee met to hear my report on how our discussions with the Chinese delegation had gone. I told them how we had changed our position a number of times and how we had finally reached a decision not to apply military force in Hungary . . . After long deliberation, the Presidium decided that it would be unforgivable, simply unforgivable, if we stood by and refused to assist our Hungarian comrades . . . So it was decided. But Liu Shao-chi . . . still thought that we had agreed not to apply military force in Hungary. We thought we should inform him that we had reconsidered our position . . . Liu agreed that our revised decision to go ahead and send in troops was right. (*Khrushchev Remembers* (Boston, Mass./Toronto: Little, Brown, 1971), pp. 417–19, emphasis added).

Perhaps the time which elapsed between Liu Shao-chi's belief that the decision was *not* to intervene and his being informed later that the Russians would in fact intervene accounts for the difference between the Chinese communiqués which Molnár records but cannot explain.

13 Bibó, 'Draft', p. 143.
14 We believe that he was simply obeying his own natural inclinations, rather than devilishly plotting with the Soviet army to nip the revolt in the bud, as many conspiracy theorists believe. But we have here no evidence either for or against this view.
15 One example will suffice to demonstrate to what extent even the feelings, let alone the opinions, of a silent majority prove to be inscrutable in these societies of dictatorship over needs. *A week before* the revolt broke out, the *Literary Journal*, mouthpiece of the rebellious writers, published a reader's letter from a certain Mr Horn, a factory technician, who expressed his doubts regarding the social relevance of the clamorous debates of intellectuals in the so-called Petöfi Circle.

'What's the use of all this?' he asked. 'The working class is, and will remain, politically passive for good, and uninterested in such hair splitting . . . and without them what good can we do?' And this inscrutability is *not* identical with the well-known problematic inherent in tacit consent. Arendt correctly argues that movements of disobedience, should they meet resistance on the part of the 'silent majority', immediately prove by the fact of resistance that tacit consent is not a totally negative principle, and is at least predictable – *to some extent*. Political inscrutability in the dictatorship over needs is, however, agnosticism pure and simple of the political observer, imposed on him or her by the atomizing oppressive character of the dictatorship.

16   Kővágó mentions the greatest example of this: Béla Kovács, the abducted general secretary of the Smallholders' Party, who had recently returned from the Gulag. We do not question the credibility of Kővágó's account, despite the scornful description of 'career-seekers' given in 1959 by Béla Kovács to the Hungarian press – a category in which he obviously included Kővágó. The gesture was not necessarily noble, but Kovács's position is understandable. First of all, he was suspicious of his ex-colleagues, who had sold him out to the communists back in 1947 but who were now full of cheap enthusiasm without being aware of Soviet resourcefulness. Secondly, they had a real political disagreement. Kővágó and others had simply wanted to return to the 1930 programme; Kovács, however (and this is very important to note when assessing the chances of success for Bibó's 'Draft' and its socialist provisos), was more realistic, and emphasized that the historical clock could not be simply turned back [see his article 'A magyar nép semleges Magyarországot kíván', *Magyar Nemzet*, November 1, 1956, p. 1. in *1956 sajtója* (The Press of 1956) (Budapest: Kossuth, 1989), p. 129.]. The description of Kovács's views by Kővágó, on the basis of a conversation between them in the late hours of November 1, reads as follows:

He knew, as I did, that the whole Hungarian nation wanted to be rid of Communism forever. There was no doubt whatsoever that this included national Communism also. But his main argument was that he knew the Russians better than I or anybody else . . . The Soviets would never permit a small nation under their domination to regain her freedom . . . His view was that the revolution must forge its own new order with bloody sacrifices. In his eyes it seemed that *this new order would not resemble a clean Western type of democracy. It would be something new in which, despite our opposition, institutions and customs established by the Communists would still remain part of the social and economic life of the country.* He was convinced that even the new order of state which was created in relative freedom in the years of 1945–46–47, belonged to the past . . . The Revolution forged the whole nation into a sacred unity against Soviet domination. *It would not be so easy to find the same unity when searching for a synthesis of the free enterprise system and socialism.* (Kővágó, *You Are All Alone*, p. 209, emphasis added).

We do not question the credibility of this passage for the simple reason that it is a testimony *against Kővágó and for* Kovács's political realism. Kovács's motives are clear: a predilection for a capitalist and liberal regime; a hatred and an unceasing distrust of *all* types of communist, including the reformists. But his political realism teaches him – and this is the crucial part of his creed – that there is no return to a Hungarian past, for this would be a return to oblivion. He attributes this mostly, even if not exclusively, to the Soviet presence in the area, while we overwhelmingly attribute it to inner factors, but the result amounts to the same: to the acceptance of a situation in which liberal freedoms and a socialist organization of the socioeconomic order must coexist. And even if the just claim is made that Kovács was not representing the whole of the Smallholders' Party it would have to be equally admitted that he was most influential within it.

17 We can see how deeprooted the Bolshevik instincts in the Nagy group initially were from a letter by Anna Kéthly, the leader-in-exile of the Social Democratic Party written on July 18, 1958 to the writers and journalists who valiantly decided, following the executions, to save Nagy's and his companion-in-arms' honor by editing a volume in defense of the executed. Kéthly describes in her letter her first (and only) encounter with Géza Losonczy, one of the most hated 'traitors' of the group, who was later simply murdered by forcefeeding in prison, taking place in 'the first moments of the revolution' (probably on October 24 or 25). She made her participation in the new government conditional on the legalization of the Social Democratic Party. In reply, Losonczy categorically stated that they intended to maintain the 'hegemony of the Party', and that they were not going to modify the single-party political structure of the country. In T. Aczél, P. Kende, and T. Méray, eds, *The Truth about the Nagy Affair*, published for the Congress for Cultural Freedom (London: Secker and Warburg, 1958), p. 62.

18 Molnár, *Budapest, 1956*, p. 124.

19 The description of this scene from the prison period and the trial stem from Sándor Kopácsi, *lu nome della classe operaia* (Rome: Edizione e/o, 1979), p. 238.

20 Bibó, 'Draft', p. 140.

21 Obviously, 'consensus in the making' always contains elements of wishful thinking, and it has remained so particularly in Hungary, where it has never come to free elections. But the following results of an attempt at a representative survey may at least suggest something of the relevance of the design of such a draft constitution. Miklós Molnár and László Nagy describe, in their *Imre Nagy: Réformateur ou Révolutionnaire?* (Geneva/Paris: Librairie E. Droz/Librairie Minard, 1959), the following surveys among Hungarian refugees of the revolution. One of these, comprising 343 refugees then recently arrived in Austria, produced the following response to the question 'Who would have been in your opinion the most desirable prime minister in Hungary in the year preceding the revolution?': I. Nagy, 31 percent; G. Losonczy, 9 percent; J. Kádár, 4 percent; T. Déry (oppositional writer), 2 percent; G. Lukács, 2 percent; various and without opinion, 52 percent. The second question was 'Who in your estimation was the worthiest of being appointed prime minister?' The answers: B. Kovács, 31 percent; I. Nagy, 30 percent; J. Mindszenty, 10 percent; I. Bibó, 9 percent; P. Maléter, 6 percent; Z. Tildy, 4 percent; others or no answers, 10 percent. In another survey, made by the Free Europe Radio in 1957, the unspecified results gave I. Nagy the priority with 35 percent of the vote. University Marquette (Milwaukee), in a survey published in January–February 1959 (but still made *before* the execution of Nagy and his colleagues) of 129 young Hungarians studying then at various American universities produced the following response to the question 'Whom do you consider to be the three most remarkable Hungarians of our century?': I. Nagy, 34 percent; Cardinal Mindszenty, 31

percent; P. Maléter, 26 percent; B. Bartók, 21 percent; Z. Kodály, 16 percent; E. Ady, 12 percent; A. József, 8 percent (the last two are leading radical national poets). We do not wish either to exaggerate the importance of such surveys, which can be methodologically criticized. Least of all would we say that under normal circumstances (or under any circumstances, for that matter) such surveys can be substitutions for free elections. They show only so much: that the people who accepted for a historical moment the 'consensus in the making', and particularly the great personality of Nagy, who died for it and in its name, had at least a relative and short-term justification for believing that they were entitled to introduce the new and final period of Hungarian and socialist legitimacy deriving from the revolution of October 23.

22   Molnár, Budapest, 1956, pp. 174–5.

23   Bill Lomax, *Hungary, 1956* (London: Allison and Busby, 1976), pp. 100–1.

24   Molnár, *Budapest, 1956*, p. 175. Molnár himself contradicts this statement a few pages later: 'The council programmes up to November 4th were a mixture of democratic and socialist, anti-bureaucratic demands, but lacking the unanimous slogan of the Soviets of 1905 and 1917: "All Power to the Soviets" ' (pp. 177–8). This is true – and this is why his earlier statement is not entirely appropriate. We only have to add that, according to our whole conception, we do not find this to be a weakness but an organic part of a new (dual) conception of power.

25   Lomax, *Hungary, 1956*, pp. 140–1. The passage here italicized by us raises two distinct problems which we are going to discuss later. [A good documentation of the role of the revolutionary workers' councils can be found in I. Kemény and B. Lomax, eds, *Magyar Mu – kástanàcsok 1956–ban* (Hungarian Workers' Councils in 1956) (Paris: Magyar Füzetek Publisher, 1986).]

26   Molnár, *Budapest, 1956*, p. 179 (emphasis added).

27   Bibó, 'Draft', p. 141 (emphasis added).

28   We shall come back to the 'trial' of Nagy and his group. Here only the following facts need be stated, which, according to the testimony of Sándor Kopácsi (and many others), are beyond any reasonable doubt. The 'Nagy case' had not for one moment been entrusted to the Hungarian–Kádárist leadership alone; it had been directly supervised by the Khrushchevite head of the KGB, General Serov, and his emissaries, who *instructed* the Hungarian political bureau rather than counselled. On the other hand, the Hungarian political leadership had to be – in fact *was* – implicated in these representative political murders. We know from those who participated in or contributed to the session that a leadership meeting in Leànyfalú (near Budapest) discussed and decided the sentences for the Imre Nagy group. In this case, Kádár, otherwise a champion of a miserable 'legality' tolerated a flagrant deviation from any legal formalities. Losonczy, the second man of the group, according to Kopácsi's testimony, was simply murdered in December 1957 (Kopácsi, *In nome della classe operaia*, p. 230).

29   In this respect, Lukács had a very negative opinion of the Prime Minister. After Nagy's first fall in March 1955, when Ferenc Fehér tried to mediate between Lukács and Nagy in order to unify the socialist opposition to Rákosi, Lukács firmly answered: 'I am an old factionalist myself [he was referring to the 1920s]. I know how to make factions. One does not organize factions with *litterati* but with *apparatchiks*. This is dilettantish politics.' General relations between the two were

fairly hostile. When Ferenc Fehér tried again, during the spring of 1956, to bring the two together with the mediation of Gábor Tánczos, the secretary of the Petöfi Circle, after a week Tánczos returned with the answer that Nagy was not interested.

30 This early period has been described in Molnár and Nagy, *Imre Nagy*, pp. 18–27.

31 Just a few months before he suggested to Tito that 'perhaps' Nagy was an agent of the Western secret services, Khrushchev was complaining bitterly to Micunović about Rákosi's stupidity and aggressiveness in ousting Nagy from the leadership.

32 Quoted in Váli, *Rift and Revolt*, p. 148.

33 An example of this will suffice. In 1967 his confidant, then ideological secretary of the central committee, G. Aczél, coined the slogan 'Not the monopoly, but the hegemony of Marxism.' That would have meant a measure of *institutionalized* freedom. Frightened by this, the apparatus obviously put Kádár under pressure, and a few weeks later he 'explained' in a speech that the slogan was correct and remains valid but does not entail that anti-Marxist or non-Marxist views may be published.

34 Molnár and Nagy, *Imre Nagy*, p. 132.

35 Ibid., p. 133.

36 Ibid., pp. 145–8.

37 Quoted from Molnár, *Budapest, 1956*, p. 96.

38 Ibid. We wish to emphasize Nagy's turn towards the *members*, not the apparatus, of a political party. In his renewed conception, sovereignty belonged, in a political party, too, to the 'masses'.

39 Molnár, *Budapest, 1956*, p. 97.

40 Molnár and Nagy, *Imre Nagy*, p. 49.

41 Molnár, *Budapest, 1956*, p. 97 (emphasis added).

42 Ibid., p. 98.

43 *History of the Hungarian Working-Class Movements*, pp. 571–8. This time we can believe them: they speak against their better interests.

44 In order to avoid idealization, we have to state here again what is generally known: that, of all the ministers of the Nagy government, Bibó alone remained in the parliament in the early hours of November; all others, including the prime minister himself, looked for shelter, he at the Yugoslav embassy. This gesture could have been the result of his habitually wrong impulses, or it could have been – as Molnár suggests – guided by the feeling that in the Yugoslav embassy he would preserve his freedom of bargaining with the Soviet leaders; and, if it had happened once already, it was not in principle excluded from happening again. [Whatever the reasons, we positively know from the important publication, Mariá Ember, ed., *Menedékjog – 1956* (Asylum, 1956)(Budapest: Izabad Tér Kiadoi, 1989), that he had rejected all offers of a compromise based on a 'self-criticism' and the denigration of the revolution. In other words, he had not simply been 'thrown to his fate'; he had *chosen* his death. The only basis of negotiations that he was ready to accept was the legitimacy created by the revolution.]

45 There can be no doubt that the trial was stage-managed by mass murderers. Here is a short biography of the man in charge, this Khrushchevite Kaltenbrunner,

this implementer of the 'restored norms of socialist legality'. Ivan Aleksandrovich Serov, born 1905, was already in the 1930s in Stalin's personal secretariat, in that innermost sanctum of super-political police. In 1939–40 he commanded the campaigns for the sovietization of Baltic countries and the liquidation of 'politically undesirable elements' there. In 1940 he was in charge of NKVD organs in the Ukraine, and in 1943–4 in charge of deporting Chechens, Ingushes, Kalmyks and Crimean Tartars from Northern Caucasus. In 1945 he was the deputy chief of 'Smersh' in the Soviet zone of Germany, and in 1954–8 (the time of our story) chairman of the Committee of State Security (KGB). *Who's Who in the USSR, 1961/1962*, ed. H. E. Schulz and S. S. Taylor (New York: Scarecrow, 1962), pp. 669–70. Definitely the man for the job – a worthy successor to Jagoda, Yeshov, Beria and Abakumov.

46   Of course, he could have simply remained silent, or – what amounts to the same thing – he could simply have stated provocative slogans as, according to all testimonies, Szilágyi did. But Nagy knew that in that case he would simply be murdered, and he needed even that minimum degree of self-expression granted by a mock trial in order to bring into play a posterity to which alone he wished to relay his message. It is also true that such behavior suited his personality better.

47   We possess a very detailed summary of Nagy's confidential negotiations with Andropov during the crucial days, which stems from György Heltai, Deputy Minister of Foreign Affairs of Nagy's cabinet. According to this, Nagy talked to Andropov in the parliament on November 1, in the early hours of the morning, and he protested against the maneuvers of newly arrived Soviet troops in Hungary, an unexpected and suspicious act which constituted a flagrant violation of the October 30 declaration of the Soviet government to evacuate the national territory of Hungary. Andropov, who had first denied having any information about such troop movements, called Nagy later (11 a.m.) and told him a blatant lie about the character of these maneuvers (the existence of which he now admitted). In a later call (11.40 a.m.), during which he confirmed the sustained validity of the declaration of the Soviet government, Andropov suggested technical negotiations concerning the details of Hungary's withdrawal from the Warsaw Pact (which the Soviet government had apparently accepted). In the afternoon of that same day, a new negotiation with Andropov took place in the parliament building (in which the Hungarian party and government leaders participated and in the course of which Kádár made the emotional statement that, as a Hungarian, he would fight with 'weapon in hands' against a new Soviet invasion). Nagy made the solemn threat that, unless the new troop movements stopped, the Hungarian government would turn to the United Nations with an official protest. Late in the night, Andropov called Nagy on the phone again, to confirm, in yet another blatant lie, the Soviet decision not to send new troops. At the same time, he asked Nagy to refrain from the official protest in the United Nations. Nagy accepted Andropov's proposal. See Aczél et al., *The Truth about the Nagy Affair*, pp. 86, 87.

48   If we accept the characterization of the Khrushchevite 'restoration of socialist legality' as a *rationalized* form of terror, we shall immediately understand that Khrushchev's cynical argument against Stalin (that the Bukharin trial was 'superfluous') and Micunović's equally cynical argument against Khrushchev

(that the Nagy trial was 'superfluous') betrayed the very spirit of this *rationalization* of terror, which boasted of being legal and humane.

49 Kopácsi, *In nome della classe operaia*, pp. 265–6. In order to avoid misunderstandings, we do not wish to state any numerical prevalence of communists among those sentenced after the revolution. Our statement is restricted to the Nagy trial alone.

50 [We now possess two statements about Nagy's last gestures in the trial from the two last surviving defendants, Sándor Kopácsi and Miklós Vásárhelyi. Kopácsi sums up Nagy's last words as follows:

'I have attempted twice to save the honor of the word "socialism" in the basin of the Danube, in 1953 and in 1956. The first time I was obstructed by Rákosi, the second time by the Soviet army. In this trial, in this tissue of hate and lies, I have to sacrifice my life for my ideas. I willingly sacrifice it. After what you have done to these ideas, my life has no value any longer. I am certain that history will condemn my murderers. One thing alone would repulse me: to be rehabilitated by those who will murder me.' (See Kopácsi, *In nome della classe operaia*, p. 266.)

Vásárhelyi denies the validity of this version in J. Ember, ed., *Menedékjog–1956*, p. 158. According to him, Nagy

declared that he had been thoroughly preparing for making a last statement but, given that the whole trial had been so illegal, absurd and flagrantly violating even the most minimal formalities of law, he was not willing to legalize it by making any kind of last statement. He showed a thick notebook in order to demonstrate: although he would have had a lot to say, he would forego his right to a last statement in this trial.

We have decided to accept Vásárhelyi's statement as the genuine version. In actual fact, there are no substantive, merely stylistic, differences between the two versions.]

51 [1989: By now we have a certain degree of clarity concerning the number of the executed victims of the revolution. We owe this clarity to the exemplary, highly committed, yet balanced and objective, research of a team whose major figure was János M. Rainer. They published the results of their research in the volume *Halottaink* (Our Martyrs) (Budapest: Katalizátor, 1989). We will deliberately omit the analysis of the technical problems these authors had to face owing to the reluctance of the cooperation of the new Ministry of Justice. The ministry released figures of and certain data about the executed victims but it still has not made the documents available. But even after leaving the most generous margin for doubt, the following can be stated unambiguously. Between December 20, 1956 and December 13, 1961, 289 persons were sentenced to death by various courts and executed for 'counterrevolutionary crimes' in Budapest and the countryside (for participation in armed insurrection or for political activity during the revolution). However, this is very far from representing the actual number of the victims of the reprisals. First, separate military tribunals tried the soldiers, the army officers and those servicemen of the police personnel who participated in the revolution. From various indications, Rainer comes to the conclusion that together with those court-martialled and executed in the course of this second type of political trials, the total figure of the victims runs as high as 320 to 360 persons and possibly more (*Halottaink*, vol. II, p. 48). From the same

source we learn that the number of those sentenced to several years in prison was upward of 16,000; the number of those interned indefinitely adds further tens of thousands to these figures. Second, following the second Soviet invasion of November 4, 1956, there were persistent rumors in Hungary of summary executions (as well as deportations in the Soviet Union) of armed insurgents by special KGB units. We have now at least one irrefutable datum of such an atrocity, the murder of two activists of the workers' council in Salgotarjan, an industrial city in north Hungary, which was perpetrated by the reorganized militia of the Kádár government without the slightest legal formalities ('Ipoly menti Antigonék', *168 óra*, the weekly of the Hungarian Broadcasting Service, vol. 1. no. 22, October 3, 1989, p. 18). Third, there are not yet ascertained statements about the summary executions by KGB units, after the second intervention, of those Soviet soldiers who had shown signs of fraternity and solidarity with the revolutionary crowd, in KGB centers in and around Budapest. An indirect proof of the veracity of these rumors is Andropov's statement to Nagy on November 2 to the effect that the Hungarian observers confused the maneuvers of these units, brought to Hungary in order to bolster the discipline of the Soviet troops, with the maneuvers of military troops preparing for a new invasion (see note 47). While the second half of the statement was obviously a lie, the first half, the deployment of KGB units was in all probability a statement of fact. It is the task of the Soviet authorities to rehabilitate their own citizens who fell victims to reprisals for acts on behalf of the Hungarian revolution. Until this happens and the figures are made available, we have to include an undefined number of executed Soviet soldiers in the sum total of the victims of the revolution.

Part III

After the Historic Year of 1956

4

Kádárism as the Model State of 'Khrushchevism'

THE GENESIS OF A KHRUSHCHEVITE REGIME

Is it reasonable to discuss 'Kádárism'? Is one justified in adding the suffix 'ism' to the name of János Kádár, who has been for decades the first secretary of the Hungarian Socialist Workers' Party? Is his regime different from those of other, past or present, communist party general secretaries? If not, then 'Kádárism' is nothing but a journalistic catchword, for it would be clearly nonsensical to list as many 'isms' in Eastern Europe as general secretaries in the region since Stalin.

There is more to the dilemma if we consider that there has always been a taboo against identifying the regimes of Soviet-type societies through the names of their leaders.[1] In Kádár's case, in the case of a man who has a sense of dignity and a cold and ruthless will to power, but who is also altogether lacking in pompousness or self-aggrandizement, the taboo is not merely personal but also social, a matter of shrewd calculation. Giving his own name to his own regime would be tantamount to the dangerous deviation of 'national communism.' This is why, one can assume, he would be happier with the (naturally, confidential) appellation of Khrushchevite. But can we define one 'ism' through another: 'Kádárism' through 'Khrushchevism'?

Since we have analyzed in detail the 'social character of Khrushchev's regime' elsewhere,[2] the recapitulation of a few major features of this regime would suffice here. 'Khrushchevism' did have its distinctive set of characteristics. First, Khrushchev put an end to the inferno of the Gulag. His decree of 1956, releasing some eight million political prisoners, perhaps the broadest amnesty on record in political history, tacitly acknowledged the unbearable tensions caused by the terror under Stalin, which threatened the very existence of the system Khrushchev himself had helped build and to which he had remained committed. Khrushchev's impromptu attacks on the 'cult of personality', which is ostensibly the most meaningless term in modern politics, as well as his experiments with founding a separate 'industrial' and 'agricultural' party, were so many acts of groping in the dark. Yet, together, these chaotic attempts can be construed as a quest for a new equilibrium which would retain the principle of dictatorship while eliminating the idea and practice of mass terror. In a word, Khrushchev was the man who closed the crippling cycle of Stalin's 'revolutions from above'.

Economically, 'Khrushchevism's' chief aim was 'rationalization'. This strategic objective had three distinct aspects. First, the Khrushchevite efforts were targeted on increasing the production of consumer goods. (According to a widely accepted interpretation, Khrushchev put an end to the priority of Sector A (or Department 1); in simple terms, to the predominance of heavy industry over the industrial sectors which were directly catering to consumption. Breslauer, however, proved that this widely held view is simply a myth.[3] Rather, it was Malenkov, during his short reformist escapade as Prime Minister of the Soviet Union, who made inroads into the sacred domain of Sector A. Ironically, Khrushchev demolished Malenkov precisely with the accusation of thus 'violating a fundamental law of socialist economy'.) Khrushchev's innovation, and his major means of increasing production of consumer goods, was, first, to launch agricultural reforms and, second, to insist on the principle of 'substantive rationality' (an appellation given to his efforts by sociologists with which the not particularly cultivated Khrushchev was obviously unfamiliar). This fairly mysterious term describes a near-religious belief in the hidden potentials of the regime actualizable by good leadership. It was Khrushchev's substitute for genuine socioeconomic reform. Hence his incessant improvisations and experiments which, though they solved nothing, upset the mental peace of his apparatus sufficiently to trigger a cycle of coups against his rule. At the same time, the new policies also spelled the recognition of the private person *qua* consumer in Soviet history for the first time since the short period of the Bukharinist New Economic Policy (NEP) in the 1920s.

The second aspect of Khrushchev's campaign of rationalization was the emancipation of natural sciences and technology from ideological arbitration. Removing the ideological umpire, and thus liberating the sciences, directly served the interests of the ruling apparatus to which the whims of the increasingly senile tyrant had done untold damage. (The army, for example, had been forbidden to apply 'bourgeois' cybernetics during Stalin's last years.) In a broader sense, this act of emancipation supported the increasing enfranchisement of critical thought, the extremely fragmented 'second Russian Enlightenment'. The third aspect of the campaign of rationalization was the *rapprochement* with the world market, the abandonment of Stalin's thesis of the existence of two parallel world markets.

Kádárism, as an ideological system and as a political structure, has come of age via the internalization of the lessons of Khrushchevism. It was the outcome of a social experiment in a country which had been shaken to its very foundations by three years of overt political crisis and the storm of a great revolution. Both the deliberately 'Khrushchevite' character of the experiment and the general lack of confidence in its durability were constitutive of Kádár's Khrushchevite improvisation. It is not the uncertainty with which the new and unknown first man of Hungarian communism was regarded that needs to be corroborated. Virtually no one, not even the boldest political forecaster, would have predicted that Kádár's regime would become fourth oldest in Eastern Europe (after those of Tito, Zhivkov and Hoxha). It is rather its consciously Khrushchevite character that has to be shown.

Two tendencies were already operative in the slow prerevolutionary recruitment of the Kádárist faction in 1955–6. The first was the principle of selection: the group only admitted those 'party reformers' who unambiguously wanted to retain continuity with the past, despite the fact that several of them had been victims of the show trials of the fifties. They also insisted upon a commitment to an absolute loyalty to the Soviet Union. The second distinctive feature of the Kádárist group was that its leading members levelheadedly understood what was fomenting around them in Hungarian society. Some of them reached the conclusion that the political system, or its way of functioning, had to be restructured if the dictatorship were to be enabled to survive.

But when their 'finest hour' came with the second Soviet intervention, which crushed the Hungarian revolution on November 4, 1956, when they were literally handpicked by Khrushchev for the task of governing Hungary for the Soviet Union,[4] they faced an almost impossible task. Even a dictatorship that rests on the narrowest minority needs a minimum of coercive and administrative apparatus, and for a historical moment it seemed as though Kádár and his group would not be able to find even this minimum. One section of the previous party apparatus had become 'traitor'; that is, they had been compromised during the revolution and its immediate aftermath. They either remained loyal to Imre Nagy or hesitated too long before joining Kádár. Another section considered Khrushchev's experiment, including his de-Stalinizing 'secret speech' at the Twentieth Congress of the Soviet Communist Party, criminal or doomed. The Hungarian anti-Khrushchevites remained gleefully passive, waiting for the collapse of the Kádár leadership. In the meantime, they were flirting with the Molotov/Malenkov opposition organized against Khrushchev, which indeed made a grab for power in June 1957, but which failed.

All this implied that the Hungarian leadership had no other choice but to remain committed to the 'politics of the Twentieth Congress'. It can be stated without exaggeration that their whole political and physical survival depended on the success of 'the line of the Twentieth Congress' and on Khrushchev's remaining in office.[5] Paradoxically, this was true the other way around as well: Khrushchev's political fate was closely linked to the outcome of Hungarian events in the first phase of his leadership. We know from Khrushchev's own memoirs (taped during his years of disgrace and smuggled out of the Soviet Union) that Molotov had warned him of the predictable consequences when the latter had read the text of his 'secret speech' before the congress. And the Hungarian chickens did come home to roost just as Molotov had predicted. This meant that yet another failure in either direction (either a too-weak Hungarian leadership allowing the tensions to approach a new boiling point or an overtly Stalinist group in power in complicity with Khrushchev's enemies) would have meant the end of the Soviet First Secretary, who had already been thoroughly shaken in his authority in the eyes of the apparatus. This is why a superficial political association initially based on an almost random choice gradually developed into a solid alliance between Khrushchev and Kádár, and in some sense into an alliance based on shared principles. As a result, Khrushchev provided the support needed by this inexperienced and politically weak leadership in its politically formative years.

There were so-called 'objective circumstances' which also facilitated the emergence of a 'model Khrushchevism'. Hungary is a small country with a small population (ten million, the second lowest in the East European Comecon countries), but it has climatic conditions which are favorable for agriculture. Although it is lacking in the raw materials needed for a Stalinist program of industrialization, even this liability was turned into an asset by the Kádár leadership. It served as a good pretext for bringing forced industrialization to a halt. Furthermore, Hungary did not have, for such a small country could not have, a significant army. Because of the revolution and the concomitant dissolution of the army, the Hungarian armed forces could not even be used, as Cuban forces would later be, to further the purposes of Soviet expansionism, as a kind of 'foreign legion'. If credence can be given to the party grapevine, an effective armament program was sabotaged by the Hungarian party apparatus itself, even after the total reorganization and the thorough political purge of the army. For a small army meant less expenditure and a limited involvement, and both were indispensable preconditions of the Hungarian experiment with Khrushchevism. Finally, the complete absence of the habitual East European explosive material, the domestic conflict between various nationalities, spared Hungary the Romanian temptation of internal Stalinism cum rabid nationalism. This special dispensation from the adversities of history and environment made it possible, as well as necessary, for the Kádárist leadership to embark on an innovative strategy in a political no man's land.

But in the main, Kádárism could become a 'model Khrushchevism' for the paradoxical reason that there were no other Khrushchevite countries around her. Periodically issued 'reminders' of Hungary's isolation or at least solitary position within the bloc, selectively addressed to various strata of the populace, have always been an absolute prerequisite of the regime's existence. It is primarily the 'ideological intelligentsia' that has been warned, naturally, in an informal and 'off-the-record' manner, about the 'danger from outside'. But messages of this kind have never been restricted to the intellectuals. In a word, not only the fact but also the consciousness on the part of the populace of being the only Khrushchevite country in a non-Khrushchevite milieu is a fundamental precondition of the Kádárist experiment.

A MACHIAVELLIAN ESTABLISHMENT

What are the constitutive features of Kádárism?

For starters, the regime was conceived in an authentically Machiavellian spirit. This is not meant in the popular sense that its leaders are ruthless or subscribers to political pragmatics without moral principles; although this, too, is correct. What we mean is rather that, in a manner of speaking, they stumbled upon certain fundamental principles of the Machiavellian *techné* of governing. First, they 'reinvented' the maxim: 'men must either be caressed or else annihilated; they will revenge themselves for small injuries, but cannot do so for great ones; the injury therefore that we do to a man must be such that we need not fear his vengeance.'[6] And they added the following maxim to this:

[Cruelties] well committed may be called those . . . which are perpetrated once for the need of securing one's self, and which afterwards are not persisted in, but are exchanged for measures as useful to the subjects as possible. Cruelties ill committed are those which, although at first few, increase rather than diminish with time . . . Whence it is to be noted, that in taking a state the conqueror must arrange to commit all his cruelties at once, so as not to have to recur to them every day . . .[7]

From Machiavelli we can learn the precise difference between Stalin's 'ill committed cruelties' which, in the postwar period of his terror, 'increased, rather than diminished with time' and the Kádárist reprisals. The latter constituted a three-year long process of brutal reprisals,[8] which totalled a number second only to that of the victims of reprisals in the wake of the Greek civil war in post-World War Two Europe (the Soviet Union being always left out of calculation). On the other hand, this drama was followed, to confirm the Machiavellian wisdom, by miraculous acts of self-moderation in the sixties.

The Kádárist organs of repression and coercion bore strongly in mind that 'people will revenge themselves for small injuries, but cannot do so for great ones.' They so increased terror and intimidation between the gloomy years of 1957 to 1960 that no one dared to think of resistance, not even in the form of a (public) statement of solidarity with the defeated revolution. Apart from cases in which they were resolved to kill their prisoners (as they were the leaders of the Nagy group), the defendant's resistance or repentance meant the difference between life and death; a partial 'self-criticism' could bring at least a significant diminishment in the length of imprisonment. But the Kádárist leadership had apparently intended from the start to impose its 'well committed cruelties' all at once, rather than increase them. After selective acts of personal amnesty in 1960, the most unexpected and sensational act of early Kádárism came in 1962: a general amnesty, six years after a ruthlessly crushed revolution. When compared to the record of other European dictatorships, one is inclined even to admire the Machiavellian brilliance of Kádárism. (Francoist Spain never experienced such a collective act of clemency, and in Greece, an incomplete amnesty came only 20 years after the events.)

The results did not fail to materialize. The populace perfectly understood that this was a regime capable of literally anything, without the slightest inhibition, when its political existence was threatened. (The highest number of women in postwar Europe were executed under Kádár for 'political crimes'; young men were arrested on their eighteenth birthdays and sent to the gallows for acts of armed resistance when they had been fifteen.) But the amnesty also proved that this government was willing to make reasonable arrangements with a populace bullied into obedience. The system of repression was 'streamlined' and 'rationalized'.

Is Kádárism still a 'police state'? Answering this question is undoubtedly difficult in the face of the ongoing cruelties of many an Asian, African and Latin American dictatorship, when one looks, as a tourist or a casual observer, at the smooth facade of Kádárist Hungary in the seventies. And there have been indeed unmistakable efforts on the part of the Hungarian leadership to reduce the repressive/police character of the regime, even beyond banning the methods of Stalinist show trials which became a common feature of Eastern Europe after the de-Stalinizing Twentieth Congress and Khrushchev's 'secret speech'. The use of torture is now strictly forbidden in dealing with 'political criminals'. The relatives of those held accountable for such 'crimes' are not automatically persecuted by 'law'. And, above all, the leadership takes extraordinary precautions to protect its own cadres from its own political police. It is a central committee mandate in Hungary, a more powerful decree than any law, that no member of the central committee can be investigated for any crime without the committee's prior approval. Police interrogations must be interrupted if the name of a central committee member surfaces during the confessions. Even if several hundred persons were imprisoned for political crimes in the seventies, as was mentioned in one of the rare quantitative reports of the Minister of the Interior to a sham parliament, Hungary still has a pride of place for moderation in the non-democratic world in numerical terms.

And yet, Kádárist Hungary has remained a police state. It is still a stated principle of the regime that legality, the law, the whole legal system is dependent on the political objectives of the party, and not the other way around. This entails more than a lack of autonomy on the part of the courts of law. It expressly means that political punishments, including particular sentences, are decided by political bodies and not by courts. At least formally, the sentencing of Imre Nagy and his colleagues was initiated by the Hungarian central committee (substantively, there cannot be the slightest doubt that it was Khrushchev's direct order). Even the very sentence, the death penalty, was a leadership decision.[9] The legal prerogatives of the police, which shield it to the extent that unauthorized public mention, let alone criticism, of their activities is declared a crime; the ban on the lawyers' independent investigation; the maintaining of the system of 'police supervision' (in simple translation, internment at home), which is an act of police jurisdiction instituted on the grounds of suspicion and for an indefinite time; the existence of a (limited number) of internment camps – all this is ironclad evidence of the continued existence of the Kádárist police state.

KÁDÁR'S ECONOMIC STRATEGY

In order to understand the economic structure of the regime, which in its main features has remained a unique subtype of 'the dictatorship over needs', we have to isolate the terms of its economic strategy. After the revolution of 1956, the major goal of the Kádárists was the termination of the so-called extensive development of the economy, and they made desperate and futile efforts to make a transition to the intensive phase.[10]

We should not assume, though, the existence of prefabricated economic blueprints in these leadership circles. Rather, they invented their economic strategy *en route*. Yet one principle has remained crystal clear from the very beginning: economic strategies must not get in the way of political pacification; rather, economic policies must guarantee the smooth functioning of the political system without spectacular disfunctions and interruptions. The inviolable rule of these policies was that there be a slow but uninterrupted growth in both the per capita product and the real wages and salaries of the employees of the state (who, until the late seventies, comprised the majority of the urban populace). This meant the shelving of all decisions which could, in the short run, lead to dangerous social conflicts. (As far as caution is concerned, Kádár the Khrushchevite has always had the exact opposite of his master's adventurous character, while, of course, remaining a super-

Khrushchevite with his national brand of 'goulash communism'.) Economic policies like this are naturally dangerous in the long run and, so far, long-range planning has been where Kádárism has proved to be most vulnerable. A striking example of what such policies entail are the decisions about infrastructure, including housing stock.[11] Since infrastructural work involves huge investments, with amortization being extremely slow, the Kádárist budget experts made incessant and desperate efforts to cut down the section of the budget reserved for such 'indirect amenities' to the bare minimum. Urgent economic decisions have thus been postponed *ad infinitum*. Such a policy is in itself a source of economic tension that in turn contributes to the postponement of further decisions some of which later cannot be made at all. The classic example of this economic prevarication is the neglected road network which could have gone hand in hand with the increase in cars; this opportunity having been missed, however, the problem became insoluble.

Subsequent to the crushing of the revolution, Kádárist economic strategy has had two basic principles: the annual and moderate raising of the standard of living (in a direct form, by raising real wages), and the recognition of the need for certain 'trendy' consumer goods (cars being their epitome). Both were politically motivated priorities. Although they were substitutes for even a modicum of political freedom, both of them had a certain liberalizing impact. As far as the first is concerned, direct rises in wages and salaries broadened the autonomy of the populace as consumers. With regard to the second, a widespread New Leftist romanticism has to be dispelled. Since the typical wage laborer in the East European countries, employed by the state, has never had the option of 'either domination over production or consumerism', but rather the other alternative of 'consumerism or dire poverty', the avenue opened up to them by Kádárism at least proved to be the better choice. Of course, the policy of consumerism was not implemented without relapses. Simultaneous with the intermittent waves of neo-Stalinist offensives, Kádár launched recurring and vehement invectives against 'immoderate consumerism'. But in between, consumption grew, and it is the leadership's firm intention that this trend should continue. A third important factor in the successful economic functioning of Kádárism is the agricultural reform. This again is an unintended result of the regime's 'somnambulist Khrushchevism', of the clarification a posteriori of its own principles.[12] In the immediate aftermath of the crushed 1956 revolution, at least the peasantry seemed to be an economic victor. In order not to be forced to send armed detachments into every village to 'pacify' the peasants, the Kádár leadership abolished a series of oppressive decrees, passed and enacted during the early fifties, which had been targets of the visceral hatred of the peasantry. 'Natural taxation', which required that virtually the entire yield for each season be delivered to the state for a nominal reimbursement, a truly ingenious scheme triggering regular short supplies in both the city and the countryside, was immediately revoked. The policy of directives issued by the 'center', meticulously prescribing both the quality and quantity of everything to be grown on the fields in even the smallest village, yet another Orwellian masterpiece, was cancelled. Agricultural prices were raised.

But 1958 was already an ominous year for the Hungarian peasant. Under Soviet pressure, the slogan 'Socialist collectivization has to be completed' was again put on the agenda of almost all East European central committees (with the exception of Poland). The following alternative solutions were discussed in the Hungarian central committee. It was hotly debated whether total collectivization, in itself a foregone conclusion, should be brought in line with the economic (primarily credit) capacity of the state, and thus economic rationality preserved, or whether the cadres should proceed with the customary vigor of the Stalinist early fifties, regardless of the economic and political consequences. In a typical Kádárist manner, the solution was a theoretically untenable compromise between the two proposals. It has been resolved that no coercion should be applied, but that the process should be politically, and not economically motivated. According to the very convincing account of Ferenc Donáth, three factors combined in the ultimately successful course of collectivization. First, the peasant felt isolated and cornered. With the exception of Poland and Yugoslavia (the latter, as a non-Warsaw Pact country, being irrelevant to Hungarian politics), the policy of collectivization prevailed everywhere. If after the revolution of 1956 and the subsequent solemn promises of the new leaders, the policy of forced collectivization was to be resumed, the peasants had to deem resistance entirely useless. The second factor was coercion itself.[13] Even if the process did not resemble the Stalinist 'heroic age' of collectivization, accompanied by armed raids on the villages and mass deportations, the exhortations of the government were amplified by court sentences for 'incitement against collectivization' and internment camps. Third, the new leadership was shrewd enough not only to punish but also to reward those complying with the new trend. By 1959, the process was completed, and according to familiar scenarios, Hungary was all set for cyclically recurring food crises.[14]

In the most 'Khrushchevite' and innovative act of its political career, the Hungarian leadership at this point suddenly understood that reconciliation with the peasantry within the framework of the collectivized agriculture was an indispensable precondition of the system's consolidation of its existence. The aftermath has been termed by Donáth the first significant (naturally, informal) 'agreement' between leadership and peasantry; this term has traditionally been completely missing from the communist vocabulary. The most important stipulation of this agreement was the creation of 'household economic units' whereby a certain quantity of land (albeit no formal ownership title) and a certain amount of free time was allotted to the peasant.

It is the consensus of agricultural experts that Hungary has not experienced the usual East European food supply crises since the sixties solely due to the existence of these units.[15]

All these economic factors together have led to the recognition of the need for, and the possibility of, a large-scale economic reform in Hungary.[16] Of course, the idea was not exclusively a Hungarian concern, although the triggers to economic reform vary from country to country in Eastern Europe. Some of these countries are relatively prosperous even when compared to the poorer Western countries, the result of a number of – inherited or extraneous – circumstances. This is the case with the German Democratic Republic, due to the economic privileges it has enjoyed in the Comecon since the 1953 Berlin uprising (which, in turn, it owes to its key strategic position); further, due to the presence of the technologically best trained workforce in the whole 'socialist bloc'; and, finally, due to the economic bonuses provided by West Germany, and through the Federal Republic by the EEC. Some other countries, for example the Soviet Union and Romania, badly need the most elementary rationalization of their very poorly functioning economies. Both types belong in the same cluster by virtue of one factor: their respective leaderships reject every idea of reform following an arch-conservative suspicion of social change of any kind.

A very sketchy typology of the motives for reform in the countries where reform experiments have been made or are in the making, reads as follows. Novotny's Czechoslovakia has actually been forced to launch the idea of economic reform under the threat of political collapse: it alone among the 'brethren countries' had to officially cancel its collapsed Five-Year Plan. By contrast, Yugoslavia's longlasting policy of drawing ever closer to the Western common market made the decision of introducing the principles of economic reform both inevitable and irrevocable. Hungary represents a third class. Because of the overly cautious Kádárist policy, there was no imminent danger of an economic collapse. At the same time, a serious economic rapprochement with the West was out of the question for political reasons. The Hungarian leadership was sufficiently motivated to introduce reforms, after having spent two years (1966–8) in intraparty debates, by its intention to continuously increase consumerism (which in turn presupposed structural rationalization), and also by the tacit but unmistakable pressure of the populace. People in Hungary claimed bonuses for their political obedience.

The basic terms of the Hungarian reform can be easily summed up. First, the legitimacy of 'socialist market relations' was recognized in principle. Of course, this was a serious theoretical offense against the 'authentic' Marxian standpoint, but the Hungarian leadership had exclusively pragmatic concerns. Secondly, a line was unambiguously drawn beyond which concessions, for political reasons, were non-negotiable. During the lengthy preliminary consultations with leading Hungarian economists and sociologists, proposals for a relative (legal, economic and political) autonomy for the factories and enterprises have emerged. These were either immediately rejected by the political leadership or indefinitely postponed. On the most crucial point, then, the Hungarian economic reform was dangerously flawed from the outset.

More important than the question of the 'specifically Hungarian' model, discussed, and to our mind insufficiently resolved, by Rezső Nyers,[17] is the other question: is it a genuine reform or merely a superficial management liberalization? In our view, given that the Soviet regime is a 'political society' or a 'dictatorship over needs', the analysis of its economy in complete separation from political power is methodologically illegitimate. Without fundamental changes in the political system of domination, no more than a technical rearrangement of the rules of economic management is conceivable in these societies; this is what has happened in Hungary.[18] The fatal weakness of this kind of flawed 'reform' is that all rearrangements of the rules of economic management can be revoked with a single central committee decision. It will suffice to quote Iván Berend, a historian who is an extreme apologist for Hungarian development, to prove this point: 'At the end of 1972, an explicit hostility to the reform emerged which led, by 1977, to the braking, in part the withdrawal, of the reforms.'[19] The Hungarian 'management adjustment', a better name than 'reform', was, as Xavier Richet correctly said, a political instrument, a much delayed answer to the revolution of 1956, a redistribution of power between the various groups of the ruling apparatus, having the objective of making the functioning of the regime smoother and more flexible than it had been earlier.

THE POLITICAL SYSTEM

The third structural element of Kádárism lies in its unique political system. Of course, the term 'unique' holds true only within the usual Leninist framework of the single-party system. The factors constituting Kádárism's unique character are numerous, but the non-legitimized, yet tacitly recognized, existence in it of pressure groups is of crucial significance. Open and legal legitimation of pressure groups would automatically lead to the loss of the party's 'primogeniture', to use Trotsky's well-known term, to a radical transformation of the whole system. Not for nothing are attempts at even collective forms of protest liable to very severe punishment in Kádárist Hungary. On the other hand, the reputation of Kádárism, so highly praised by a totally uncritical Western press, of not just solving but preventing open social conflicts rests precisely on the never publicly acknowledged fact that Kádárism tacitly recognizes the existence of at least the following pressure groups. The foremost negotiating partner of the Kádárist leadership is the so-called 'ideological intelligentsia', once the hotbed of rebellion, these days lamentably tamed and corrupted. Next come the arch-conservative leaders of the Hungarian churches who are, nevertheless, willing to become the advocates of the regime's political interests and decisions in their sermons and pastoral letters as well as in their authoritative and confidential advice given to their believers. This dubious attitude is all the more easily practiced as being religious in Hungary these days does not imply a greater degree of discrimination than being an atheist in a Catholic and undemocratic country in the nineteenth century. A third group consists of leading technocrats, some of them party members, others 'fellow travellers', who, regardless of their party affiliation, have material and intellectual interests distinctly different from those of other pressure groups. Eventually, a further pressure group has been constituted by chairmen of collective farms. Even decisive sectors of the political bureaucracy have themselves become pressure groups. Typically, however, the pressure group which would be the least recognized and tolerated would be the one emanating from the official 'ruling class', that of the factory workers.

What were initially spontaneous canalizations of social conflicts have been solidified into a *techné* during the long years of Kádárist rule. A certain type of tension defusion has become a routine Kádárist scenario. Initially, negotiations on areas of potential conflict are handled by semi-official emissaries of the center out of the presence of official authorities. The latter only appear on the scene once an informal pact has been hammered out, in order to formally ratify it. Machiavellianism operates here as well: a fiasco by the authorities would mean a loss of face, forcing them to quell disobedience by coercion even if the use of force were not in their better interests. Furthermore, official negotiations would confer legitimacy on the opposition. But the emissaries, while they have the verbal mandate of the center, are neither official representatives of the authorities nor their plenipotentiaries. The center jealously guards its prerogatives even with regard to these emissaries. And, although this complicated ballet works in the majority of cases, overt and uncompromising acts of protest and disobedience are immediately crushed. This is what happened to the spontaneous nationalist demonstrations of high-school students celebrating the anniversary of the 1848 Hungarian national revolution and war of independence in 1972 and 1973.

A second basic element of the Kádárist political system is the deliberate de-politicization of everyday life. This tends to be seen as a concession and a relief by the populace, in a certain sense quite rightly so. The forced atomism, or, in Lukács' vocabulary, 'the brutal manipulation' of the Stalin era has been replaced in Kádár's times by 'refined manipulation' (which always implies the potential use of coercion). 'I prefer them to go home and watch the TV,' the ideological secretary of the Kádárist leadership remarked in the sixties in confidential circles.

The Kádárist campaign advertising the charms of a conservative family life is a simple extension of this policy. Just as in Gaullist France and in the United States, divorce in Hungary is a setback for a political career; if leading functionaries wish to retain their positions, they must ask for permission to divorce. Premarital and extramarital sex are accepted as an ineradicable evil, but the 'display of disgusting sexuality' is sanitized from movies, television and literature. Feminism is suspect, lesbianism and homosexuality are considered aberrant by both government and populace (homosexuality was, up until recently, punishable by law). But even in this regard, the combination of common sense and Machiavellianism puts a limit on Kádárist Victorianism. Up until 1973, abortion was legal and free, and even the present restrictive regulations are not enforced beyond the point where they would make life unbearable for the unmarried, the poor and the ill. But the principles of the traditional nuclear family can have no competition. When Agnes Heller and Mihály Vajda published an article on alternative forms of family in 1972, the then prime minister commented on the 'immoral' authors: 'We are going to take the pen out of their hands.'

Mass tourism, unique in the bloc countries, is part and parcel of the functioning of the regime. Of course, the state retains its patronage over the citizen in this respect as well. Characteristically, Kádár once gave the following answer to the question of a UPI reporter as to whether Hungarians have a right to hold a passport: they have the right to apply for a passport. But, in fact, the Kádárist state promotes tourism. Although Hungary is an extremely currency-hungry country, its citizens are annually or biannually allotted a small amount of foreign currency which is sufficient for a short stay abroad. There are several reasons for this policy. The leaders want to advertise their liberality both to the West and to the Hungarian populace, and this is the most painless way of doing so. They want to diffuse the politically dangerous atmosphere of collective claustrophobia, a typical sociopsychological disease of the Soviet populace. Finally, mass tourism, and the concomitant currency black market, guarantees the influx of much sought-after consumer goods, which would otherwise be a heavy item on the state budget.

The price for the de-politicization of daily life, for the protective aura surrounding the conservative family, and for mass tourism is unconditional political obedience. This is why, in analyzing the political mechanics of Kádárism, one must consider the decision-making centers alone. We are convinced that these centers and the distinct *modus operandi* of their aggregate is far from uniform in all communist countries. Although the seat of decision-making in all of these countries is ultimately the political bureau and the secretariat, while the central committee has been normally reduced to the role of a posteriori sanctification of motions carried by the supreme bodies, post-Stalinist Eastern Europe exhibits the most surprising variety. Furthermore, the central committee has played a crucial role on certain junctures in the Soviet Union. It was this body that first, in 1957, quelled, and then, in 1964, brought to victory the coup against Khrushchev. Alongside that it may be put that there is no knowledge that Yugoslavia's central committee perpetrated a single act of disobedience to Tito.

In the case of Hungarian Khrushchevism, the central committee had to play a key role for the simple reason that, despite certain well-rehearsed scenarios, the new, handpicked leaders had no idea of how and where to steer a revolution-torn Hungary in November 1956. During the first years of his leadership, Kádár had to fight an uphill battle to impose his gradually developing policies on his own apparatus. For a while, in 1957 and early 1958, his crypto-Stalinist opposition was openly organizing itself. Kádár's grip over the central committee became firm only after this group was disbanded. But even thereafter, he had to strictly observe the 'rules of collective leadership'. Kádár suffered repeated defeats in the central committee. It is reasonably certain that the outcome of the collectivization debate of 1958 meant at best a compromise for him. More importantly, the resolution of the November 1972 plenary session, inaugurating the temporary victory of the neo-Stalinist opposition, was an outright condemnation of his policies. On the other hand, Kádár, like all first men in communist apparatuses, gradually shifted decision-making towards the political bureau, which consisted of his own handpicked men. This trend was backed by his increasing authority inside and outside the party. In 1957, he was regarded by the populace as a Quisling, and by the majority of his apparatus as a dubious ex-apparatchik, compromised by his behavior during the 'counterrevolution'. Over the years, he came to be considered Hungary's best king in centuries by the man in the street and as a shrewd tactician by his own startled apparatus. This reputation has not granted him Tito's prerogatives in the central committee, but it certainly lends an added weight to his opinion in the decision-making process.

Kádárism, restored to full power after its temporary setback from 1972 to 1976,[20] now faces a 'natural' dilemma and three alternative courses. The dilemma is Kádár's age in a society where so much depends on the personality of leaders. The first alternative for the regime is that it continues its present course unchanged for as long as Kádár lives. The second is that the regime relapses into oldfashioned Stalinism pure and simple. The political forces necessary to bring about such a change are always present, but the task would not be an easy one. Even a violent backlash on the part of the populace could not be excluded given such an eventuality. The third alternative is only now beginning to take shape. The most significant development in recent years is the emergence of a Hungarian *samizdat* representing a degree of free press and free public opinion. Until now, it has been tolerated by the authorities. Its institutionalization, together with a measure of actual independence for the trade unions, an unlikely event after the crushing of Solidarity but one which cannot be excluded with absolute certainty, would point to a 'Titoization of Kádárism'. But such a possible Hungarian Titoism clearly lacks one of two necessary foundations for existence: national independence or a major change in the Soviet Union.

1978–1983

NOTES

1 To our knowledge, this significant fact has never been analyzed: not even the omnipotent Stalin ventured to establish his own 'historical epoch' designated by his name. Of course, confidential party gossip – probably emanating from that last, most servile, political bureau 'elected' by the Nineteenth Congress – to the effect that 'Stalinism' was in the cards, circulated during his last years. But with the tyrant's death, it remained gossip.

2 See the analysis in 'The social character of Khrushchev's regime', in F. Fehér and R. Miller, eds, *Khrushchev and the Communist World* (London: Croom Helm, 1983), reprinted in A. Heller and F. Fehér, *Eastern Left, Western Left* (Cambridge/Atlantic Highlands: Polity Press/Humanities Press, 1987).

3 G. W. Breslauer, *Khrushchev and Brezhnev as Leaders: Building Authority in Soviet Politics* (London/Boston/Sydney: Allen and Unwin, 1982).

4 The most detailed story of Kádár's random selection by Khrushchev during the stormy days of the Hungarian revolution has been recounted in part II.

5 One can ascertain from the confidential statements of these leaders the degree of threat from their own apparatus amid which they lived. Kádár himself told the most telling story. In his then unpublished address to the first national conference of the Hungarian Socialist Workers' Party in 1957, he mentioned the symptomatic case of an investigating officer of the 'new' secret police who, during the interrogation of a 'counterrevolutionary' suspect, the writer L. Szilvási, made the following remark about the general secretary of his own party: 'Kádár's case too will be reopened in due course.' The transcript of the national conference was confidentially circulated in 1957. Since no confidentiality is absolute, not even in the 'dictatorship of the proletariat', we had the opportunity to read it; hence the information. [Addendum: Typically, however, the above section is expurgated from the first publication of the speech. See 'Az ideiglenes Központi Bizottság beszámolója a Magyar Szocialista Munkáspárt országos értekezletének a politikai helyzetről és a párt feladatairól', in *Kádár János Művei* (Budapest: Kossuth Könyvkiadó, 1987), vol. 1 (1956–9), pp. 169–219. *1989*]

6 Niccolò Machiavelli, *The Prince* (New York: Random House, 1950), p. 9.

7 Ibid., p. 34.

8 See above, note 51 to chapter 3, p. 125.

9 Personal communication of G. Marosán, then secretary of the central committee, to these authors.

10   [Hungary has the best and largest contingent of 'critical economists' who, despite enormous difficulties of decades of repression, censorship and an almost pathological official secretiveness, did a model job of critically dissecting the command economy. We refer the reader to the works, some of them available in English translation, by J. Kornai, T. Bauer, A. Bródy, T. Liska, M. Tardos and several others. *1989*]

11   See the criticism of Kádárist housing policies in Ivan Szelényi, *Urban Inequalities under State Socialism*, (Oxford: Oxford University Press, 1983). This book has become an East European sociological classic for Szelényi did much more than merely expose the inadequacy of housing, and social services in general, in Hungary in the sixties. He also revealed that the distribution of apartments amounted to the systematic creation of inequalities on behalf of the nomenklatura.

12   In the analysis of the agrarian question, we are relying on the best expert and historian of the problem, Ferenc Donáth, in the fifties a prime defendant of Stalinist secret trials who, after being released, became minister of state in Imre Nagy's second government, and was later sentenced and imprisoned again. See his *Reform és forradalom: A magyar mezőgazdaság strukturális átalakulása 1945–1975* (Reform and Revolution: The Structural Transformation of Hungarian Agriculture, 1945–1975) (Budapest: Akadémiai Kiadó, 1977), described above, p. 83.

13   The use of coercion against reluctant peasants is now openly and cynically acknowledged by the official historians of the regime. See, for example, the contribution of András Gergely to the volume *Küss die Hand, Genossin* (My Humble Respect, Lady Comrade) (Hamburg: Rowohlt, Spiegel Bücher, 1983), p. 104.

14   Donáth, *Reform és forradalom*, p. 120 and *passim*.

15   It is Donáth again who sums up the main results of this policy: 'Hungary has the highest per capita agricultural production among the Comecon countries. In all of Europe, she is second only to Denmark. Given that the population growth is very small in Hungary . . . through the doubling of the yield of agriculture not only the food supply of the growing urban population can be ensured without problems, but also an ever increasing amount of agricultural products are exported. The export computed in US dollars already constituted two thirds (exactly 72.6 percent) of the export of the country in 1980. More than a third of the net agricultural production goes abroad.' *Küss die Hand*, p. 149 (our translation).

16   The best source on the Hungarian economic reform is P. Hare, H. Radice, N. Swan et al., *Hungary: A Decade of Economic Reform* (London/Boston/Sydney: Allen and Unwin, 1983).

17   Rezső Nyers, 'Jede Epoche bedarf einer neuen Demokratie', in *Küss die Hand*, pp. 42–3. Xavier Richet, a French expert, compiled an eight-point list, included in his contribution to Hare et al., *Hungary*, of technical changes in economic management which, as a rule, are pompously called the 'Hungarian economic reform'. We agree with both the realism of Richet's treatment and the appellation of the issue.

18   [The most prominent Hungarian critical economist, János Kornai, thinks otherwise. In his truly classic summary, 'The Hungarian reform: hopes,

illusions, perspectives', in F. Fehér and A. Arato, eds, *Crisis and Reform in Eastern Europe* (New Brunswick: Transaction Press, forthcoming), he diagnoses a genuine, but extremely hindered and retarded reform process. Much as we respect the authority of this outstanding scholar, we have to contradict him on this point, relying not least on his own lecture, given at the New School for Social Research on December 5, 1988, in which he expressed resignation, if not outright despair, over the systematic sabotage of reformist trends. In Kornai's terms, instead of market regulation, a new network of bureaucratic control moved into the vacuum created by the relinquishment of certain state prerogatives in the Hungarian economy. *1989*]

19 Iván T. Berend: 'Veränderungen waren notwendig', in *Küss die Hand*, p. 125.

20 Kádár's actual comeback (nominally he always remained the first man) can be accounted for by various factors. The Soviet leaders needed, after signing the Helsinki Agreement, a 'liberal' communist who had a pleasing image in the Western press. They had no other choice but Kádár. After the Polish uprising of 1976, which already foreshadowed the collapse of Gierek's regime, they did not want to add to their own difficulties. Finally, Kádár had a 20-year long reputation of keeping Hungary under control without bloodshed. Gossip also has it that the Eurocommunists, primarily the Italians, made Kádár's stay in office the precondition of their presence in the conference of European communists.

5

The Place of the Prague Spring

I

Four main types of social unrest can be identified in post-Stalin Eastern Europe. The first type is mainly characterized by incidents of famine mutiny, but it has occasionally had other causes, such as an unbearable norm readjustment period in factories, or the sort of fiscal reform which wipes out all the savings of large parts of the population in one stroke. Incidents of this type occurred in Berlin in 1953, in Pilsen in 1956, in Novocherkassk in 1962, and in the Zhil Valley in 1977; and the trend no doubt continues in many other places of which we are not yet aware. These upheavals display certain characteristic features. They are overwhelmingly spontaneous, unconnected to critical activity which may be fermenting in the rest of society. Sometimes they assume violent forms, as was the case in Berlin and Poznań, where the conflict was fought out on the barricades between demonstrators and armed forces. But they are not revolutionary. The ominous 'hydra of revolution' which is supposedly incipient in all strikes was not present in the famine riots, not even in their violent versions, which governments generally survived. After a short transitory period, the riot in Berlin resulted in an even firmer hold by Ulbricht over East Germany. In Poland, it took the propaganda campaign of the Gomułka group to undermine Ochab's short-lived rule and sweep him from power; by itself, Poznań could not accomplish it.[1] In none of these cases was the demonstrators' aim to overthrow the government. Their actions were spontaneous, desperate, non-ideological, limited in space and shortlived in time. However, they might be read as signals of a gathering storm, which indeed was the case in Poznań in 1956.

The second type of social unrest in Eastern Europe is represented by a singular event: the Hungarian revolution of 1956. We have discussed the revolution in detail in part II and so here a brief characterization will suffice. From the first hours of its dynamic existence, the 1956 Hungarian revolution, which was both radical and total, questioned and eventually rejected the communist one-party system. In fact, for its short duration, the revolution completely overthrew that system. Precisely due to its uncompromising radicalism, the Hungarian revolution did not and could not become a *paradigm* of action for other nations in the region. Nonetheless, we believe it remains a 'regulative idea' for an anti-authoritarian revolution in the sense that it was the exclusive work of the crowd in momentum, which had not the slightest inclination to make concessions to new or old oppressive authorities, but always remained determined to self-manage its own destiny.

The third type of social unrest, and again the only one of its kind, was the Czechoslovak attempt at structural reform. Since the specificities of this event will be fully considered below, here we only indicate its presence in our typology.

In the fourth type, exemplified by the events in contemporary Poland, we see the culmination of a decade of social struggles marked by desperate, sometimes bloody battles between the state and the huge, mostly industrial crowds of state wage-earners. In the 18 months before martial law the Polish situation was unique, but the general hysteria and confusion of the ruling apparatus was unmistakable evidence of their fear of a dangerous precedent which threatened to engulf the rest of Polish life.

In characterizing the Polish events as *a revolt of civil society against the state*, we will use the terms of Andrew Arato, supplemented by some of our own.[2] We may begin by pointing to the antagonistic symbiosis of a mutinous populace on the one hand, and a totalitarian state on the defensive but steadfastly claiming its right to rule on the other. Although this antagonistic symbiosis can be longlasting, it cannot yield any structural solutions or give rise to any institutions or drafts of a social contract which are capable of providing the basis for a lasting state of normality. It can only produce a temporary stalemate. Such an equilibrium, arising from a stalemate, is completely unstable. At any moment it can be tilted to one pole or the other by a random move on the part of either antagonist. This creates an atmosphere of uncertainty in the totality of social life, where flare-ups of hope are followed by deep depressions, and where there is duplicity on both sides.

The atmosphere in Poland typifies such a situation. Prior to martial law, the party apparatus daily assured the population of its sincerity and goodwill, while at the same time most of them eagerly awaited their first opportunity to crush the mutiny and punish those responsible. On their part, the representatives of civil society, who were bounded by the heterogeneous conglomerate calling itself a trade union (but which was both more and less), assured the government through released communiqués that it intended no actions other than those implied in the current situation. The truth, however, according to numerous spontaneous testimonies (and all too well understood by the Soviet leadership), was that at that moment people lacked the hope and therefore the audacity to go any further.

This strange symbiosis, in which both sides waited for a social miracle to happen, did not contain the specific elements of the *Czechoslovak option*, that is, it did not harbor illusions of reforms implemented in and by the party. In the concatenation of events in Poland, some of which had already occurred and some of which were about to occur, the elaborate ballet danced by certain party functionaries took on secondary importance. It is most telling about the East European state of affairs that this perhaps most inorganic and conservative of all possible solutions will eventually prove to be the most widespread, resulting in neither economic nor social stability, but instead containing the potential for exploding at any moment in the face of the social actors. And its significance can be traced precisely to the last factor: to its *revolutionary* potential.

II

Unlike the spontaneous behavior of the first type, the second, third and fourth types of mass movements have three characteristics in common. First, they were all preceded by economic crises which, although different in nature, affected the power bases of their respective societies. In Hungary in 1953, the collapse of one of Europe's finest agricultural systems was caused by a hyper-Stalinism which endangered the existence of the regime's very policy of industrialization – which was itself deeply irrational. Czechoslovakia in the mid-sixties was perhaps the only 'socialist' country that formally and publicly had to cancel its Five-Year Plan, an unusual admission of failure given that the editors of the official statistics were far from exact regarding the data they published. In Poland, a decade of wishful thinking about the economy ended in one of the most spectacular bankruptcies in postwar Europe, which had been predicted even by laymen.

Second, at the political level as well as the economic, the roots of these events can be traced back to a time well prior to their dramatic eruption. The Hungarian revolt of October 23, 1956, the Prague Spring intitiated by the January 1968 session of the central committee, the Polish breakthrough during the August 1980 strike, all were preceded by longstanding social crises in which many social actors sought to influence a public opinion *in statu nascendi*. Regardless of their conscious intentions, these actors eroded the power bases of their regimes to a considerable, though varying, degree.

Finally, they all shared a common peculiar rhythm. Following a long period of apathy, during which a numerically weak cohort of militants – the so-called dissidents – seemed to be eccentrics rather than social actors to be seriously reckoned with, there came an abrupt acceleration and extension of social interest and involvement.

Here is where the similarities end regarding the Hungarian, Czechoslovakian and Polish types of unrest. In order to further the analysis, we now need to address their differences and contrasting features.

A main line of division can be drawn between the Hungarian and Czechoslovakian movements on the one hand, and the Polish process on the other. The former, of short duration, were initiated and consummated by oppositional and reformist communists at various levels of the social hierarchy; in other words, by both intellectuals without power, and well-placed functionaries. Both the Hungarian and Czechoslovak reform programs were prepared and designed as grandiose acts of self-criticism, a kind of communist movement's 'homecoming'. At least some in the movement genuinely realized what crimes they had committed in the name of socialism, both against their own people and against their own socialist ideals. This generated a number of beliefs which most of us would today call illusions, but to which we then resolutely committed ourselves. In contrast, after Gomułka's regime betrayed its 1956 promises, the Polish movement from the middle of the sixties onward ceased to nurture reformist communist illusions. This was no doubt its *forte*, although it exposed the movement to the dangers of a new fundamentalism. The last expression of communist self-criticism in the Polish process of radicalization, the 'Open Letter' of Kurón and Modzelewski to the members of the Polish Communist Party, called for an uprising in the spirit of socialism against the 'new class'.[3]

Another feature distinguishing the movements in Hungary and Czechoslovakia from the Polish process can be found in the background of international events. Both the Czechoslovak and Hungarian radicalizations took place in the face of a *change of leadership* in the Soviet Union, the area's primary power. In the case of Hungary, this change signalled a dramatic crisis in the post-Stalin power vacuum. In the case of Czechoslovakia, where the course of events after Khrushchev's fall was smoother and outwardly less spectacular, Novotny's regime quickly consumed its limited reserves of confidence. But regardless of its form, a change of Soviet leadership has always meant uncertainty (or new options) and the disintegration of some of the mechanisms of domination, that is, certain formerly unassailable 'laws of Marxism-Leninism' which overnight become completely irrelevant.

The relative openness and choice of options introduced by the post-Stalin and post-Khrushchev changes provided the Hungarian and Czechoslovakian movements with a certain amount of self-confidence. This leads to social action, but it can also give rise to a dangerous kind of heightened self-assurance we may term 'social somnambulism'. In Poland, by way of contrast, suffering under Brezhnev's conservatism, the seventies seemed to offer only the impenetrable darkness of an ossified social immobility. The great accomplishment of the Polish workers and radical intellectuals was to find the stamina, the courage, the methods and the ingenuity to create the landslide victory of August 1980 and thus provoke a legitimation crisis for the regime – without triggering Soviet intervention.

There is, of course, one particular standard of comparison which sets apart the Polish and Czechoslovakian struggles from the Hungarian: namely, a historically developed awareness of the dangers inherent in radical action.

Occurring after Hungary 1956, both the Czechoslovak and Polish movements were able to appropriate some of the Hungarian lessons. Two are notable. One was the realization that the Soviet Union would in all probability intervene if the communist party dictatorships were threatened. This explains the repeated declaration of the Czechoslovak and the Polish actors that they were not questioning the communist party's monopoly of power. Second, judging by the Hungarian experience, the future protagonists of change knew with reasonable certainty that the Western powers would not take any positive non-military action to dissuade Soviet intervention. The theatrical and ineffectual machinations in the United Nations after the Hungarian revolution remained vivid in people's memories. A fact formerly only presumed to be true, that President Johnson simply gave the go-ahead to Brezhnev, was documented in 1980 by Zdeněk Mlynář's book *Night Frost in Prague*.[4] Adam Michnik's article 'What we will and what we can', as well as outspoken references to Hungary by the Polish public, showed that the Polish movement was fully aware of the danger of any reformist course.[5] And the Prague Spring also took place beneath the shadow of Hungary. Despite certain gestures which might be called, in retrospect, exuberantly optimistic, the historical and 'progressive' naïveté of Hungarian radicalism was absent from both Czech and Polish aspirations.

Despite the statements of both foes and pusillanimous friends, neither the Hungarian nor the Czechoslovak nor the Polish courses of social reform were doomed from the start (although we might mention our extremely skeptical view regarding Poland's chances). In writing on Hungary 1956 we showed that there were perhaps several moments during the turbulent 13 days, and certainly *one* moment, when the Soviet leadership, together with a Chinese delegation, seriously considered a more conciliatory course than the one actually taken. Moreover, despite a lack of concrete proof, we are certain that the same kind of deliberations took place during the Prague Spring, and during the Polish process as well. The lessons to be drawn from such a vague statement, of course, are not unambiguous. Even after their advice has become obsolete, and even after the play has ended, some chroniclers continue to suggest a posteriori that the Hungarian actors should have acted more considerately in their historical drama, and that the Czechoslovak ones should have acted more audaciously in theirs.

What remains beyond doubt is the fact that the Soviet leadership always meant to intervene in the event of destabilization in their sphere of influence, particularly if they could do so without undue cost. Therefore it is incumbent upon the East European emancipatory movements to make the price of Soviet intervention as high as possible, as well as being in their best interests. Two other conclusions can be drawn. We must consider the general irrationality and unpredictability of Soviet behavior in both foreign affairs and – more particularly – their 'imperial politics'. For example, what constitutes a counterrevolution in Soviet eyes? If we take the view that *Two Thousand Words*, a moderate manifesto of the Czechoslovak reform communist-socialist intelligentsia, was an undeniable sign of 'peaceful counterrevolution' in Czechoslovakia, then undoubtedly Poland too experienced a year and a half of a counterrevolutionary process, but no repressive domestic or external action took place in Poland. On the other hand, if occupying communist party buildings, arming the population, and demanding a multi-party system – all of which occurred in Hungary – constitutes a counterrevolution, then Czechoslovakia 1968 was certainly *not* a counterrevolution, and yet an intervention still was made in Czechoslovakia.

Second, regardless of the viewpoint of the Soviet leaders, nothing is more crippling and paralyzing for a mass movement than to be convinced in advance of failure. Such a feeling can produce a tragic *grandezza*, and who would know this better than the Poles? In fact, what Eastern Europe demands now is a tenaciously prosaic realism and stamina.

III

We can now proceed to a characterization of the unique position of the Czechoslovak attempt at social reform. But first the position of these spectators must be identified. We take the view of a Hungarian, and generally East European, radical; or to put it even more cautiously, a position identical with one of the radical views in the present Hungarian opposition. However, in order to present the fairest possible account of the Prague Spring, we must distinguish our present views from our previous ones.

The news about Czechoslovakia in 1968, which was filtered through all the usual unofficial East European channels of communication, engendered an immense sense of relief in Hungary, particularly when the reforms announced in January 1968 became the official policy of the Czechoslovak Communist Party. This feeling of relief affected three different actors with separate ways of reading the events. First, paradoxically, was the Kádárist leadership. A considerable number of this leadership, although not a majority, felt encouraged. For two years they had been tinkering with the idea of, and even with detailed plans for, an economic reform, but had felt hopelessly isolated after the fall of Khrushchev. Although he would not necessarily have sympathized with the idea of reform, Khrushchev was at least an experimentalist in spirit. But by 1968 the Soviet leadership had developed its arch-conservative and immobilist stand, refusing to consider even the idea of innovation. There was nowhere else to turn until Czechoslovakia. The regime of Gomu*ł*ka in Poland, having begun with surging hopes for emancipation and human dignity, was just then nearing its despicable conclusion in an anti-Semitic campaign and a massacre of striking workers unprecedented in postwar Europe. To be sure, in Yugoslavia an over-reformist mood prevailed, and even the abdication of the power prerogative by the League of Communists was discussed more or less publicly by a younger generation of functionaries. But Yugoslavia signalled danger, since no Warsaw Pact country that wished to remain on good terms with Brezhnev and his cohorts wanted to share common ground with the still heretical Titoism. For the Kádárist leaders the Czechoslovak turn came as an unexpected godsend, promising a new ally and an important new factor in East European politics.

Sharing the Kádárist optimism in the first weeks of the Czech reforms – for different reasons – were the intelligentsia and the technocrats. Arguing what they called 'socialist democratization' and 'the renaissance of Marxism', some members of the intelligentsia had become victims of the heavy post-1956 persecutions, and some were survivors on the regime's political-cultural margins. While always retaining suspicions and sometimes even hatreds of Kádár's Khrushchev-created regime, and while displaying varying degrees of skepticism, most of the intelligentsia nevertheless allowed the possibility of collaboration with Kádár's reformist aspirations, following the Czech pattern. Between January and June 1968, it appeared that both the leading Hungarian functionaries and at least half of the oppositional intellectuals – who were still under suspicion and even occasionally under police surveillance – shared concerns about Dubček's harassed government.

The third group of actors was the non-ideological technocracy, that is, technological intellectuals and managers, who were primarily interested in an economic rationalization, and regarded both party apparatchiks and 'romantic ideologues' as questionable and unreliable allies. Nevertheless, for all intents and purposes and for several reasons, they joined the pro-Dubčekist alliance. Since they were lacking autonomous political power, they could only express their aspirations through the mouths of the ideologues, whom they otherwise regarded with suspicion. Moreover, since Dubček's own program included economic rationalization, their only option was to bargain with the party bureaucracy.

Each with different objectives, the three groups of Hungarian actors had very different expectations regarding the course of Czechoslovakian events. The Kádárist leadership wanted a simple duplication of its own politics. Mutual and concerted, its recommendation amounted to a call for a 'return to the Leninist norms of legality', that is, in somewhat more prosaic words, a formal rehabilitation of the communist – and perhaps other leftist – victims of the sham trials of the fifties, thus defusing the mounting social tensions. This kind of concession meant that certain needs of the population would be recognized as justified, but that the populace would still be excluded completely from shaping the direction of the political course.

The ideologues wanted a theoretically founded 'socialist democracy', although they were in a state of general confusion about its specific content.

Some of their demands included the active participation of the citizenry, and considerable (that is to say, institutionalized) political change. Therefore their reading of Dubček and his leadership envisioned something like a triumphant Imre Nagy group firmly in power, at least for a few months.

The technocrats, for their part, had never been over-enthusiastic about popular participation in matters they believed should be left to experts; hence their natural and spontaneous alliance with the Kádárists, whom they otherwise saw as nuisances. Their reading of Dubček and his entourage was simple. They believed that after many blunderers the Czechs had found in the person of Ota Šik an expert who could accomplish the task of pulling Czechoslovakia out of its economic crisis. Šik and his people, with their up-to-date technology, could also serve as reliable allies of Hungarian modernization. Everything else, including semi-free trade unions, seemed to them to be either a dangerous fantasy or a sign of incompetence.

The differing expectations within this random alliance necessarily created inner tensions, and they began to surface in June, when the Czech leadership was officially taken to task. When the invasion came, and the Dubček leadership signed the humiliating 'Moscow agreement', the reactions of the various Hungarian actors were drastically different. The pragmatists lost faith in any change. The Kádárist leadership capitulated even before the Soviet dictates of late July–early August, and so became 'an accomplice before and after the fact'. As for observers like ourselves, the oppositional social reformers, the reaction was quick and final. Most of us unconditionally rejected and publicly condemned the Soviet invasion,[6] and along with it, any Leninist vestiges of thinking (for those who still held them). But while we publicly showed solidarity with the victims, our inner fury increasingly turned against its halfheartedness, its lack of resolve to press ahead with reforms, and its lack of will to defend against the aggressor. After the defeat, and to a great extent after the self-humiliation of Czechoslovak reformism, we fell back into the darkness of that endless tunnel in which we had lived before January 1968, and particularly the early sixties. We felt engulfed by a new dystopia. We had the sense that nothing could happen any longer in Eastern Europe, and that the clock of history had stopped for good in our godforsaken part of the world.

From the beginning of the Dubček experiment, we had had the clear awareness that only the spectacular and decisive fiasco of Khrushchevism could polarize the trends of East European social development, at least in countries like Bulgaria and the German Democratic Republic, where there was total social immobility anyway. We had seen Romania resolutely (or perhaps hysterically) embark on the path of combining inner repression with an increasingly chauvinistic, mostly economic, and partly political independence from the Soviet Union. Now we also saw Gomułka in Poland execute a *coup de grace* to the shabby vestiges of his once-reformist course by becoming a hardliner against Dubčekist Czechoslovakia. Most importantly, we clearly saw that Kádár's reluctantly given commitment to the Soviet action meant an end to the *pax dei* which had reigned in Hungary since the general amnesty of 1963. By virtue of Kádár's participation in the interventionist contingent, if only symbolically, the fate of Czechoslovakia became a Hungarian responsibility as well. Recalling the mournful days of Hitler's agreement with Admiral Horthy, the abominable sight of Hungarian troops in Czechoslovakia was only slightly mitigated by the fact that there were Hungarian intellectuals (although not many) who felt the shame of this self-inflicted humiliation.

Needless to say, the invasion sealed the fate of any Hungarian aspirations for reform. Hungary was now isolated in a milieu hostile to all such ideas. However, for Kádárism, certain chickens came home to roost. In the view of the ever-present arch-Stalinist faction of Kádár's apparatus, which had always mistrusted what they saw as the dangerous game of irresponsible changes, August 1968 was irrefutable evidence of the correctness of their suspicions. For the first time in a decade, some of these Stalinists almost publicly turned against Kádár and appealed to the Soviet Union.

At no time did we believe that Husák could consolidate his regime's hold on power in the same way that Kádár did in the early sixties. However, this statement calls for some qualifications. We do not mean it to imply either a romantic overestimation of the Czechoslovak reserves of resistance, or an apologetic evaluation of Kádár's performance. As to the first, widespread national stereotypes prompted realism. As to the second, our firsthand experience of the total but selective and shrewd character of the Kádárist oppression gave us an understanding of its consolidation. The contrast between the two regimes was clear. While both the Kádár and Husák leaderships were created by a foreign occupying army, the first came into being after a desperate and all-embracing revolution, which was followed by a wave of reprisals more severe in terms of executions and long imprisonments than any other in postwar Europe with the exception of the Greek civil war. As a result, the Hungarian population was resigned to the permanence of terror. Paradoxically, because of this totally negative expectation on the part of the Hungarian people, Kádár had something to offer them: his regime's easing of terror. An undeniable capacity for statesmanship enabled Kádár to grasp this historical opportunity, instead of continuing a foolish policy of revenge. That the option existed at all, however, was not due to him, but to the situation.

In another set of contrasts, Husák was of course personally superior to Kádár, being more cultivated, equally as shrewd, and in possession of an incomparably more heroic prison record. Moreover, because he had come to power after a period which even the Soviet propagandists had to recognize as *peaceful* counterrevolution, Husák could not embark on any kind of 'salutary bloodletting' (a fact which infuriated the Soviet leaders). Thus, a course of progressive moderation was simply not open to the new Czechoslovak leadership. They were able to offer nothing politically. Economically, with respect to balancing an economy which was near collapse in the mid-sixties, they could and did offer the public certain options. But although they could also have introduced a measure of sensibility into their policy of revenge and harassment against a wide stratum of the participants of the 1968 events, they never did.

For us in Hungary, the Prague Spring raised this initial question: was social reform in East European countries feasible in terms of party reform? Further, was it a reasonable way of reforming society? We obviously had in mind a social solution which would create new and more widely accepted institutions in a general atmosphere of *social contract*, whether tacit or explicit. Today, we would give neither a simple affirmative nor a simple negative to this question. Historically speaking, no one can deny that for the French monarchy in 1789, there existed the abstract possibility that France would take an English course. Similarly, regarding East Europe, no one can rule out the abstract possibility of a social reform overwhelmingly confined to a reform of the party (which would, of course, also involve the reform of several extraparty institutions). An opportunity was missed three times: first with Khrushchev, then with Gomufka, and third, and in our view next to last, with Dubčekist Czechoslovakia. In Poland, characteristically, even the more or less sincerely reformist elements of Polish communism played a secondary role in the process prior to martial law, and the trend in the party went *against* social reforms. The unique feature of the Czechoslovak movement of 'social reform from above' can be grasped by regarding it as the historically penultimate incident of East European social reform, one primarily designed and executed as a reform of the party.

More important than missed historical opportunities, however, are the considerations contained in the second part of our question. Specifically, is such a reform a reasonable historical settlement of affairs? Does it create new institutions, a new social contract, even a consensus? In fact, when such an arrangement is granted an initial vote of confidence, as the Dubčekist leadership was, we do not deny the existence of more 'organic' elements within it; unlike the case in Poland, where the symbiosis of two barely reconcilable extremes coexisted in a somewhat disguised but unmitigated enmity. In the acceptance of single-party rule, there may exist both positives and negatives to shape, if not a consensus, then at least a majority opinion. Submitting all reformistic ideas to this universal premise, we may say that the negative is grounded in general apathy and the fear of worse to come, the positive is rooted in an appreciation of some outstanding, usually patriotic deed of the political force in question. (An example is Yugoslavia, where both factors now perhaps merge.) However, we regard the inorganic element as more influential than the organic one. Even when social reform is at its most liberal, when it is implemented primarily as the reformed rule of the party over society, it always presupposes two negative factors: paternalistic supervision of the state over social life; and the political immobility of the 'citizenry'.

No doubt it was an unintended result of the Czechoslovak movement for social reform to give vent to such considerations, and expose the conservative – even if perhaps lasting – character of any social reform which is primarily a reform of the party. Even though in a totalitarian system it is difficult to move beyond the inscrutability of political attitudes, at least for external observers, it seems to be the case that no party leadership ever received such far-reaching and voluntary support as Dubček's. No such support was ever given to Khrushchev, and he himself did his utmost to destroy even its appearance. In Poland, the Polish masses accepted Gomu*ka only in the face of an invading army, although with a measure of optimism and a limited confidence, while the Hungarian revolution began with the gesture of radically dismissing any single-party rule. In this sense the Czechoslovak situation was again unique, and particularly instructive. As we now see it, without Soviet intervention, at best Dubček's leadership could have achieved another version of Titoism. This would have been incomparably better than the cynical, oppressive, morally and politically sickening world of Husák's regime, but it is certainly not an ideal to which we would commit ourselves.

It must be added that this is not entirely an historical or abstract theoretical question. Some expert observers still contend that if the Dubček regime had been consolidated, it would have grown gradually into a consensus for a multi-party system without violent social conflicts, in an atmosphere which would have been imperceptible to the Soviet leadership. However, the unique character of the Prague Spring leads us to conclude precisely the opposite. Although not professional historians, we must challenge a view which is generally accepted in the historical discourse concerning the Prague Spring, to wit, that the 'support from below' and the popular unrest, which were manifestations of an independent will, appeared too late, due to a 'natural' and 'naturally slow' growth of consciousness at the social base. The Hungarian revolution teaches us totally different lessons. The often cited and much demeaned masses needed hours, not months, to pick up momentum. In Czechoslovakia, if such a popular initiative demonstrably appeared at the end of the Dubček era and not earlier, this is evidence of the mutual incompatibility between liberal-reformist party tutelage and the emancipation of the masses. As long as people had a dual confidence in Dubček, in other words, as long as they believed, first, that he was serious, and second, that he would deliver the goods, they remained passive and unemancipated. Only when they realized that Dubček might be able to fulfill the first promise but could not fulfill the second, did they start to generate their own dynamics.

At this crucial point, let us set the record straight. By arguing for the ultimate futility of any social reform designed exclusively, or even primarily, as a reform of the party, and by using the Prague Spring as our most illustrative example, we do not intend to imply that the Prague Spring was 'superfluous'. Such a statement would be arrogant and meaningless. Anyone who made such a statement would be arrogating to himself a position of infallibility *vis-à-vis* all historical protagonists, and the statement would be meaningless insofar as it would be equivalent to addressing the protagonists in terms of a concluded chapter of history.

A second question is generally raised in the aftermath of the Czechoslovakian events: was the communist appeal to the masses for a new vote of confidence simply the new phase of a longstanding 'Trojan horse' strategy, or was it an act of insolence after what they had done to the nation? When one considers the whole of East European history, and when one observes the maneuvers with which the Polish communist leadership stalled for time between Gdansk and martial law, waiting for their moment to crack down, the question is far from baseless. Czechoslovakia 1968 was both unique and characteristic, for the ČPC (Czechoslovak Communist Party) was perhaps the region's only party which still had the right to appeal for another historical chance on the basis of its past record, and despite its recent deeds. It was the only Eastern European equivalent to the German communism of Weimar or the communism of prewar France, where a legal mass party built an ever-increasing electorate, with Stalinist ulterior motives but with a practical observance of the rules of the parliamentary game. Furthermore, even if it could never become a party of 'national salvation' like Yugoslav communism, it was not a party of continuous high treason against the nation like the Polish communist party. Although Polish communists had fought valiantly against *German* occupation, they easily lived with Stalin's deliberate inaction during the Warsaw uprising, and moreover, they adjusted to the brutal greed with which Stalin seized and subjected the nation to his will. This is equally true of the Hungarian communists, who were the first to praise whatever the Soviet Union did to humiliate their own nation.

In a way it was easy for the Czechoslovak communists to remain patriotic during the dark days of Munich, since the whole country, including its liberals, looked upon the Soviet Union as their hope of liberation. In addition, Czechoslovak communism very reluctantly appropriated the Stalinist norm of self-decimation. During the Stalinist purges, it had the historical good fortune to be protected by its country's 'bourgeois parliamentary system'. By the time the Czechoslovak communists were forced to emigrate, the wave of inner-party purges in the Soviet Union was over, or at least past its peak. In contrast to the Hungarian and Polish communist parties, which were almost wiped out, after which the survivors internalized the norm of fratricide as an acceptable – even salutary – rule of conduct, different *mores* operated in the Czechoslovak Communist Party. As attested to by the Pillar document,[7] for a long time even Gottwald advocated an absence of treason in the Czechoslovak Communist Party, citing the fact that the leaders had known each other for a sufficiently long time to have mutual trust. During the fifties, however horrendous might have been the final outcome of the Prague events, it can be said in all fairness that a considerable number of the leading Czechoslovak communists, in contrast to their peers who volunteered for the role of murderer, were 'Leninist' in the sense that they tried to observe the words of the dying Lenin to Rykov: 'Blood should not flow among you.'

Finally, it is perhaps not unfounded to say that the slow process of the sixties can be called proto-Eurocommunist, that is, an attitude characterized by a regaining of conscience and sense of responsibility for Stalinism, as well as a partial realization that the system's outward strength and solidity were facades behind which lay undefusible tensions. It is very far from accidental that Eurocommunism proper was born in the stormy aftermath of the invasion of Czechoslovakia. These factors make a very strong case a posteriori for Czechoslovakian communism and its national vote of confidence. However, it clearly follows that only in the presence of the above conditions, namely, democratic and patriotic promises and expectations, and under no other conditions, can a communist party appeal for confidence. This makes the Prague Spring a truly unique event.

Yet at certain historical junctures, movements are like individuals: when they are unwilling to undergo a radical process of relearning, they tend to repeat the fatal mistakes of the past. François Fejtő's book[8] describes how timidity, greed and hunger for power in February 1948 allowed Czechoslovakian communists to be pushed into the Soviet coup, thus wiping out a system of parliamentary liberties from which they had benefited for over two decades. It is also remarkable that the leadership core of Czechoslovak communism never had the audacity to stand resolutely by what they had conquered, as Tito did in Yugoslavia. Despite what later occurred between presidents Brezhnev and Johnson, the Czechoslovaks did have a chance for autonomy in the immediate postwar period. In spite of the very limited flexibility provided by the Yalta system, and in spite of a widespread belief to the contrary among the non-professional Czech public, Czechoslovakia did not belong to the Soviet sphere of influence. (Part of the wideranging ambiguity can be seen in the fact that everyone concerned flatly denied that spheres of influence existed at all.) Indeed, in the West, the February 1948 coup provoked a universal outcry. That Western public opinion felt surprised, deceived and even ambushed, is evident in the phraseology of editorials of the time.

In such an atmosphere, it was an objective possibility that the Czechs could have joined the Yugoslavs, instead of condemning them alongside Stalin's obedient minions. This would have enormously weakened Stalin's prestige, and perhaps even to some extent reduced his field of maneuvering. But instead, the desire for short-term preservation and the instinct of adjustment to Bolshevism proved overwhelming, and for the second time in a year the leaders of the CPC chose a truly fatal course.

Something similar happened in 1968, although partly for different reasons. It is difficult for those not involved to argue for armed resistance (or perhaps it is much too easy). In all fairness one must acknowledge the argument once put forward to us by Antonin Liehm: if the Czech leaders could not guarantee the broadcasting of the state radio in an hour of emergency, how could they guarantee the loyalty of their staff officers, indoctrinated with the spirit of absolute dedication to the Soviet Union, and infiltrated at all levels by agents of the Soviet secret service? Moreover, in an atmosphere where the Czech leaders well understood the West's neutrality, and sometimes its outright and barely disguised indifference, an enormous responsibility was felt for human lives.

But even if guesswork can never be proved, one fact seems to be irrefutable: the defeatism of the Czechoslovak leaders was a direct encouragement to the Soviet politburo. In full awareness of both Czech irresoluteness and the Czech determination *not* to meet force with force, the Soviet politburo measured gains against only very limited losses – mostly in terms of angry editorials. (The emergence of Eurocommunism in the wake of the intervention was an unpredicted, although not fatal, byproduct.) We think there is no historical justification for the capitulation which took place in Moscow during the so-called 'August negotiations' between the Soviet politburo and the abducted Czechoslovakian leaders. It is true, there is a very delicate balance between arguments 'for' and 'against' action in the case of a superpower ready to go to any lengths to achieve its aims. Beyond any doubt, if the Czech leaders had not capitulated, they might have shared the fate of Imre Nagy. Again, we do not intend to give advice in the past tense, and in particular we do not mean to suggest that anyone should have made the ultimate sacrifice. But nevertheless, we have the legitimate right to our judgment. This is not only a right but a precondition for learning from history. This particular historical juncture, we feel, offers only two alternatives to political protagonists: they have the choice of disappearing from the scene at a time when they can still do so without cowardice and without damaging the nation; or they have the choice of going to the extreme, as did Imre Nagy, whose heroic resoluteness to the bitter end in Hungary provided a binding norm for all reformist leaders of this region.

One unique feature of the Czechoslovak movement for reform did provide a positive and binding norm: the norm of synchronization of the forces and efforts of East European progress. There were earlier occasions in the region, of course, which called for concerted action on behalf of 'progress'. However, from one period to another, and in every situation, the subjects who represent it differ. The year 1948 presented an initial opportunity, when country after country fell victim to a totalitarian takeover in a classic example of the political domino theory. But the national liberal and democratic parties who might have participated in a synchronized action at the time (with some socialist forces among them) were politically and ideologically unprepared for such a role.

A second opportunity emerged a few months later when the Yugoslavians were excommunicated. They as subjects for binding synchronized action were different, as was their situation. But like their predecessors (and fellow victims), they missed their chance, even though they had already had training in concerted international action, and even though they should have realized it was a matter of self-preservation.

The third opportunity, in 1956, for whole nations, produced at least some elements of action in solidarity. One must not forget that the Hungarian revolution developed from a mass demonstration which was organized in sympathy with Polish events. But even for those longing for synchronized action, 1956 presented a special difficulty, for an immediate question needed to be asked: solidarity with whom? An active solidarity with a nation in full revolt was next to impossible. The Hungarian revolution was so radical that if it could not make a separate treaty with the Soviet Union (which was not absolutely out of the question at that historical moment), not only individual acts of solidarity with Hungary but even simple expressions of sympathy for Hungary were dangerous, as the tight clampdown in Romania and elsewhere showed clearly. Moreover, the Gomułka regime in Poland, having achieved what it wanted in its first round, morally and politically abandoned the Hungarian revolution, and so any solidarity with Poland was either ambivalent in value or superfluous. In the event, responsibility fell squarely on Hungarian shoulders alone.

A unique situation came to pass in August 1968, not only offering the possibility for acts of solidarity, but demanding them. This time there was a new group of actors, the dissidents. It offered a possibility because in communist terms the Dubček leadership was legitimate. It had policy objectives (economic rationalization, political rehabilitation of the victims of nearly two decades of repression) which presented no serious challenge to the power prerogatives of its own regime or any other regime in Eastern Europe. (According to the statements of the Dubček leadership, they did not even imagine renouncing these prerogatives.) This made it possible for both individual and collective actors to express active solidarity with the Czechoslovak course, without taking the extreme risk for which very few dissidents were ready at the time.

And yet solidarity was never achieved, at least not in a politically effectual form. This is not the place to discuss the reasons for such a tragic failure. Our concern here has been to emphasize what was unique about the Czechoslovak course, what remains relevant, and what has become a binding norm. To briefly sum up the last point, the subsequent Soviet leaderships, not particularly strong in the classics, nevertheless managed to learn three Latin words which constitute the key to their domination in Eastern Europe: *divide et impera*. And forces of an opposition movement intending to emancipate themselves from Soviet domination must bear in mind, whenever another country in the area is in turbulence, three other Latin words: *tua res agitur* (they act for your cause).

1982

NOTES

1 [Decades later, Ochab himself described the Poznań revolt as an event which was perfectly understandable, given the justified dissatisfaction of the workers. But he also hinted at the possibility of a provocation by his Stalinist colleagues organized against him, the reformist. See his interview in Teresa Torańska, *Them*, trans. A. Kolakowska (New York: Harper and Row, 1987), p. 60. *1989*]

2 Andrew Arato, 'Civil society against the state: Poland 1980–1981', *Telos*, Spring 1981. See also Maria Márkus, 'Crisis of legitimation and the workers' movement: understanding Poland', *Thesis Eleven*, 3 (Melbourne, 1981).

3 An analysis of the content and context of the 'Open Letter to the Party' by Kurón and Modzelewski can be found in P. Raina, *Political Opposition in Poland* (London: Poets' and Painters' Press, 1978), pp. 121–3.

4 See Zdeněk Mlynář, *Night Frost in Prague* (London: Hurst, 1980), p. 241.

5 For the Hungarian translation of Michnik's article, see the Paris emigré journal *Magyar Füzetek*, 7, 1980.

6 [The phrase 'public condemnation' refers to the August 1968 statement to the French press agency, Agence France Presse, by five Hungarian philosophers (Agnes Heller, György and Mária Márkus, Vilmos Soós and Zádor Tordai), in which they roundly condemned the invasion of Czechoslovakia and the role their own government played. Miklós Vásárhelyi, a survivor of the Imre Nagy trial, in a television interview in 1988 later described the Korčula protest as the first ray of hope in the inscrutable darkness of the Kádárist regime. The Hungarian parliament gave satisfaction to the protesters in its declaration of August 20, 1989, in which it apologized to the people of Czechoslovakia for the Hungarian role in the invasion. *1989*.]

7 Pillar, a member of the Dubčekist politbureau, was assigned an investigation into the sham trials of the fifties as the head of a commission including politicians, apparatchiks and historians. The Dubček leadership promised publication of the collected documents and commentary, but this plan, of course, was doomed by the Soviet invasion. Nevertheless, certain Dubčekist cadres leaving the country in the post-invasion confusion were able to smuggle out copies of the documents and publish them in several European countries.

8 François Fejtő, *Le Coup de Prague, 1948* (Paris: Editions du Seuil, 1976).

6

Eastern Europe Enters the Eighties

In relevant, that is, confidential and 'un-self-censored' conversation between critical-minded and clear-sighted East Europeans, the crucial question that frequently arises is: 'what will come "afterwards"?' or, rather: 'what *should* come "afterwards"?' Interest in current political rumors ('Who said what at the last session of the central committee?') is, of course, still vivid but even moderate hopes for short-term and substantial changes are definitely waning. The new feature is the *regime's total loss of credit*. Obviously that does not refer to national oppression by overwhelming Soviet military might, nor to the 'lack of freedom' in general terms, nor to the lower standards of living (even when compared to leading Western countries that have now been in crisis for a decade). These are all truisms for the 'man in the street' in Eastern Europe. To understand what is really meant by 'the total loss of credit', it is necessary to discuss changes in this region during the 1970s.

The first thing to mention is the nearly total disillusionment with 'reforms from above'. In 1953 Stalin died only physiologically. His political agony took place during the 'secret session' of the Twentieth Congress of the Soviet Communist Party and on the streets of Budapest in 1956. Similarly, Khrushchevism, at least in the form of hopes of 'reforms from above' and vague perspectives, did not disappear immediately after the coup against the First Secretary in October 1964 but only in 1968, with the invasion of Khrushchevist Czechoslovakia. It is the dubious distinction of the present Leninist opposition (Bahro and Medvedev) that it courageously keeps 'squaring the circle' by upholding Khrushchevism ideologically and with a wholly obsolete vocabulary. 'Oppositional Leninists' are not only conservative but also superfluous: the much-quoted man in the street learned the lesson without their aid. Even when they were driven to despair by police salvos, in 1970 the Polish workers knew when to stop before the Soviet invasion came. Workers learned from the consequences of Czechoslovakia in 1968. They knew that they could strike back, but they could not reform an inflexible and irreformable regime. We do not mean to advocate 'social inertia': our whole argument aims at *pragmatic* and *limited*, but actual, changes. We only wish to speak against those high-soaring dialectical dreams (which we shared in the sixties) according to which one can change everything while everything remains, at least politically, unchanged.

Secondly, the seventies were the decade in which, strange as it may sound, the opposition became a structural feature of East European social life. Of course, its strength varied from country to country. It is oppressed everywhere and its *guiding* role in social conflicts is insignificant. But since such is the predicament of every opposition in every non-genocidal (non-Hitlerist, non-Stalinist) tyranny, this does not diminish its importance. For those acquainted with Leninism, there is no need to explicitly state how scandalous the very existence of any overt opposition is. Further, in moments of heavy social convulsions such as the Polish workers' riots in 1970 and 1976 this opposition sometimes extends beyond intellectual circles which are the hotbed of 'free thinking', and thus gives added weight to its mere existence. Finally, with its sporadic and persecuted counter-press, the *samizdat*, always confiscated and destroyed but always resurrecting, it became the embryonic form of a *new public sphere*.

A third feature of the seventies was the final collapse of official ideology. Those who called Lukács, Kołakowski during his Marxist period, Kosik, the *Praxis* group, 'indirect apologists' for the regime, were correct at least to the extent that the type of Marxism which retained any cultural reputation existed only through them, in opposition to the long since dead official version. The novelty of the seventies was the following: at the top, this atmosphere produced a new type of pragmatism, compared to which the much-reprimanded Khrushchev and his consumerist 'goulash' communism were highly doctrinaire. Today, the first secretary's advisers are technocrats and security experts – electronic gadgeteers rather than Grand Inquisitors. Professional ideologues, especially if they take the pseudo-theoretical aspects of their duties seriously, are troublesome, if not altogether dangerous, types. The reason for this is clear. Maoism made the 'ideological fanatic' suspect. Their passion can lead to 'Chinese escapades', and can throw doctrinaire obstacles in the way of the unprincipled compromises by means of which all post-Stalinist governments operate. Djilas was right: East European leaders no longer give a damn for what they publicly call the 'purity of our ideas'. In the face of a sometimes overt opposition, the complicated rigmarole of disciplinary measures for deviations from the holy gospel has a blunted edge. If such measures are still used, they are only fronts for intricate political games under the surface, such as in the case of the Hungarian ideological purges in 1972–3. On the other hand, within the depth of social life, there is an increasing parricidal passion to 'kill Marx' – the once religiously respected forebear whose original sin allegedly caused all the problems. This morbid passion turns into an often undisguised anti-Enlightenment vision and complements the hostility of the local ruling strata to any genuine culture. Thus, it indefinitely buries Eastern Europe as an ideologically influential area.

The fourth feature is the emergence of a new phenomenon: a limited and Soviet-dependent state nationalism which, in some countries such as Romania, had already emerged in the late 1960s and whose social function is to replace earlier versions of 'national communism'. National communism looked up to Tito, and its objective was to regain genuine, even if 'Finlandized', national sovereignty. Its last representative was Dubček, whose political fate dissipated any lingering illusions concerning its possibilities. Limited and Soviet-dependent state nationalism ranges from a cynical and programmed pseudo-centrifugalism by satellite governments (for example, in economic relations between East Germany and the Soviet Union) to a precarious balance between unfriendly and spectacularly disobedient gestures on the one hand and subsequent 'remaining within limits' on the other (for example, recent relations between Romania and the Soviet Union). Whatever its particular character, limited and Soviet-dependent state nationalism has no illusions regarding the possibilities of genuine sovereignty in an age of Soviet expansionism. Yet, it is an annoyance for the Soviet government, which, consequently, tries to nip such attempts in the bud (as it did with Moczarism in Poland in the late 1960s, which was too close to a Polish version of Ceauşescu's regime).[1]

Various limited and Soviet-dependent state nationalisms also differ in their social functions. Some build nationalist images in order to continue semi-Stalinist practices in the post-Twentieth Congress period (this was the starting point of Romanian separatism under Gheorghiu-Dej). Such intransigence, however, exposes them to dangers 'from below': Stalinist or semi-Stalinist governments rarely like to be left alone with their own population. Therefore, an opening towards nationalist groups was and is aimed at widening the regime's power base.[2] Other similar tendencies, such as Moczarism, are narrower in scope. In the case of Moczarism, its social function was, through the mass rehabilitation of the *Armija Krajowa* (the non-communist insurgent army whose members were persecuted in the fifties and just tolerated afterwards) and other measures, to mobilize nationalist masses against rebellious intellectuals and university students with a basically chauvinistic and anti-Semitic 'Black Hundred' ideology. Whatever their objectives, none of them seeks any longer to introduce political reforms in the way 'national communists' did. The hallmark of limited state nationalism is to build essentially phony national images such as that of a non-existent Great Romania based on Dacian cultural origins, or of an 'East-German' nation and culture. Even Kádár, whose regime is the only conservative-*liberal* and not 'state-nationalist', has lately introduced categories like 'Hungariandom' whose bulk is 30 percent larger than the number of Hungarians living in the Hungarian People's Republic. The allusion was made mostly to Hungarians living in Romania, Czechoslovakia, Yugoslavia and Russia as national minority groups who for consecutive Hungarian governments for 30 years have never been Hungarians, but citizens of the respective countries in which they resided. Partly, the message was broadcast to masses of emigrants who are still ready to maintain relations with the old country. This is, of course, considerably less than seeking national independence but more (and therefore more dangerous) than mere windowdressing. This 'nation-building' which includes, among other things, hysterical waves of sports chauvinism, is part and parcel of typical efforts of any ruling strata in permanent crisis frantically trying to channel social dissatisfaction into nationalist fervor.[3]

Another complementary feature of 'limited state nationalism' is *permanent economic conflict* between individual countries and, occasionally, between all of them and the USSR. The main issues on this invariably stormy agenda are the usually unjust mutual clearing system within the Comecon (whose 'rectification' is an unending problem), the tolerated extent of being partially integrated into the Western economic system which decides the industrial financing strategies of all East European countries, the prices of Soviet raw materials (the USSR being the major raw material exporter to practically all its satellites), the necessary contribution of each country to the Warsaw Pact military budget (regarding which all presently display great and understandable reluctance), and the like. All this points towards a kind of conservative 'imperial reconciliation' between the ruling strata of the Soviet empire. This would not be altogether new in Eastern Europe. That, in fact, was the solution by which the Habsburg monarchy postponed its collapse for half a century after its defeat by Prussia. But even if this is correct, this is the very first step of a development which will narrow operating room for small nations even more than did reconciliation in the Habsburg monarchy. Unlike the Austrian empire, the Soviet one has a very strong national center – historical Russia – with a population equivalent either to all East European countries or to that of other nations within Soviet borders. This makes it less vulnerable and more arrogant. Furthermore, it is not a traditionally conservative-autocratic system but rather a totalitarian one for which the prerogative over military, foreign and financial affairs, centralized in the imperial capital but to some extent shared with 'partner nations' (as was arranged in the Habsburg monarchy), will not suffice. Soviet leaders retain control over 'international security' and the secret police.[4] Also, they will at least keep interfering with the planning of particular economic strategies – although here they are gradually losing ground.

These negative features clarify the nature of the single major (and novel) development of the seventies: the regime's total loss of credit (which is not to say it is close to collapsing). But there were also many positive features in the seventies that must be taken into account when evaluating Eastern Europe's predicament in the eighties. First of all, this was the decade of Soviet expansion beyond the Yalta line. The new conquests are not significant in terms of geographical dimensions, population or natural resources. They are mostly *African* satellites.[5] There are a few Arab satellites (first of all South Yemen) which guarantee the easy access to this vital area for the growing Soviet fleet, and some highly unreliable close allies (such as Syria, Libya and the Palestinian movement). There is growing Soviet influence in the vacuum created by the American defeat in Indo-China but, given the efforts of Vietnamese party apparatus to turn the whole area into *their own* satellite, this is rather a shaky and temporary influence: the Soviet presence is only one power factor among many.

On the whole, the following can be said: until the seventies, both East and West regarded the 1945–7 situation as 'ultimate and unchangeable' (in spite of attempts to expand on the part of the Eastern bloc, for instance, Korea, or Nato's 'rollback' propaganda). Lately Soviet leaders seem to feel that they can get away with expansion, and this understandably whets their appetite. Whereas during the Suez crisis of 1956, they had the courage to send an ultimatum to France and Great Britain only when they realized that the United States would not support the latter, and they backed out quickly from the Cuban crisis, Admiral Zumwalt has testified that, in 1973, when the Egyptian President Sadat was clearly losing and the Egyptian invasion army was on the brink of destruction, they sent an ultimatum to the United States and actually undermined an Israeli victory.

Secondly, the weakening of the West is equally beyond doubt. This started with Vietnam, which, apart from the deep psychological defeatism it generated, became at least one crucial factor among many in the present crisis of capitalism. Through its enormous military expenditures, the Vietnam war upset the equilibrium of the American financial system on which the whole Western financial and credit system had rested since the political-economic settlement of the Second World War. As Kissinger has correctly pointed out, a second factor is the ongoing crisis of the executive arm of the American system: the presidency. Since 1960 it has been the fate of American presidents not to fully serve their elected time because of being murdered or driven out of office, or to be the unelected bearer of this all-important post (as with Ford), or to have so clearly failed that he did not even run for a second time (Johnson). Needless to say, this circumstance paralyzed Western decisions and was an important factor in the South Vietnamese collapse.

Thirdly, as a result of the above, as well as other reasons, Nato has undergone a growing crisis. Finally, Western capitalism has run into a new adversary in Moslem fundamentalism which, because of its natural resources, has a certain unprecedented hold over industrial countries. In terms of the problem under discussion, all of this means that *the West has no East European policy* – something the Hungarians have known at least since 1956. The only time when this could have had any military meaning was when the West had a nuclear monopoly (up to 1949–50). At that time, the only beneficiary was Yugoslavia, which survived Stalin's official and public anathema partly because of Soviet fears of Western nuclear retaliation. Ironically, the 'roll-back' policy was advertised at a time when the means necessary for it were already waning. This has been shown by the Korean 'no-win-war'. Hungary in 1956 is a classic case study. Radio Free Europe, sponsored by the American Congress and undoubtedly under CIA management – thus expressing an official or semi-official American position – pushed ever further the revolt's objectives to the point of driving Imre Nagy and all leftists out of office while promising, even if in vague terms, some Western aid. Everyone knows that this was just a cynical game and nothing happened. But the fate of the Helsinki Agreement and the failed boycott of the Moscow Olympics clearly show how even that much concerted effort cannot be expected from Western governments concerned with avoiding a resuscitation of the Cold War. At any rate, this would not really help those who actually fight for freedom; it is instructive, at least, in the sense that freedom can only be regained by the fighters' own efforts.

Thirdly, the one competition the Soviet leadership feared in Eastern Europe, Eurocommunism, came to an abrupt halt due to the weakening of the Spanish, and the predictably perfidious behavior of the French communist parties. There is no need to exaggerate the Eurocommunist threat to Soviet interests in Eastern Europe. On the one hand, the relation between East European opposition and Eurocommunism has always been highly pragmatic, limited and insincere. They used each other for their own practical ends, without much reciprocal trust. On the other hand, this is an ideological and political, rather than a power influence. The Eurocommunists provided at least a *language* for the public articulation of a certain type of East European opposition which could only be condemned with the final excommunication of the Eurocommunists, for which the Soviet leadership is not prepared. Should, however, the Eurocommunists speak the same language as Moscow does (as in the case of the deplorable demagogy of the French communist press in connection with Afghanistan), this relatively progressive role immediately disappears.

Given this state of affairs, one could outline what can be expected in Eastern Europe during the 1980s. First it is important to point out the limits beyond which political developments are very unlikely to go. The first is a *wholesale return to Stalinism*. The Soviet leadership closed the period of Stalinist 'revolutions from above' with Khrushchev and his successors. It feels much more secure without them, and the apparatus, the only possible 'agency' of mass terror, lacks the determination to impose a semi-militarized life on the country and, mostly, on itself. The second improbability is the dropping of any country out of the Warsaw Pact. Since the Prague Spring, watchful eyes follow the slightest suspect signs. Finally, the inner collapse of the Soviet system itself is highly unlikely. Within these limits, the following major conflicts will determine political developments in the region.

First there is the tension caused by the contradiction between Soviet global imperialism and its influence over East European economic and social life. It will suffice here to mention only one characteristic example. Ten to fifteen years ago, East European governments did not even suspect that there could be such a thing as a short supply of oil: Soviet resources seemed inexhaustible. Now, the Soviet leadership tries to pass on at least part of its burdens to its satellites and, for the first time in the economic history of these states, the Soviet government demands world market rather than 'political' prices for raw materials. Understandably, the East European leaders are outraged and, as cautiously as they should when dealing with their touchy master, yet firmly, they point out that mutual relations between 'brother countries' are based on 'fraternal principles', that is, on politically created, not economically calculated, prices.

The second likely future conflict will take place between certain 'limited state nationalisms' and Soviet military and diplomatic monopoly. There have been reports of growing jealousy and resentment against Soviet chauvinism, arrogance and unquestionable privileges. There is no doubt that the civilian and military East European apparatuses want their share of military command, political and diplomatic key positions, and they will tolerate less and less being informed about crucial events only *ex post facto* (as they most likely were in the case of Afghanistan). The role of a regional superpower with nuclear weapons, which imperial Iran briefly played within American strategy, is highly attractive to East German, Polish or Bulgarian military and political leaders. By the same token, it is seen as a serious danger by the Soviet leaders who do not regard their allies as being as reliable as themselves.

Thirdly, there is the problem of the coming changes in Soviet leadership. Not only will Brezhnev die, but also the majority of the politburo and a huge part of the central committee will have to leave active politics during this decade. These are bodies that represent gerontocracies to the same extent as they are bureaucracies. Although it is a normal event without dramatic consequences in *every* country for leadership to rotate under the pressure of age, things are not quite that simple – even in Western liberal capitalism where the electorate's impersonal will rather than the politicians' personalities seem to dominate the political scene.[6] This is even more valid for the Soviet Union. First, this is because whoever wins the political competition is a total enigma, given the anonymous character of Soviet politics and its intolerance of policy differences – especially those attributable to distinct persons. The winner thus has to create his public image with unexpected gestures.

If a change of this type were to take place in the Soviet Union, everyone would be affected and the confusion would be general. Shrewd political hacks slip, lose their well-trained survival instincts, and sometimes make irreparable mistakes.[7] Secondly, and more importantly, the winner's position is initially very weak. He has no legitimation whatsoever. Thus, he desperately needs spectacular successes which are direct threats both to domestic tranquillity and the general equilibrium of world powers.

Thirdly, East European leaders are likely to take a bigger role in the appointment of the new Soviet leaders than has hitherto been the case. Or, more realistically: *some* of them are going to play *some* role in it.[8] Very likely, all potential successors to Brezhnev's position will involve Hungarian, East German, Bulgarian, and Polish lobbies[9] in the preliminary skirmishes since in the Soviet systems there are no legal processes of succession. Fourthly, and finally, the coming change of Soviet leadership is an event which does not necessarily imply only negative possibilities. The new leadership average age will not be below 60 (in this 'revolutionary' society one has to be well up the rungs of the gerontocratic ladder to carry any political weight). Even so, these new politicians will be part of a generation whose formative experience was the war and the immediate postwar hopes for a 'milder' regime, rather than men of the 'heroic' and ideologically committed 1920s and 1930s. In Soviet politics and in Marxism-Leninism, the fewer the principles, the better. Thus, while the new generation of leaders will seek to keep together, or even expand, the Soviet empire, they may also be receptive to various 'openings'.

A fourth type of conflict will in all probability develop between the increasingly nationalistic satellites themselves. One instance of this new conflict has already emerged in the seventies between Romania and Hungary. For a variety of reasons, the Hungarian government had been traditionally almost pathologically anti-nationalist, to the extent of being blind to the most understandable national aspirations of its population, such as the defense of the rights of national minorities living outside of Hungary. The Kádár government attacked the Romanian leadership only in order to toe the Soviet line. But internal pressure groups have gradually forced the Kádár leadership into a national strife which may slip out of Soviet control to the point of endangering one of the most sacrosanct elements in Soviet politics: postwar borders. This type of conflict is unprecedented in East European history since the beginning of Soviet domination. Previously, some country was occasionally assigned the role of 'loudspeaker' against certain others, or assumed the role voluntarily (such as Hungary against Tito in 1948–9, or East Germany against Dubček in early 1968), but the tone, duration, and vehemence, as well as the beginning and the end of the attacks were all dictated from Moscow. It is impossible to predict what configurations these nationalist conflicts among satellites may take. Although painstakingly concealed, there are indications of a growing friction between Polish and Ukrainian nationalism, a collective resentment by most other countries against increasing East German chauvinistic arrogance, a Polish–German conflict, and strained relations between Romania and Bulgaria over territorial questions. These conflicts are an inexhaustible source of nuisance to the Soviet leadership. They cannot favor any particular satellite without threatening their own interests in the other country, since they constantly have to supervise them – possibly without direct or even military interference. On the other hand, in the well-known spirit of 'divide and rule', these conflicts are in the interests of the Soviet leaders who see imminent danger in the slightest tendencies toward confederation.

The next cluster of possible conflicts is generated by the gradual transition of the Soviet economy from an *extensive* to an *intensive* phase. In principle, such a development would result only in beneficial consequences. Given the fact that the Soviet Union is the largest economic unit of the area and *potentially* one of the world's greatest wheat producers, the introduction of intensive methods into the Soviet economy promises blessings for the region. But, for reasons too long to even enumerate, the transition to the intensive phase is more of an exigency than a likelihood in Soviet economic life.[10] In addition, a considerable amount of these rationalizing efforts will be at the expense of East European countries. The conflict will result from an overall change of economic strategies and interrelations. The question concerning whether the Soviet Union exploits East European countries was already raised in 1956, in the wake of the Polish and Hungarian uprisings. The best answer has been provided by Sartre who pointed out that Eastern Europe displays a system of *mutually disadvantageous* economic relations dominated by force and the prevailing *political* interests of the stronger partner, the Soviet Union.[11] This situation is now slowly changing, but in a 'Prussian', rather than in an 'American' way. The Soviet leaders pursue the unattainable dream of rationalizing a society economically but not in terms of an overall social rationality. One could say that the Soviet leaders want American economic efficiency based on Russian bayonets and widespread KGB bugging technology.

Apart from the question of realizability, the policy objective is meant only for Russian purposes, which hides a latent but inevitable conflict – not only with the 'people' but also with Eastern European *communist governments*. These governments are themselves in the process of rationalizing. They are either in the process of moving beyond extensive development, or have been well past it, as in the case of Czechoslovakia or East Germany during the whole postwar period, when they were only forcibly slowed down by the

Soviet presence. These ruling groups, and even more eagerly their national technocracies, may rightly claim that the pattern of industrial development was literally forced upon them and that they had to renounce the most lucrative postwar opportunities of economic collaboration with the West because of Soviet demands.[12] In exchange, the Soviet Union offered them unlimited resources of raw materials at so-called 'political prices'. Should the Soviet leadership change this without taking into consideration its satellites' particular interests, the whole edifice threatens to collapse. East European governments are increasingly blackmailing Soviet leaders with the phantom of a coming 'counterrevolution' in case of a constantly worsening economic situation resulting from one-sided Soviet economic rationalization. This internecine strife has actually begun between the Soviet Union and Romania. What lends support to the East European argument is that Russia can produce short-term economic 'injections', can help sustain small entities such as Cuba on a subsistence level, but simply does not have the resources to rationalize at home *and* keep bigger East European countries on the near West European level at which their population wishes to live, 35 years after the war. Finally it is unavoidable that during the eighties in certain countries open social conflict will break out in order to bring about a modicum of political pluralism. Whereas, especially since Tito's death, the explosion is generally expected from Yugoslavia,[13] there is little doubt in our mind that Poland is again likely to have the dubious distinction of becoming a world-historical nation: the center of the gathering storm.

None of the mentioned factors is news to the experts, or even to observant readers of periodicals. What is significant is their ensemble. First of all, Poland is a large European nation of 33 million people with an army of more than 300,000 men. While the Soviet army has no equivalent in Europe, nevertheless in the case of a Polish army revolt a limited 'police action' for the Soviets as in Hungary in 1965 or Czechoslovakia in 1968 would still be ruled out. Secondly, Poland is the country where social dissatisfaction not only became explicit, but extended far beyond the intelligentsia: here the working class is gathering an apparently unstoppable momentum. The scene is nightmarishly reminiscent of the late nineteenth-early twentieth-century socialist image of proletarian revolution – or, at least, its modest beginnings. At this stage, Polish workers are not fighting for direct democracy or political pluralism but for much more limited nineteenth-century gains which they lost through 'socialist emancipation': free trade unions. Thirdly, apart from the semi-legitimate organizations of the opposition, there is one visible national organization, the Catholic church, which is wiser than to play an oppositional role prematurely, but which is more intransigent and influential than its other East European counterparts. As a result, it could not be assimilated into the regime, and it retained far-reaching spiritual and political powers.[14] Given that there is now a Polish Pope, and given its immensely increased hold over social life gained during the complicated conflicts of the post-Gomułka decade, the Catholic church is one of the most important power factors in the coming collision. Further, the oppositional intelligentsia very wisely avoided the 'lobbying' policy of many of its East European colleagues and became the mouthpiece of universal national grievances, particularly those of the industrial working class – the spearhead of social rebellion in Poland.

Thus, for the first time in the history of East European dissent, the critical and even openly oppositional intelligentsia has roots and a protective 'shield' in the industrial workers. Should the secret police go too far against them, there is at least the danger of a nationwide political strike. On the other hand, the workers have a multilingual and dedicated agency, with good connections in the foreign press to create instantaneous world publicity for all their demands. Finally, the Soviet leadership has hardly any other option but the military one to put down rebellious Poland. Traditionally, the nation is passionately and chauvinistically anti-Russian. The equally traditional myth of Polish irresistibility is rapidly gaining ground. Economically, 33 million want affluence, or at least decent West European standards and, needless to say, the Russian option is ludicrous.

The above sketch may not be dramatic enough to emphasize the situation's seriousness. But it is on this battlefield that the coming fate of Eastern Europe for this century will be fought. All attentive observers of post-Second World War history know that while many options were undecided in 1944–5 (Finland, perhaps even Hungary, Austria and Czechoslovakia), and despite the fact that the Soviet army was exhausted, there was one objective for which Stalin was even prepared to start a new war: the domination of Poland. His unceremonious policy towards the Lublin Committee (the Moscow-appointed government of Poland which simply declared a minority communist group the 'sole and legal representative of the Polish people' while the war against Germany was not yet over) leaves no doubt about the importance he ascribed to Poland. Nor is it reasonable to assume that this ever changed for any Soviet government, except in the sense that the Poles now could count on no Western allies. This leaves one logical conclusion: should a rebellious population endanger the communist party's ultimate rule or threaten Poland's defection from the Warsaw Pact, the Soviet government would go to *any* length to stem the tide. It could mean the destruction of major Polish cities, mass deportations and executions, a military and police rule and martial law. Similarly, no other parts of Eastern Europe would remain unaffected by these waves of neo-Stalinism.

A Polish civil war developing into a direct Polish–Soviet clash is the only thing that would resurrect the ghosts of Yeshov and Beria. On the other hand, the Soviet apparatus is just as hesitant to take the fatal steps or even precipitate them. The apparatus loathes the perspective of a recurrent

Stalinism and its imminent dangers for *itself*. They are also aware of the unpredictable consequences a 'Polish war' could trigger at home. Finally, they have no doubt that the 'spirit of Munich', which is now so widespread in Western politics, would disappear in a moment should they do the irrevocable. While they are glad to toy verbally with the 'danger of a new Cold War', they would not welcome its actual recurrence. The only hope is that, while on the one hand both parties are adamant concerning at least a good portion of their demands, on the other, both are aware of serious, or even fatal, consequences of foolhardiness. This suggests a possible partial restoration of political pluralism, that is, free trade unions, freedom of religion, a broader scope for limited private economic initiative, a relative separation of the judiciary from political authorities (at least in non-political matters), an increased and formalized legal tolerance towards the private person within the sphere of private law, a gradual emancipation of the workforce from the compulsion of labor and the corollary restrictions afflicting private persons in their capacity as wage earners, guaranteed freedom of travelling. And such positive changes would not necessarily be limited within the Polish borders. Poland, her working class and dissident intelligentsia could become the first real liberator of Eastern Europe. They could also precipitate a collective catastrophe.

In conclusion, three dilemmas of East European history, all likely to intensify during the eighties, should be briefly discussed. The first can be summed up by this question: is the 'Finlandization' of Eastern Europe possible? Whereas Western European nations regard 'Finlandization' as a serious danger, Eastern European ones regard it as a considerable relief from their present situation. Characteristically, the most vehemently negative answer comes from Finnish observers. Since Finnish politicians occasionally take more than their share of humiliation from Soviet leaders, they tend to see their situation as the unlikely upshot of their unique and inimitably wise efforts. Yet, apart from seeking the domination of Poland, from extending his influence in the region as far as possible and from the general wish of grabbing as much spoil as he could, in 1945 Stalin had no definite strategic plan regarding Eastern Europe. Later, two disparate considerations combined to lead to his decision. The one was political: the belief that only a monolithic communist party rule imposed on East European nations could adequately serve Soviet interests. After 30 years of nearly uninterrupted uprisings, it is superfluous to comment on the practical value of this idea. In the ultimate analysis, to have or not to have an empire is reasonably decided by whether it brings more profit than it imposes burdens on the mother country.

The other consideration was military, shaped according to an 'infantry strategy' which was already obsolete at the time of its conception. The Finnish example is again useful: Finland's borders were fixed so that no first waves of an infantry attack against Leningrad would succeed. No remarks are needed concerning how fruitful such a strategic vision is in the age of global missiles. Considering the obsolescence of the underlying military doctrine, and the enormous fiscal burdens of garrisoning huge occupying armies, it is not unrealistic to claim that *dependent but not simply occupied*, that is, 'Finlandized', buffer countries would better serve even the purposes of the Soviet military.

The second dilemma is the following: should the restoration of Western-type liberal capitalism be the goal of oppositional movements? At first glance, this seems farfetched and irrelevant for the eighties where even in terms of a not entirely pessimistic view, the most one can expect is some limited concessions on the part of Soviet and national ruling strata. Yet, social strategy is never irrelevant and has an impact on short-term behavior of political actors. And if one speaks of 'Finlandization' it should be remembered that Finland is a liberal capitalist country.

As George Konrád argued in a recently published *samizdat*, capitalism cannot be restored *democratically* in these countries for two main reasons. One is Isaac Deutscher's argument that such a restoration is physically impossible since the development of a gigantic industry occurred in an area that had never been previously industrialized to such an extent. While this may apply to the Soviet Union, it does not necessarily extend to the smaller East European countries, which could easily be integrated into a system of multinational organizations. But there is another argument that has to do with the split consciousness of the state wage-workers in Eastern Europe. This social agent is vehemently anti-communist and anti-socialist as far as ideology is concerned. In Poland, it is also under the direct influence of the church which advocates the most conservative social views. But when acting out its social impulses, the state wage-worker is anti-authoritarian and would hate to trade its impersonal master for a restored personal one. It was out of this 'social impulse' that the Hungarian workers' councils were born in 1956.

There is no physical or social impossibility of a restoration, but this disobedient and rebellious subject has to be tamed first in order to be turned into a proper subject of a restored liberal capitalism. Of course, the social equivalent of 'taming' is authoritarian conservatism, not democracy. Therefore, all those seeking democracy as a future for Eastern Europe have to consider socialism understood as a self-managed society. Unfortunately, an opposite tendency can be readily discerned among those who are politically active. The opposition already includes a new group of non-theocratic radical conservatives for whom democracy is a prime suspect. Since the so-called 'subjective factor' and its preliminary political 'schooling' are crucial to influence the convulsion to come – even if the convulsion is not likely to come in the 1980s – the clash within the opposition between conservative and democratic-socialist tendencies has a definite bearing on the future.

Finally, there is the third dilemma: can activities in different nations be synchronized? Is there such a thing as an international opposition? The importance of synchronized activities is paramount. Thus the spontaneously synchronic Polish and Hungarian 1956 revolts reciprocally affected each other. Similarly, the Soviet hesitation in October 1956 which provided a leeway for the Hungarian revolution and a chance for the Polish 'flood' to break through peacefully was caused by the fact that the Soviet leaders had two problems on their hands, rather than just one.

On the other hand, in 1968 Dubček could not have strayed much farther than the early Gomułka regime. He could never consolidate his system even on the most modest reformist basis, owing mainly to the 'desynchronized' character of East European history, particularly evident in the fact that Gomułka's regime, the only possible obstacle in the way of Soviet and East German pressure hysterically gathering momentum, was on the decline. When Dubček rose, Gomułka was about to leave the scene as a reformer. His regime had deteriorated for years and the reckonings came, in the form of the March 1968 Warsaw demonstration, precisely when Dubcekism was gaining ground. So, instead of looking for a reformist ally, Gomułka was haunted by the ghost of an 'international counterrevolution' and thus joined the inquisitors. That was a signal for Dubček's last and always overcautious protector, Kádár, who backed out. With this defection, Dubček's fate was sealed.

But even if such a cooperation is necessary, it is unclear whether it is possible. At this point all ideas of a Central European confederation are futile and dangerous dreams. But even if it were possible, three major obstacles militate against it. The first is the nearly hysterical sensitivity Soviet leaders have always shown towards confederative ideas. An example of this is the then unprecedented open Soviet attack against Tito's and Dimitrov's joint statement about a possible Balkan confederation in 1947, at a time when Stalin was frantically attempting to keep up the appearances of a communist 'phalanx without inner rift'. Secondly, these nations have such diverse histories, sometimes even without ever having had independent states, that when 'compressed' into one confederation, as with Yugoslavia, they present immense problems for their national leaders. Thirdly, any confederation, even under ideal conditions, would mean a duplication of bureaucracies, and there is nothing worse than a supranational bureaucracy responsible to no one. But if the idea of confederation should be discarded, the intensification of separate national chauvinism should equally be rejected as even more dangerous. These nationalist ideologies simply serve Soviet aims to divide and rule, the classic example of this being the systematic anti-Ceauşescu propaganda within Hungarian intellectual circles with tacit government consent: a political subculture in which it is increasingly argued that 'even Soviet intervention would be better than Ceauşescu's cultural genocide.' There is no question about the Romanian government's crimes in culturally and politically oppressing the Hungarian minority. Since East European governments do not tolerate, and the Western media are not interested in unmasking these hard facts, it is a duty of the opposition to make them public. But to see this as the central Hungarian and Romanian social question is a fatal blind-alley and one day those who claim this could find themselves in the position of indirect agents of a Russian invasion in Romania. This type of intensification of nationalist ideologies is the shortest avenue to produce the new poison: a new conservative elite in the nineties.

December, 1979

NOTES

1   General Moczar, a once famous underground fighter – a strange mixture of a nationalist and a hardline pro-Soviet Stalinist – led an influential faction of the Polish central committee, which was politically annihilated by the Gierek leadership.

2   The most intransigent and brutal of these systems, Albania, went beyond the limits of Soviet dependent state nationalism, left the Warsaw Pact – which always constitutes the line of demarcation – and thus falls into a different category not to be analyzed here.

3   In his autobiography, Ernst Fischer relates how German communists, led by Ulbricht, jubilantly cried in 1940, in the Hotel Lux (the Comintern hotel): 'We have captured Paris!' Eastern Europe is not far from the time when such gestures will become officially accepted elements of 'socialist patriotism'.

4   No major appointments could be made in this field without Soviet blessings: KGB advisors directly control local activities.

5   They are mostly remnants of the collapsed Portuguese colonial empire, plus Ethiopia and, until the conflict with Ethiopia in which the Soviets sided with the Menghistu regime, Somalia. Independently of this development, Brazzaville Congo should be included in this region.

6   If one considers that at least a considerable part of the pettiness typical of today's French public life can be accounted for by the fact that de Gaulle built a system of 'presidential Bonapartism' with very mediocre candidates to the role, it is easy to see the overwhelming importance of changes of political personnel in *every* country.

7   One of the most famous examples is Kádár's memorable speech highly apologetic of Khrushchev after the coup, which was obviously made in a moral fit. Since Soviet memory is long, some eight years later this nearly cost him his post.

8   Gomułka was already used by Brezhnev and Kosygin as an *ex post facto* legitimizer of their newly established rule which was questionably legitimate even by Soviet standards. The Polish General Secretary readily delivered the useful lie about Khrushchev's 'personal confession' to him of his intentions to retire.

9   Certainly not the Romanian and probably not the Czech, which even they consider a quisling government.

10 For an excellent discussion of these problems, see Antonio Carlo, 'The crisis of bureaucratic collectivism', *Telos*. 43 (Summer 1980), pp. 3–32.

11 Cf. Jean-Paul Sartre, 'Czechoslovakia: the socialism that came in from the cold', in his *Between Existentialism and Marxism* (New York, 1974), pp. 84–117.

12 This is primarily true of Czechoslovakia, the only European country in 1945 with an intact and powerful heavy industry.

13 Cf. Sharon Zukin, 'Beyond Titoism', *Telos*, 44 (Summer 1980). pp. 5–24.

14 Once, in 1956, it more or less played the role of the arbiter, spelling out, through Cardinal Wyszynski, how far Gomu*ł*ka's 'reformist communism' should go to be acceptable for the nation, and how far the nation should not go in order to be still acceptable to the Soviets.

Part IV

Soviet Strategy before Gorbachev

7

Target Europe

THE CHARACTER AND MOTIVES OF SOVIET EXPANSIONISM

Soviet expansionism remained somewhat tarnished under the inwardly murderous and outwardly cautious first decade and a half of Stalin's rule. Its first signs only became visible during the Molotov–Ribbentropp pact.[1] While this event can be interpreted in whatever way the interpreter wishes, the 'minor blemish' of devouring Poland together with Hitler cannot be explained away: *it was the first act of Soviet expansionism.* Stalin, as shrewd as he was ruthless, went one major step further after the victory, and within three years he completed the occupation of Eastern Europe. Although his armies had moved deeply into Germany, however, he held Austria in a state of suspension and, while occasionally he neared various parts of Scandinavia, never made one further dangerous move. It is now a generally known fact that he even tried to discourage the Chinese communists from a final offensive because, as the most commonly accepted interpretation goes, he considered the Soviet Union to be too weak as yet to venture any further. This explanation could be entirely true, but as far as we can see, it has to be reinterpreted. There are few signs that indicate either that this concern was technological in nature or that Stalin had drawn major technological-strategic consequences from his devastating defeats during the first year of the war. The Soviet army continued to suffer difficulties during Stalin's last years. Its best generals were either politely exiled (Zhukov) or used for political purposes (Rokossowski, who became 'our man in Warsaw' for the Soviet government). Several ideologically motivated bans on technological research and on the use of applied technology remained in force and slowed down development in military technology. (The most famous example is the ban on 'bourgeois' cybernetics, without which modern warfare and military training are inconceivable.) Yet Stalin learned other lessons from the war. Official propaganda notwithstanding, he must have clearly known how shaky the foundations of the Soviet regime had proved to be during the war wherever the Soviet army had pulled back from a region. He was also well aware of the extent to which Hitlerite brutality and ideological fanaticism had been needed to guide a jubilantly anti-Soviet populace back in the direction of a reluctantly pro-Soviet stance. He watched with even greater suspicion the newly occupied Eastern European countries. As the true creator of the regime for which expansion without all-embracing control was worthless, he must have felt that control had to be further strengthened and intensified; the new territories had to be absorbed and governed with an iron hand. In all probability, it was primarily the fact that social control was not sufficiently deeply rooted, not sufficiently all-embracing, rather than military considerations that commanded a halt to Soviet expansionism.

The new features, the whole novel framework of present-day Soviet expansionism, were designed under the confused and contradictory but historically crucial period of Nikita Khrushchev, in whose policies there was, despite undeniable contradictions and spectacular and seemingly irrational changes and improvisations, a much firmer consistency than is generally assumed. In the area of foreign policy Khrushchev is regarded, more often than not, as a shallow clown who liked to travel and behaved on his trips in an unstatesmanly manner, gave speeches on questions he was totally unfamiliar with, and took action with a degree of improvisation (from Berlin to Cuba) that thoroughly endangered the peace of the world (or, viewed from another angle, the well-considered interests of the USSR).

While the details can be correctly assessed, we find the verdict is as a whole a complete misreading of Khrushchev's incomparably more complex political personality. In his autobiography, he narrates an extremely telling story which sheds much light on the origins and genuine objectives of his later foreign policy. As a pillar of Stalin's last politburo but as a politician who, up until then, had hardly had any experience in foreign politics, Khrushchev had vigorously encouraged Stalin to display a full and open Soviet commitment to North Korea in the Korean war and give all the military aid 'the Korean comrades need'. It is clear from his own description that Stalin had fenced him off with a measure of disdain, giving him a few quick lessons in the basics of 'socialist foreign policy'.[2] The conflict, obviously not serious for Khrushchev had survived, was largely one between two generations of Bolshevik functionaries. For Khrushchev, the postrevolutionary communist, the victorious Soviet Union was strong enough after the war to embark on its historical mission in the rest of the world without hesitation and double talk about non-interference, with all the external insignia of the liberator. It is well known how surprised John F. Kennedy was during their Vienna talks to hear, after the endless, albeit transparent, diplomatic lies of Stalin and Molotov, clear language from Khrushchev. The First Secretary stated without camouflage that it was the 'duty' of the Soviet Union to lend support – if need be even military support – to so-called wars of liberation everywhere. (Earlier it had been almost regarded as a crime against the state to assume that the Soviet Union had anything to do with any of the communist-led rebellions, revolutions or partisan wars throughout the world: the 'exporting of revolutions' was a Trotskyite idea.) In fact, the 'struggle for peace' (the Khrushchev period abounded with his clamorous and wholly unrealistic offers of almost complete disarmament) and the insistence on the 'world revolutionary process', on the 'worldwide victory of communism', form one unitary process. The Soviet Union would not launch a thermo-nuclear war (Khrushchev seemed to have honestly believed in the universal destruction that would follow in the wake of such a war), but it would develop, whatever the costs, its nuclear strike force, in part as a deterrent (Khrushchev still faced a West that had guts and had not, at least not formally, resigned from the policy of 'rolling back' communism), in part as a means of terror and blackmail. It would support uprisings and rebellions of *all kinds*. Khrushchev's great, then unacknowledged, invention was that he regarded Lenin's Machiavellian suggestion ('let us support the emir of Afghanistan who is more progressive than Kautsky because he is hostile to Western imperialism') a useful, operative idea. Following closely this principle, he decorated Gamal Abdel Nasser as a hero of the Soviet Union. It is less understood that his policy toward Yugoslavia was instigated according to the same principles. Not for a moment did he believe that Tito had 'corrected his mistakes' (the resolution of the Soviet Communist Party on the intactly preserved revisionism of the Yugoslavs in the aftermath of the Belgrade meeting testifies to this). But for Khrushchev it was towing the Soviet line that counted, not ideologies, and he hoped, mistakenly, that Tito would tow that line. Maintaining the nuclear balance, increasing Soviet superiority to a point where its power could arouse fear and could be used as a means of bargaining without ever contemplating, however, the possibility of an all-out nuclear war; being able nevertheless to conquer the world through fear, to exploit weakness, subversions, and rebellions of any kind: this was and has remained the master formula of Soviet expansionism under all successors of Khrushchev.[3]

Everything that has happened after Khrushchev (and this statement now already covers two decades of Soviet expansionism) has to be understood, in our view, against the double, extremely complicated background of the increasing self-confidence and inner despair of the Soviet oligarchy. The self-confidence, which fuels their self-conceived historical mission of uni-versal expansionism on all continents, is nurtured by three factors. First, the Soviet oligarchy feels, for the first time in Soviet history, that they have time, that they are not threatened with 'running out of time'. Second, despite all duplicitous lamentations to the contrary, the Soviet leadership does not have the slightest fear of the West. American military morale in Vietnam and the outcome of the Watergate affair (the near impeachment of an incumbent president is a sign for them of the contemptible weakness of Western democracies) were the last symptoms that were needed to convince them. Further, if the West was not able to attack them when it could have done so with a very good chance of winning and getting away with it, it would hardly do so now. Finally, they realistically know that there is no Western strategy, rather a progressively diminishing degree of Western unity.

Such increasing self-confidence would suggest strategic optimism, were it not more than sufficiently compensated by the inner despair, the result of the unsolved, protracted, and apparently insoluble inner crisis of Soviet society, which can be summed up in the following terms. The Soviet oligarchy could have eliminated the most imminent danger of a general explosion following the death of Stalin, which threatened for three explosive years (1953–6), from Berlin to Georgia, the edifice of 'completed socialism' with 'counterrevolutionary' explosions, by rejecting Stalin's murderous 'revolutions from above'. But they have never been able to achieve a genuine transition into a so-called intensive period of industrialization. Industry, except the military-industrial complex, works inefficiently and Soviet society remains technologically dependent on the West; the agricultural crisis cannot be overcome or compensated by an industrial boom; standards of living have been lagging far behind Western societies, and this is still true despite the longest depression capitalism has ever known. André Glucksmann sums up this situation in the following, picturesque way:

The wind of spirit has turned. It is the West that makes the East dream. Bourgeois Europe has become the concrete utopia of the workers, peasants and intellectuals of Soviet socialist Europe. In 1945, the experts of the right despaired of, and the intellectuals of the left were enthusiastic about the idea that Western enterprises could be exploded by a revolutionary and communist ideology, while the system of private property was condemned to crises and catastrophes. Ever since, it is the turn of the masters of the Kremlin to denounce the fifth column which, in the inside of the factories, seizes the minds of workers and provokes 'insurrectionist' strikes for such obsolete and formal rights as the freedom of opinion, right to assembly, the right to pray.[4]

Without a doubt, the Western way of life, and not the American army, has remained the most powerful challenge for the nomenklatura, actually the only threat they are afraid of, and the one they wish to eliminate, for otherwise, as they believe, there can be no end to internal turmoil and unrest. But the subject in tacit disobedience (and sometimes in open revolt) that they are facing is now twofold. There is the aforementioned, the 'fifth column of the Western way of life'. But there is a novel one as well: *the anti-Soviet but anti-Western* Soviet Russian fundamentalist, the gigantic image of which can be found in Solzhenitsyn. In an act of statesmanship (which considerably surpasses the capacities that could have been expected from this power elite), the nomenklatura has come up with a twofold recipe against this new danger:

the 'Soviet way of life' and an updated version of Dostoevsky's 'Russian idea'. Both grow out of a situation in which the word 'communism' has lost all seriousness, both at the top and at the social base. Victor Zaslavsky has analyzed in detail what 'the Soviet way of life' means: paternalism and guaranteed security at the price of total depoliticization and automatic obedience, 'order', the cult of authority and conservative ways of life, no social reforms or 'improvisations', xenophobia with almost public anti-Semitism.[5] One has to add only a short quotation from Dostoevsky to understand precisely what the 'Russian idea' means:

A truly great people can never reconcile itself to playing second fiddle in the affairs of humanity, not even playing an important part, but always and exclusively the chief part. If it loses that faith it is no longer a nation. But there is only one truth, and therefore there is only one nation among all the nations that can have the true God even though other nations may have their own particular great gods.[6]

If one were to translate Shatov's aggressive and laconic text into the banal language of present-day Soviet 'literature', one would understand very well what is meant by the 'Russian idea'. However, the 'Soviet way of life', the 'Russian idea', and the ideological struggle against Westerners can achieve their aim only in the event of an utter humiliation, preferably total defeat, of the West. Therefore, expansionism remains vital for a system in crisis, even if the situation is incomparably more complex than Glucksmann's formulation suggested.

But if this is so, is it not reasonable to conceive *the Soviet Union as a military society*, a conception which would have been ridiculous under Stalin but which recently has gained an ever wider audience? It has found its best, deepest and most ingenious formulation in Cornelius Castoriadis's *Devant la guerre* (Facing the War), which analyzes the Soviet Union in terms of a 'stratocracy', a military society.[7] Shortly after the book was published, Wojciech Jaruzelski and his way of 'pacifying' Poland seemed to present a spectacular corroboration of the theory.

We shall present here our arguments in refutation of Soviet societies as military societies, but we wish to emphasize that there is absolutely nothing in Soviet societies that would interdict with the force of 'historical necessity' a regular and visible military takeover. The ineptitude of the Soviet bureaucracy could reach such a level in internal affairs, the danger of general chaos could be so imminent, that the military, motivated as always by so-called patriotic considerations, could sweep party apparatchiks out of power. Such a turn would be clearly visible, however, and in our view it would have the inevitable economic consequence of restoring a market economy for the Soviet Union (with as much state supervision and protection as in many Latin American countries) and leading it to join the capitalist world market.

The advocates of a military society can argue in one of two ways. One is to state that the military now in fact occupies the dominant positions in the Soviet hierarchy, and that the Soviet Union is a military society in precisely that sense. There are frequent attempts made to interpret each and every Soviet politician as a direct or indirect representative of the 'military complex', but the facts, which deny rather than corroborate the theory, are so obvious that this is to be regarded as the weak version of the theory. The strong and much more sophisticated version is argued by Castoriadis. According to him, and his theory of the 'imaginary institution', there is not and will not necessarily be any 'red Bonapartsky'. No visible military takeover is needed to assume the actual existence of a military society: no statistical analysis of the members of the central committee is required to make this theory more convincing, whatever the findings. There is, however, a social 'imaginary institution', the military conquest of the world, operative in the Soviet society, which works through agents regardless of the external contingencies of whether they wear a uniform or civilian clothes. In this sense, the Soviet Union of the last two decades has gradually been self-transformed into a 'stratocracy'.

Our first argument against the theory is that the telos we have suggested lies within Soviet societies, namely, the expansion of socioeconomic control embodied in social structures and institutions, among others, the 'goal of production',[8] is at least equivalent to the imaginary institution Castoriadis argues for. At the same time, it accounts for the whole of Soviet history, not just a chapter of it. Secondly, Castoriadis has never renounced his theory of Soviet society as a type of capitalism. If this is the case, either there is no need to posit any special telos or imaginary institution for expansionism, assuming that the military telos is a factor common to all capitalist societies (which is at least questionable), or there are some special structural elements in 'Soviet capitalism' that make it a military society. These, however, have never been elaborated by the theory of 'stratocracy'.

The main question that any theory of the Soviet Union has to address is the following. If we conceive of the party bureaucracy, or apparatus, as the civilian-clothed agent of an impersonal military telos, which at a certain point must mean that it merges, even sociologically, with the army, can this apparatus fulfill all the roles generally ascribed to the party bureaucracy, internally and externally? We believe it cannot, for the following reasons. The political-universal image attributed to the party by itself is a constitutive element of the regime. The party apparatus is the leading stratum required by a political society (a society in which political ideas, goals and considerations dominate all other life activities) for its longevity, while the military simply cannot fulfill the same functions. This means that if the party is to be reduced to the role of the civilian-clothed agent of the military, it cannot function as a party any longer. There will indeed be a vacuum as Castoriadis himself surmises, but the vacuum would have to be filled *in a public and visible manner*, not just clandestinely, thereby transforming political rule into military rule pure and simple. Further, one of the sources of legitimation of the party, and the basis of its capacity for integrating the Soviet regime, is its non-particularistic character. All organizations, associations, and institutions of Soviet society are particular; only the party is general. It is judge, supervisor, arbiter over all particularities in a capacity it could never uphold were it to be degraded, even if 'clandestinely', to the role of a civilian-clothed agent.

Secondly, and more important, the party is 'international', the military is, perforce, national. There is no such thing, not even in hypotheses or ideologies, as an 'international army'. An army is always the agency of a particular nation, and its rule over another nation is *overt occupation*. If the party were viewed publicly as the civilian-clothed agent of the military, the extension of the Soviet regime would be simply identical with overt foreign occupation. But is it not so now as well, some will ask. Our answer is that the situation is more complex. Except in East Germany, where they are a 'legitimately' occupying force, Soviet agencies make serious efforts to achieve covert rather than overt forms of occupation. While in Eastern Europe the Soviet regime is indeed the result of continued Soviet occupation, this is not the case everywhere (for instance, Vietnam and Cuba). Nor are the integrating functions of the Soviet regime exhausted by the term 'occupation'. Therefore, even if the party were to keep its uniform in mothballs, it could not fulfill its international function as a civilian-clothed agent.

Further, there have been short periods in Soviet history in which some sectors, first of all the party apparatus, were militarized (most of all during collectivization, when 'party armies' fought a desperate war against millions of 'kulaks' doomed to destruction). But on the whole, the Soviet way of taming the disobedient could never be adequately described by the word 'militarization'. It is particularly so in the most recent phase of the 'Soviet way of life'. A militarized society has a martial culture with open contempt for peace, with an exaggerated emphasis on valor. Soviet society, precisely in the period covered by Castoriadis's analysis, is dominated by the pharisaical phrase of 'love of peace', the flagellation of 'warmongers' and 'militarists'. Further, all military regimes understand themselves by definition in terms of the dichotomy 'military–civilian' which presupposes the existence of civil society of a kind. However, all attempts to validate the claims of the 'military' (as an openly corporate entity) over the 'civilians' to certain crucial prerogatives constitute an open challenge to the party's rule. Without such attempts a military society is inconceivable; with such attempts the political society of 'dictatorship over needs' is equally inconceivable. Not even the relative but important socializing role of the Soviet army, so correctly emphasized by Zaslavsky, could be understood in any sense other than in terms of socializing the youth within a framework established *not* by the army, but by the party oligarchy. Finally, we believe that while, as observed by Castoriadis, Zaslavsky, and others, the Soviet army and its separate industrial complex represent a bulwark of rationality in Soviet society in that they operate according to rationalized standards, under the effective control of a consumer, and the like, this too can only be achieved because the army is part of the regime and not coextensive with its leading stratum, either directly or indirectly (through the 'imaginary institution'). The regime as a whole, as it stands now, is not rationalizable.

All this is not, of course, to state that there have been no changes in the Soviet power structure in the last two-and-a-half decades. Instead of personal tyranny, a collective rule of an oligarchy has emerged that has legitimated, even if not publicly, the role of certain influential lobbies and power brokers in presenting their relatively distinct interests and policy recommendations. Because of both its innerly rationalized structure and its more prominent role in the Soviet–American competition, the army comes out on top of the list of competitors. The relative proportions in this competition have considerably changed, not primarily for technological reasons, but because of the lost strategic confidence in the West. In this altered situation, the role of the army, not as a means of all-out warfare but as a means of blackmail and the guarantor of each and every anti-Western uprising, coup and revolution, has grown tremendously. As we have shown elsewhere,[9] the legitimation of the Soviet regime after Khrushchev has been increasingly based on a paternalistic and nationalistic ideology (albeit the Soviet regime never would, and never could, give up its 'internationalist' function). This also squares well with the heightened role of a powerful national army, the symbol of a 'great nation'. All this and several other factors cannot, however, alter the ultimate fact that the party has remained in power, although with a totally empty, entirely iconographic ideology. Failure to see this caused the pessimistic, tragic tone of Castoriadis's book, and not any 'latent anti-humanism' as his biased critics would maintain.

THE 'FINLANDIZATION' OR THE 'VICHYIZATION' OF EUROPE?

What exactly does the Soviet threat mean? Does it imply the goal of a global nuclear war on the part of the Soviet Union? The answer is negative. The meaning of the threat is equivalent to asserting Soviet expansionism with global aspirations of *total domination*. Should someone deny this as a social and imminent tendency of the Soviet system, one would be theoretically compelled to give some very serious explanation about the fate of Eastern Europe.

Although they have never ceased to be interested in Europe, it was at the end of the 1970s that the Soviet leadership ostensibly returned to the idea of a primarily European expansion. Earlier, there had been few encouraging signs for them. The governments of the crucial countries, as well as the bulk of the opposition in those countries, were strongly pro-Atlantic, or at least clearly hostile to the Soviet Union. Eurocommunism, now a spent and failed attempt to provide an alternative, had nonetheless temporarily deprived the Soviet leaders of their two most influential and strongest allies, for which an emerging, entirely Stalinist, and, in relative terms, not insignificant Portuguese communism was no compensation. Francisco Franco's death offered no opening to the Soviet plans on the Iberian peninsula for a number of reasons – the king's determined stance for democracy, the socialists' growing influence, Santiago Carillo's verbally energetic, even excessive, Eurocommunism (which in the light of his new pro-Soviet turn has proved a mere ploy), and the like. The economic situation in Europe, although deteriorating in some countries faster than in others, nevertheless remained generally tolerable. Germany, potentially the political center of the European scene, has for many years remained unaffected by the gravest symptoms of crisis.

All this changed, for a number of reasons, in the late seventies, turning Soviet expansionism resolutely back to the European theater. It is a matter of special consideration to what extent any Russian leadership (Soviet or non-Soviet) has historically felt itself to be either culturally European or the bearer of a 'special Russian mission'. (There is a good deal of evidence to suggest that the centennial discussion between neo-Slavophiles and 'Westerners' goes on covertly in Soviet cultural life.) But a decision on this question is one thing; denying a *traditional Russian interest in politically dominating Europe is quite another.*[10]

The prime objective of Soviet expansionism, then, is the Finlandization, or, rather, Vichyization of Europe. But why the second term? What justifies speaking of a European Vichy? Finlandization means, as everyone knew once upon a time, when it was not yet an almost honorable title, limited sovereignty. The term derives from the limited sovereignty enjoyed by Finland. This involves a formal ban on Finland's participation in any treaty or organization which the Soviet Union regards as dangerous or damaging to its interests. Presidents and governments of Finland, duly elected in free elections, have to be approved by the Soviet Union; indeed, elected governments have been dismissed because of the lack of such approval. There is an almost equally formal limitation imposed on freedom of press in Finland. The Soviet Union does not allow the Finnish press to criticize it. (Thus, when the press revealed the condition of the port cities after the Soviet evacuation, there was such vehement protest on the side of the Soviet Union that the reports had to be cancelled.) Within this framework, the Finns can freely live the life of a liberal parliamentary political system and a market economy. Such conditions are 'not too bad', argue some Western leftists who otherwise regard the introduction of identity cards as the absolute proof of 1984. Others would argue that our sovereignty under American hegemony is limited as well, so why the fuss? We reject this identification as entirely hypocritical. American hegemony means, beyond any doubt, a supremacy over nuclear weapons that are American-made and American-financed but stored in Europe, a system which in its present form is unacceptable for Europeans of all persuasions and common sense but which is not identical with American use of such weapons *ad libitum*. Second, it means that one country, which was formally the loser of the Second World War and which still does not have a peace treaty, suffers from certain limitations imposed on its armament policy, and this is, indeed, a certain limitation of sovereignty. Third, it means that each administration of the United States did, and will do, everything in its power (financially, politically, as well as through its clandestine channels) to reverse all political decisions unfavorable for America, and in doing so, it will mostly follow egoistic American interests (as the US role in the Greek colonels' coup or in the Turkish regime demonstrates). But American hegemony does not mean the formal right to dismiss governments disliked or mistrusted by the US administration (not only social-democratic governments but the presence of Stalinist French communists in François Mitterand's cabinet testify to this). Further, it does not mean that the United States can impose its will on any major (or increasingly, even minor) European country if it is determined to make an anti-American decision. If one needs proof, one should think of the break of Gaullist France with the Western alliance. Anti-nuclear propagandists who find all media channels open to their anti-American propaganda are the best persons to decide whether there is any (formal or informal) obstacle to propaganda in Europe hostile to America.

However, 'Finlandization' as an exceptional solution (which would certainly still be a dream for Eastern Europe) rests on three special factors. Finland, despite its political regime, was not part of the victorious democracies. For very clear historical reasons, it unforgivably sided with Hitler; even if it was Hitler's strangest ally, only the flexibility of its political elite (which managed to change sides much earlier than the shrewd Romanians) saved it from sharing the fate of the Eastern European countries. Second, Finlandization has remained what it is and not worse, namely, complete Sovietization, because not only the Scandinavian countries but also the United States, which felt obliged to show loyalty toward the small country, protected it against Stalin. Finally, precisely because of the above two factors, there is a *national consensus* in Finland guaranteeing the conditions of a peacefully limited national sovereignty. This is a consensus that today seems to be shared alike by ultraconservatives (who know that they cannot get better) and pro-Moscow communists (who know that perhaps even the Soviet Union would not be happy if they now upset the equilibrium).

We are entitled to speak of the Vichyization rather than the Finlandization of Europe above all because such a national consensus about the self-limitation of national sovereignty cannot be attained peacefully in any other country, and therefore it has to be imposed coercively. *In fact, the slogan 'better Red than dead' is a call for civil war,* between those who are either Red or would prefer to be, and those who would prefer death to this alternative. The parties could never find consensus (exactly because of the manner in which the question is posed), therefore the goal would not be a peaceful Finland but a European Vichy, with national KGBs or Gestapos. Further, 'better Red than dead' in itself means more than the slogan of 'Finlandization', as careful reading will show. 'Finlandization' means the serious limitation of national sovereignty; 'better Red than dead' is an injunction to submit to an alien, hostile *social system*, which is regarded even by those who coined the term as something very negative. Such a submission never takes place without the brutal crushing of huge social groups who would prefer death to being 'Red' (whatever this connotes). And if someone thinks that such alternatives are purely hypothetical, one should think of the boat people of Vietnam, who indeed risk no less than death when they take to the sea in their miserable vessels. Finally, for 'Finlandization' to be relatively mild, there must be a West European and American background that supports Finland, or at least, to formulate it more accurately, the opinion of which, for the time being and for one reason or another, is taken into consideration. In the case of the Finlandization of the whole of Europe, such a protective background would no longer exist, and therefore there would be no restraint on the part of the victors.

What are the objectives of a long-term 'Vichyization' of Europe as the Soviet strategic goal? First, the expulsion of the United States from Europe, preferably by the Europeans themselves. This would be a resounding political victory for the Soviet system, the trigger to a political crisis of unheard-of dimensions within the United States itself, and it would establish the Soviet Union in a political position just as unchallenged, or perhaps even stronger than, that of the United States in 1945. This would mean a total reversal of the results of the Allied victory, a landslide power shift without a war.

Second, Vichyization would transform a considerable and highly developed part of the capitalist world market into the 'catering periphery' of the Soviet world system. The Soviet leadership has very good reasons for wanting to achieve such an end: they have simply been unable to negotiate the transition to an 'intensive period of industrialization' with its accompanying material benefits. At the same time, while 'the perfecting of the economic system' is constantly splashed across the headlines of Soviet newspapers, even the vaguest ideas of genuine economic reform are regularly dismissed. This is so in part because there is no longer unanimity concerning what precisely such reforms would mean. The simple formulae for reform, seemingly panaceas after the total irrationality of Stalin's world, proved worthless, or only extremely relative palliatives. As well, there is a constant and strong fear of social change of any kind in an immobilist oligarchy: they are suspicious of experiments, which invariably bring 'counterrevolutions'. However, exporting the economic reforms, in the form of subjecting the industrial giants of Western Europe to the political predominance of the Soviet Union, bullying them into conditions that are advantageous to the Soviet leadership, would be an ideal solution. For the time being, it is entirely idle to speculate or 'predict' whether such a transformation could in the end be achieved through an extremely narrowminded Sovietization of the West European economies (which would destroy precisely the preconditions of their present effectiveness), or whether it would be a 'Finlandization' in the strict sense, in that a functioning market economy subsists but under political dictates. Indeed, such speculation would hardly just be idle, but would be pernicious as well: 'dreaming the dreams after defeat' is support lent to a future occupation. Nonetheless, the strategic objective seems to be extremely realistic.

Third, Vichyizing Europe would also mean a *cordon sanitaire* around rebellious Eastern Europe. A Vichyized Europe, even without the direct assimilation of the Soviet system, would be a very effective means of final (or at least a lasting) pacification of turbulent Eastern Europe. However much East European nations have known that they could not expect anything substantial from the West, there has always remained the faint hope that the West (and, in a geographical and perhaps economic sense, above all Western Europe) is ultimately sympathetic to their aims, and that in the unlikely case of a country's withdrawal from the Warsaw Pact they could rely on this sympathy in several respects. A Vichyized Europe would be a hostile environment for East European emancipatory movements, which are in any case facing an adversary with incomparably more powerful means. Finally, Vichyization would create an ideologically favorable atmosphere around the Soviet Union, which, as an ideologically constituted system, has always been very vulnerable to ideological criticism and 'subversion'.

This too, however, is already part of the present, in the form of a voluntary and anticipatory self-Finlandization. In Germany, Rudolph Bahro can be credited with embracing the 'Finlandization option' of his own will. When one sees similar symptoms, however, from the authoritative writer and anti-Fascist Günter Grass, who is undoubtedly in the mainstream of public opinion and not the *enfant terrible* of *Nationalbolschewismus*, one has to realize that the process has indeed gone a long way already.[11]

How should we imagine the Soviet *marcia su Europa?* The sarcastic anti-nuclear critics of Nato war games are certainly correct, partly because things almost never happen in the way strategists preconceive them on their computer or television screens, partly, and more importantly, because there is one particular scenario, precisely the one most analyzed by the Nato analysts as the unlikeliest course of future events: a frontal assault, conventional or nuclear, against one or all of the major West European countries (West Germany, France, Italy and Great Britain). Let us repeat again and again: there is absolutely no necrophile element in the intellectual make-up of the Soviet apparatus. While it is undoubtedly true, and a source of great internal Nato tensions, that, as Glucksmann put it, Americans in Dallas will not automatically die a nuclear death because Soviet tanks are in Frankfurt, nonetheless, such an assault is still the most probable trigger to an all-out nuclear world war. As things stand now, and as long as the Western alliance exists at least in name, it would be almost impossible for an American administration to convince American public opinion of the superior wisdom of standing by idly while one of the major West European countries is destroyed and occupied. But the alternative is only nuclear war, gradually or directly.

Therefore it is the *southern flank*, the soft underbelly of Europe, where we can expect, under circumstances favorable for the Soviets, the most vigorous Soviet actions. There are immediate and traditional Soviet strategic interests (first of all, gaining direct and unperturbed access to warm-water ports and to the Mediterranean); there are conflicts to be exploited, old debts and 'grievances' to be settled; there are even allies they can rely on. The first, cautious step would be an internal Warsaw Pact affair to which the West could not object with too much vigor: the removal (by a coup or otherwise) of the clique of Nicolae Ceauşescu and the establishment of a loyally pro-Soviet leadership, as well as a redeployment of the Soviet army on the territory of Romania. A logical further step would be the exploiting of two major Southern European tensions: the Greek–Turkish and the Yugoslav–Albanian conflicts. Local wars in both cases (encouraged clandestinely by Soviet diplomacy) would be, whatever their outcome, exclusively to the advantage of the Soviet Union, which would act as the main ally of one party (in the Greek–Turkish conflict, without a doubt, the ally of the former; in a Yugoslav–Albanian conflict by keeping their options open) and a supreme arbiter over all of them. Such a conflict, if wide enough and skillfully exploited, could lead to the following crucial results. Turkey would be constrained (either in the Finnish way, that is, by a 'lend-lease' agreement, or otherwise) to make the Dardanelles a free and uncontrolled channel for the Soviet fleet. (The 'Sovietization' of Turkey would lead, in all probability, to a long and bloody partisan war, and here there would be no economic advantages for the Soviet Union, but certainly strategic ones.) Greece would be 'Sovietized' or itself fall prey to temptations. The country has a relatively strong communist party, the morality and 'sociology' of which can be traced back to the unbroken self-confidence of the Stalin years (which is a more than adequate qualification for the political and police apparatuses that would be required for the task). Andreas Papandreou's Socialist Party, a new creation without long traditions, under a popular, shrewd, and extremely demagogic leader in whom sincere anti-Americanism and anti-Turkish feelings blend with an insincere pro-Soviet stance, could not present a serious obstacle to this. There is a widespread and legitimate anti-American feeling in Greece because the decades of tyrannically conservative rule could never have existed, as part of the 'free world', without overt American support, and the latter was a luxury even in terms of American strategy at the time. In addition, Nato's incapability or unwillingness to guarantee certain vital Greek interests against another Nato member is a further powerful factor weakening the resistance to Soviet expansionism. Such a turn could bring about the reunification with its Greek motherland of Cyprus (a small country but important as a potential naval base; it already has a relatively strong absolutely pro-Soviet communist party), an event which would undoubtedly raise the following question: as far as the Turkish minority is concerned, are we not going to face something similar to the Armenians' fate?

Soviet expansionism, interestingly, is likely to meet more obstacles on both sides in its attempts to exploit a potential Yugoslav–Albanian conflict. Both countries are traditionally jealous of their national sovereignty; both have, almost alone in Europe, a brilliant record of indomitable partisan wars against foreign invaders. It is worth considering whether the Soviet Union, facing a number of Afghanistans, would be ready to use tactical, 'Hiroshima-scale' nuclear weapons for purposes of intimidation. Whereas all this is speculation, if one takes into consideration the historical morality of the nomenklatura, there can be little doubt of its possibility. They could even use the American argument, namely, that all this is necessary to defend Soviet lives. But the main lever would be utilizing the Yugoslav–Albanian conflict centered on Kosovo, which, if the Soviets wisely side with the Yugoslavs, would inevitably mean the collapse of Enver Hoxha's disobedient regime, the installation of a pro-Soviet leadership (not a complicated matter, for in all communist apparatuses, quite naturally, there must be a latent pro-Soviet faction). Lending a hand to Yugoslavia could result, particularly if accompanied by the application of some pressure, in Yugoslavia joining the Warsaw Pact (perhaps with some special guarantees and certainly with safeguards for its considerably different social structure). Let us emphasize that if all this is handled with sufficient finesse (and Poland in 1981, the only resounding political victory of the Brezhnev era in Eastern Europe, demonstrated that certain lessons have indeed been assimilated), the West can only stand by and observe events (including such additional moves as the incorporation of

Malta into the 'Soviet naval line of defense') in a state of immobility. As things stand now in Western Europe and America, the West would not be in a position to act otherwise.

There is only one region where resolute direct, overt Soviet expansionist action is imaginable: ironically, in Finland. As its fate has constantly hung precariously in the balance, as soon as the Soviet leadership is convinced that the nuclear deterrent has been sociopsychologically eliminated and conflicts within Nato are vehement enough, the Sovietization of Finland will take place, accompanied by some lively but peaceful and shortlived inner protests. The Finns, who have no great confidence in Western valor, are not likely to put up an excessively heroic and costly armed resistance without potential allies. No further moves would be expected in the immediate aftermath of the Sovietization of Finland against the core of Scandinavia: Sweden, Norway and Denmark. The first is one of the two symbolically neutral countries of Europe; violating its integrity would provide only harmful publicity. The two latter are members of Nato (while Greece is only partially under the Western umbrella) and 'organically Western countries' with traditions of liberal regimes. Their ill fate could provoke unexpected West European or American reactions.

Such vigorous movements on the southern and northern flanks by the Soviet Union would complete a gigantic pincer maneuver and leave Europe wide open to any military move, if need be, from any direction, and would inevitably place the Mediterranean under Soviet dominance. This having been completed, there are three weak spots of the Western system where the Soviet leadership could attempt political pressure combined with military blackmail. Holland, for reasons that are beyond our comprehension, is obviously the weakest spot of the Western alliance. The anti-nuclear movement there has become, in relative terms, the strongest contingent within the European movement. It embraces all parties, political positions, and avenues of life. Clearly, a country in which the soldiers of the army demonstrate in uniform against their main ally is, for all practical purposes, a member of the alliance in name only. If in an hour of national crisis the Soviets are shrewd enough to offer one of their endless and meaningless treaties of mutual non-aggression (and a leadership that firmly believes in the Turkish principle of politics – an oath made to the giaour (infidel) is not binding – can easily do so), it would propel Holland out of the Western alliance toward a Swedish position, which would be a resounding political victory for Soviet strategy.

The second, always open field of expansion is Portugal, which for many reasons has not been economically or sociologically stable since the 1973 revolution. Its moderate and democratic military officers have up until now saved it from a totalitarian takeover, and the hold of the military over the civilian society, a danger in itself, irrespective of the eventual political affiliation of the army officers, has been considerably weakened. However, with an unrepentantly Stalinist communism still strong, a coup or even a civil war can never be entirely excluded. While all this would happen closer to the heart of the West, the degree of Western commitment to resisting such an eventuality is still not clear.

Austria is the last possible direct target. The neutrality of the country was the greatest, perhaps the only, concession the Soviet Union has ever made to the West. For almost 30 years now Austria has cautiously observed Soviet strategic interests and only touched upon Soviet sensitivities with gloved hands. There is absolutely no inner support for any pro-Soviet turn in the country: the anti-nuclear movement is insignificant, social democracy is firmly anti-totalitarian. The Soviet leadership has in fact 'Finlandized' Austria in the sense that the country's abstention from alliances is not optional but mandatory. Further, its Finlandization, or the formal ability to influence the internal affairs of the country, is not entirely excluded under circumstances favorable for the Soviet Union, but it is highly unlikely.

GERMANY, EUROPE'S POLITICAL STORM CENTER

In Europe, however, everything depends on Germany, and in the last three to four years we have witnessed what earlier would have been totally unexpected – an explicit German nationalist upsurge, which is increasingly cross-class, transcends ideological barriers, and unifies even traditional enemies who for decades have not been able to sit down at the same table. *Der Spiegel*, with a pathos somewhat incongruous with the language of its otherwise ironical, cynical journalism, recently stated that the movement has created a national unity on the missile issue unparalleled since the national unity movement in 1848. The current national unity movement is, in an extremely heterogeneous orchestration but ultimately *unisono*, anti-American and extremely understanding toward the Soviet Union. Symbolically, during the huge October 1983 demonstrations all over Europe against the deployment of the Pershing and Cruise missiles, Soviet television did not show pictures of the massive Italian demonstrations (for at least the slogans there were evenhanded). On the other hand, they televised *without distortion* the German demonstrations, which only protested the presence of American missiles in Europe. Does this mean that we have to do with a gigantic 'tacit collective conspiracy'? Is the anti-nuclear issue, which a decade ago was weak and insignificant in West Germany (in contrast to Great Britain) and has now grown into this tidal wave of enthusiasm, a Trojan horse behind which there is an awakening new Germany eager to be released from bonds and have its own nuclear freedom? This view, which has begun to emerge in various parts of Europe, above all in French public opinion, which is traditionally sensitive about German nationalism, is certainly a crude sociological simplification. However, let us quote from a splendid article to demonstrate that even according to German testimonies it has a considerable basis in reality:

Nato's double decision focused public concern on two issues: the sovereignty of both German states and their populations' chances of surviving a limited nuclear war. The extent to which the reactions to these issues have a nationalist character can be ascribed to elder spokesmen of the SPD [German Social Democratic Party] who, while not part of the peace movement, influence it nonetheless. Participants like Hellmut Gollwitzer and Heinrich Albertz sound very much like Guenter Gaus and Egon Bahr . . . Bahr and Gaus argue that reunification and, ultimately, the restoration of national identity should be German politics' immediate concern: 'if a German tells you that the national question is no longer important, do not be so sure. Do not believe him. Either he is dumb or he is not telling the truth, and both positions are dangerous.'[12]

It is precisely this covert and inauthentic character of the new German nationalist upsurge that causes immediate concern for the observer. The proof of a sudden change is beyond doubt: all analyses of the anti-nuclear issue conclude, either directly or with a detour, in establishing the moral and political foundations for German reunification. (Grass's interview mentioned earlier proceeds directly from the condemnation of American missiles, and a very reluctant allegiance to the Western alliance, to a nuclear-free zone in Europe, which is, to all intents and purposes, identical with the process of confederating the two Germanys.) The general social discourse, except on the aggressive right, has changed dramatically as well. The leading liberal journals *(Die Zeit, Der Spiegel)*, without weakening their traditional total contempt for 'socialist utopias', have become excessively uncritical toward the Soviet Union and its East European empire and harshly critical of the United States, in the case of *Der Spiegel* very often in the tone of a traditional 'cultural superiority'. Jaruzelski emerges from their pages as the savior of Europe, the man who prevented an unruly population from triggering a world war (which is as far from historical reality as any German historical legend could be); Kádárist Hungary emerges as the *ne plus ultra* of human freedom. The Hungarian revolution of 1956, once the favorite child of liberalism, now appears in the presentation of David Irving, a 'historian' who has termed himself 'mildly Fascist', as a mob uprising serialized by *Der Spiegel*. And while the criticism of the United States, in particular for the policies it pursues in Central America, is entirely justified, it is a telling historical fact that many of its anti-communist and anti-totalitarian critics in Germany needed this particular historical hour to understand what has always been clear to any objective observer: the deep contradiction within American foreign policy between defending the global interests of world capitalism and defending democracy. The translation of this fact into the formula that 'America betrays her ideals' is little more than a depiction of the latecoming self-illumination of the German liberal.

How did this nationalist upsurge come about? Any approach to the 'German issue behind the issue', namely, national unity through the anti-nuclear protest, has to start with *la condition allemande* in 1945, when not only the Reich lay in debris, but the very right to be German, even more a German nationalist, had been questioned by all victims of Hitler's aggression. Our analysis suggests a different approach. First, we believe that admitting the legitimacy of every single nationalism other than the German, or watching it with exaggerated suspicion just because of what transpired in an earlier phase of German nationalism, is racism with reversed signs. Either no nationalism at all or each and every nationalism has to be historically legitimized as long as it does not aim, explicitly or implicitly, at the extermination of other human groups. Second, annoyed observers of the reemergence of a German nationalism often miss the important point that there is a self-critical element in the very structure of the new German collective feeling: *it is the nationalism of the German nation, not that of a future German Reich.*

The best characterization of the German destiny after Hitler is given, in our view, in the document of a small group of 'Titoists' and Trotskyites (the so-called Independent Labor Party of Germany) in 1951:

The contradictions between the Western capitalist powers and the Soviet Union led, through the occupation of Germany and *the absence of a German revolution,* to the partitioning of our country. The collectively conceived Potsdam decrees of the superpowers about the subjugation and exploitation of Germany did not prevent the victors from adjusting quickly their respective zones of occupation to the structure of their own countries . . . The reunification of Germany must not be the political victory of either the SED [East German Communist Party] bureaucracy or the Western capitalists.[13]

Here, the reference to a German revolution that never came in from the cold is vital. In fact, a German revolution in 1944 seems to be the last historical moment when Germany could have escaped being partitioned by putting a resolute end through German acts to the shame and misery Germans caused to endless millions, by setting their own house in order and thereby protecting the old edifice. It is not our concern here whether such a German revolution was 'likely' or 'unlikely'; we only would like to point to theoretical possibilities. Germans on the left have argued in the last decades that a great opportunity for a leftist victory in 1945 was miscarried by conservative Anglo-American policies. If half of this claim is true, the adherents of the left must have been there in 1944 in sufficient number to use July 20, or any other occasion, to turn the Nazi tide. This is all the more so as Nazism, despite its omnipotence on the surface, in 1943–4 must have already been very weak. In particular, in 1944 the writing was clearly on the wall: the German armies were in retreat, German cities lay in debris, almost all its allies – Fascist Italy, half-Fascist Romania and Hungary, pro-German (or rather, anti-Soviet) Finland – had all deserted the Nazi cause, so many signs and facts that not even Goebbels' propaganda could reduce them to 'hostile figments of a feverish fantasy'. However, *unbewältigte Vergangenheit*, 'the unmastered past', this hackneyed phrase of German self-understanding, again produced a miracle. The historical legend of the *Dolchstoss*, in November 1918, stabbing the knife in the back of one's own fatherland, the compulsory mythological explanation of the first monumental German defeat, worked as a negative categorical imperative. Millions, in particular on the left, who hated Hitler as no one else, who expected no better fate than peril at the hand of Hitler's myrmidons or the victors and were therefore led not by fear but by despair, still did not act, when they could have for the last time with historical efficiency, because they were not prepared to take the stigma of patricide, the *Dolchstoss*.

Once this historical moment for a German revolution was missed, partitioning became inevitable, and German history up until the present *has developed in antinomies that have been lived by the overwhelming majority of Germans as suffering.* What is felt to be suffering *is* suffering. Germans were lucky, however, in that the majority of their occupied territory and populace fell into Western hands, and not those of Stalin. Whether one applies 'bourgeois-liberal' or 'socialist' standards to the assessment of historical events, the fact remains that even Konrad Adenauer's extremely restrictive, conservatively liberal *Obrigkeitsstaat*, this paragon of the cold war West, was a measure of freedom when compared to Ulbricht's and Honecker's 'real socialism'. In addition, the Western occupants learned at least one lesson from Versailles: exploiting and humiliating the bulk of the German population is simply bad politics. Therefore the West 'donated' a liberal system to Germany (or imposed one on it). This, together with the extraordinary talent of the conservative and misanthropic statesman, Adenauer, comparable only to that of Charles de Gaulle, plus the efficiency of his cynical power elite, created what the world saw as a genuine miracle: the strange 'victory' of a Germany after a war without peace, which is the other face of the 'German condition'.

What can be said were the antinomies of the German situation after 1945, after the *de facto* partitioning? The first pair of antinomies was presented in the following option: either a collective passive resistance of all Germans against all occupying forces as a long-range policy, or a collaboration with them on both poles, in both spheres of influence. And here, there was indeed no third option, nor any 'redeeming' choice between the two existing options. In fact, to our knowledge, no serious political factor appeared, either on the right or on the left, that would have prompted the Germans in 1945 to opt for

Gandhi's strategy of non-collaboration. There were indeed very good moral and political reasons against such a choice. First, democratic and socialist Germans, and often even religious Germans without any political creed, felt so deeply remorseful for the terrible crimes committed in the name of Germany and by German hands that they could not mobilize the necessary amount of self-assurance required by such a long-range boycott. They also felt that they would become stooges of a clandestine Nazi resistance manipulating them shrewdly from behind the scenes, which beyond any doubt could well have become the case. But it was also true that all the trumps were in the allied hands, and that the leaders of the victorious powers had already toyed with the idea of turning a defeated Germany into a new Carthage. An all-German boycott could have triggered an Anglo-American and Soviet reaction of this kind.

The other option inherent in the antinomy was accepting the politics, the strategy, the hegemony and finally the social system of one of the victors. The embracing of a Western hegemony and alliance offered two possibilities. One was represented by an SPD led by Kurt Schumacher. In order not to appear biased, we simply accept Brandt and Ammon's description of Schumacher's policy as accurate:

From now on, the line of Kurt Schumacher has broken through permanently. Schumacher, who had spent ten years in a concentration camp during the Third Reich, emphasized like no one else since the Spring of 1945 the necessity of a radical self-purification and social change as the right of the German people to national unity and equal rights. At the same time, he criticized with unusual outspokenness the occupying powers, in particular the USSR, so that he was regarded as a 'nationalist'. Apart from fundamental convictions, the underlying idea of Schumacher's patriotic rhetoric was also the fear that once again, as in the Weimar Republic, it could be the 'false powers' (as in his view the communists and the right were), who would exploit for their purposes certain existing national problems. Schumacher was convinced that Germany could only be reconstructed in a 'socialist' way, and that German democracy had to be founded in a socialist manner in order to last; the socialization of fundamental raw materials and key industries as well as the big banks belonged to this. Schumacher claimed the politically leading role for the SPD as the only undeniably democratic, freedom- and socialism-oriented, at the same time internationalist and patriotic party, which he wanted to realize in sharp confrontation with the bourgeois right and center parties and the communists. Above all, he made the reproach to the KPD [the West German Communist Party] and SED that they were oriented exclusively toward the interests of the USSR, instead of those of the German working people. For him, the USSR was a non-democratic and non-socialist state, while he saw socialist trends emerging in the Western states (New Deal, Labour governments) . . . From the start, Schumacher was West-oriented . . . In contrast to Adenauer, he did not commit himself unconditionally to an alliance of the western zones of occupation with the West. Although he did not reject later the German contribution to defense in principle – at any rate, he combined it with unacceptable conditions – the emphasis of his conceptions has always been on the democratic and socialist 'magnetic appeal' of West Germany to East Germany, instead of on military terrain.[14]

It is at this point that we can grasp the historical responsibility of the Western powers for the emergence of a conservative Germany for a period of two decades. This was the second possibility flowing from an acceptance of the Western alliance. America was naturally mistrustful of the socialist conceptions of Schumacher, as was, equally naturally, the British Tory establishment, whose political and military infrastructure was the *de facto* administration in the British zone. (And not even a victorious Labour Party found the determination, for nationalist reasons, to side with a natural ally.) It would be an exaggeration to say that the British and the Americans 'suppressed' the socialist option (although they were all-powerful during those years and did everything to obstruct it). But the simple fact that Schumacher's strategy was for them clearly and publicly unacceptable, and not even negotiable, miscarried the chances of a radical social democracy from the start. The Western powers needed Adenauer, the anti-Bismarck, the man who had the moral courage to divide his own people in order to recreate its role as a powerful nation; who was, however, Bismarckian enough to tolerate government through parliament only to the absolutely necessary minimum degree. With this Promethean act of a conservative nation-creation barely four or five years after the war, an achievement nobody believed possible in 1945, a set of negative features that have never been eliminated or rectified emerged as characteristic of West Germany. First, and this is borne out by key documents of the West German trade unions from the Adenauer era, Adenauer's victory was not just accompanied by the emergence of an extremely restrictive and authoritarian state, hardly reformed later by social-liberal governments, but it also embodied the purest capitalist domination of economic and social life in liberal Western Europe. Of course, the reverse side of this situation has been a policy of gradually raising standards of living over a period of more than 20 years, during which West Germany has become the most prosperous nation of Europe. The completion of Bismarck's policy, the coupling of an arch-conservative political regime with a generous system of social security, also belongs to the picture. But the new German prosperity favored above all an ostentatious, repressive, and uncultured class of *nouveaux riches* whose roots go back to a shady prehistory during the Third Reich. Further, once a 'donated sovereignty' has been accepted, sovereignty is stipulated as a fact, never shaped in a nationwide consensus. Independence existed without a declaration of independence (just like peace without a peace treaty), and therefore it could be, and in fact has been, called a non-independence; more particularly, a non-sovereignty. Statements such as these may be exercises in demagoguery or at least exaggerations, but they are certainly not lacking altogether in historical foundations.

Third, on this basis no peace treaty could ever be concluded. The end of the war, just as the beginning of sovereignty, was an act without ratified agreements, something of a mythological event whose interpretation is truly open-ended. Finally, consistent de-Nazification simply could not take place, and the reasons are deeper than just a series of cover-ups on the part of an arch-conservative establishment. Adenauer's West Germany was a nation that regarded itself as sovereign, but which had no instrument of sovereignty; a nation that regarded itself as defeated and dispossessed of a quarter of its territory by the USSR but was powerless in translating such perceived injustices into an outright condemnation of the terms of Germany's defeat because of the Western powers it had to rely on; a nation that was used and greatly favored as a political and military instrument against the USSR but which was, at the same time, publicly mistrusted; a conservative state that could hardly fool its own electorate about having postponed reunification *ad calendas Graecas*, and which, therefore, had to be extremely sensitive about the past and the deeds of that same electorate; in sum, Adenauer's West Germany, caught in the web of all such contradictions, could do little other than circumvent the 'Hitler syndrome' by a superficial rhetoric about barbarism, instead of radically eliminating at least those roots of Nazism that were incompatible with a Christian culture.

However, the alliance with or integration into the 'West' of Adenauer's Germany has set in motion a new pair of antinomies. On the one hand, a 'European', a 'Western' Germany was hardly less of a rupture with German traditions than Hitler's, albeit a beneficial one. Politically, it meant a radical abandonment of any idea of a Reich. The CDU–CSU [Christian Democrat Union – Christian Social Union] circles could make as much noise as they wished about expelled Germans, against the loss of territory on behalf of Poland and the USSR, but the *Bundesrepublik* would be no conduit for any messianic empire to come, rather an integrated (or, as Germans still tend to believe, overintegrated) part of an alliance. Culturally, it meant the far-reaching Americanization of West Germany, a trend which, of course, finally could not shake the self-confidence of what has remained one of the leading cultures of the world, but nonetheless a trend against which Germans now fight with good reason, even if often it is under the sign of questionable objectives. Most importantly – and today this is a typical criticism levelled on the left against Adenauer's policy, but increasingly in the center (and perhaps soon on the right) as well – the integration into the Western alliance, the politics of *Alles oder Nichts* meant a perhaps deliberate and certainly a final abandonment of German reunification (short of some miraculous turn in history). The other side of this antinomic situation, however, is that this new Germany, which went the farthest in 'self-Westernization' and the abandonment of the imperial idea, could not allay suspicion in either the East or the West. As far as the East is concerned, up until 1970 consecutive Soviet leaderships had played on the 'danger of German revanchism'. Of course, it is always difficult to determine whether such perceived threats are real or whether they are merely exploited for political purposes, but it is an indubitable fact that, excepting China and the 'yellow peril', the only instance of a coincidence of government and popular perceptions in foreign policy in the USSR has been this common fear of a new German power. As far as the West was concerned, the rise of a new German power, however integrated, simply could not fail to trigger immediate French suspicions. The last years of the Fourth Republic were spent in nervous debates about the French role in Nato were West Germany to join it as a full-fledged member. There could be, and indeed there was, no mistake either in the United States or in the Federal Republic that the Gaullist decision to leave the military alliance was triggered to a very large extent by the German rise to quasi-independence. De Gaulle publicly warned about a complete French volte-face and, if need be, a revival of the traditional Franco–Russian pact, in the event of a German nuclear rearmament. West Germany has, then, remained the Western continental power par excellence, with all the burdens, risks, and duties that go with such a role, but without the trust and recognition that normally accompanies such a role within an alliance. This is indeed an antinomic situation for both West Germany and its allies.

A third set of antinomies came about in the relationship of the Federal Republic to the eastern part of Germany, which Adenauerian Germany, with an unusual lack of realism, kept calling SBZ (*sowjetische Besatzungzone* – Soviet zone of occupation) and was not prepared to regard as a state with at least formal sovereignty. There was, of course, more to this than just foolhardiness. It was integrally bound up with the whole system of *Ersatzlegitimation* of Adenauer's historical option. That he chose, via an 'integration with the West', a particular German state which was the only possible German nation meant that he was necessarily bound to regard the rest of Germany as a Soviet colony. For a very long time the Adenauer propaganda worked not just because of the sheer brutality with which the Soviets handled the German question (in particular, we have in mind the tragedy of millions of Eastern *Volksdeutsche* who were expelled from their homes and native countries in the most horrendous way), but also because of the attitude of the East German apparatus itself, which, while wishing for the permanence of its position, was quite unsure about its master's intentions. In their quick justification of whatever atrocities were committed against German prisoners of war and *volksdeutsch* Germans in the USSR and in East European countries, and their direct dependence on Soviet military commanders, the East Germans indeed resembled much more a colonial administration than even a subservient government. It was precisely the Adenauer solution, however, that had accelerated matters: the deeper the Federal Republic was integrated into the Western alliance, the quicker the formalization of an at least nominal East German sovereignty proceeded, very much against West German intentions and interests.

This, of course, raises the well-known question: Did Adenauer *et alii* deliberately sabotage a possible German reunification based on Soviet offers of negotiations in 1952 and later in 1955, by pursuing their policies of *Alles oder Nichts*, in order to save their political hegemony? As a direct answer to this would demand not only incomparably more knowledge of German history than we command, but even introspection and illumination in certain dark historic spots, we would rather try to answer a broader question: Could these Soviet offers represent an *objective possibility* for German reunification? We believe that the Soviet offer certainly did not mean such a possibility in 1952, though it could have meant an opening in 1955, when the initiative was in the hands of the United States rather than in West German diplomacy. As to the first offer, all available historical evidence refutes unequivocally any serious and honest intention on Stalin's part to let Germany reunite itself even on a Finlandized basis: he could only lose considerably and gain nothing. Given Soviet economic conditions right after the war, a unified and even Finlandized Germany had to loom as an economic giant over the USSR, boosting Western rather than Eastern economies. Although the Western nuclear monopoly had disappeared, there was no telling when the West could have won over the whole of Germany once the Soviets allowed East Germany to slip from their grip, leaving them only the option of war should they wish to rectify a disadvantageous strategic situation. At that time, the Gaullist option was yet to emerge; a German–Russian relationship that was too close could only forge much closer ties between the United States and the rest of Western Europe. All this is a strong refutation of the genuine character of Stalin's offer. Much more likely, it was an attempt to decelerate West German integration into the West.

The situation changed, however, after Stalin's death. A mysterious document, published by *Der Spiegel* in 1978, entitled the 'Manifesto of the Union of Democratic Communists in the GDR' saw the situation in the GDR as follows: 'All power struggles in the political bureau – Ackermann, Zaisser, Herrnstadt, Oelssner, Schirdewan, Ulbricht against Honecker – were connected with the national problem.'[15] In addition, in our account of the Hungarian revolution,[16] we have argued that the first post-Stalin leadership, being in throes of infighting and rebellions affecting almost the whole of the empire, at least could have been amenable to early openings to détente. Therefore, that this historic opportunity was not used is, to a very great extent, a Western responsibility.

The German constellation underwent a gradual but radical change from the early sixties onward, the most visible political result of which was the end of the political hegemony of the CDU-CSU and the gradual conquest of power (in alliance with the Free Democrats) by the SPD. The causes of the change can be summed up in a laconic way. First, the Adenauer option had been fully implemented: the Federal Republic not only had been integrated into the Western alliance as an (almost entirely) sovereign state but it had also become its main 'continental' power. As this feat completed the historical task Adenauer had vowed to achieve, and as it had unwittingly accelerated the emergence of the GDR, in itself a symbolic sign of the impossibility of German reunification on Adenauer's premises, there was indeed no historical mission the Christian Union (CDU-CSU) could have further fulfilled. Second, whereas the German *Wirtschaftswunder*, which was a miracle indeed in the sense that it transformed an almost destroyed Germany into the wealthiest nation of the European West was a kind of 'consolation prize' for an irretrievably lost national unity and hurt national pride, there emerged certain structural social problems that a conservative government could not change. The time was ripe for a change, even if later the change brought more disillusionment than fulfillment. Third, after the Berlin crisis, the cold war started to 'slacken' and give way (in the form of confidential communications between Khrushchev and Kennedy) to what later became Kissinger's strategic option. The Vietnam war rechanneled tensions away from Europe to Asia, so that a central argument of the Christian Union, that their unyielding vigor alone could protect the new state, could no longer captivate the majority of an electorate whose needs and political priorities were altering. Finally, social democracy, too, underwent a number of changes under the impact of a new generation of leaders. On the one hand, the social democrats gave up Schumacher's nationalism and accepted the integration of West Germany into the Western alliance, while on the other hand, they tamed (in Bad Godesberg) their socialist ambitions. They gradually became sensitive to a new opening, which later gained notoriety under the name of *Neue Ostpolitik*, and which, in objective terms, completed Adenauer's mission. While the conservative chancellor reassured the West that the Federal Republic was a German nation-state and not a nucleus of a German Reich, the social democratic chancellor reassured the East (that is, the Soviet Union) that a Germany led by his party had abandoned forever any idea of going beyond the Oder–Neisse line. In this sense, Adenauer and Brandt are not so much political enemies as complementary figures of a postwar German history.

The real content of an impending and important political change is spelled out by Rudolf Augstein. This is how he saw *Neue Ostpolitik*, long before *Der Spiegel* became a mouthpiece for Brandt's policy:

Supposing we had, despite everything, a government capable of action, what could it do? As a first task, it ought to perceive that a threat of war in Europe does not arise from itself, not because of the devilishness of the godless Bolsheviks, but above all, because of the intricacies of the German question. The present borderlines must be recognized, in order for Poland and Czechoslovakia to proceed further toward independence. The pressure of German revisionism, I deliberately use here an originally communist vocabulary, has to be eliminated from the whole of Eastern Europe. Friendly relations of all kinds, obviously diplomatic relations as well, should be cultivated with governments of the former satellite countries. This in itself would be a lot. Secondly, one must not sabotage, ridicule or countermand the operations of both world powers for they cannot withdraw from the center of Europe without endangering the European balance, and as such their presence should be constructively supported. Without a nuclear-free zone in Central Europe, without a disentanglement of the military blocks, without armament control and the reduction of troops in a limited area . . . there is no chance for an inner-German rapprochement, no chance for the re-Europeanization of the former satellite countries. An absolute reconsideration is necessary here, and in a very un-German fashion, namely, reconsideration as non-wishful thinking. If the Soviets left just Poland, Hungary and Germany, progress would be guaranteed. If the Americans left the continent, de Gaulle, or whoever steps in his boots, would be obliged to be satisfied. Clearly, without the USA as a guarantor of a European settlement there could be none. Just as France and Sweden guaranteed the Treaty of Westphalia, so too the USA and the USSR, whether we like it or not, are the guarantors of all systems in present Europe. Thirdly, and finally, the GDR, with all the false pretenses conveyed in her name, should be brought, through collaboration, through manifold economic merger, even through economic aid, to a higher level. Whether its government is a German government is a question which, for very good reasons, is at least open to doubt; that it is a *de facto* authority, even a government is not. . . . It is in our interests that the GDR authorities should become a government without inverted commas, a more independent, more self-conscious body. Our interest is that the GDR government should be more German, a German government. . . . Be it communist or whatever else you wish to call it, this should not bother us.[17]

The balance of the *Ostpolitik* can be summed up in the following terms. The new leaders of Germany, who made it public knowledge that they felt shame and remorse for the horrendous deeds committed in the name of Germany and by German hands, who in a way had taken the responsibility upon themselves, although often they had been victims or targets of persecution themselves, fulfilled a historical duty for their nation and for the rest of humanity, without which there could never be reconciliation. It should be added that this duty has never been done in a sincere way by the politicians of the conservative parties. Not independently of the aforementioned, *Neue Ostpolitik* has defused the tension from the Soviet–German relationship, not only at an official level, but also at the social base. The 'German revanchist' scarecrow could be brought into play during the Dubček period by Soviet propaganda, but no longer. These two factors were considerable contributions to defusing the Cold War in general. The process of 'merging' the GDR economy with the West German, making Honecker's Germany a silent partner in the European Economic Community through West German channels, was also an organic part of *Ostpolitik*. If this opening is assessed from an exclusively nationalistic point of view, it was, of course, successful in the sense that the GDR, promoted by both the Soviets and the Federal Republic, has attained the best standard of living within the Eastern block and thus could further pass certain economic burdens to the West German taxpayers. If this process is evaluated from the value of freedom (democracy), however, it was a total flop. No serious liberalization of the GDR has been achieved, or demanded, other than some increase in family reunions. Honecker's 'workers and peasants republic', about which the West German left regularly lapses into delusion, has remained, together with Romania, Turkey and Albania, the most repressive country of Europe since the overthrow or gradual demolition of dictatorships in Portugal, Greece and Spain (if, of course, the Soviet Union is not included in this cluster). However, the basic ideological self-delusion of the Brandt-Schmidt era became gradually manifest. The SPD, which had abandoned Schumacher's nationalism but which had come to power with a criticism of the Cold War romanticism and with the promise that the realism of its piecemeal engineering would produce results that could not be produced under CDU-CSU illusionism achieved exactly the same as its predecessors: no progress at all.

What are, if any, the abstract-logical chances of a German reunification in such a situation, seen from a Western as well as an Eastern point of view? For the GDR, only logically speaking, the Beria option has always existed, that is, being sold out to the West by the Soviet masters in return for some kind of a global bargain between the superpowers. If we mean by 'GDR' the ruling apparatus and not the populace (for the latter it would be, of course, liberation), this has, in our firm view, never been an option seriously considered by the overwhelming majority of the apparatus. Further, again purely logically speaking, there is the chance of 'Yugoslavization', that is, a considerable degree of inner liberalization together with an increasing measure of relative independence from the Soviet Union. As a hypothetical possibility, there could emerge a 'gradual unification', a 'piecemeal merger' of the two new German states. Willy Brandt and the SPD nurtured some such hopes; their incomparably more realistic GDR counterparts, however, never have. Willy Stoph made this very clear during the 1970 Erfurt meeting of the delegations of the two German states: 'In fact, the two sovereign states, the GDR and the FRG, do not lend themselves to unification because contradicting social systems cannot be unified.'[18]

The GDR has always recommended a single solution: *confederation*. This would provide a symbolic satisfaction for the Western part, and several invaluable advantages for the East German apparatus. The single Western satisfaction would be *cultural-spiritual* unity at the price of self-Finlandization of the whole of Germany. It is easy, however, to enumerate the Eastern advantages. It would be a tremendous political victory for an oppressive apparatus, an actual confirmation for the most cynical of East German slogans, 'Wer mit der Sowjet-Union ist, ist mit dem Sieger', ('Who is with the Soviet Union, is on the side of the victor'). The *economic* advantages of such a confederation for a highly industrialized country that suffers, because of its social system, from incurable diseases as far as economic-purposive rationality is concerned, are equally conceivable. Politically, the terms of a self-Finlandization of the whole of Germany would allow the East German apparatus to take any course it deemed fit. The most likely one would be to carry on business in as harsh a manner as usual, with one exception – that it would have to make (and is in fact now already making) concessions concerning travel of citizens within Germany.

However, in discussing the *realities* of German reunification, one particular option has to be addressed above all, the one we have termed the 'new Rapallo'.

THE OPTION OF A 'NEW RAPALLO'

The motives on the part of *Germany* leading to Rapallo have been succinctly summed up by a monographer of Brockdorff-Rantzau, the first conservative German diplomat working on the reconciliation of German conservatism with Russian Bolshevism:

After the military collapse of Germany, the plan for an honest rapprochement with the former wartime enemies in the West, in order to fight Bolshevism together, played a certain role among the considerations shaping future foreign policy of Foreign Minister Brockdorff-Rantzau. The precondition of the success of such a politics was the implementation of the promised just peace. Instead, the Western powers displayed an unforgiving attitude in Versailles; as a result of a failing readiness to understand the exigencies of the most simple life conditions and vital rights, the German nation had been completely neglected and dismissed.[19]

E. H. Carr further elaborates on this generally known premise of Rapallo:

The choice between east and west, which was forced on the German Council of People's Representatives within a few hours of the armistice by the offer of two trainloads of Russian grain, was a permanent dilemma of German foreign policy, especially when the choice had to be made from a position of weakness. Of the German political parties under the Weimar republic only the SPD had its roots in the west and was consistently western in outlook. It was linked with the other parties of the Second International whose main strength was in western Europe; it was traditionally hostile to Russia, which was regarded not merely as reactionary but as backward and barbarous; and, having . . . rid itself of the revolutionary purity and intransigence of Marxism, it had imbibed much of the bourgeois-democratic radicalism of the western European Left. Thus, almost alone among German parties, it turned a receptive ear to Wilson's democratic pacifism, embodied in conceptions such as national self-determination and the League of Nations. During the first period of the Weimar Republic, when a western orientation was essential to Germany, the SPD held the reins of power; its importance declined as Germany became capable of pursuing an independent foreign policy. Of the other parties the Catholic Centre had western leanings. But, being based on confessional rather than political loyalties, it rarely spoke with a firm or united voice on major issues, and could for the most part act only as a balancing force. None of the other forces in German political life looked primarily to the west. The extreme Left . . . stood for an alliance with Soviet Russia. The parties standing to the right of the Centre were all in a greater or lesser degree hostile to the west. The nucleus of these parties was formed by the two powers which, behind the facade of the Weimar republic, continued to rule Germany, as it had ruled it under Wilhelm II: the army and the heavy industry. The officer class of the defeated army nourished almost to a man longterm ambition of avenging itself on the west; and for this, alliance with the east would be indispensable. Heavy industry excluded from western and overseas markets, could find an outlet nowhere but in the east. The forces favouring an eastern orientation were already powerful in the Germany of 1919, even though they had few means of giving effect to their views and their ambitions.[20]

When a Western politics based on a continued indifference to vital German rights and preconditions of national life coincided with an express Soviet wish to enter into alliance with anyone who would help break the *cordon sanitaire* around Russia, when even such convinced partisans of the rapprochement with the West as Rathenau were dismissed, often in insulting terms, what had been intended to be a conference of the Western powers (Genoa, 1922) turned into Rapallo, the first secret agreement between Germany and Soviet Russia. The gist of the agreement is, again, best summed up by Carr:

The fact of signature was more important than the formal contents of the treaty. It provided for the mutual renunciation of all financial claims, including German claims arising out of Soviet nationalization decrees, 'on the condition that the government of the RSFSR does not meet analogous claims of other states.' Diplomatic and consular relations were to be resumed; and the most important article of the treaty dealt with economic relations . . . The effect of this clause was to ensure the exclusion of Germany from any international scheme for exploitation of Russian sources and the establishment of a common economic front between the two countries . . .[21]

Beyond and above all such details, Rapallo was a *symbolic*, but in that function, crucial, event. It showed, first, that a defeated Germany and a weakened and besieged Soviet Russia reentered the heart of international politics as major forces to contend with, and secondly, that in a world of

Machiavellian politics neither widely diverging social structures nor equally diverging, even conflictory, ideologies are absolute barriers to strategic alliances.

However, for an event so widely accepted by 'mainstream' German opinion to come about, 'marginal' agents were needed in German politics, the main one being *Nationalbolschewismus*. Let us hear again Carr's presentation:

The Russian revolution exercised a fascination on vanquished Germany which went far beyond the narrow circles professing sympathy with Bolshevik doctrine, and was felt on the nationalist Right as well as on the communist Left. For many Germans whose tradition was wholly of the Right, including German officers, it seemed in 1919 that the only path to salvation for Germany lay through revolution. The mood of sheer despair counted for much in this vision of destruction: the German Samson in the hour of defeat and humiliation would call the dark powers of Bolshevism to his aid to pull down the pillars of the temple and cheat the Philistines of their triumph. But the vision also had its positive sides, which would not necessarily clash with the aims of the Russian revolution. The blow would be directed against the west and against liberal democracy: it would be authoritarian, but would recognize the new power of the urban proletariat; and its aim would be the revival of German national military power. Thus an alliance between nationalist Germany and Bolshevik Russia might be sealed by a common hatred of the west, determined by ideological antipathies as well as by conflicts of interest with the western Powers. The idea was at first sight fantastic and might have passed for a typical concoction of politically unschooled officers and harebrained young men. But it had its counterpart on the extreme Left. Laufenberg and Wolffheim, the leaders of the Left group expelled from the KPD at the Heidelberg congress in October 1919, were sponsors of a doctrine which came to be called 'national Bolshevism' and invited German communists to proclaim a 'revolutionary people's war' against the Versailles treaty and thus win the support of German nationalists for the proletarian revolution . . . About the same time an anarchist intellectual, Eltzbacher, wrote a pamphlet entitled *Bolshevism and the German Future*, in which he argued that Germany could obtain deliverance from the slavery of the Versailles treaty only by accepting Bolshevism, which could then sweep over western Europe and destroy it: for this end he was prepared to reckon with disorder, terror and hunger. In a confused argument the themes of ideological and political union (*Anschluss*) with Russia became indistinguishable . . . From this extreme of revolutionary intoxication to the opposite extreme represented by Seeckt and the Reichswehr generals, of hard calculations of the value of a Russian alliance, the prism of German opinion about the great neighbour in the east showed every variety of hue. What was common to all these groups was hatred of the west, admiration . . . of Russian power, and the hope and belief that this power could somehow be enlisted in the struggle against the victors of Versailles.[22]

In this context, it is clear that 'marginal' positions were expressive of 'mainstream' opinion. And it is only against such background that we can understand the consistency of the otherwise seemingly confused careers of actors, such as that of Ernst Niekisch (see his autobiography, *Gewagtes*

Leben[23]) moving between the communist revolution of Munich, 1919 through a friendship and alliance with the Strassers on the 'left' of the Nazi Party to Stalinist communism after 1945 in East Germany and concluding in a Leninist opposition to the GDR. But even if we move further to the right, and read what at first sight appears to be an incredible entry in the young Goebbels's unpublished diary (February 15, 1926), we have to understand it in the context of *Nationalbolschewismus:* 'Hitler talked for two hours. I feel as though someone had beaten me. What sort of a Hitler is this? A reactionary? Altogether lacking in poise and assurance. Russian question: quite off the track. Italy and England our natural allies. Terrible! Our task, he says, is the destruction of Bolshevism. Bolshevism is a Jewish creation. We must break Russia. A hundred and eighty millions! I am unable to say a word. I feel as though someone had hit me over the head . . . how my heart hurts! . . . I should like to cry . . .'[24]

As far as the *goals* and *substance* of the Rapallo agreement is concerned, the first was spelt out with unusual clarity and levelheadedness on both sides. Referring to Brockdorff-Rantzau, Helbig writes:

In no way did he think from the start of entering into an alliance. Should, however, the allied powers intend to annihilate Germany and this, he argued, was, for all appearances, occurring, so that it would not only be much more dignified, but also politically more clever, to actively interfere in the world development and at least to make an attempt to spiritually take over the leadership, instead of the passive endurance of fate. Above all, Moscow had to be assessed as to whether there are indications of the revolution turning into evolution. But at any rate, he found the unity of the Reich less endangered through a rapprochement with Russia than by the politics of the Entente.[25]

On the Russian side, a few months after Rapallo, Radek, then very much still an official spokesman of Russian policy:

defined this relationship in terms of the eternal interests of Russia and the traditional requirements of the old diplomacy: 'This policy of strangling Germany implied in fact the destruction of Russia as a great Power; *for, no matter how Russia is governed, it is always to her interest that Germany should exist* . . . A Russia weakened to the utmost by the war could neither have remained a great Power nor acquired the economic and technical means for her industrial reconstruction, unless she had in the existence of Germany a counterweight to the preponderance of the Allies.'[26]

As to the substance of Rapallo, Helbig denies that Rapallo contained secret clauses and that it was the preparation for a military alliance, a first act of the Molotov–Ribbentrop agreement.[27] However, he cannot deny, he even proves, that something like that was the underlying Russian intention. Let us quote a conversation between Brockdorff-Rantzau, then ambassador of Germany in Moscow, with Rykov, for a while President of the Council of People's Commissaries (Prime Minister) on February 25, 1925.

The President touched upon the suggestions made by Chicherin and set forth that without any doubt, after Versailles two power groups had come about, each intending to surpass the other. The victorious states had made efforts to win over Russia, though at the same time, there were attempts being made to create a united front against the Soviet Union. However, Rykov and the Russian Government were not inclined to be won over for such plans, and had instead decided to enter into a closer relationship with Germany, after giving due consideration to the fact that there were still in Germany tendencies aiming at forming a united front of the Entente against the Soviet Union. Despite this, he would suggest an alliance.[28]

This was certainly a historical offer of some significance. Were it realized, the whole postwar history of Europe would have taken a different course. Weimar Germany was, however, so deeply undermined by the meteoric rise of Hitler's National Socialist Party and therefore clearly unreliable for the purposes of a German-Soviet alliance, that the Soviet leaders gradually turned toward the equally traditional idea of a Franco-Soviet alliance.

It would be a serious misreading of our text were it to be seen to be an attempt at an unmasking of 'criminal German-Soviet intentions'. In terms of a pragmatic conception of politics (and this was the language both Soviet Russian and German politicians used), Rapallo was a perfectly reasonable move for both parties. Russia, as the internationalist and non-Russian Radek pointed out quite correctly, had from her own nationalist viewpoint persistently shown a keen interest in a non-subservient and strong but friendly Germany. On the other hand, German-Prussian politics (roughly since Frederick the Great, when the race for German unity around a Prussian nucleus commenced, through Bismarck and up to the end of the Weimar Republic) had always been governed by three factors: the West, the Russian empire, and the 'medium powers' (of which the Habsburg monarchy, for reasons which cannot be discussed here, had always been a special factor). This means, firstly, that 'Germany' (Prussia) regarded herself *as distinct* from both the West and (the Russian) East. This was not just a geopolitical question, but also reflected certain philosophical considerations. Secondly, 'Germany' even if conceived of as a Reich, with decidedly imperialist aspirations outside Europe, and unmistakably intending to dominate her weaker neighbors as all imperialist powers do, nevertheless did not make any attempt to create an 'artificial empire', but strove rather to unite German-speaking states and ethnic groups into a 'Great Nation'. (Reaching out for the Ukraine in 1917 was not just a spectacular 'overreaching' of themselves in the light of the German collapse a year later, it was also dangerously out of pattern with traditional German politics, and in that sense, in retrospect, an anticipation of Hitler.)

Precisely because 'Germany' from Frederick to the end of the Weimar Republic was not an 'artificial empire', but an expansive nation, it was not a matter of principle, rather, simply just a matter of pragmatic expediency for German leaders of all shades whether they were fighting the West in alliance with the East or the other way round. Both 'East' and 'West' were separate, and, as it seemed to a traditional conservatism or a traditional liberalism, *eternal* factors of power politics, in themselves neutral. It was not regarded as a betrayal but rather an observance of principles for German statesmen to ally their expansive nation once with the West, once with the East. However, this explains that the German nightmare of 'fighting on two fronts' was more than a strategic principle; it organically followed from a historical conception of the European world in which there had to be a distinct 'East' and distinct 'West'. It was, in terms of this conception, futile, even lunatic, to imagine that one could 'eliminate' any of these distinct and eternal entities (even more to aim at eliminating both). Therefore taking on two was certain defeat, whereas a quick victory over one, with the other in alliance or, at least, neutral, was certain victory. It was precisely in this sense that the conservative German generals misread Hitler. The Führer was simply not interested in the conservative nation, only in his 'artificial empire', nor was he, as a consistent irrationalist, interested in the 'succession of time', but just in the 'eternity of the moment' which knows no posterity, only the present tense of a pagan Nazi mythology. He needed *total* victory or nothing. He needed the obliteration of both 'West' and 'East' and a world unified in the sign of the swastika over endless hecatombes, otherwise the war was hardly worth being waged. This negative consistency, and not the alleged 'ignorance of the corporal' had made him totally impervious to arguments coming from the Moltke-Schlieffen school. However, social-liberal and conservative German statesmen of the Weimar republic who had nothing to do with Hitler's new empire simply believed, and in terms of a 'naturalistic' conception of politics where human 'nature' is conceived of in Hobbesian terms, with very good reason, that they were following the traditional patterns of 'German' policy: bringing the 'natural' Eastern ally into play when the West had become intolerably self-righteous and oppressive. In fact, they were right in many respects, and hardly any *moral* reproach can be made to them even in retrospect. Above all, there is no such moral authority in the name of which such remarks could be made. Wilson's moralizing politics were the least suitable for the role of an arbiter because his liberal pacifism lent itself easily to the chauvinistic-egoistic interpretation of German responsibility by Clemenceau, a chauvinism which ended in Versailles, and in the simple reversal of an unjust *German* peace dictated to France in 1871. Further, it is simply not true that France or England were champions of democracy as against

Rapallo Germany. The post-First World War English record in Ireland, the establishment of, or benevolent support lent to, mini-dictators in Eastern Europe as guarantees against communism by French and British politicians, are sufficient refutation of such claims. Nor is the standard criticism (otherwise valid), according to which Rapallo made it possible for the German military to transgress the Versailles restrictions particularly convincing morally. On the one hand, Versailles regulations were no absolute obstacles to war, on the other hand, Hitler cannot be 'deduced' from von Seeckt's complicity with the Soviet military, from the latter's efforts to maintain a legitimate level of national defense. There was, however, one point, and an ominous one in view of the possibility of a *new Rapallo*, which *cannot be morally defended* at all: *the treaty was clearly and consciously aimed against Poland, her strength, even her existence.* The liberal Wirth, then Chancellor, spoke a language in his conversation with the conservative Brockdorff-Rantzau, July 19, 1922, the message of which Poles would never forget for more than half a century: 'I state something without reluctance: Poland must be finished. This is the goal at which my politics is aiming . . . I will not sign any treaty through which Poland would be strengthened . . . in this point I am in full agreement with the military, in particular with General von Seeckt.'[29]

The main beneficiary of a new Rapallo can only be a conservative Soviet nomenklatura which intends to maintain the present system of oppression without even the most meagre inner reforms. The latter, the resolute rejection of all social reforms, has been, since the overthrow of Khrushchev, so manifestly a collective will of the nomenklatura that it can only be missed either deliberately or by what can only be termed a narcissistic preoccupation with one's own interests and problems. And for an arch-conservative and oppressive USSR of the post-Khrushchev era a 'new Rapallo' would bring, above all, a necessary *cordon sanitaire* around an unruly Eastern Europe.

A second, even more obvious pro-Soviet result of a new Rapallo would be the expulsion of the United States from the European continent by Germans and therefore in a way which does not imply direct American–Soviet confrontation. Such an action by the West Germans would be the only way to achieve an American evacuation of Europe given the specific instability of the American political atmosphere after Vietnam and the extent of the present crisis. A direct Soviet demand would be ignored; a threat would be resisted with almost universal consensus; a German demand, on the other hand, would be treated with disgust and resentment but its effect could only be a new isolationism for the USA together with a new Franco-American treaty, with which the United States could respond to such a demand. It is inconceivable that, under present circumstances, any American administration would put down (if it could at all) German resistance to American presence by force. Therefore, should the USSR have the political courage to take the steps necessary for achieving a new Rapallo, should the nomenklatura find a German partner to this crucial turn, the Second World War would end with an American withdrawal from, and a Soviet tutelage over, Europe.

A further yield of the new Rapallo for the USSR would undoubtedly be its ability to 'import economic reforms'. This has the following meaning. From the early sixties onwards, since the public mention of the necessity of an economic reform is no longer absolute heresy, there have always been public statements, sometimes authoritative central committee decisions, to the effect that the system of the 'socialist economy' has to be altered. But attempts at reform have either remained empty declarations or failed disastrously (with the sole exception of Hungary which advertised a – never realized – *full* reform but which managed to implement a *partial agricultural* reform) because the nomenklatura has always wanted the impossible: economic change without social change. The very idea of conceiving a developed economy which works according to the standards of purposive rationality where the very basis of such rationality, a market of a kind, is fragmented by tyrannical political intervention, is a new chapter in the timeless chronicle of squaring the circle. On the other hand, even the distorted consciousness of the nomenklatura realizes that restoring a genuine (non-simulated and non-fragmented) market implies social consequences that could prove uncontrollable for the *nomenklatura*. A new Rapallo would solve all the dilemmas of the nomenklatura from an economic viewpoint, at least in the short run. A confederated Germany, which would produce according to the standards of purposive market rationality (*in this respect*, the GDR would, in all probability, be integrated into the whole of Germany) is a sufficiently large unit to cater for the ardent needs of the USSR; its very existence would solve the East German problem. 'Catering' means here investments and the supply of high quality products both for industry and household consumption in exchange for Soviet raw materials and East European agricultural products. For all practical purposes, this would solve the economic tasks of economic reforms in Soviet societies without the need to change anything in terms of social structure, the supreme wish of all modernizing, but arch-conservative ruling elites.

What would be German, Eastern and Western, gain from a new Rapallo? Above all, the *symbolic satisfaction* of national unity of a kind, German confederation, *a cultural*, rather than political, unity, and, as we have argued, one based on a considerable reduction and self-reduction of liberties. Such a symbolic-cultural German reunification would not exist without new contradictions; for example, Germany would become, especially as a result of the vacuum created by the American abandonment of its commitment to Europe, much more powerful than it has hitherto been, while at the same time, being dependent on the USSR in all external matters, Germany could not put this increased power to use (which would thus become the source of a new European tension). However, with all these provisos, Germany would no longer be a *defeated country* following a new Rapallo, a status that has persistently plagued the whole nation for four decades now. For any community for which this symbolic restoration of self-esteem is more important than political freedoms and the freedoms of her immediate neighbors, this is a satisfactory solution.

Furthermore, there are quite obvious *economic* advantages offered by a new Rapallo for at least two German generations. Recession has finally hit the powerful West German economy and there is, this time, no 'American medicine'. On the contrary, the United States passes on a good portion of its own economic burdens, in particular those stemming from its gigantic budget deficit, to European countries, and in this scenario, it is the most powerful who suffers. But, in a broader sense, at least one of the factors causing the present depression is that Western capitalist industry has arrived, once again, near to the 'limits to accumulation'. A new Rapallo, with the vast possibilities of investments in an underinvested Soviet Russian economy could provide a stimulus to profits and employment, in Germany. In fact, this could become a West German version of the Marshall Plan, with beneficial results for at least the donor, and with some specific advantages. One of them would be that Eastern Europe could be turned into a vast supply region for agricultural goods for Germany with a price structure lower than those of the EEC and which is guaranteed by the *political* structure of prices in the Soviet systems. The guarantor of such a price system would be, of course, the main beneficiary on the Eastern side, the Soviet nomenkla-tura. Further, the confederation would integrate East German industry into an all-German market. No doubt this would not proceed without contradictions and unpredictable results precisely because economic changes always imply social changes. But if it can be implemented, German industrial might would know no competitor in Europe, and only the United States in the Western world. Finally, German investments in Soviet societies would enjoy an almost colonial advantage: the labor force there is not unionized and does not, therefore, enjoy any collective rights to protest.

As perhaps the most unequivocally victorious party, the status of the GDR leadership would be greatly enhanced in the wake of a new Rapallo. Its leaders could congratulate themselves on achieving one of the most resounding and most unexpected political triumphs in modern history. If a new Rapallo did eventuate, Ulbricht, this dislikable satrap of Soviet hegemony, would appear in retrospect as a German Cavour. For, indeed, such a victory would have been achieved against overwhelming odds: not just against the might of the USA, against the determination, evident some decades ago, of almost the whole German nation, to eliminate the 'Soviet zone of occupation', but occasionally against the will of the Soviet masters as well. The GDR leadership, this most tenacious, and at the same time, homogeneously reactionary social force, which played a pioneering public role in the elimination of the Czech reforms (for which reason one can suspect a similar clandestine role in the case of the Polish reforms), would become, after the Russian apparatus, the leading political power in all matters East European. This, again, is a fairly logical conclusion of a new Rapallo, for two reasons. The relative economic weight of the 'socialist federative state of Middle Germany' would, in comparison to other countries of the region, grow tremendously as a result of confederation; it would not only outweigh a chronically bankrupt Poland but its traditional industrial competitor, Czechoslovakia, as well. Further, while the GDR, as a member of the German confederation, would have a decisive say in internal German affairs (which means a say in crucial European events), it is inconceivable that it should sever ties, political, economic *and military*, with the Soviet bloc.

At this point we must address the likely effects of a new Rapallo on the future of European military alliances. The neutralization of Germany, which would be the main effect, does not 'involve', but literally means the end of Nato. And there is no point here to try to foretell what foreign policy alternatives the rest of Western Europe and the United States would opt for in such a situation. As far as the Soviet bloc is concerned, however, at this juncture the *formal* dismantling of the Warsaw Pact would seem to be a logical step which, of course, would require some kind of an ideological resolution on the part of the nomenklatura. But one must not forget that Stalin, precisely at a time when he strengthened his hold over communist parties which were coming to power, dissolved the Comintern. The nomenklatura has traditionally had the courage to make apparently momentous, but in fact only nominal, decisions to change or disband seemingly eternal institutions. In addition, while dismantling the Warsaw Pact would have an obvious propaganda advantage, it would not affect the Soviet political and military integration of Eastern Europe (of which the Warsaw Pact is a facade and an external outcome, not its basis or its genuine organizational framework). Finally, and perhaps most importantly, it would leave the Soviet Union with any number of available options.

A more immediately tangible effect of a new Rapallo would, of course, be a *German peace treaty*. Khrushchev tried to blackmail the Western powers during the Berlin crises in the early sixties with a separate Soviet–East German peace treaty. A new Rapallo would, or at least could, bring a separate peace treaty between a (confederated) Germany and the USSR, with the following immediate results. Firstly, in all probability, such a separate peace treaty would not be recognized by the Western powers, allied in a war against Germany, and above all not by the United States. Therefore such a result for a new Rapallo would leave Germany, obviously only formally, but not insignificantly, in friendly relations with the USSR, having a formal peace treaty, but in an extremely unfriendly relation to the West, in a formal state of war. Secondly, this turn of events would *formally* put an end to the Yalta system of partitioning the world between the superpowers into agreed (or covertly recognized) zones of influences, a system which, strangely in this world of rampant conspiracy theories, has operated almost unnoticed for 40 years, if not without hitches, nonetheless continuously.

However, the major issue involved in discussing the 'new Rapallo' is the fate, perhaps even the nominal sovereignty, of Poland. The simple raising of the question of Polish nominal sovereignty seems to be absurd. However, our reason for raising the matter is that it stems from so-called authoritative Polish sources. We recall that among all the thinly veiled threats addressed by consecutive Polish governments to an unruly populace in the turbulent years between 1968 and 1981, but with special emphasis in the last months before the introduction of martial law by the government of General Jaruzelski, the first and foremost was the remark, strange in itself, that Polish sovereignty was being endangered by oppositional demands, in particular by Solidarity activity. Now this momento can mean only one thing: the Soviet leaders, who had already spelt out similar threats through Marshall Grechko in Spring 1969, forcing Dubček to resign, had made it clear that, should Solidarity go too far, or rather should it not withdraw from its actual positions, and should Polish communists further hesitate to crack down on the rebels 'because of false patriotic feelings incompatible with the class positions of Marxism-Leninism', the problem would be resolved directly by Soviet Russian actors, the sovereignty of Poland will be abolished, and the country integrated into the Soviet Union. For such an act there are, apart from the long forcible affiliation of parts of Poland with the Romanov empire, historical antecedents in the ideology and consciousness of the nomenklatura. Kristian Gerner correctly remarked about the Soviet view of Polish sovereignty: 'The Bolsheviks could apparently never reconcile themselves with the fact that the resurrected Polish state slipped out of their hands and that they could not bring it under their own domination in 1920: the Soviet Foreign Minister from May, 1939, Molotov, called the Polish republic "the monstrous bastard of the Peace of Versailles" and Stalin mocked "pardon the expression, a 'state' ".'[30] But, deeper still, the following general considerations of Gerner have to be taken into consideration when we try to size up the chances of Poland after the new Rapallo:

The Polish nation is situated, on the east–west axis, between Germans and East Slavs – the latter dominated by the Russians. Whenever Prussia or Germany and Russia or the USSR have been strong, the Poles have had great difficulties in defending their national independence. It is significant that Polish state sovereignty was reborn in 1918, when both Germany and Russia were temporarily weakened, and that sovereignty ceased once these countries had regained strength again and joined forces in 1939 . . . relations with Germany are, so to speak, the other side of the Polish–

Russian/Soviet ones. The original reason behind the establishment of the South-East and Central European empire of the USSR was to help safeguard the Russians from any possible threat from Germany. Seen from a Polish perspective, the nature of *her* relations to (West) Germany should affect her relations to the USSR as well. The agreement with Bonn in late 1970 eroded the very foundations, at least theoretically, for Poland's subordination to the USSR, i.e. the USSR in its capacity as the power which could – and would – defend the western frontier of Poland against (West) German revanchism and revisionism. The potential significance of Bonn's *Ostpolitik* in fact was touched upon in the Polish press.[31]

The following conclusions can be drawn from these correct and seminal remarks. Firstly, as Poland has always had her chances when Germany and Russia (USSR) were simultaneously weak, and inversely, it has invariably proved fatal for her sovereignty (in the nineteenth century, in 1939) when both were strong, it follows, at least logically, that a new Rapallo poses an equal threat to Poland. Secondly, while it is theoretically true that the *Neue Ostpolitik* could have eliminated a good part of the legitimizing ideology of Soviet predominance over Poland, and could have contributed to its increased sovereignty, the fact is that it did not. Moreover, to the extent that increased West German nationalism and concessions to an expansionist Soviet politics eroded the emancipatory potentials of the *Ostpolitik*, it turned into an *objectively anti-Polish* policy.

What we are confronting here is the whole internal tension of *Ostpolitik*. *Ostpolitik* was originally conceived as the reconciliation of Germany and the Soviet Union (together with other East European nations affected by Hitler's devastation) and as nothing else. This original goal has been achieved with flying colors, to the lasting glory of its architects. East Europeans who had experienced another Germany, are in no position to deny this. However, in practice, *Ostpolitik* has increasingly been harboring other initiatives. For instance, German 'advice' and German 'mediation' in relation to East European affairs is frequently given, though, apart from some limited success with the GDR, these have been utterly ineffectual. But at least it can be stated in all fairness that, up until Poland 1981, such efforts were at least aimed at charitable relations with the persecuted.

This ineffectual but benevolent model changed dramatically with the attitude adopted by German Social Democracy towards the last Polish revolution. Since this is vital to the debate over a possible new Rapallo, we quote extensively from the Polish democratic opposition. *Uncensored Poland*, a news bulletin of the opposition, carries the following statement:

In an open letter with today's date [18 November, 1985], Professor Edward Lipinski, the economist, 97, a founding member of KOR (and we would add, a lifelong socialist from legendary, almost prehistoric, times), tells Brandt that he has earned a great deal of sympathy and respect in Poland. Therefore, the Professor is all the more saddened by the news that Brandt is unable or unwilling to accept Wałesa's invitation. Lipinski notes with bitterness that a long line of politicians from the SPD have visited Poland since the introduction of martial law, *but have avoided like the plague all contact with Solidarity or opposition figures.* When Brandt arrives, says Lipinski, he will meet politicians who deprived Polish workers of their own free trade unions, who sent troops and police against them, who on a daily basis violate, or tolerate the violation, of human and civil rights, who keep Solidarity and opposition activists in prison. Lipinski says that he has lived a long time and knows that at times it is necessary to seek understanding even in situations like this. But he does not think it necessary or useful for the political interests represented by Brandt for him to discuss German–Polish relations only with the authorities of 'this part of the great Soviet empire,' while ignoring the opposition which represents a substantial section of the nation, perhaps the majority . . . *There are good reasons for fearing that, if SPD politicians go on maintaining contacts exclusively with the authorities, independent opinion in Poland will interpret their attitude as a consequence of German–Russian relations rather than as something aimed at bringing the German and Polish nations closer together.* The Professor believes in Brandt's good intentions but *stirring up fears in Poland that the Germans are playing a political game directed against the majority of the nation,* or which at least ignore its aspirations, would be a disservice to our common future.[32]

The detailed analysis of the internal German situation in dealing with Soviet strategy is important because it is only on this basis that we can understand the main strategic line of Soviet expansionism in Europe. The Soviet Union combines the policy of making open threats (referring, of course, to its vulnerable position) with suggesting (and perhaps secretly making) offers of a way out of the unification impasse. While it sometimes commits mistakes (such as the mass arrests of independent peace activists in East Germany in the aftermath of the Bundestag's decision to deploy the Pershing missiles, an act which provoked protest even from Petra Kelly), it is not likely to repeat such mistakes. It will obviously wait either until the CDU-CSU regime is voted out of office in a new election and a (then) overtly unilateralist SPD returns to power or until this trend spills over to part of the right and a national consensus emerges concerning the abandonment of the Western alliance. This would be the historical moment to make a fundamentally new offer for a kind of German reunification. Stalin's successors would make a strong contribution to the legitimization of their repressive rule, if they could come up with one at the right moment. There is no telling whether they will indeed have the historical lucidity adequate for their historical chance. Once, in the hour of despair in 1941, they were capable of doing so. Throwing overboard a policy of divisiveness, they preached and reached a relative national consensus (of course, with the background support of Hitler). The fact is that, adding to the general picture the British situation, where the open crisis of the alliance is only postponed by the renewed Tory electoral victory, a disaster for the country socially and economically, but where the Soviets have no particular move to make, it suffices to wait and see. The Soviets have never had in 40 years such historical openings as these.

1984–5

NOTES

1 Adam Ulam, *Dangerous Relations: The Soviet Union in World Politics, 1970–1982* (New York: Oxford University Press, 1983).
2 Nikita Khrushchev, *Khrushchev Remembers* (Boston: Little Brown, 1971), pp. 332–8.
3 Admittedly, this continuity is not complete. Khrushchev was sometimes much too concerned with inner Soviet political stability to enforce budget cuts that the military resented and which have never happened since. He underestimated, inconsistently, the role of the surface fleet in an expansionist policy. His famous remark made during a visit to London testifies to this. There he suggested that the cruiser *Sverdlov*, on which he made his trip, could be purchased then and there, as only imperialist powers need gigantic fleets (a remark which would not have been to the liking of Admiral Gorshkov, the head of perhaps the greatest single fleet in the world). However, these were inconsistencies *within* a policy formula that has remained valid.
4 André Glucksmann, *La Force du Vertige* (Paris: Grasset, 1983), p. 52. Our translation.
5 Victor Zaslavsky, *The Neo-Stalinist State* (Armonk, NY: M. E. Sharpe, 1982).
6 F. Dostoevsky, *The Devils* (Harmondsworth: Penguin, 1957), p. 258.
7 Cornelius Castoriadis, *Devant la guerre* (Paris: Fayard, 1981), especially pp. 251–64.
8 See F. Fehér, A. Heller, G. Márkus, *Dictatorship over Needs* (Oxford: Basil Blackwell, 1981). [See a slightly different interpretation of Castoriadis's position in Andrew Arato, 'Facing Russia', *Revue européenne des sciences sociales*, 27:86 (Geneva, 1989), pp. 269–93. *1989*]
9 See Agnes Heller, 'Legitimation' in Fehér, Heller and Márkus, *Dictatorship over Needs*.
10 One such attempt to deny this can be seen with Rudolf Augstein who, in the pages of *Der Spiegel*, relies on the authority of Roy Medvedev, the oppositional Khrushchevite historian. Against this legend the following facts should be recounted. From the time (mainly under Catherine the Great) when Russia began to modernize and 'Europeanize' its bureaucratic system and social affairs, including its legislative processes, a Russian political presence in European affairs, especially in Central Europe (by which we mean the areas now called Germany and Austria and related parts of what was then the Habsburg empire) was clear, unambiguous, and menacing. It is the authoritative view of Albert Sorel that, in its early crucial years, the French revolution was saved by the fact that both Austria and Prussia, fighting each other to partition Poland, were

mesmerized and paralysed by their common fear of Russia. After the collapse of Napoleon, when the legendary Cossacks were very materially present in Paris, two of *Metternich's*(!) main dilemmas (see H. Kissinger, *A World Restored* (Boston: Houghton Mifflin, 1957)) were whether the Russian army would return at all and, generally, how to terminate the 'revolutionary' policy of Alexander I (where 'revolutionary' simply meant the upsetting of the conservative *status quo ante*). Ever since the French revolutionary wars, in which Russian armies and fleet fought in Italy and Switzerland and tried frequently to gain strongholds in the Mediterranean, Russian imperial interest in the disintegrating Turkish empire and in the revival of more or less independent Balkan countries with strong pro-Russian loyalties (especially Greece) has been explicit. In the 1848–9 revolutionary crisis, Russia served first as a general warning to the much too sanguinary revolutionaries in Germany and the Habsburg monarchy and later as the actual savior of the monarchy against Hungarian republicanism. Louis Bonaparte was greeted, as newly elected president, as the happy medium between the 'Reds' and the Cossacks, both actual French alternatives.

Although suffering a reverse in the Crimean war, after a second wave of modernization, the 1861 emancipation of the serfs, Russia was back in full swing at the center of Bismarck's strategic considerations. He simply could not imagine German unification without at least tacit Russian backing. All this has hitherto been common knowledge. It needed a unilateralist historical consciousness to create a legend of a Russia that is traditionally uninvolved in attempts at dominating European politics.

11   See Bahro's statement in *Le Nouvel Observateur*, June 26, 1982, p. 37. G. Grass said the following to *Newsweek* on September 5, 1983, p. 52: 'In the long run we should aim at developing a new security system, a nuclear-free zone, for example, that would make Nato and the Warsaw Pact unnecessary. If that is "neutralization" or "Finlandization", I say, "Why not?" I admire the Finns, these people who have managed to preserve their independence in spite of their long and open border with the Soviet Union.' Grass is as ruthlessly outspoken here, as in his earlier, overwhelmingly anti-Soviet period. He hardly beats about the bush, and as it is very unlikely that he would not know *what kind of independence* the Finns are able to preserve, we can see a glimpse of a new Europe that embraces Soviet predominance for more limited gains (or illusions), nationalist in nature.

12   Sigrid Meuschel, 'Neo-nationalism and the West German peace movement's reaction to the Polish military coup', *Telos* 56 (Summer 1983), pp. 119–20.

13   Peter Brandt and Herbert Ammon, eds, *Die Linke und die nationale Frage* (Hamburg: Rowohlt, 1981), pp. 97–8 (our translation). In what follows we take our documentation mostly from this volume. We radically disagree with the editors on all counts, but we regard their selections as the paragon of an objective and knowledgeable presentation of an extremely debatable and sensitive problem complex.

14   Ibid., pp. 36–7. We identify with Schumacher's conceptions to a very great extent and simply cannot see any reason other than Brandt and Ammon's Leninism (within their 'national Bolshevism') that would justify their using the term socialist in quotes with Schumacher. (For Schumacher's option meant

accepting the Western alliance, but *not* the Western system.) In particular, we endorse fully his conception of the Soviet Union.

15 Ibid., p. 343.
16 See part II above.
17 Brandt and Ammon, eds, *Die Linke und die nationale Frage*, pp. 244–5. (The text was published in *Der Spiegel* in 1965; our translation.)
18 Ibid., p. 310.
19 Herbert Helbig, *Die Träger der Rapallo-Politik* (Göttingen: Vandenhoeck and Ruprecht, 1958), pp. 38–9 (our translation).
20 E. H. Carr, *The Bolshevik Revolution*, (Harmondsworth: Penguin, 1973), vol. 3, pp. 306–7.
21 Ibid., p. 375.
22 Ibid., pp. 311–12.
23 In *Erinnerungen eines deutschen Revolutionärs* (Memoirs of a German Revolutionary) (Cologne: Verlag Wissenschaft und Politik, 1974).
24 From the preface to Goebbels's published diaries of his later years, *The Goebbels Diaries*, tr. and ed. Louis L. Loechner (London: Hamish Hamilton, 1958), p. xx.
25 Helbig, *Die Träger*, p. 49.
26 Carr, *Bolshevik Revolution*, p. 380 (emphasis added).
27 [However, there are people who, for eminent reasons, cannot be convinced of the validity of this argument concerning either the 'old' or the 'new' Rapallo. Let us listen to Adam Michnik – from 1990: 'German resistance to Polish participation in the two-plus-four conference that will arrange for reunification suggests that Chancellor Helmut Kohl yearns nostalgically for grand diplomacy in the style of Rapallo or Yalta. But Poles remember that from Rapallo a straight road led to the Ribbentrop-Molotov pact and the invasion and occupation of their country.' Adam Michnik, 'Notes on the revolution', *New York Times Magazine*, March 11, 1990, p. 45.]
28 Carr, *Bolshevik Revolution*, p. 380.
29 Helbig, *Die Träger*, pp. 168–9.
30 Kristian Gerner, *The Soviet Union and Central Europe in the Post-war Era* (Lund: University of Lund Press, 1983), p. 56.
31 Ibid., pp. 41, 62.
32 *Uncensored Poland*, 23 (December 10, 1985), p. 7 (emphasis added).

Part V

Gorbachev's Long March

8

Red Square: The Inglorious End of the Brezhnev Era

CONSPIRACY

The novel by E. Topol and F. Neznansky, *Red Square*, is a story about conspiracy which is in part fiction, in part interpretation, certainly not a document.[1] It is, however, interpretation of a kind whose ultimate 'historical truth claim', although cannot be confirmed, can be very strongly supported by scholarly works of 'Kremlinology'.[2]

The plot, but not its deeper implications, can be summed up in a laconic manner. On January 19, 1982 Semyon Kuzmich Tsvigun, General and First Deputy Chairman of the KGB, Brezhnev's brother-in-law (Tsvigun's wife and Viktoria Brezhneva are sisters), the Secretary General's personal watch-dog around the overambitious Andropov, dies at the age of 64. Although his obituary released by the Tass agency mentioned a 'longlasting illness' as the cause of death, the leaders, so the novel suggests, were fully aware, and the Western press surmised that to all appearances Tsvigun died a violent death, albeit by his own hands. An unusually wide anti-corruption campaign, codenamed Operation Cascade was under way in parallel (this is how Neznansky and Topol account for their case), significantly one which had been instigated by the central committee secretary and the second man of the Soviet oligarchy, Suslov, but *not* by the whole of the *politburo*. (This is, to repeat, part of the narrative, not a documented historical fact.) As a result of this campaign, approximately 1,500 leading Soviet functionaries and underground economy wheeler-dealers were arrested on the very first day. In the novel, all evidence seemed to point to Tsvigun as the main protector of, and chief profiteer from, a vast network of corruption (termed the 'underground economy'). Tsvigun seemed to have committed suicide, after a violent showdown with the 'purist' Suslov, in a KGB 'safe apartment', to avoid legal consequences. Apparently, Brezhnev accepted the bitter facts. The politburo instructed the legal authorities and the press that, 'in the interest of the party', the compromising fact of the involvement of the second highest KGB functionary in corruption and blackmarketeering, as well as his subsequent suicide, should not be publicized. However, and this could not escape the attention of Russia-watchers, Brezhnev did not sign the obituary of his brother-in-law (nor did, of course, Suslov). This circumstance further corroborated the assumption that Brezhnev accepted the KGB version of Tsvigun's death, although he had very good reason for doubt: there were unmistakable indications that 'Operation Cascade' had been undertaken against him. Despite Brezhnev's apparent resignation, the novel starts with the surprising mission assigned to Igor Shamrayev, a middle-aged and middle-placed legal bureaucrat, a senior investigator from the chief public prosecutor's office, to investigate Tsvigun's death and its *genuine* circumstances. Shamrayev was curtly ordered back from a frosty, but long-awaited holiday in the Crimea by instructions sent him via secret army telecommunication channels. This could only mean that, although no one questioned the KGB version openly, Brezhnev smelled conspiracy.

But does this whole plot make sense to anyone with an elementary knowledge of Soviet reality? Does the all-powerful secretary general, the head, if only a *primus inter pares* of a tremendous power machine need a non-entity to 'investigate' a political case, in a society where the 'legal' or 'illegal' character of criminal cases is defined, not uncovered, by the state? What can a Shamrayev find out that Brezhnev cannot by simply issuing a few orders through his habitual channels? In fact, Brezhnev, who is in this novel an almost perfect copy of the cornered, shrewd and ruthless Louis XI in Walter Scott's *Quentin Durward*, was perfectly aware, despite delusions on all sides, that Tsvigun had not committed suicide at all, rather that he had fallen victim to a KGB ambush. However, for reasons that will gradually become clear to the reader, at the given moment he was simply not in the position to order wholesale arrests and fathom the mystery. Further, he had to find out who (meaning which of the rival security organizations) liquidated Tsvigun, and, above all, to what extent they had penetrated Tsvigun's secrets.

The confused political situation in early 1982 unleashed a bitter struggle of rival power centers. 'Operation Cascade' means 'KGB versus KGB' (Andropov against Tsvigun), but it also means the Suslov-backed KGB leadership's bid for the position of the secretary general (Andropov versus Brezhnev). For the time being, the arch-rivals, the KGB and the MVD (the latter is an equivalent to what is called Ministry of the Interior in Western countries with, of course, incomparably wider powers) forget about their usual interdepartmental clashes. They combine forces to fight the 'Brezhnev clan' with Suslov's political support, and whereas Suslov dies during the course of the plot, Andropov, the new candidate for supreme power, emerges from the background silently, ominously and unperturbed by the momentary fiasco. Further, the combined KGB-MVD forces have some of their customary

skirmishes with another investigating and prosecuting organization, the chief
public prosecutor's office, a largely ineffective and nominal body which,
although it has armies of special investigators and possesses wide formal
powers, is in fact totally dependent on the central committee or the KGB or
both. On his part, Brezhnev, for the moment not controlling either the KGB
or the MVD, his usual power instruments, fights back with the tremendous
reserves of the army in his double capacity of 'Marshall' and 'Head of the
Defense Council of the USSR'.[3] Whenever Brezhnev needs something, he
uses the army communication system, the army personnel (to which at a
certain crucial point of the plot he even gives the order to *crush* an eventual
KGB-MVD resistance with arms, if need be), the army intelligence network
(to have the protagonist Shamrayev murdered, once the work so crucial for
Brezhnev has been done). The second weapon Brezhnev uses is less
definable, even in Soviet terms. There is a network at his disposal which can
only be called 'The Secretary General's personal guard and apparatus', an
organization which certainly does not have an even semi-legal standing in any
Soviet government and party charter. His chief bodyguard, General Zharov,
a fairly unsophisticated but shrewd giant, commands a contingent of armed
men (who eventually disarm an MVD surveillance team and dismantle their
electronic equipment spying on Shamrayev). There is no telling to what
authority, if not to Brezhnev personally, these people belong or are accountable. Further, there is Brezhnev's 'personal office' which issues binding
orders to all levels of authorities (army commanders, the Main Directorate of
all camps and prisons of the USSR, passport office heads and the like), and
which constitutes his 'private estate'. In perfect imitation of Scott's absolute
rulers, Brezhnev gives a written mandate (as kings used to give their seals to
their confidants which carried their authority) to instruct every private
person and state official to obey unconditionally the insignificant Special
Investigator, Igor Shamrayev, then badly needed by the ruler, but already
marked for violent death.

But, one might ask, is the nonsensical issue of 'whodunnit' the cause of all
this paraphernalia? Does Brezhnev have such a sentimental heart to seek
personal revenge over the murder of his brother-in-law, and if so, is he
lacking the means of doing so other than a Soviet James Bond? Of course,
Brezhnev could not care less about the personal aspect of the story. It is also
true that there are simpler ways in the Soviet regime to establish responsibility. In an outburst of what is for the moment an impotent rage, Brezhnev
yells 'Let's have the whole MVD Intelligence Section arrested! We shall soon
find out whose orders they were carrying out!' (p. 342). To repeat, unlike
'normal' cases in Soviet government procedures, this time Brezhnev is only
boasting. A politburo meeting is convened for February 4, on which, and
Brezhnev knows this all too well, his enemies plan to produce *material*
evidence that not just his totally corrupt family, but Brezhnev himself is a

seriously compromising factor for the regime. Until the meeting, his powers are limited, and if he loses on February 4, he will have lost all.

The paradox of Soviet law comes to the surface on this basis. On the one hand, the period of Lenin and Stalin, that of Tchekist *troikas* (three Tchekists 'sitting in court', establishing 'evidence', spelling out sentences and occasionally executing them personally) is over. Over and done with the 'heroic age' of Soviet jurisprudence in which vast terrains of social life were not covered by legal regulations at all: as, firstly, law was anyhow a 'bourgeois formality', and, secondly, such formalization of rights and duties would have been a waste of time in a context where people disappeared by the millions at a hint of the supreme ruler (or minor rulers). Since Khrushchev, this has gradually changed. There is now a vast body of Soviet legislation, laws and decrees formulated in a manner which is technically not very unlike the legislation of Western countries. There are learned Soviet lawyers and investigators who are well versed in their profession, capable forensic experts equipped with the most modern gadgets. But what is the function of all this? Simply to serve arbitrary and tyrannical actions, authorities and persons who are totally impervious to such niceties as 'the truth of the matter', 'legal facts', 'evidence' and the like. Just a few examples taken from the novel will suffice here. Pirozhkov, Deputy Chairman of the KGB, plainly tells Shamrayev, in reply to the latter's annoying queries about the *real* causes of Tsvigun's death, 'The press announcement about General Tsvigun's illness was a decision of the Politburo' (p. 37), and in Soviet terms, this is a *legally satisfactory* explanation. The *binding orders* issued by Brezhnev's office are *personal* decrees of a sovereign which have no legal standing even in terms of Soviet legality, but which are the expression of the will of a sovereign.

The genuine and in no way romantic need for a shrewd investigator, who otherwise is a political nonentity, is the following. One of Tsvigun's cronies and gobetweens in the shady deals, a young Georgian, had installed a secret and very sound-sensitive tape recorder in Brezhnev's family dacha, partly because he was infantile enough not to know what kind of fire he was playing with, partly to take a personal revenge on Tsvigun. The tapes recorded Brezhnev's totally cynical conversations about his own regime, in a tone of utter contempt, which, except for the 'purists', seems to be the prevailing tenor of the apparatus about their externally much advertised soviety. If the tapes reached Brezhnev's enemies, they would constitute material evidence of his 'unworthiness' to be the head of the Soviet state and of the party. And since the enemies believed that the tapes were in Tsvigun's apartment, they had him murdered. Brezhnev is then not involved in any kind of sentimental puzzle-solving concerning Tsvigun's death. In the mirror of this popular fiction, he appears as the paragon of shrewd and ruthless sovereign ruler. Had he had his own way, he would have whole sections of the Soviet intelligence organizations arrested, for the only question bothering him is their loyalty or disloyalty to him. Anyhow, his myrmidons would eventually find the person who was, in a physical sense, the murderer of Tsvigun, and if not, the General would be just added to the hecatombes on which Brezhnev, and Tsvigun himself, ascended to power. *But the tapes have to be found and destroyed;* this weapon has to be extorted from the hands of his enemies. Therefore, in this unique case, Brezhnev is interested *in facts,* and he needs a skillful and experienced investigator. This is why the historical novel *à la Walter Scott* dons the guise of a thriller.

What is the *social content and function* of the conspiracy (beyond the usual frictions and jockeying for more power between leading figures of a totalitarian apparatus)? The authors invent an extremely important document, the so-called 'Program of the New Course Government' which was found in Suslov's writing desk right after his death and which, in all probability, is the common work of Suslov and Andropov. We are going to quote this important and lengthy document in full not, of course, because we believe in its authenticity but because we regard it as the *best interpretation* of what Andropov's rule was destined to be. The unique document reads as follows:

Points for February 4

1   Report: "Evils of L. I. Brezhnev's cult of the leader"
    a Defeats in foreign policy:
        – failure of peaceful occupation of Afghanistan in 1978, feet-dragging in active Sovietization of Afghanistan today;
        – delayed reaction to outbreak of anti-Soviet trade-union movement in Poland, prolonged liberalism towards Solidarity leaders:
        – indecisiveness over expanding Soviet spheres of influence in Middle East, leading to weakening of our bargaining positions for an outlet to the Persian Gulf and loss of control over Arab oil.
    b In internal policy:
        – liberalism (afraid of the West) over anti-Soviet dissident movement. Solzhenytsin. Sakharov; permitting Jewish, Armenian and German emigrations, which has led to re-emergence in Union Republics of nationalistic aspirations directed towards secession from USSR;
        – collapse of planned economy and emergence of "unofficial" economy (figures and materials from Cascade);
        – members of Brezhnev's family involved in bribery and corruption (Cascade materials);
        – result of above points – weakening of ideological education of workers, destruction of Soviet people's faith in Communist ideals, critical attitude of people to existing authority.

2   Decisions of Politburo meeting:
a Suggest Brezhnev retire. In case of agreement by him, not publish report "Evils of the cult of the leader", see Brezhnev off with honor, awards, etc. In case of refusal, remove from Politburo, publish report "Evils of the cult of the leader" to May Central Committee plenary meetings;
b form "New Course Government" to ensure following measures as soon as possible.

In foreign policy:
– immediate total Sovietization of Afghanistan;
– final destruction of Solidarity forces in Poland;
– take decisive advantage of West's inability to oppose active moves by Soviet Union, as indicated by events in Afghanistan and Poland. Therefore, maximum military support for pro-Communist popular movements in Middle East countries, including direct military intervention to secure control within next one to two years of Persian Gulf and Arab oil;
– extend military and other support for Communist and anti-Imperialist forces in countries of Latin America and Africa;
– take advantage of growing rift between NATO-countries, widen it, and bring about isolation of USA in Capitalist world.
– Successful realization of these points within a concrete timespan (1–2 years) will be final stage in preparation for Sovietization of Europe, Middle East and American continent.

In internal policy:
– harsh eradication of dissident movements, religious and spiritual sects, cessation of all forms of emigration;
– census of population capable of working and mandatory attachment of workers to enterprises, collective and Soviet farms. This will guarantee sharp improvement of economy and permit supply of food products through network of industrial distributors exclusively to working population;
– eradication of all forms of "unofficial economy" and other manifestations of anti-Soviet and Capitalist aspirations. For this purpose conduct series of exemplary trials with public execution of capital punishment;
– in connection with new foreign and internal policy tasks, increase numerical strength of Soviet Army by increasing compulsory service period from 2 to 5 years in land forces and from 3 to 7 years in Navy. (pp. 258–60)

Later we will return to the social and political problems involved in the 'New Course Government Program'. At this point, the relevant question is as follows. Does a historical novel based on, and dealing exclusively with, conspiracy *theory* provide an explanatory framework for a rational understanding of the word?

In Soviet history, it was Stalin's rule that brought conspiracy theory to full bloom as a universal world explanation. Under Stalin, belief in the omnipresence of old-time and more recent 'conspirators' against the new order was required by everyone. All problems were blamed on these conspirators, and a rational understanding of the new society was replaced by a totally mystifying indoctrination. The spirit of witchhunt, thus released, reached its peak with the Moscow trials. Khrushchev did what he could to eliminate the omnipresence of conspiracy theory. His so-called 'secret speech' made it sufficiently clear that whatever one thought of the defendants, conspirators they were not. His first, very reluctant, steps to unravel the famous case that had triggered the avalanche, namely the murder of Kirov, proved that probably one single conspirator may have been responsible: Stalin himself. Further, whenever genuine conspiracies did take place (as in the case of Beria, in 1953, or in that of his unrepentantly Stalinist colleagues in April, 1957), he made these events public.

But the advent to power of the collective body of the Soviet oligarchy represented a *spectacular return to conspiracy*, but not as a theory, rather as the normal form of power struggles at the top. To start with, the very rule of the oligarchy was established in a formal coup against Khrushchev, in October, 1964. Further, although the power centers have been to some extent separated in order to prevent any one man from becoming dictator over a whole social stratum which runs a totalitarian dictatorship, this separation of centers of power only opened a period of constant conspiracies as the unacknowledged course of Soviet policy-making. Conspiracies invariably aim at redistributing power positions already occupied by other individuals and groups. Thus, it is proper to approach major political changes of Soviet society as an uninterrupted series of conspiracies. For this reason, *Red Square*, a story about conspiracy, is a fullblooded historical novel, rather than just a 'Soviet thriller'.

THE UNDERGROUND ECONOMY

In terms of the novel, the overt goal of Operation Cascade was the liquidation of the 'underground economy' which exists in reality, not just in this fiction, and which is a complex network of heterogeneous but, as far as Soviet law is concerned, equally illegal, activities. The volume of these 'underground economic activities' (according to the anti-fraud group and the chief public prosecutor's office), as estimated by the novel, can be put somewhere around 20–30 billion dollars, a staggering figure (if, of course, one accepts the official rouble–dollar parity). The agglomerate of these operations consists of disparate activities, such as common fraud, embezzlement of state funds, bribery from individuals and from collective economic units (factories, kolkhozes and the like) in exchange for such 'favors' as admission in tertiary education institutions, release of prisoners from camps, state allocation of better flats, etc. Andropov even casually mentions to his fellow conspirator, Scholokov, the Minister of the Interior, that to his knowledge, in Azerbaidzhan even the position of a district party secretary has a fixed price: 120,000 roubles (p. 324). A more dangerous but far from unusual form of underground economic activity is the smuggling of precious Soviet raw materials, canned goods and agricultural products out of the country to the West, disguised as cheap commodities. This, for instance, is how the best Russian caviar was continuously smuggled out in tins wearing the label of a very ordinary sort of fish. The profiteers, among them the All-Union Minister of Fisheries, who was later executed for such transactions, sold the precious goods for huge profits, which they either kept in numbered Swiss bank accounts or, eventually, smuggled back to the country, which was yet another violation of Soviet law. Other underground economic practices are, however, in terms of business ethics, beyond reproach. They are regarded as illegal only under prevailing conditions of Soviet irrationality. Transactions of this kind are, for example, the forbidden marketing of fresh vegetables and flowers from Georgia grown on small household plots.[4] Dealings in hard currency, as well as in all sorts of Western consumer goods, make up an integral part of this unofficial network. However, one important feature of this aspect is to be found precisely in the fact that it cannot be pursued, given the strict state surveillance over tourists, without KGB officials being themselves on the take. Yet another sector of the underground economy strives to produce certain consumer goods in the USSR (naturally, outside the framework of state-planned operations), which are either unavailable for the consumer or available only to those members of the nomenklatura who have access to closed shops.

What is the explanation for the emergence of this vast network of illegal economic activities? The authors' answer is simple but convincing: Soviet society's total technological dependence on the West. *Red Square* is a mini-encyclopedia documenting the presence of Western goods in Soviet life. Consider the following few examples from an endless catalogue. Karakos, head of the investigation department of the chief public prosecutor's office, 'was invariably dressed in a smart general's uniform made of fine English wool, bought in a special foreign-currency shop, although the fashionable shirts and stylish French ties which he sported were out of keeping with it' (p. 45). In the murdered Tsvigun's 'safe apartment' (which also served as a 'love nest' for his permanent lover and the hard currency prostitutes she procured for him): 'All rooms were decorated with vinyl wallpaper imported from Finland and embossed with a pleasant design – wallpaper that would have been the dream of many a Moscow housewife' (p. 71). The noiseless elevator that brings the protagonist to Malenina's office in the anti-fraud squad bears the inscription: made in Germany. She only smokes Marlboro cigarettes and the gadget with which she bugs Galina Brezhneva's love-making scene with her 'Gypsy lover' is American (pp. 100–5). The files the KGB uses are 'not made in our country'; an arrested prostitute who was watching smart apartments for a gang of thieves to which she belongs remarks about the apartment of a foreign-trade ministry functionary: in his flat, which they robbed, 'even the tiles in the lavatory are foreign, and there is a pink wash-basin marked "Made in Sweden" ' (p. 207). The wives and relatives of those arrested in Operation Cascade bring to the Butyrka, the famous Moscow prison, 'French cosmetics that mingled with the aroma of . . . Finnish brisket, Dutch cheese, Arabian fruits . . . – all foreign produce' (p. 227).

Whatever the reason for the underground economy's emergence, the visible result is an ever wider social inequality. On the one hand, 'all Moscow knows that fresh bread made from pure wheat flour can only be bought in four places' (p. 152), all of which are near the areas where the nomenklatura lives. Everyday life for an average Soviet citizen is spent in an incessant standing in line as well as begging for the most insignificant favors in the most humiliating ways (including permission to be buried with one's loved ones, a remarkable scene in this realm of 'realized freedom'). Petty scarcity extends even to the paper used to wrap the high-quality fish the investigators of the chief public prosecutor's office get from the Special Supply Depot (in itself a social prerogative). Thus, sometimes they end up having to wrap the fish in official documents – even sometimes top-secret ones. The protagonist, Shamrayev, lives in such a rundown one-room apartment that the first thing General Zharov, Brezhnev's *garde-de-corps*, offers him for his services is a brand-new one which has perhaps two rooms (p. 145). On the other hand, the apartments of Kosygin's and Podgorny's daughters (in the same building as Tsvigun's 'safe apartment') are equipped with indoor swimming pools. Mrs Mzhavanadze, the wife of the ex-first secretary of the communist party of Georgia (a crony of Brezhnev who, nevertheless, had to be demoted because his shady dealings had become embarrassingly public knowledge in the USSR) is the patron saint and main profit-taker of the diamond black market. At the same time, she is a pal of Galina Brezhneva. The leaders of the worst types of underground economic activities (themselves members of the nomenklatura or persons closely associated with them) have *personal fortunes* that amount to millions.[5]

There is a wide and heterogeneous range of assessments of the underground economy in *Red Square* (and, obviously, in Soviet society as well). The proverbial 'man in the street' regards the tsars of the underground economy (including the Brezhnev clan) as common, albeit successful, thieves. The purists, partisans of the 'New Course Government', have an equally straightforward view – although one that stems from different motives – of this network of economic relations. Baklanov, Shamrayev's colleague and the main conspirator in the chief public prosecutor's office, gives a laconic summary of the purist position: 'The people are used to stealing. In one Georgian film this man says quite openly to his neighbor: "How do you survive? There is nothing to steal at your factory except compressed air!" And even if you jail three million of them it will not help because the rot starts at the top . . . this ruling family has created a vast unofficial industry in the country, a *second New Economic Policy* . . . but we need to unite . . . and bring the country back to health. So that we have people in power with clean hands' (p. 247, emphasis added). This position contains undeniable elements of truth and has the appeal of speaking out against corruption. But the program for which Baklanov engages in conspiracy prescribes 'mandatory attachment of workers to enterprises, collective and Soviet farms' which in plain language means serfdom. Furthermore, Baklanov's main objection is that all this represents a new NEP, that is, a social and economic 'loosening of the screws'. This is why his conversation partner, Shamrayev, calls it, rightly, a policy of 'clean fists', not of 'clean hands'. While corruption at least allows for a certain perverted indulgence, in the complete absence of public liberties all trends that aim at social purification generate a cycle of reprisals resulting in a world worse than the one it replaces. This kind of dynamic can only end up in one of Stalin's 'revolutions from above'.

There is another view of the underground economy – one that is tolerant, albeit skeptical. This is set forth in a remarkable scene involving Brezhnev's policy advisers in a confrontation with Shamrayev that resembles a chapter out of Konrád and Szelényi's *Towards a Class Power of Intellectuals*. All constitutive elements of the book are there: the intellectuals' craving for power, the naïve and complacent belief that Brezhnev, the ruler, is in fact dependent on them, and that he can only choose among the alternatives they recommend (whereas in fact the *only* thing Brezhnev learns from them is faking illness whenever his enemies are too strong); the hope that they only need one or two more years and then, miraculously, a wholesale rationalization of Soviet society will spring out of the will of the 'good' tsar.

Of course, the Brezhnev faction is not entirely amateurish, nor are they 'messianic politicians'. Rather, an unsavory atmosphere of the cynicism of the 'inner circle' reigns supreme among them. They have serious, positive or negative arguments, although usually the negative ones are the stronger. One of them paraphrases the paradox that Besançon has formulated as follows: corruption in the USSR is the embryonic form of the struggle for emancipation of a brutally oppressed civil society.[6] The adviser tries to convince Shamrayev:

A word about the 'unofficial economy.' What is it? A chance phenomenon? A cancer on the body of socialism? Or the consequence of the fact that the collective farms have not justified themselves and our planned light industry is totally useless? And so the 'unofficial' economy appears to compensate for the shortcomings of the official one: it meets seventeen percent of the population's needs in food and industry today . . . If we remain in power we shall have to take the final step – legalize a certain amount of private enterprise. (p. 267)

What is important, and grotesque, is not that all this daydreaming takes place in the antechamber of Brezhnev, whose exclusive parallel preoccupation is planning how to liquidate his enemies (and some of his rescuers). The genuine weakness of such daydreaming, which constantly takes place in 'socialist reality', not just in novels about it, is the one-sided idealization of underground economy as *productive*, a view just as biased as that of their opponents who see only its corrupting effects. However, the negative argument of the adviser is valid beyond any doubt: the New Course government would introduce serfdom, if gradually.

The struggle between the two positions ends in a stalemate that is an almost prophetic anticipation of the stalemate between the Brezhnev and Andropov factions under Chernenko, many years after the novel was written. On a deeper level, these are but two typical reactions to the fundamental feature of Soviet socioeconomic life: *the simultaneous production of scarcity and waste*. Although the New Course document concentrates on the staggering dimensions of waste, everyone with an elementary knowledge of these societies can assess the prospects of predictions about 'the sharp improvement of the Soviet economy' that this unique document contains. However, their critical argument about waste remains valid.

CULTURE

It would be redundant to belabor the obvious in *Red Square:* the total corruption of Soviet intellectual life and the truly barbaric need structure of the nomenklatura. The more interesting question raised by the book is the culture crisis of the 'Soviet way of life' and its cheap domestic palliatives.[7] The main dilemma is *social sanity* versus the *illness* of the social body.

To repeat, the purists have their point: a world whose 'culture' is based on drinking bouts, black market operations with gold and diamonds, orgies with male or female prostitutes, with hoodlums involved in all of these transactions, cannot be a sane society. But who are the advocates of social sanity? First, the various Suslovs and Andropovs, not just politicians responsible for crimes of almost genocidal magnitude, but also sick, misanthropic old men jealous of all pleasures their healthier and younger colleagues can enjoy. Misanthropy and envy are the guardians of social sanity in a society from which joy is banned, motives are kept strictly under surveillance, and the rebellious will is 'scientifically' crushed. This is the sanity of serfdom. Another form of 'social sanity' is represented by the perfectly healthy body coupled with the spiritual make-up of a *Lager Blockführerin*. We are speaking here of Malenina, the head of the anti-fraud squad, an earlier Master of Socialist Sport in gymnastics. Malenina is indeed the ultimate product of a 'civilizing process' with its roots in the Gulag. Like those talented folk artists in Bergen-Belsen who made pretty lampshades from human skin, she is beyond morality. After drinking heavily and listening with Scholokov and other KGB and MVD generals, in Galina Brezhneva's copulation scene with the 'Gypsy', she is so aroused by the exacting task of 'protecting socialist achievements' that she unceremoniously lays the hero in her enormous study, after the following unhypocritical introduction: 'I'll be honest with you. I am a bit drunk. We've just been doing an old bird, listening – you know, there is this American gadget, it can hear you screwing your girl in the bathroom a kilometer away . . . And can you imagine – this old cunt was at it forty minutes and could not come. And the man, he was terrific, kept banging away. It quite took my breath. I got really worked up . . .' (p. 105). True enough, no electronic surveillance experts of any secret service are likely to assess their findings in the language of Santa Teresa. But Malenina's habitual 'fuck your mother' style, tacitly accepted by her superiors, is the routine language of an otherwise hypocritically macho culture. And here the tolerance displayed toward her linguistic excesses suggests the same sort of indulgence which *Blockführerinnen* enjoyed in the camps in exchange for the 'burdens' of their 'heavy task'. For, in the final analysis, Ilse Koch's pastimes were not part of the public image of German artists even under Hitler. Furthermore, Malenina is not a rebel against hypocritical morality. She simply does not believe in the boring social game called morality, only in a culture where performance is the exclusive value. This is why she appreciates the 'terrific' Gypsy and despises Galina Brezhneva. Yet, despite the esteem for the good performer, the 'Gypsy' was eventually found hanged in a Butyrka cell. The Master of Socialist Sport is a passionate subscriber to the iron fist and to ultimate, unquestionable authority. But precisely for this reason, her symbolic figure tells everything about the predicament of the New Course activists. Although the New Course program complains about the public disappearance of both conscience and the sense of shame, can it really believe in restoring either one with the Maleninas whose intemperate bestiality is so badly needed by the conspiracy?

Precisely because of this unfulfillable need, the other need for self-glorification is inherent in the 'culture' of the nomenklatura. The biggest hit on Soviet TV is the series *The Seventeen Moments of Spring* – a story about the 'holy Tchekist' disguised as a Gestapo agent who accepts the ultimate sacrifice: that of his conscience. Hand in hand with a lifestyle including orgies with hard-currency prostitutes, blackmarketeering and dealings in stolen goods, and corruption, the Tsviguns' life also includes 'literary' and 'film-making' activities. Both man and wife are passionate producers of self-glorifying trash about their 'heroic past'. It would be simplistic to reduce this yearning for self-glorification to mere neo-Victorian hypocrisy. When the Tsviguns accept to remain anonymous, as writers of their memoirs, when they send all of their honorary to warstricken Vietnamese children, when this type of 'creative activity' remains the only bond in a dissolved marriage, when, finally, seeing their next movie about heroic Tchekists on the screen becomes a veritable obsession with Vera Tsviguna, all this is much more than mere acting. The oligarchy's main cult figure is the sentimental and dilettantish poet, who was at the same time a narrowminded and ruthless Great Inquisitor: Feliks Dzherzhynsky, the founding father of the Tcheka who constantly yearned for saints but invariably trained mobsters. It is symbolic that Malenina, another good performer who climaxes quickly, perhaps in record time, stands stark naked after copulation under Dzherzhynsky's portrait (which decorates all rooms in the security services) and silently ponders ways of deporting Soviet Jews.

Red Square, this alleged 'Soviet thriller', is indeed a traumatic message from a godforsaken world. A society where conscience as a regulatory mechanism never worked for historical and political reasons, now has also lost shame as a regulatory agency to the extent that it has become a social handicap even for those who have consciously created this situation. This hysterical craving for a regulative authority by those who always went beyond all limits and are ready to do so again, shows the fatal consequences of the new Soviet oligarchy's lifestyle. The weakening of the leader's power, a subsequent separation of powers and the like, were all social preconditions of the semi-liberties the oligarchy now enjoys. But the price for it is that now there is no real or imaginary authority left in their world. This world is godforsaken precisely in this sense. For in a society which is fundamentally, rigidly and unquestioningly authoritarian but which, simultaneously, lives in a state of constant conspiracies, *all authorities must eventually collapse*, and they indeed do. Brezhnev is regarded in the public consensus as the head of a clan of thieves and an imbecile, the only mistake about this being that in actual historical fact he was indeed a Godfather, but also a very shrewd operator and powerbroker. Suslov is called a Fascist in the novel both by the liberalizing advisers of Brezhnev and the arch-Tchekist Tsviguna; Scholokov, a partner in conspiracy, suspects Andropov of Jewish descent, which means questioning his authority before he ascended to power.

Anti-semitism, which plays such an important role in this novel, is the negative theology of a godforsaken world. The phenomenon is coextensive with Soviet society; from Brezhnev to the head of the local bakery, almost everyone is *publicly* anti-Semitic. The charming atmosphere of Tsarist Russia has returned to full bloom. The difference between the two parties, the Brezhnevite and the 'purists', is only one of degree. To start with, in case of a full victory of the New Course program, Jews ought to prepare for pogroms and perhaps for deportation. It is the symbolic figure of Malenina once again who reveals the genuine objective. In making love with Shamrayev, she fulfils a 'political assignment': the conspirators want to seduce, one way or another, Brezhnev's emissary. But there is also an element of perversion in the story so well known for those who have read Julius Streicher's *Stürmer:* Malenina–*Blockführerin* has an obsessive curiosity for circumcised men which, however, remains unsatisfied after making love to Shamrayev. Immediately after her climax, she remarks: 'What are we to do with your lot?' And to Shamrayev's surprised question as to the meaning of her question, she cryptically answers: 'Well, I don't mean you. You are like us. You are not even circumcised' (p. 106). The answer, however, loses its cryptic quality if we recall her angry outburst against one of her (obviously Jewish) subordinates, one scene earlier, during the listening to Brezhneva's lovemaking with the 'Gypsy'. 'We are going to drive those dirty Jews out of the security services, Comrade Minister, we are going to drive them out' (p. 102). And perhaps it is not just the security services from which the purists want to drive out those dirty Jews. Malenina's remark entails *formalized* racial discrimination which is always the prelude to segregation or coercive population transfer – simply put: deportation.[8]

The functions of this 'socialist anti-Semitism' are manifold. First, problems of a practical nature emerge with the awakening of the Jews' collective consciousness. They emerged, and here the New Course Program is correct, as a result of Brezhnev's tinkering with détente. Second, this problem is not just an internal one, but it involves foreign policy as well. Tolerance towards 'Zionists' hardly meshes with the ideological and political requirements of many of the USSR's allies. However, we are convinced of the mainly *projective* character of Soviet anti-Semitism. Various forms of racisms are emerging within the Soviet Union, and the best way of manipulating them, whenever coercion is not sufficient, is to find a common demon towards which all hatreds can be projected. Further, negative theology needs a visible incubus. There are no authorities in this society, not even manmade ones. All authority evaporated from it, although society itself is as authoritarian as it can be. It does not have positive principles, not even in the form of widely shared ideological delusions. It is no longer possible to blame the regime's self-generated problems on readily available collective subjects (Trotskyites, kulaks, etc.). But a *collective demonology* can do the job. The struggle with the mythical agent of genuine social malaise intensifies hatred, the only antidote against total moral decay – an antidote which, in turn, calls for an authority with an iron fist.

It is on the margin of this society that the only hope, the only authority that commands respect, appears here and there: simple, non-ideological, directly personal *love*. Its only bearers, in the best tradition of Russian literature, are women: Nina, the circus artist, Shamrayev's lover who is brutally murdered by the conspirators, and Anna Finshtein, the Jewish girl, whose indefatigable love for the imprisoned young Georgian triggers the whole plot. However, tragically but not uncharacteristically, these affections find relatively unworthy subjects, particularly in the case of Anna. The message of this historical novel is therefore bitter and resigned. It reads as follows: in order to find gratification in real love one has to leave this world of hatred and corruption. But even if one succeeds (Anna does, Nina does not), it remains an open question whether it was worth the efforts. Is there a more discouraging view of the state of affairs in the Soviet Union under Brezhnev's final days?

1984

NOTES

1   Edward Topol and Fridrikh Neznansky, *Red Square* (New York/London/ Melbourne: Quartet, 1983), translated from the Russian. Topol and Neznansky are Soviet emigré writers who left the Soviet Union in the late 1970s and are now living in the West. Both held sufficiently high positions in the USSR, in the film industry and in the office of the public prosecutor respectively, to be kept abreast of the constantly circulating political rumors. They spell out their intentions of writing a historical novel, not merely a thriller, in the motto of the book in an ironical fashion: 'All the characters in this book, including Brezhnev, Suslov, Andropov, Tsvigun, their wives and children, as well as the events described in it, are entirely fictitious. If, by chance, any of them should happen to coincide with Soviet reality, then so much the worse for the latter.'

2   A reconstruction of Brezhnev's final days can be found in Ilya Zemtsov, *Andropov* (Jerusalem: IRCS, 1983), which is nightmarishly similar to that in *Red Square*. In addition, almost all fragments and details of the story surfaced in the Western press in an incoherent and often self-contradictory form.

3   This is an extremely illuminating example of how the Soviet Union is ruled, not governed. For organizations like the Defense Council are simply undefinable in legal terms. Usually, but not 'constitutionally' (whatever the word means in the given context) the title of being the head of this council goes with being the President of the USSR. However, again practically and not constitutionally, being the President derives from being the Secretary General. (But, as the first months of Andropov's short rule demonstrated, even this is not automatic.) Another example given by *Red Square* is the following. Initially, the KGB was meant to be a simple investigating body (which, of course, was never the case in practice), subjected to the Council of Ministers of the USSR, and personally to the Prime Minister. When, however, Kosygin became a nuisance for Brezhnev, the latter simply rebaptized the powerful body 'KGB USSR', and subjected it directly to himself, as *party secretary general.*

4   Inevitably, there are certain illegal aspects even in these transactions so beneficial for the Soviet consumer. For example, Aeroflot pilots have to be bribed to transport the goods from Georgia to Moscow. But who, if not the 'omnipotent planners' of the regime are responsible for this 'illegal', although extremely beneficial, activity?

5   Should anyone point to the Tanaka case, and the Lockheed scandal in general, by way of a rejoinder, two remarks would be appropriate. First, societies in which instances of this kind of corruption happen do not call themselves socialist and have a public admiration for wealth coming from 'honest' sources. Second, one can sometimes, far from always, read something about such dealings in the press. Most importantly, no one is executed for embezzlement in Western countries.

6   See Besançon's preface to the book by I. Zemsçtov, *La corruption en l'URSS*, (Paris: Fayard, 1982).

7   In his *Neo-Stalinist State* (New York: Sharpe, 1982), Victor Zaslavsky analyzed the social conditions presupposed and implied by the seemingly neutral substitution of the slogan 'the Soviet way of life' for 'the construction of communism' in vogue under Khrushchev. In short, it shows the ineffectiveness of the dominant Marxism–Leninism and the rise of chauvinism.

8   The deportation of the Jews in the USSR, a country whose official ideology is the counterpoint *sui generis* of racism, seems to be impossible even for those who condemn the regime in the strongest terms. Recently, Victor Zaslavsky has voiced his skepticism about such a perspective. But let me quote Zaslavsky against Zaslavsky. In his new book on *Soviet-Jewish Emigration and Soviet Nationality Policy* (London/New York, 1984), he describes (p. 71) the typical case of a Soviet Jewish engineer who, up until 1974, had never even thought in terms of Jewish identity. Then he had to attend a so-called 'closed lecture' held by an emissary of the central authorities who argued that: just as we had to deport our Volga Germans to Siberia during the Great Patriotic War . . . so we have to be careful of the Zionists among us now.' Everyone familiar with Soviet reality knows that no emissary of the center, in 1974, would dare to air options which were not also under consideration in the 'upper circles'. Therefore, deportation does not seem so impossible even in Zaslavsky's own book. Historically, W. Korey convincingly demonstrated in his book, *The Iron Cage*, that in 1953, during the hysterical weeks of the so-called 'doctors' plot', there had been far-reaching preparations for a 'protective' mass deportation of Jews against 'popular fury'. Among other things, a petition of Soviet Jewish intellectuals was submitted to the Soviet government (obtained by the usual threats) in which they requested, in the name of the Jews endangered by an ever-increasing atmosphere of pogroms, triggered by that same government, to guarantee their safety by transferring them to some distant and preferably unpopulated areas of the USSR. And the regime's ideological character was more emphatic under Stalin than under any of his successors. Technically, the whole matter is simply exercise in terminology: eventually, they would not deport Jews, but 'Zionists'. The counter-argument, which makes this option a weak one, is the fact that any mass deportation in the post-Stalinist era would cause such an internal turbulence that the Soviet leadership would consider it carefully before implementing it. Thus, we regard the deportation of Jews in the USSR as an implicit danger but one the actualization of which is highly unlikely and connected with one particular social alternative: a new version of one of Stalin's 'revolutions from above'. But the perspective being analyzed on the basis of *Red Square* – a work of fiction and interpretation, not a document – is precisely such a 'revolution from above', Andropov's short rule must be seen precisely in such terms, and similar attempts cannot be ruled out in the future.

9

The Gorbachev Phenomenon

THE FACTS

One of the most surprising phenomena of the present (leftist and rightist) admiration of Gorbachev in the West is the inverse ratio between the enthusiasm exhibited for the Soviet New Team and the facts which would support such a response. This fairly irrational attitude is, of course, easily explicable in terms of the long frustration so many actors and observers in the 'first world' have felt about a conspicuously conservative and immobile society during the long ice age under Brezhnev. However, as long as the relevant facts are not isolated, identified and classified into clusters, theorizing about the new situation is not possible; the field remains a free hunting-ground for myth makers.

We propose to acknowledge two different sets of facts after two years of Gorbachevschina. One cluster is constituted by 'significant facts', that is, ones which have a direct significance for, and a direct impact on, the whole social context. Another set of facts is constituted by events received with understandable relief by the populace of the USSR, which, however, remain socially irrelevant and without consequence as long as a particular new scenario does not emerge. Once embedded in such a new scenario, these facts, which are irrelevant in themselves, could gain a new significance.

A clearly identifiable cluster of socially significant facts has emerged during the short rule of the New Team: the mounting, indeed irrefutable, evidence of *the push towards a change of the elite*. And if it comes to pass, this will be the third wave of elite change in Soviet history after Stalin's Great Terror and Brezhnev's thorough, albeit bloodless, 'housecleaning' which completed Khrushchev's legacy, and which at the same time deflected it from its initial objective.

The waves of elite change were constituents of different strategies and followed, therefore, different patterns. Stalin crushed with the sword the Bolshevik old guard in order to ground a society which would thereafter live in the permanence of 'revolutions from above' and in the cult of the Leader. Emotional Stalinists though they were, Khrushchev and Brezhnev were rather committed to the closure of the revolutions from above, the first in an inconsistently reformist, the second in a consistently conservative manner. Brezhnev's *modus operandi* was a complete dismantling of the old (this time Stalinist) apparatus without shortening its members by a head. A strategy of gradual, rather than dramatically publicized, demotions, wholesale pensioning, a further extension of the system of group privileges *and* the tacit tolerance towards corruption, did the work just as effectively from the viewpoint of the Brezhnevite strategy as the mobile execution squads of Yezhov had done in the thirties. In Gorbachev's case, the will to the change of the elite derives from *the will to modernization* which is the main strategic objective of the New Team. Therefore, its methods are perforce different from those of both Stalin and Brezhnev. Gorbachev simply cannot employ Yezhov's apparatus, the technology of mass murder; it would be dysfunctional for his purposes. Nor would Brezhnev's cynical pragmatism be entirely adequate for the strategic goals of the New Team. The Young Turks have to adopt a publicly moralizing stance. The latter also has the implication of introducing 'the protestant work ethic' as an antidote to the oriental immobility and ossification of the Brezhnev era.

The elite change which is now being engineered by the New Team is the only visible trend, the only identifiable cluster of events which can be said so far to have had any general social significance. If the New Team will be able to complete its project, the political and economic structure of Soviet society will remain fundamentally the same but 'life quality' will be different. Although the term 'modernization' is clearly too polyphonic and it carries too many shades of meaning (which in what follows we will try to briefly define), a 'modernized' Soviet regime would be, despite and beyond all varieties of meaning, different from Brezhnev's gerontocratic rule.

A totally different picture is presented by several additional sets of events that are typically in the forefront of media curiosity and which are perceived with understandable relief by the Soviet intelligentsia, but which in themselves have no general social significance at all. Unless these events, semantic, legal and ideological, form part of some emerging scenario with social thrust, they are, and will remain, inconsequential and will be buried, together with so many other flare-ups of the reformist will in Russian and Soviet history, in a common grave without sequel. Three groups of non-significant, albeit 'relieving' facts can be identified in the present context. These are the releasing of a few hundred political prisoners on the basis of a selective amnesty, the policy of 'language reorientation' (to use the term coined by the American expert A. Arato) which of course includes the policy of *glasnost*, and, finally, certain isolated but important acts pointing to a somewhat more realistic reinterpretation of Soviet history.

The interpretation of Gorbachev's clemency may vary from observer to observer. It can be seen as an act of mere windowdressing with an eye on

Western loans or as some kind of *captatio benevolentiae* towards the opposi-tional or semi-oppositional intelligentsia, aimed at convincing them to jump on the bandwagon of the New Team. It can even be understood as a sign of the ruler's excessive personal generosity. Finally, it can be seen as the combination of all three aspects. Whatever particular shade of interpretation an analyst will select, even if it is their combination, one conclusion can hardly be avoided. Gorbachev's clemency remains an isolated act in Soviet policy, insofar as it does not imply the slightest reform of the Soviet legal system or the penal code. If the latter eventuates, it would, of course, be a change equal in importance to the change of the elite.

The case with 'language reorientation' is similar. This term is roughly coextensive with *glasnost*, that is, with the regular flow and public availability of reliable information about major domestic and internal events through official media (channels as opposed to just confidential party channels) – which is, of course, a major novelty in Soviet history. *Glasnost* also includes critical reports on social facts (regarding short supplies in indispensable commodities, ecological threats and the like) in the official, and not just oppositional (*samizdat*), media. The significance of *glasnost* for the life quality of a populace which has been kept for decades in almost total darkness on all major issues, has to be emphasized for those who have never experienced the charms of Stalinist and post-Stalinist 'public information'. However, the interpretation of 'language reorientation' varies again from analyst to analyst. It can be argued that the new policy is the only possible bargain the Gorbachev team can offer in exchange for Western loans. It can equally be argued that *glasnost* is needed for the leadership itself: in the self-inflicted darkness they too had problems of vision. This has been fully demonstrated by Chernobyl. Finally, there is a more sophisticated argument in terms of which the spirit of *glasnost* is symbolically needed for the purposes of modernizing Soviet society. Unless one accepts the last shade of meaning as the only valid one, 'language reorientation' remains an isolated fact without general social significance.

A partial, but realistic, reinterpretation of Soviet history has presented itself in two conspicuous cases. The rehabilitation of Pasternak is well under way; one can even predict the poet's 'nationalization' in a manner very similar to the nationalization of Lukács in Hungary. More dramatically, Trotsky and Bukharin have emerged, in a drama written in 1962 but published in *Novy Mir* just recently, not as flawless figures like Lenin, the paragon of perfection, but as revolutionaries nonetheless. Furthermore, and most importantly, Bukharin has been fully rehabilitated by Gorbachev, and he is now being hailed as the hero of the New Economic Policy of the 1920s. All of this is, of course, a serious step towards the restoration of common sense in a society which has been so thoroughly lacking in it. Interpretations of this change may again vary. One can argue that the gesture is of symbolic relevance: it ushers in the era of the restoration of a sense of justice in Soviet society. It can also be seen as a superlatively shrewd pragmatic gesture. With all its gloomy dramas and theoretical hairsplittings, Soviet history *qua* history has lost all of its doctrinaire relevance for the overwhelming majority of the populace which was born or socialized after the Second World War. It only serves as a myth of genesis in which single figures, instead of representing distinct political options, can fulfill a *function* in the great tableau. The interpretation of Soviet history will lose its political tension, becoming, rather, a ceremonial-ritualistic activity. From either scenario, a clearing of the intellectual climate in the USSR can be inferred, but a strategic turn cannot.

Two remarks must be made in conclusion of this section. First, it is not accidental that economic facts have not been listed here. While the New Team has indeed softened its initially harsh ideological stance on market mechanisms, the introduction of the latter in a controlled form and on a scale similar to the Chinese experiment has so far not been in evidence. At the very best, an increased tolerance towards the second economy, in particular towards its service sector, can be noted. Nor is there any sign of structural changes in the system of economic management. Secondly, facts belonging to the 'socially significant' cluster and those having no social significance are not necessarily interconnected in Gorbachev's politics. The Gorbachev strategy is, rather, a montage in which one element could easily be replaced by almost any other.

PARALOGISM OR ALTERNATIVE SCENARIOS

The definition of paralogism is: a type of speculation in which one infers the existence of something on the basis of hypothetical facts. It is our conviction that almost all recent interpretations of the Gorbachevschina operate as paralogism. This is so for two reasons. First, because every eventuality which has surfaced in the recent atmosphere of 'let a hundred flowers bloom' has been used by commentators as an actuality. The second reason is that the majority of overly optimistic interpreters have been operating if not with fictitious events then certainly with *fictitious actors*. However, unless we declare the present turbulence in the USSR a figment of Western journalists' imaginations (which we did, but no longer do), paralogistic thinking is inescapable in analyzing, or fantasizing about, current Soviet politics. For everything is fluid there and we have no certitude. But whatever comes to pass in the Soviet Union has an obvious, and tremendous, relevance for the rest of the world. Our own whole exercise rests on the identification of mostly hypothetical actors within the alternative scenarios. As far as we can see, current Soviet history harbors the possibility of the following scenarios:

modernization as mere technological reform (this is the only scenario which has an actual, and not just a hypothetical, actor); modernization as technocratic-economic reform; modernization as an attempt *from above* to double the social actor and create 'socioeconomic partnership'; and modernization through the military. Since radical democratization from below, or revolution, is merely a logical possibility, we have not included it in our paralogical exercise.

Modernization as a mere technological reform seems to be the particular option which the New Team could accept as its new political strategy, most likely after long and vehement internal debates. Gorbachev's Young Turks clearly regard themselves as the historically predestined, sole implementers of this major overhaul. The dilemma to be eliminated can easily be circumscribed in their terms: a dangerous lagging behind, caused by Brezhnevite 'conservatism' in the technological competition with the West which will soon have a crippling effect, above all, on the USSR's military might. They seem to be prepared to admit a technological, but not an economic, crisis with the difference being that the latter would also imply drastic changes in the economic mechanisms and system of management.

Modernization as technocratic-economic reform is 'the intellectuals' scenario'. Its hypothetical actor is 'the intelligentsia as a class'. Although the actor is hypothetical, from the quick and almost uncritical embracing of the New Team's policies by Sakharov one can come to the conclusion that this particular actor is *ante portas*. The analysts of the intellectuals' option locate the source of evil deeper than the mere obsolescence of current Soviet technology. Their objective lies in the introduction of market mechanisms into the Soviet economy, an updating of the existing system of management and, more generally, a 'limited Enlightenment', that is, a restoration of elementary common sense in Soviet society. At the same time, the intelligentsia is not promoting political changes of any kind. As a dissident critic of Sakharov's quick identification with the new line has correctly pointed out, these intellectuals, courageous though they were, never opposed paternalistic and patriotic authority as such, but only its excesses and unrestrained irrationality.

Modernization as an attempt to overhaul the political structure from above, the option of Imre Nagy (before the revolution of 1956), that of Gomu*k*a (immediately before and after seizing power but not later) and that of Dubček, is the reformist communist scenario. Up until now, reformist communism has never been a significant actor on the scene of Soviet history although it can be derived from Khrushchev's breakthrough. Much as he changed the course of events in his country more than anyone after Stalin, Khrushchev nonetheless cannot be identified with reformist communism. The latter is invariably the opposition within the party for a shorter or longer period of time, an opposition which never abandons fundamental communist tenets. (Whereas Khrushchev was never an oppositional force but always the representative of the summit of power; moreover, he not only triggered, but also crushed, reformist communism in many countries.) The internal duality of reformist communism, its insistence on changing the political system on the one hand, which must ultimately remain the same on the other hand, is the unresolvable paradox of this option. It has not yet made its appearance in Soviet history (or only sporadically did in the recent past), but it is, in a vague sense, on the cards.

Modernization as an attempt at artificially creating socioeconomic partnership with the omnipotent political, authority is a scenario with one initial actor, the party apparatus, which then gives birth, of itself as it were, to a junior partner, the system of workers' self-management. The latter is a strictly *economic*, not a political, authority but one which has political implications. When a particular communist apparatus has proceeded far on the road of economic reform but without the slightest intention of sharing power with other groups, it might, but not necessarily will, compensate for this unshared power through the creation of a (fictitious or real) junior economic partner. But this option can only emerge after a long period of economic reforms; therefore, it is not a very topical item on the Soviet political agenda.

Modernization through the military, the last hypothetical scenario, has an easily definable actor: the army in power. There has been so far not a single precedent for army rule in Soviet history. Ever since the short, chaotic and far from absolute political domination of the *streltsy* during the regency of Peter the Great's sister, even old Russian history has known only one example of the (short and covert) rule of the army. For the period of a few years after the great reform of 1861, when the countryside was shaken by peasant rebellions and *haute société* was alienated from the court, Alexander II could arguably rule only by relying on the army. However, a lack of precedents is no absolute argument against future occurrence. Moreover, the thesis of C. Castoriadis, the theory of 'stratocracy', assumes that the rule of the army, admittedly without 'men in uniform' at the helm, is not a future option but the actual reality. Even if we disagree with this diagnosis, the possibility of an army takeover, if modernization in one of its 'civilian' ways gets bogged down again, is far from impossible.

Which is the likeliest scenario? The problem with all possible answers given to this question is that they can only be supplied within a hypothetical history. The latter is not necessarily complete nonsense, or a mere guessing game. It has two objective bases of extrapolation: the *past* frequency of certain events, similar to the one whose emergence we predict (always assuming that we believe in a degree of historical continuity); and *present* cultural patterns. On the basis of such parameters, scenarios number one and number two (modernization as technological reform and the intellectuals' blueprint) appear to be the likeliest candidates, while scenarios number three and four are the unlikeliest ones. Scenario number five (modernization through the military) is the dark horse. The main weakness of all predictions within a hypothetical history is, however, that it operates with a static, not a dynamic model. When the new actor appears in historical reality, it always generates new dimensions, new strategies and new reactions in response to its presence. And the latter simply cannot be figured out with the parameters of hypothetical history.

The actor of which particular scenario of this hypothetical history has the strongest chance for victory? The difficulty in answering this question is that the term 'modernization' changes its meaning from scenario to scenario, and with every shift of meaning the chances of the blueprint being implemented also change. Modernization is a deceptively simple task in the first version, one which is basically equivalent to the overhaul of current technology. But it is precisely this deceptive simplicity that offers the trap. Even if the target could be achieved with enormous Western loans, thereby increasing the already enormous Soviet debts, it would be a one-time success, and the next round of technological competition could easily be lost. For apart from moral exhortations, scenario number one provides no mechanisms which would ensure a continuous competitive edge in the technology race.

Incomparably more complex would be the hypostatizable concept of 'modernization' in scenario number two, in the intellectuals' (or technocratic) project. Since this particular actor would be concerned with the perpetuation of the Soviet capacity for technological competitiveness (this is precisely the meaning of economic versus technological change or reform), the intellectuals would try to push through more thoroughgoing changes. The ensuing greater complexity of their concept of modernization would provide better chances for, as well as put severe limitations upon, scenario number two. The serious and complex approach to social problems inherent in this version could generate an enormous economic momentum in the initial phase. Its almost total indifference towards political change would inevitably result in an insurmountable impasse at a very early stage. Finally, it is literally impossible to make statements of any kind about the actual form the respective concepts of modernization would take in scenarios three, four and five. Nor is it therefore possible to predict their (stronger or weaker) chances for implementing their respective projects. At this point, we are groping in the impenetrable darkness of hypothetical history.

However, our typology of possible scenarios was not entirely based on the parameters of hypothetical history. In fact, the distinct versions were borrowed from a very real history: the East European. It is easy to identify scenario number one with the East German blueprint of modernization. In the East German case, we can isolate the following constituents of a (relative) success: a technologically efficient managerial elite, a workforce with a protestant work ethic, a continuous, almost inexhaustible source of capital investment which is located *outside* the system and a machinery of repression which remains unaffected by technological modernization. Scenario number four, a system of dual (socioeconomic) partnership created from above, is clearly identical with the structure of the Yugoslav experiment during the last more than 20 years. The equivalent to scenario number three, the reformist communist, is Dubček's Czechoslovakia but similar trends were discernible in the very early phase of Gomułka's rule also. Scenario number five, the army-based modernization, is a blueprint-in-progress in Poland. It is debatable to what extent the army is a distinct social power in that context (distinct, that is, from the party) and to what extent its share in power has diminished. However, it would be difficult to deny altogether the army's massively increased presence in both the political policing and the economic modernizing functions of the regime. Finally, scenario number two is the replica of the Hungarian model. Experiments with the introduction of market mechanisms, the increased role of (a primarily technocratic) intelligentsia, the emphasis on ideology-free purposive rationality together with an essentially unaltered power structure, whose behavior however is one of cautious and realistic repressive tolerance – all of this bears strong resemblance to Kádárist Hungary. Paralogism therefore cedes place to the analysis of genuine historical alternatives in departing from the actual, and highly distinct, histories of the countries of periphery. It is the ironical revenge of history for more than 30 years of Soviet immobility and miscarried embryonic reforms that the leaders of the center now have to turn to the periphery for guidance in their own alternative scenarios.

TRANSITION FROM HYPOTHETICAL TO REAL HISTORY

Gorbachev himself, as well as the New Team as a whole, are presumably aware of the fact that their possible scenarios of 'modernization' are Eastern Europe's actual, alternative, versions of the post-Stalin change. One finds references, owing to the Great Russian chauvinism of the nomenklatura, not too frequent ones, to the East European stimulus. However, those who encourage the Soviet leaders to swiftly press ahead with one of the East European blueprints (the one most often recommended being the Hungarian) do not seem to realize what enormous complexities are inherent in translating hypothetical history into a course of practical action.

The first complexity, or rather danger, is best summed up in a political joke of Czech provenience (and in Soviet society, jokes are the best indicators of political climate, particularly in times of change). The Moscow politburo is in full session discussing the issue of dismantling the kolkhoz system in order to promote agricultural modernization. Gorbachev's secretary appears in the middle of the session and whispers something in the ear of the First Secretary who, pale and trembling, interrupts the meeting and makes the following announcement: Comrades, the armies of the Warsaw Pact are approaching Moscow – what shall we do? The evident absurdity of the joke carries the following message. First, if indeed modernization presses ahead, and insofar as it implements any of the scenarios which transcend the level of mere windowdressing (especially if it adopts the reformist communist scenario), then the Moscow politburo itself will be virtually indistinguishable from that center of 'peaceful counterrevolution', the Dubček leadership in 1968. But hatching plans for a 'peaceful counterrevolution' is the historical moment when the armed forces of the Warsaw Pact, whose nucleus is of course the Soviet army, would intervene to save the 'socialist achievements'. However, who would intervene if the Moscow politburo becomes the center of 'peaceful counterrevolution' in order to save them from themselves? The comic schizophrenia of the joke covers a serious and threatening dilemma for the Soviet leaders, a danger that has never been experienced by East European modernizers. Whenever the latter got the green light from Moscow, they charged ahead without ever looking back, for the ultimate trump in case of failure, namely Soviet intervention, was, as a guarantee, behind them. But what kind of trump can Gorbachev produce in an hour of crisis?

The second dilemma is the following. All East European attempts at modernization took place in countries which were ethnically not homogeneous but which were not empires. And while neither of the above-mentioned scenarios implicitly or explicitly contains a solution to the problems of the empire, each and every serious scenario of change, particularly the fifth, that of modernization through the military, is implicitly bound to bring the problems of the empire to a point of near-explosion.

The third dilemma and danger is as follows: the dimensions, the economic potential as well as the dysfunctions, and the military might of the USSR are so enormous that the difference between it and any East European country tinkering with modernization is qualitative. If the ailing, but tremendous Soviet economy were organically integrated into the world economy, this integration would result in the emergence of the world's largest debtor country, one whose economic behavior is unpredictable and hardly influenceable. This country's eventual failure to pay its debts could trigger the collapse of the world economy. Its eventual transition to a military dictatorship would turn Western technology against the West, and it would bring the world to the brink of a global war. If, alternatively, the USSR would pay for loans with obedience and the abandonment of expansionist projects, this behavior would be tantamount to what economic language calls 'dependent integration' into the world system, which would then question the very legitimation of the system.

These and similar dilemmas are so serious that the respective advantages and threats which the distinct scenarios imply for various actors both inside and outside the USSR have to be put under careful scrutiny. The scenario of military takeover and subsequent modernization would be devastating for almost everyone inside and outside the USSR. Of course, it would bolster the 'imaginary institution' of Russian–Soviet nationalism. But it would perforce oppress all initiatives of liberalization or democratization within the Soviet Union perhaps more brutally than that which happened under party rule. It would be tantamount to the military dictatorship of the Slavic component of the empire over the non-Slavic, above all the Muslim, contingent. And it would inevitably sharpen the conflict between the USSR and the West. Total militarization of Soviet life would be crippling even for the traditional (reformist or non-reformist) communist political imagination. Not even the most experienced dialectician could conjure up the image of the motherland of the world revolution in a country living under the dictatorship of the Russian army.

Alternatively, the most beneficial scenario is the one which projects a dual social partnership, the system of workers' self-management which would complement the politically monolithic rule of the state. (This statement is of course not equivalent to the other that self-management is the economically most efficient system.) A (highly unlikely) outcome of the Gorbachevschina favouring self-management would naturally be a tremendous stimulus for a broadly understood Eastern and Western democratic left. It would be a politically neutral event for Western liberalism but certainly change of a kind which would not threaten the Western establishment with a more aggressive wave of expansionism.

Scenarios two and three, the intellectuals' scenario and the reformist communist alternative, would have varied results. The first version in particular would favor the Russian element within the USSR and would in all probability heighten ethnic tensions. At least in the short run, it would improve economic effectivity. Both versions would prepare the ground for a more comprehensive détente, and the beneficial impact of an international thaw on Western economies and social policies needs no comment. At the same time, two predictable negative features of these hypothetical courses should be noted here. First, these scenarios, especially the first of increased effectivity without political guarantees for the workforce, would inevitably increase social differences and would create a *new* type of economic inequality in the USSR. Secondly, if one of these scenarios proves successful and the Soviet economy gathers momentum while no change eventuates in the political system, the main beneficiary would be an expansionist party apparatus which would return to its projects of global domination with a heightened self-confidence and an increased military might.

There is of course one universally beneficial, and eminently fictitious, scenario in terms of which all actors of Soviet society, now for the most part only embryonically existing, would convene for a domination-free discussion

of the most adequate, and the most generally acceptable, project of modernization. This extremely peaceful event would be the day of the most radical
Russian revolution.

HISTORICAL EPILOGUE: KHRUSHCHEV AND GORBACHEV

Genesis is the clue for explanation, and the respective stories of birth and
emergence in the cases of Khrushchev's and Gorbachev's 'new trends' are
widely different. Khrushchev's failed attempt had grown out of a *legitimation
crisis* and *the crisis of the empire*. Gorbachev's 'drive for change', an extremely
incomplete story as yet, has been emerging out of an *economic crisis, a crisis of
the ruling stratum with wide sociological implications* and a *demographic crisis*
which has equally far-reaching implications for the regime's social policy.

A very simple fact lay at the root of the legitimation crisis that Khrushchev
inherited. Stalin had become an independent, destructive, and at the same
time cementing historical force, a force from which the country suffered
immensely but on which its political cohesion rested. When this charismatic
tyrant died, neither the country nor even Stalin's own loyal apparatus seemed
to be prepared to tolerate the emergence, and the future role, of a new
charismatic tyrant. Khrushchev showed his mettle when he came up with
two apparently plausible answers to the crisis, one to cater for the party, the
other to cater for the country at large: *collective leadership* and *substantive
rationality*. The first was to become the accepted political mechanism of the
nomenklatura under Brezhnev only. The latter, 'substantive rationality', a
term coined by observers and one which the not particularly erudite
Khrushchev never used, has a straightforward meaning, which has been well
known since Max Weber's anatomy of rationality. Socialism, Khrushchev
contended, is a regime which is superior to all others in its very substance,
that is, potentially. If Soviet socialism does not function adequately to its
'substance', malfunctioning is solely due to the tyrant's personal irrationality,
his caprices, and to the artificially created chasm between science and
political leadership. Once a realistic body of strong, self-appointed but
collectively acting politicians was at the helm (Khrushchev never abandoned
an unmistakably authoritarian model), once, furthermore, science was given
its fair share in policy making (a change which never eventuated largely
because of Khrushchev's own caprices), socialism would show its hidden,
superlative substance, the United States would be overcome in terms of per
capita production by 1980, and communism would be built. Khrushchev's
political vocabulary had remained to the end homogeneously 'Leninist'-
ideological.

The gradual unfolding of the crisis of the empire, which was accelerated by
the fears and anxieties of the Soviet leaders themselves, had a tremendous

impact on the Soviet political drama at home. Immediately in the wake of Stalin's death in March 1953, symptoms of an East European unrest appeared, reaching its first culmination in the June uprising in Berlin. The main political battlefields were Poland and Hungary, whose upheavals and revolutions shaped crucially the political physiognomy of Khrushchev's shortlived regime of reform. Here, too, Khrushchev produced a number of elastic political formulae, but at this point he did not find even a temporary answer. Rather he passed the burdensome legacy of the crisis of the empire on to his heirs.

Gorbachev in turn has inherited no crisis of legitimation. Brezhnev's 20-year-long rule had created a new and lasting formula of legitimation. Under Brezhnev, the conservative and nationalist tradition, the tradition of an already long Soviet history, which had become national history in the war and had thus embraced important elements of traditional Russian nationalism, became the principle of the regime's legitimacy. All signs indicate that Gorbachev's team intends to remain within the apparently safe walls of this establishment. However, Gorbachev has inherited the onerous legacy of an *economic* crisis from Brezhnev, a crisis which had become manifest in the almost zero growth of the Soviet industry for the first time in 50 years. Khrushchev, too, had of course arguably inherited an economic crisis from Stalin. Rapid though Soviet postwar industrial reconstruction was, neither the very modest needs of the populace nor the far larger needs of the army could be satisfied by Soviet industry in the fifties. The daily calorie intake of the populace hardly surpassed their intake at the time of the war, due to chronically stagnant and ill-performing agriculture. But economy in the USSR, a political society, is the function of the political structure. Economic crises or malfunctions in the Soviet regime do not have 'objective' indicators. They change their meaning and forms of manifestation with the changing malfunctions and strategic priorities of the political structure. Thus Khrushchev had economic dilemmas precisely because the principle of legitimation no longer functioned. With Stalin dead, it was necessary for Khrushchev to assuage a dissatisfied populace in order to be able to introduce new principles of legitimation. Similarly, Gorbachev now has economic problems precisely because the traditionalist-nationalist legitimation is vigorously alive, but the ailing industry cannot live up to its duties. It ought to cater for the expansive strategy of a superpower; at the same time it ought to satisfy at least some of the needs for consumer goods of a populace which is determined to take seriously the propaganda statements that they are the denizens of the leading nation of the world, and draw pragmatic conclusions from them for their household budget. Since neither of these needs can be satisfied with zero growth, economic crisis now becomes manifest in an untarnished form. However, in Soviet media it is presented as a result of technological backwardness, not that of political obsolescence. The political dimension has since the first steps of Gorbachev's rule been treated as *ancilla technologiae*.

More directly political in nature are the symptoms of the crisis of the ruling stratum. They are directly political and sociological insofar as Brezhnev's gerontocracy had been blocking the career ambitions and chances of a whole new generation of younger functionaries. In addition, the crisis is directly moral because the nationwide plague of corruption had raised a dual and seriously threatening dilemma for the ruling apparatus. For corruption means here more than bribing and bribe-taking. It implies the relative independence of the apparatchik from the apparatus through illegally accumulated private wealth, as well as the gradual emergence of a *class* from the ruling corporation. The first trend runs counter to the corporative interests of the nomenklatura, whose discipline and unity of will is undermined if it is increasingly composed of private proprietors. The second trend threatens the credibility of one of the main ideological claims of the ruling corporation: the claim that its strategic goal is a 'classless society' radically different from the Western pattern.

The present Soviet *demographic crisis* has many facets. The first aspect is a slow population growth which is probably caused both by the recurring demographic catastrophes of Soviet history and by the present low standards of urban living, in particular housing conditions. In the USSR alone among industrially developed countries, we find a decreasing life expectancy, probably a conjoint result of massive alcoholism and the inadequate health system. The Slavic component of the empire is decreasing in the face of a Muslim contingent which experiences a population explosion. The political implications of the demographic crisis are obvious. With a slowed-down population growth it is impossible to maintain a huge army and navy as well as supplying young manpower for industry on the required level. Nationalist-traditionalist legitimation, its pride and pathos, is seriously infracted if the nation is not healthy enough, if it cannot control its self-imposed plagues, if it sends fewer children into the world in replacement of the older generations than 'the greatness of the fatherland' would demand. Finally, without a strong and growing Slav, above all Russian, component the home empire is in jeopardy.

The *modus operandi* of the two periods of 'drive for change' are widely different. Khrushchev appeared on the scene as a reformer after decades of mass terror when even doubt was criminalized. In an atmosphere like this, the self-appointed reformer could not count on any support from 'society' which had for decades been lying prostrate at the feet of the charismatic tyrant. He perforce had to be a conspirator and a gambler who pulled off his liberating, mostly bloodless coups in a deliberately theatrical manner. Khrushchev, the master gambler, was an expert of his *coups de théâtre*. This was his forte as well as the major structural weakness of his position.

Improvising the reform from one coup to another proved a weakness, for whatever had been repeatedly gained through the brilliant performance of the master gambler, without the support, or even the participation, of 'society', stood or fell with the Great Improviser himself. A further structural weakness consisted of the enormous stubbornness of the opposition Khrushchev had to cope with, one he could not ultimately overcome. The cause of this dogged resistance was twofold. First, Stalin's apparatus could not but think in Stalinist terms; for them defeat meant the execution cell. Secondly, this apparatus still possessed an enormous amount of historical self-confidence. Their philosophy of history encouraged them to justify mass murder as 'historical necessity', as 'the necessary price paid for progress'. These structural weaknesses had predestined Khrushchev's incursion in the phalanx of apparatchiks to be an isolated bridgehead which could be, and eventually was, eliminated.

By contrast, Gorbachev's offensive has been for some time an unbroken triumphal march almost without resistance. It is precisely this self-accelerating pace of the new line that creates the as yet undeserved aura of radicalism and thoroughgoing change around Gorbachev's trend. Self-acceleration has three disparate reasons. First, Gorbachev's opponents no longer fear for their lives as did Khrushchev's opponents. Under Khrushchev and Brezhnev, the Soviet ruling apparatus had indeed 'returned to Lenin' at least in one respect. They now heed the advice given by the dying Lenin to Rykov, the advice which was so curtly dismissed by Stalin: No blood should flow between you. The second reason for this conspicuous lack of resistance is a moral disarray among the Brezhnevites. It is an inhuman paradox of politics that self-justification for heinous crimes on a mass scale can at least be attempted for they had allegedly been committed 'on behalf of the common weal'. However, corruption, this collective vice of the Brezhnevites, cannot be publicly excused. There is no public recognition for private acts of greed and self-interest, not even in terms of a twisted philosophy of history. The third reason for this self-acceleration is that Gorbachev has been selecting and finding allies with great tactical skill from the start. While his leadership is thriving on the Brezhnevite principle of legitimation, it is also parasitic on the Khrushchev period in another respect. It is precisely the old Khrushchevite intelligentsia, which had survived the Brezhnev period either at the price of humiliating compromises or by living beyond the pale of official tolerance, which now constitutes the spearhead of Gorbachev's incursion in the phalanx of the apparatus.

'Substantive rationality' and 'modernization', Khrushchev's and Gorbachev's programs respectively, have, despite certain features in common, widely different premises as well as social implications. 'Substantive rationality' was a heavily ideological blueprint designed by a leadership which was subscribing to Stalinist tenets while it was fighting Stalin's shadow. Khrushchev had directly inherited the thesis from Stalin that there were two separate and competitive world systems. He never intended to abandon this self-claimed autochthonous character of 'the socialist world market'; he only sought to run the latter efficiently and 'scientifically'. Khrushchev's hostility towards, or rather total contempt for, any genuinely structural change in the economy (which of course would have implied the establishment of new sociopolitical structures) was therefore no simple concession to his apparatus. The attitude followed from his own, sincerely felt ideological bias. Khrushchev's inherent ideological conservatism had two seriously negative consequences. He did not aim at reshuffling, he remained content with 'reeducating' his own Stalinist apparatus. If he, one of Stalin's closest lieutenants, could become the main de-Stalinizer, there was no reason for others not to follow his example, Khrushchev obviously contended, and it is well known what price he paid for his unexpected anthropological optimism. (Ironically, the drastic change of personnel took place under Brezhnev, and for different reasons.) Furthermore, his own Stalinist training made Khrushchev insensitive toward such subtle and complex sociological terms as 'public opinion' and the intellectuals' role in influencing public opinion. At any rate, in a totalitarian society, leaders could easily delude themselves that public opinion did not exist. While himself breaking powerful, seemingly eternal and inviolable Soviet taboos, Khrushchev continued to treat the intellectuals as learned servants who could be used for limited assignments and sent packing when importunate. His extremely brutal handling of the Pasternak affair now provides a unique opportunity to Gorbachev for exercises in tact and generosity.

Gorbachev's strategy of modernization has an implicit axiom which the Young Turks are in no particular hurry to spell out: Western economic performance and technology is the criterion of what is modern. And in the new generation of apparatchiks who had been living in an almost total disintegration of Soviet Marxism and the quasi-public indifference of the Brezhnevites for their own official doctrine for two decades, there are no internalized ideological taboos. In their perception there is one world technologically with two sharply different ways of life, Western and Soviet. The interests of the 'Soviet way of life' – those of a strong, conservative and oppressive authority not reducible to mere ideological prejudices, which Gorbachev wants to update but not to fundamentally alter – will decide to what extent the New Team is going to copy Western principles of economic organization.

As a result, Gorbachev cannot use the Brezhnevite apparatchiks with their fossilized sets of bias, ingrained habits of corruption and baffling inefficiency. Nor does he entertain illusions about 'reeducating' them. Therefore he has been moving since the first days of his ascendancy to power to replace them *en masse*. The new social actor, and, in all probability, the main beneficiary, of 'modernization' is the patriotic and efficient, ideologically neutral and flexible functionary, who does not deviate from the interests of the ruling corporation either in the form of corruption or through excessive social pluralism, who will be permitted to travel to the West and buy modern gadgets, who will be prepared, and competent, to conduct civilized conversations with businessmen in their own languages and who can, no less than their predecessors, draw the line beyond which pressure from below is not permitted.

The strategy of 'modernization' furthermore prescribes a pattern of relating to the intelligentsia which is different from Khrushchev's methods. Clearly, the Soviet leaders' main preceptor in devising a new attitude to the intellectuals was Kádárist Hungary in its 'liberalizing' phase. While their corporative and organizational autonomy continues to remain nil, intellectuals are being tacitly but persistently encouraged from behind the scenes to freely indulge in their alleged political and historic role. Thus they become better propagandists of the regime than under the petty and tyrannical tutelage of central committee departments. Moreover, intellectuals can *individually* join the apparatus in increasing numbers while remaining in complete self-delusion about their own social status, the latter making them all the more convincing in their former capacity. In addition, intellectuals are indispensable in another function. For the purposes of copying Western economic and technological arrangements, experts will do. But who would support the patriotic and authoritarian, yet 'rationalized' and 'efficient' 'Soviet way of life' better than the intellectual ideologue who maintains, perhaps candidly, the deceptive façade of intellectual autonomy, and who anyhow does not sport excessively democratic predilections himself?

Can Gorbachev be more successful than Khrushchev in the dual sense of implementing, not just promising, lasting changes *and* outliving Khrushchev's term in office? Five conditions have to be met for Gorbachev to last longer than the duration of a mere episode. The New Team has to find Western financial support in order to import sophisticated technology. It has to defeat its conservative enemies in the apparatus without major social upheavals. (The latter would either result in the restoration of Brezhnevism of a kind or they would trigger a Soviet 'cultural revolution' which for the time being has been unprecedented in Soviet history.) The New Team has to enjoy unambiguous but passive popular support in the process of implementing its strategy. It has to destroy several taboos of a half-century's standing but it has to preserve the taboo of the party's political prerogative. Finally, the New Team has to invent and introduce new social structures which would keep the results of the modernizing momentum alive in institutionalized channels.

Gorbachev has better chances than did Khrushchev as far as the first three preconditions are concerned. Gorbachev is, like Khrushchev, détente oriented, for détente does not imply renouncing expansionism, it only demands different, less overtly confrontationist methods. Once the Reagan period is over, or perhaps even in the last phase of Reagan's paralyzed presidency, Gorbachev could achieve his targets while Khrushchev had to struggle in vain against the double burden of still vigorous Cold War biases and the correct Western perception of his occasional expansionist and menacing escapades. We have seen why Gorbachev's conservative opponents are a collective sitting duck almost incapable of resistance. In this sense, time is on Gorbachev's side as it had worked against Khrushchev. If the remaining nuclei of the Brezhnevite apparatus will not act in concert within a year or two, their unlikely last card can only be a military coup against Gorbachev. It is no compliment to Soviet society when we predict a possible popular support which is unambiguous, which therefore paralyses Gorbachev's conservative enemies to a degree, but which is passive. Active popular support inevitably concludes in the demand of rights and pluralism which would be as unacceptable for Gorbachev as for his adversaries in the apparatus; or so it seems for the time being. Unfortunately, it is a long tradition of Russian history to hail the man on the summit without making the effort to share in his power. Gorbachev might just capitalize on this Russian tradition.

More difficult is the task of breaking, and with the same gesture preserving, taboos. Khrushchev for his part had spectacularly failed with this enterprise. When he broke the charismatic taboo and questioned Stalin's authority, he let the genie of an irreverent Enlightenment out of the bottle. And Gorbachev has to go even further than Khrushchev. For modernization to succeed, the whole fossilized body of Marxism-Leninism should be, preferably publicly, buried. But what if either the army generals or the proverbial 'masses' draw such conclusions from the iconoclasm of the top as are incompatible with the Soviet system as it now stands?

And one condition clearly cannot be satisfied on Gorbachev's own premises: the creation of institutional frameworks which perpetuate the modernizing momentum if it can be set in motion. In this respect, Gorbachev is truly an heir to the worst illusion of the Khrushchev era. He too keeps squaring the circle, reducing what is a social and political problem to the level of a mere technological dilemma. And yet, if there is a single major lesson to be derived from the economic reforms in Eastern Europe, from reforms which have been suspended or suppressed in most countries, lastingly experimented with in others, it is the inseparability of social change from economic modernization.

1987

10

Crisis and Crisis Management under Gorbachev

THE MEANING OF CRISIS IN THE SOVIET SYSTEM

The meaning of the term 'crisis', an apparent truism, turns out to be one of Churchill's famous 'mysteries wrapped up in an enigma' once we make a serious attempt at grasping its economic, political or cultural nature in the Soviet regime.

In order to illustrate this, we have selected the cases of agricultural crisis and inflation in the Soviet system. During the past 30 years, chronic agricultural stagnation has been covertly acknowledged in official Soviet vocabulary. Frequent references at party congresses to the necessity of 'solving the food problem' bear this out. Euphemisms such as 'agricultural impasse' or 'stagnation' appear as signs of crisis in the imagination and daily conversations of average Soviet citizens, who still manage to spend an annoyingly large amount of time standing in line for the staple articles in their diet.

As far as the official (party) position is concerned, it was only for the short period of Khrushchev's rule that the state of collectivized agriculture was acknowledged in the official media as being in a state of deep crisis. Khrushchev even went so far as to make the solution of the Soviet agricultural crisis his first political priority.[1] By contrast, until the ascendance of Gorbachev the term 'agricultural crisis' or 'the critical state of Soviet agriculture' completely disappeared from the lexicon of Soviet political life since Khrushchev's fall. Further official references to the continually unresolved 'food problem', as well as all objective descriptions of Soviet daily life in the Brezhnev era, suggest that while the term may have disappeared from use, the syndrome certainly remained.

The example of inflation is even more telling, since a debate on this problem has recently been raging in the Soviet media between journalists and economists on the one hand, and leading apparatchiks on the other. The debate concerning Soviet inflation turns, partly, on whether real wages are keeping up with consumer prices. In one article, *Literaturnaya Gazeta* reporter Anatoli Rubinov, who collected hundreds of letters from Soviet readers concerned about rising prices, writes that 'in recent times prices have risen out of proportion to wages . . . and not by kopeks, not even by just roubles.' But there is another story as well. Nikolai Belov, First Deputy Chairman of TSSU, the country's bureau of statistics, disagrees, saying that Mr Rubinov is 'not competent to draw conclusions' about inflation. Mr Belov called a news conference to announce that retail prices grew by only 8 percent from 1970 to 1986, while average monthly wages rose 60 percent from 122 roubles to 195 roubles. 'There can be no question of inflation or a drop in living standards in the Soviet Union,' he insists.[2]

What is at issue then is no less than deciding whether there has been a sharp inflationary trend in Soviet economic life, an unmistakable sign of the existence of crisis symptoms, or whether, on the other hand, there has prevailed in the USSR a deflationary politics for the last 16 years, something which would be almost unparalleled in any modern economy (and which, incidentally, is not necessarily a sign of sound economic performance). These two examples should suffice, perhaps, to bear out the truth of our statement, that is, that in the Soviet economy and in Soviet politics the meaning of the term 'crisis' is far from self-evident both with regard to its existence and its particular character.

There would seem to be an easy way out of this theoretical impasse. 'Objectively', many might argue, there have been easily definable periods of crisis in the Soviet economy, which are only covered up by false data, or often by simply not releasing statistical reports at all, which has, for example, been the case in China for decades. Yet, where are the 'objective criteria' on the basis of which the analyst can proceed to establish the 'objective existence' of economic crises in the USSR? The spectacular fiasco of CIA research on Soviet crude oil production a few years ago, the gross error of a study that predicted the sharp decline of Soviet production within years, proves the difficulty, if not the outright impossibility, of unveiling such 'objective criteria'. The CIA forecast turned out to be a total misreading of signs and symptoms in the Soviet economy despite the enormous funds presumably spent on research, and also despite the fact that the report was commissioned in order to advise administration policies rather than for propaganda purposes. From a technical point of view, it is the much-discussed enigma of reading Soviet military expenditures in the budget that underscores the difficulties caused by this almost impenetrable darkness.[3]

The causes of this opacity are well known. The Soviet economy is a command economy,[4] a *politically* integrated system in which the economic behavior of sectors and units is defined by the strategic will and decisions of 'omnipotent planners'. In its prime, the Soviet economy was devoid of publicly recognized, independent economic actors from whose behavior certain objective forecasts might be inferred. (Where independent actors did make sporadic appearances, these were, of course, economically marginalized.) In this system, the market was definitively abolished, or at least far-reachingly fragmented. Soviet investment strategy is politically, not economically, defined. Prices are political. The 'law of value', as Stalin himself correctly pointed out in the twenties, and repeated in the fifties, has no overall effect within it.[5] As a result, costs of production are also politically defined, which makes them, despite more recent and strenuous efforts by planners, economically incalculable. Finally, despite the ever-increasing ratio of foreign trade in the Soviet budget, the Soviet economy is not integrated into the world economy. Soviet economic behavior cannot, therefore, be influenced by external factors, an added difficulty in deciphering its mysteries.

The above remarks are well known to Soviet studies. The only reason for repeating such truisms here is that the logical conclusions have not yet been drawn from them regarding the meaning of the term 'crisis in Soviet society'. Our own conclusion is the following. 'Crisis' in Western capitalist economies can be defined as a shorter or longer period of economic malfunction, during which investment strategy remains unconfirmed or rejected by market indicators (the stock exchange being one of the most important); bankruptcies snowball and unemployment rises sharply; economic actors, from businesses to trade unions, publicly voice their lack of confidence in prevailing governmental economic and fiscal policies. And finally, unmistakable signs of the political disintegration of governments begin to emerge. If this is our working definition of 'crisis', then simply, and 'objectively', the term bears no relationship to the Soviet economy. Analysts and observers can go on endlessly looking for the 'objective criteria' of crisis in terms of the above definition, but they will never find them. The majority of indicators are simply not present in the Soviet system. While certain projects can be cancelled, the economy is *politically* coerced to maintain its dynamic (though at what level of growth cannot be established). Moreover, the Soviet economy *can* maintain this dynamic because production within it is not market-related. Buyers' opinions, and their general economic behavior, is irrelevant, or it is only politically, but not economically, relevant. As a result, the symptoms of a 'no-confidence vote' on their part are forcibly suppressed. Given that in the Soviet regime, the economic and the political cannot be separated from one another even temporarily, there is only a single criterion of Soviet economic crisis: a statement by the leadership to that effect. So understood, economic crisis has up until now surfaced only once in the USSR. It was there in the Khrushchev period when the First Man himself declared economic (and above all agricultural) affairs to be in a critical state. A similar example has been offered by China during the last seven to eight years, when Deng

Xiao-Ping described the state of the Chinese economy as one in turmoil since the cultural revolution.

The enigma we confront in exploring the term 'crisis' in Soviet society is not caused by a mere 'manipulative cover-up'; it is a much more 'objectively' impenetrable darkness for two reasons. Firstly, not only external observers, but *also the Soviet leaders themselves* are facing perpetual mysteries. An extremely interesting recent document sheds light on this perplexing phenomenon. András Hegedűs, once himself a major producer of doctored statistical yearbooks in post-1956 Hungary, gives the following account of this puzzle in his 'Autobiography in Interviews'. The existence of two distinct sets of statistical data, he states, one falsified and the other correct (the latter kept in a secret safe), is nothing but popular legend. As a matter of course, he remarks, statistical data were doubly forged by the central bureau of statistics. First, they were 'adjusted' before they went to the politburo, which most of the time wanted to see only 'optimistic results', and then again later, before data were released to the public. However, it is simply not true that the initial data would have represented an 'objective picture' of the state of the economy. The forgers themselves were collecting data which, they knew full well, had already been doctored by the ministries and economic units. Therefore, even in the rare moments when leadership *did* want to face up to reality, it could not do so.[6]

The second cause of this impenetrably opaque character of Soviet economic reality derives from the fact that Soviet leaders define crisis symptoms on the basis of strategic-political considerations, and not on that of economic indicators. (This is consistent with the main features of their regime.) It follows from this that what is regarded as 'critical' varies in Soviet society from period to period, from leader to leader, and from strategy to strategy. In fact, Soviet history proper began with a 'hermeneutical debate' (with terrible pragmatic consequences) on the meaning of 'crisis'. For Bukharin, the advocate *par excellence* of the NEP, the slow growth of Soviet industry was a totally acceptable phenomenon as long as the slowly growing Soviet industry supplied a sufficient amount of consumer goods to keep agricultural production for the market alive. For Stalin and the majority of the party apparatus, slow growth presented a major crisis. Nove shows how Stalin and his entourage interpreted the sudden decrease in marketed grain in 1928, a minor dysfunction that could have been easily eliminated by a shift in pricing policies, as the sign of an impending catastrophe. This again was not inconsistent with the general terms of their strategy.[7]

The exclusively political distinction between what is 'critical' in Soviet economic life and what is not critical, can best be understood if we cast a glance at 'mature' Stalinism. Soviet agriculture never performed more terribly than under Stalin, and yet this great designer of manmade famines remained totally unimpressed by acute stagnation or sharp decline. In terms of his strategy, these phenomena were not critical factors. Therefore, under Stalin there was no agricultural crisis in the USSR, not even when millions died of starvation and when agricultural production fell, according to the testimony of Khrushchev, below the level of the last peace years under the Tsar. On the other hand, it is quite legitimate to read his enigmatic *The Economic Problems of Socialism in the USSR* of 1951 as an indirect, and somewhat coded, message about a dangerous crisis symptom. We now know from accumulated evidence that in 1950–1 Stalin predicted that the outbreak of World War Three would occur in the near future.[8] Thus, it can be said, that Stalin legitimately regarded the economic situation of the 'socialist camp' as critical around the years of 1949–51. The postwar reconstruction in several 'people's democracies' had not even come to an end, not to mention their concerted embarkation on an accelerated rhythm of war economy. The control over agricultural production, a major factor in a war economy, was far from completely in the hands of the various communist apparatuses. The smooth economic cooperation of the national communist leaderships under the tutelage of the Soviet politburo was not even in an embryonic stage. If, therefore, we read Stalin's text as the (covert) expression of the Soviet leadership's 'crisis consciousness', and we contrast it with its imperturbable attitude toward agricultural stagnation or decline, we can grasp the meaning of the *political* definition of *economic* crisis in Soviet society.

This is why the Gorbachev strategy of 'modernization' becomes the key concept in fathoming what the terms 'crisis' and 'crisis solving' denote in current Soviet politics and economic affairs. To our knowledge, the word 'crisis' has not been officially used by the Soviet leaders, yet the often tense tenor of Gorbachev's speeches and the artificially created atmosphere of urgency does suggest a 'crisis awareness'. The single, and at the same time sufficient, proof of the existence of an economic crisis, namely the leaders' public discomfort about economic performance, is clearly in evidence in the USSR.

What precise content does the leadership give to the crisis? What are their proposals for crisis solving? What are the alternative scenarios observers may infer from the presently available symptoms?[9] The immediate objective of the new leadership is twofold: a drastic change in the elite, a preferably complete reshuffling and replacement of the 'conservative', 'inefficient', and 'corrupt' Brezhnev gerontocracy, *and* the overcoming of the current Soviet stagnation in industrial growth and its technological lag. Although it is never publicly stated, the Soviet emphasis on bringing the American experience with the Strategic Defense Initiative to a halt (a major preoccupation of the Soviet leaders, who ostensibly take the project incomparably more seriously than critical Western scientists), shows that the main motif of this second aspect of their strategy is *fear*. They are visibly concerned that current stagnation has dangerously affected Soviet military might.

The Gorbachev scenario is only one of the presently possible alternatives which could be played out in the USSR with an actually existing actor. This actor is the so-called 'progressive wing' of the apparatus, which seems to be ready to admit the existence of crisis but only in the narrow sense of a temporary failure to compete against Western technology. Well-definable perspectives of, and limitations on, future political action follow from this reductive definition of the crisis as 'technological'. The new leadership, as well as its partisans, pride themselves on being non-ideological and 'scientific'; they reject all sorts of taboos where technological modernization is concerned.

In fact, the criterion of what is modern has been borrowed by them from Western (and Japanese) technology. Moreoever, the new leadership flirts with the introduction of 'certain market elements' but, at least for the time being, its definition of crisis stops short of structural reforms in the Soviet economic, not to mention political, system. For the first time since Khrushchev, the Soviet perception of crisis is therefore lucid and realistic; it is also dangerously self-reductive. This is so because, even if the West is prepared to fund the New Course with extremely generous loans, Soviet society still has very little hope for regaining its competitive edge in the technology race as long as its self-definition of crisis remains exclusively technological.

There are three major hypothetical, alternative scenarios of modernization,[10] each of which for the time being has only a fictitious, and not actual, agent but each of which presumably proposes a distinct definition of crisis. For the intellectual-technocratic scenario the crisis is explicitly economic, rather than merely technological. Its forerunners, vociferous critics of the inconsistencies of the new leadership, are already gathering on the margins of the terrain mapped out by the present 'thaw'.[11] For them, the cause of the deep and frustrating economic, and not just technological crisis, is easily identifiable in the system of a 'command economy' *as a whole*, which they may or may not identify with 'socialism' as such. The partisans of the intellectuals' scenario are in this sense radical. But where the *political* aspect of the crisis solving is concerned, they propose no significant changes. They are patriotic (in a Great Russian sense); the grandeur of the Fatherland is crucial for them. They are liberal-minded as far as the protection of the private sphere from state intervention is concerned. But they are not democrats in the sense of being committed to a free public sphere and political pluralism.

It is perfectly clear (to the extent to which anything can be clear with respect to the future behavior of hypothetical actors) what 'crisis' will mean for the reformist communist as well as the military, if and when these actors appear on the Soviet political scene. For the reformist communist, the crisis will appear as 'political', one caused by the 'decay', 'obsolescence, 'perversion', or 'aberration' of the political system. For the topranking officers of the army, the definition of the 'crisis' is an even more simple operation. Each and every phenomenon that reduces Soviet military might, above all slow economic growth and lagging behind Western technology, constitutes a crisis symptom. The army, presumably, has no doctrinaire postulates concerning the means of overcoming the crisis. Literally every move that accelerates growth and technological development would be acceptable for the military. This is why the army is, in all probability, going to be a passive but trustworthy ally of the new leadership in the initial phase. But this is also why it will inevitably become an extremely dangerous and uncontrollable factor if 'modernization' again fails to deliver the goods.

ALTERNATIVE CULTURES OF CRISIS SOLVING

We have seen that there are no 'objective criteria' of crisis that exist independently from the 'crisis consciousness' of the USSR's only public actor, the party apparatus. Further, alternative meanings of 'crisis', and therefore alternative crisis scenarios, are similarly constituted by the distinct type of 'crisis consciousness' affecting the party. Thus, the problem of 'crisis' can only be solved if a powerful and dominating 'culture of crisis solving' appears on the scene.[12] This is why a solution to crisis in Soviet society can never be entirely pragmatic, and is always incomparably less so than in any other society. Crisis solving is, of course, inseparable from correct economic strategy, but it is at every level a more complex task than the construction of mere economic blueprints.

Gorbachev has apparently grasped aspects of the need for a new 'culture of crisis solving'. A single example will suffice to prove this assumption: his crusade to root out alcoholism. Without doubt, the plague of Soviet alcoholism, its crippling impact on an already serious demographic crisis (the USSR is the only industrially developed country with a *decreasing* curve of life expectancy), and the burden it adds to a thoroughly inadequate health-care system, would be major concerns for any Soviet government. And yet these pragmatic concerns do not account for the centrality of the anti-alcoholism drive in Gorbachev's policies. This campaign has a *symbolic-cultural* function which is closely related to crisis solving: alcoholism is a metaphor for the politics of modernization. It is the traditional, national and cultural, diseases of Soviet Russian life that the metaphor stands for: listlessness, passive and suicidal endurance of the calamities of life, collective, organized, and even glorified self-destruction, and a massive loss of personal dignity. Furthermore, it demands a new code for its resolution. Paradoxically, the Soviet politics of modernization have quickly reached the stage of 'postmodernism';

that is, that of a health cult as ersatz for religious foundations in Gorbachev's campaign against alcoholism.[13]

How wide and deep are the domestic reserves of alternative cultural scenarios for crisis solving? In raising this question alone, we are in the midst of the crisis itself for the answer is that almost nothing in the present Soviet cultural arsenal provides even the raw materials needed for new cultures of crisis solving. This is the historical hour when the oldfashioned as well as the new kinds of illness found in Russian Soviet history now present their bill to the Soviet leaders, who are sifting the debris of the Soviet cultural wasteland for the stimulating ideas and elements of a new code, only to end up empty-handed. 'Marxism-Leninism' was already dead during the decades of the Brezhnev gerontocracy. It is the terrible irony of history that the Brezhnevites had given it the *coup de grace*, not so much by the jetsam and flotsam they heaped upon its anyhow defunct corpus but by reducing reformist communism, as well as the 'renaissance of Marxism', to impotence and humiliation. For Hegel was perfectly right: a church is vigorous and alive only so long as it is capable of splitting. Marxism as a 'philosophy of praxis' proved true to itself in its demise also. It ceased to exist in Eastern Europe and the USSR at the moment when there were no longer actors who would have committed themselves to it.

The only new ideology emerging in the last 15 years or so is actually very old. It is traditional Russian nationalism in its most obscurantist version, with or without an alliance with equally traditional religious creeds. In the case of Solzhenytsin, a very traditionalist Russian nationalism, in terms of which the broken continuity of national history is the cause of all ills, has regressed to the master plan of Ivan Karamazov by grounding the new Russian state in the monastery. With such movements as Rodina in the seventies and Pamiat more recently, Russian nationalism has only one religion, and it is the religion of the mob: a hysterical and mythologized anti-Semitism. And the new leadership cannot smoothly navigate on these fairly dirty waves of Russian neonationalism for three reasons. First, neonationalism is *Great Russian* chauvinism; its excessive patriotic zeal might do untold damages to imperial interests. Secondly, although the Soviet leaders of today are no longer concerned with the doctrinaire issues of the Soviet past, they still cannot declare the genesis of their regime, the seizure of power in October of 1917, the exact point of time when the fatal breach of continuity occurred, a non-event. Finally, Russian neonationalism cannot serve as a new culture of crisis solving due to its own traditionalist features, and thus its inherent suspicions of Westernist 'modernization' itself. In Solzhenytsin's famous *Letter to the Leaders of the Soviet Union*, ideological parochialism uncovers its explicit sociological basis: the project of a country which is based on a sturdy, conservative, religious and industrious class of farmers.[14] This rural idyll is, of course, entirely incompatible with the tastes, interests, and the political-economic objectives of the modernizers.

The much too homogeneous vision of a uniform Soviet cultural wasteland, of course, evaporates as soon as we begin to analyze the (actual and hypothetical) cultures of 'crisis solving'. Modernization as the cultural solution of technological crisis has a quite unique flavor. The 'background feeling' from which this culture has sprung in the last two decades is a probably widespread conviction among the younger generation of functionaries. From their view, the gerontocracy has three characteristic features: incompetence in all matters requiring expertise (not just doctrinaire hairsplitting); corruption on a scale known only in oriental empires unfamiliar with the terms 'public interest' or 'common weal'; and, finally, not merely immobility or conservatism but the outright rule of *Russian laziness* (*Russkaya leñ*). By focusing on Russian laziness, the new leadership has come up with what constitutes their single original insight and cultural recommendation so far, and, in doing so, have joined a venerable trend in Russian culture. 'Oblomovism', this self-imposed paralysis both at the top and at the bottom of Russian life, has been the target of visceral hate by all those intent on modernizing Russia from the last quarter of the nineteenth century onwards. Lenin poured vituperative attacks on it. Bolshevism in its initial phase can be regarded as a crusade against Russian laziness, to which a cult of efficiency and feverish activity was opposed (with its well-known conclusion: the 'industriousness' of enslaved millions in Stalin's camps). The underlying originality of Gorbachev's conception of modernization consists in making a direct connection between laziness and corruption at the top and at the bottom. Gorbachev's philippics against the corruption of 'the great families' *and* the popular habit of swindling and lazing around show a degree of insight into the unity of a morbid culture.[15]

However, Gorbachev's campaign against 'Russian laziness' is extremely one-dimensional. The missing dimensions are, above all, the historical ones. Any society undergoing so violent a rupture as Russia did, not even a century ago, lives perforce in vehement spasms as long as it does not find an ideology and cultural pattern for 'a reconciliation with the past'.[16] Without a cultural pattern for such a reconciliation, there can be no national regeneration or crisis solving of any kind. But the new leadership lives in antinomies. It cannot entirely abandon the particular principle of legitimation, Soviet Russian nationalism, on which its power has been resting for 30 years. Moreover, it is due precisely to its nationalist legitimation that the leadership can find some semblance of common language with its arch-reactionary opposition. Nor can it, however, entirely shed the vestiges of its own conception: Soviet annals have to be written *ab urbe condita*. This, then, brings the new leadership on a collision course with rightist-fundamentalist nationalism.

The modernizers will face further grave dilemmas once they transcend, if they do so at all, their own extremely narrow definition of crisis, their one-dimensional campaign against 'Russian laziness' and when they try to embark on the process of redefining Soviet culture. The immediate questions to be addressed by them are as follows. What is 'Soviet culture'? Is it 'European'? An answer in the affirmative would put them in the cluster of 'Westernizers', a label no Soviet leader after Lenin has wanted to accept. At the same time, it would also bring them into serious conflict with traditional Russian nationalism. An answer in the negative would render the whole strategy of modernization empty and meaningless. Is, further, Soviet culture 'specifically Soviet'? Is it, rather, 'Russian'? All possible answers to these questions, which are inevitably posed once the struggle with technological backwardness and 'Russian laziness' transcends its most narrow framework, harbor such difficulties that the new leadership is not adequately equipped for coping with them. Insofar as the Gorbachev team seriously intends to cure the chronic crises of their society, they will have to launch an overdue edition of Russian reformation that will imply a new moral code, a novel type of work ethic, and therein a roster of values unprecedented in Russian Soviet history. Thus far, they have barely glimpsed the enormity of their task.

Technocrats and intellectuals, who interpret the crisis as 'economic', seem to be incomparably more confident from a cultural point of view. Their program is, as mentioned, one of a limited Enlightenment. In many ways, their conception of rationality is a fairly archaic one. They continue asking the classic questions of a very early stage of the Enlightenment, without apparently being in the slightest aware of the deep crisis of rationality that exists today. This blindness is their forte as well as their weakness. It is a forte insofar as they have a doctrinaire feeling of certitude about what crisis means and its remedy. Armed with this unassailable knowledge, and apparently unaware of the historical storms each and every therapist of modernity has unleashed when these wise doctors sought to cure modern society through the self-regulating mechanics of the market, the intelligentsia enters the arena to sell the panacea of the full, emancipated market system. For a number of reasons, this same doctrinaire streak is their fatal weakness. They are rationalist Westernizers, and yet at the same time they are Soviet patriots. (Sakharov is the paragon of this combination.) As long as the Bolshevik revolution appeared at least to sections of the Russian intelligentsia in the twenties as a new and universal stage of Western rationality, no problem seemed to exist with this combination. But for present Westernizing Soviet intellectuals, the term 'socialism' has either lost all meaning and relevance, or it is a hostile force. (L. Popkova puts it bluntly: either socialism or market relations. The two are incompatible.[17]) If, however, in this combination of West-oriented rationality and Soviet patriotism, the 'Soviet dimension' no longer carries universalistic connotations, if it is simply identical with the Westernizer's allegiance to the nation-state, their flank is no longer protected against the barrage of Russian traditionalists. The latter are either universalists in the sense of propagating the universal panacea of Russia as 'the third Rome' or they are late Slavophiles, apostles of Russian singularity and segregation. In both cases, they will regard the Westernizing rationalists as a force not less alien to the Russian spirit than Bolshevism itself. The conflict between the two seems inevitable.

Furthermore, it is the Westernizers' patriotic allegiance to the Soviet state that, just as it limits their conception of Enlightenment, makes them politically indifferent. They are opposed, often in a heroic manner, to the excesses of the Soviet state. However, on the personal level, insofar as this state is prepared to endorse a minimal degree of rationality and embrace a market economy, its members are not particularly busy with the promotion of alternative political structures to the one presently existing. The Soviet system, as it now stands, seems to be to them Soviet history, and as such, it is untouchable. In the writers' view, this voluntary abandonment of the democratic alternative, that of the citizen, dooms their 'culture of crisis solving' to failure from the start.

Looking at the present, still unfolding, political drama from a historical perspective, both nascent 'cultures of crisis solving' appear as repetitions of centennial dilemmas and antinomies of Russian history. This history has always been full of *étatiste* reformers, from Peter the Great via Alexander I and the Jacobin Pestel to Alexander II. In his own way, not one of them was prepared to resign the idea of a strong central power, traditional or modern-Bonapartist, as the *locus sui generis* of modernizing Russian society. Their dogmatic emphasis on the first aspect invariably frustrated the pragmatic efforts of the reformers in power with respect to the second: their projects always remained one-dimensional. From the mid-nineteenth century onwards, the liberal actor also surfaced with its advocacy of formalized, purposive rational relationships, preferably in all areas of social life excepting the political. In the latter domain, they displayed an enormous and fatal pusillanimity as well as a misplaced respect for what seemed to have been the political tradition. Apparently, we are going to live a new chapter of the old drama if Gorbachevschina gets off the ground at all.

Paradoxically, the road to crisis solving in Soviet society leads to short-term intensification of the crisis itself. In order for all interpretations of crisis to appear in sharp relief, for all scenarios and 'cultures of crisis solving' to fully unfold, all actors, embryonic or even for the time being merely hypothetical, have to appear on the scene. Furthermore, they have to enjoy the amount of tolerance necessary to formulate their own recommendations and submit them to a nascent public opinion. This would make the crisis political in nature. But then the only chance Soviet society has for solving the crisis is in raising the debate from a technological, or merely economic, level into the domain of the political.

1988

NOTES

1 A detailed analysis of Khrushchev's position on Soviet agricultural crisis can be found in G. Breslauer, *Khrushchev and Brezhnev: Leadership Styles* (Berkeley: University of California Press, 1982).
2 'Soviet media admit inflation's existence', *Wall Street Journal*, Friday, May 22, 1987, p. 15.
3 The mystery that envelops the part of Soviet budget spent on military expenditures has been sufficiently analyzed by A. Nove in his book, *The Soviet Economic System*, (London/Boston/Sydney: Allen and Unwin, 1978), see pp. 237, 239.
4 While the term 'command economy' is commonplace in the literature on Soviet societies, we use it in the specific sense we have given the term in our book, F. Fehér, A. Heller and G. Márkus, *Dictatorship Over Needs* (Oxford: Basil Blackwell, 1983).
5 J. Stalin, 'Economic problems of socialism in the USSR', in Bruce Franklin, ed., *The Essential Stalin* (New York: Anchor Books, Doubleday, 1972), pp. 458–63.
6 András Hegedüs, *Elet egy eszme árnyékában* (Vienna: Z. Zsille's edition, 1986), pp. 227–33. The degree to which the most critical economic issues remain opaque can also be seen in a more recent and revealing example: 'Last month, in the newspaper *Sovietskaya Rossiya*, a senior member of the prestigious Moscow Institute of Economics, Alexei Sergeyev, attacked the credibility of the TSSU and said Soviet industrial production is at least 3 times lower than shown in official statistics. In a denunciation of the country's statistical reporting, the February edition of the journal *Novy Mir* indicated that Soviet economic growth during the past seven decades had been exaggerated more than ten times.' 'Moscow seeks more accurate economic data', *Wall Street Journal*, April 6, 1987.
7 A. Nove, *An Economic History of the USSR* (Harmondsworth: Penguin, 1979), p. 144.
8 E. Ochab and Jakub Berman, both leading Stalinist functionaries in Poland during the Stalin period, explicitly followed Stalin's conviction that World War Three was impending. Ochab had even participated in a meeting, presided over by Stalin, in 1950 in Moscow, in which Stalin treated World War Three not as a possibility but as a certainty, and demanded increased, and more concerted, efforts for preparations for war in the East European economies. See Berman's and, in particular, Ochab's statement in Teresa Toranska, *Them: Stalin's Polish Puppets* (New York: Harper and Row, 1987), p. 46. I also know from the personal communication of G. Lukács that he had been advised by J. Révai,

number four in Hungary's Muscovite leadership, that the war, in Stalin's authoritative assessment, would, by 1953, be inevitable.

9   We have analyzed the alternative (hypothetical) scenarios in the previous chapter. Therefore I can be brief here.

10 In the previous chapter, we mentioned two further hypothetical scenarios: that of a radical-democratic revolution (which is clearly only a logical possibility) and that of a dual socioeconomic partnership (workers' self-management). However, these scenarios can be left out of consideration in discussing 'crisis' in Soviet society.

11 An example of such criticism is the letter published in *Novy Mir* written by Larisa Popkova, an economist. She remarks sardonically on the proposed introduction of a 'certain degree of market relations' that 'we cannot be a little bit pregnant.' See 'Soviet article doubts economic line', *New York Times*, May 9, 1987.

12 The term 'culture' is roughly equivalent here to what C. Castoriadis terms 'the imaginary institution of signification', that is, to the collective, and more or less institutionalized, capacity of a society, or at least of a dominant social group within it, of creating such ideas, values and collective images as generate autonomous action aiming at the implementation of the project inherent in the 'new imaginary institution'.

13 And the campaign is understood precisely as metaphor, as an attempt at a culture of crisis solving, for example, by the Pamiat group, a movement that liberal Russians describe as heirs to the Black Hundreds. As we see from the article 'Russian nationalists test Gorbachev', *New York Times*, May 24, 1987, p. 10, the Pamiat activists interpret the anti-alcoholism slogans as the first step toward restoring traditional Russian dignity and historical spirit.

14 Aleksander Solzhenytsin, 'Open letter to the Soviet Union', in *East and West* (New York: Harper and Row, 1980).

15 Popular fiction is sometimes a good indicator of such feelings *en masse* which, for one reason or another, have not gained expression in 'high culture'. This is why we regard the thrillers by two Soviet writers, E. Topol and F. Neznansky, for some time living in exile, as stunning portrayals of this morbid culture (see, above all, *Red Square* – see our review in Chapter 8 above – and *The Corpse in the Sokolniki Park*).

16 Raymond Aron claimed to his last day (see R. Aron, *France – Steadfast and Changing* (Cambridge, Mass.: Harvard University Press, 1959), p. 33, that France never regained complete political equilibrium, and certainly never reached consensus on its constitutional-political forms after 1789. It was the unique wisdom of the American republic that its political class could find its way back to the constitution and the principles of its origin after the violent drama of the Civil War. And it is a strange irony that the main victor and the main defeated from the Second World War, the USSR and Germany, have been living for 40 years, in different forms, but yet alike, in the torments of *Bewältigung der Vergangenheit*.

17 See note 11 above.

11

Eastern Europe Enters the Nineties

GORBACHEV-CUNCTATOR

Fabius Maximus Quintus was the Roman general whose unorthodox strategy of delaying every major decision at the beginning of the Second Punic War gave Rome the time and chance to gather her forces and brace for victory. Hence his appellation 'Cunctator', or the Delayer, which at this time was a title of flattery and recognition. Likewise, Gorbachev's four years in power are best summarized by giving him the title of Gorbachev-Cunctator, for he too has used a similar strategy. But these years did not bring triumph to either him or his cause, no matter how one defines the cause. Nor did they grant Gorbachev safe leadership or general accolade. And yet, this appellation still best summarizes the story of an ambitious apparatchik's gradual rise to statesmanship.

For all the major changes associated with his name, such as the coming end of the Cold War, the gradual liberation of Eastern Europe, and the releasing (if within limits) of free opinion and freedom of association from its bonds at home, result from his systematic delaying of making momentous decisions. 'Delaying' has a dual meaning in this context. First, Gorbachev refrained from violent intervention in social turbulences (except when they threatened elementary social order, primarily in the case of ethnic conflicts, when it is every government's common duty to appear on the scene with arms and authority). So far, he has not ordered military intervention when national republics have organized patriotic fronts with the explicit purpose of (minimally) reshaping the empire or when miners went on strike. He occasionally thunders against the 'irresponsibility of journalists', demands the resignation of editors, and uses all sorts of devious methods to narrow the scope of the opposition's printed voice. But press freedom has been growing steadily because Gorbachev-Cunctator ultimately recoils from coercive actions.

The second meaning of 'delaying' is 'restraining others'. In the world of international relations, there never and nowhere has been full *glasnost;* therefore we are abandoned to the grapevine when discussing Gorbachev-Cunctator's restraining actions (or rather: non-actions) with regard to Eastern Europe. One can guess fairly accurately what his reply was to the evidently hysterical Rakowski's phone call in the final hours in Poland when the communists were forced to power-sharing by a victorious Solidarity. For Soviet intervention did not come, and the communists had to sit down to the bargaining table. One can do more than guess, one knows (for the story has already been leaked to the press), what Gorbachev replied to Honecker whose only therapeutic recommendation in the gravest hour of a national crisis in East Germany was the 'Tiananmen Square treatment'. Even if Gorbachev did not boot him out of power in the unceremonious fashion of Khrushchev and Brezhnev, he restrained him by denying Soviet army backing in case of a revolution provoked by bloodshed; and Gorbachev's non-action proved a major trigger to releasing popular energies.

'Refraining from' and 'restraining' is not tantamount to a *liberté sans rivages.* The limits, although not the rules, of the game are firmly set. They are imperial unity, membership in the Warsaw Pact, and the defence of communist power from *violent* takeover. This is why he still delivers arms aplenty to the despicable Afghan regime; this is why he insisted on keeping the Polish armed forces under communist control. But where the communist power erodes of itself and where thus violence would be the method of those who intend to maintain the *status quo ante,* as is clearly the case in Hungary, East Germany and Czechoslovakia, Gorbachev-Cunctator has so far behaved in the fashion of a benevolent, albeit critical, observer. Moreover, the recantation following the Malta summit of the five Warsaw Pact countries of their former governments' decision to invade reformist Czechoslovakia in 1968 was tantamount to a *formal* pledge to authorize changes.

Can we guess the presence of a set theory and a consistent strategy behind this pattern of systematic delaying? There are two options Gorbachev–Cunctator deliberately foregoes, two historical precedents of change that must have haunted his memory during his early days of ascendancy to power: those of Khrushchev and Mao. Khrushchev's name is an equivalent to stormy experiments with the system's ultimately unaltered and repressive structure in the name of 'substantive rationality' (a term which stands for the fathoming of the regime's allegedly existing profound rationality reserves, and a freer application of science with authoritarian interruptions). There is every reason to believe that the technocrats and intellectuals, future advisers of Gorbachev, who were tinkering with reforms during the last years of Brezhnev (and whom we have tried to characterize in the analysis of *Red Square*), had already lost faith by the early eighties in Khrushchev's panaceas. As for Mao, his name carries a substantive and a methodological connotation.

The first is tantamount to the rule of a tyrannical and anti-modernizing egalitarianism which, by definition, cannot be Gorbachev's option. The methodological connotation is 'revolution from above'. We suspect that Gorbachev indeed once flirted with the idea of a 'revolution from above' and later abandoned it. Proof of this 'theory experiment' was the vehemence of his public attacks, at the Twenty-Seventh Congress and after, on the corrupt, gerontocratic and inefficient apparatus he inherited from Brezhnev, the dismissal of apparatchiks by the score, the evident signs of the intention to change the power elite as a whole and the publicized preparations for a series of trials of highstanding ex-Brezhnevites for abuse of official power. But the gathering storm in the political heavens has by now quieted down, and the new 'revolution from above' did not occur.

From the abandoned options, certain positive conclusions can be tentatively drawn. Gorbachev himself was politically socialized in a period when the whole country was almost mortally sick of the continuous omnipresence of unrestrained violence by the state. He must have understood at some point that, whatever the goals he had wanted to achieve with a 'revolution from above', the concomitant waves of destruction exact too heavy a price on everyone. Perhaps he also sensed that certain objectives, above all modernization, are unattainable by the methods of Stalin and Mao. He equally must have been aware, sooner than others, of the unbearable tensions produced by the Brezhnevian combination of economic stagnation and heightened military expansionism. Proof of his awareness is his audacious cancellation of the war in Afghanistan. His exhortations also suggest that he does not have an extremely high opinion of the Russian Soviet society's capability of taking the initiative and implementing reforms of itself.

Adding to the above, if we say that the whole process also must have been one of self-education (Gorbachev in 1989 is clearly not identical with the ambitious Young Turk of 1985), we are perhaps justified in drawing the following conclusion. A combined awareness of society's lethargy in the face of a new cycle of violence; of the complexity of a program of modernization; of the recognition that blueprints for change simply do not exist; of the depth of crisis and the absence of creative energies (but of the presence of destructive and divisive furies); these must have led Gorbachev-Cunctator to the conviction that he has to buy time and delay irreversible decisions. Time for what? For us, it seems likely that Gorbachev's ultimate hope lies in the very process of the self-awakening of intellectual and moral energies coming from different directions. 'What we don't know, we shall figure out together' – this seems to be the new leader's guiding maxim. Gorbachev apparently does not intend to give a definite direction to the process because he does not want to pretend that he is aware of the only correct direction. For this maxim to be put to use, people simply have to learn, both on the top and at the social bottom, how to coexist peacefully and how to launch a course of violence-free debate. This is perhaps not a Periclean wisdom but, short of better action plans, and above all, short of more vigorous and resourceful social actors, it will do for a while.

But for how long? And this question touches upon areas where 'cunctator-ship' is clearly an inadequate strategy: changing the political institutions and reforming the economy. In these crucial aspects, the bottom line of Gorbachev's performance is negative. Moreover, the Cunctator threatens the very existence of his course by delaying action permanently. This is not an appeal to 'change now' in Yeltsin's cavalier fashion, an appeal without the slightest inkling of what to change and how. It is, rather, a memento that, in discussing constantly shelved institutional and economic changes, we have arrived at the limits of Gorbachev's room for maneuver. The regime cannot be reformed on its premises (a statement whose truth has been sufficiently borne out by the revolutions of Eastern Europe), and the character, the direction, the potentials, as well as the predictable results of any change of consequence are not defined by the man at the helm but by his partners. This warrants the reconsideration of the social space around Gorbachev-Cunctator.

We already performed a similar analysis in early 1987 (see chapter 9 on 'The Gorbachev Phenomenon' above). But the two-and-a-half years that have elapsed have been crucial in one respect: the dichotomy 'state–civil society' no longer provides a suitable framework for analysis. First, the 'state' (or the party-state) now appears in two entirely different guises. Its civilian and military branches act differently, and Gorbachev cannot be said to be entirely identified with either of them. Rather, he serves as an umpire between the different factions. A further complicating factor, and not just for Gorbachev or for the analyst but also for the populace of the USSR at large, is that the official ideology and power habits are still strong enough to inhibit full and free self-expression of the various factions. In Hungary in 1989, the spokesmen of the army made heavily political statements in a spirit contrary to the opinion of the then formally still ruling party, which, in turn, became publicly faction-ridden. Statements of the army's non-political character have recently been released by its spokesmen in Czechoslovakia and East Germany. For the time being, but no one knows for how long, this would be inconceivable in the Soviet Union.

With this proviso, which indicates that we are still facing sociologically largely unfathomable entities, the following can be stated of the predictable behavior of the various sections of 'the state'. The party apparatus still burgeons as an ever-present threat to Gorbachev's experiments (and the more East Europe's liberation progresses, providing an instructive story for them, the more so). But the apparatchiks have evidently lost a good deal of their arrogant self-confidence by exposure to the barrage of an increasingly free public opinion for at least three years. They would not dare to take the decisive step without the army. At the same time, using Hungarian parallels, one can even assume that a considerable part of the apparatus has already built up private economic empires, having accumulated investment capital as well, and that they are eager to shed the straitjacket of an overcentralized state. The self-transformation of a ruling corporation into a class pure and simple, a phenomenon analyzed by us in this volume, may have progressed far enough for this change of mind.

The army has so far given a vote of confidence to Gorbachev's strategy of letting loose domestic public opinion and Finlandizing Eastern Europe. This surprising tolerance is due in the main, we guess, to their similarly eroded self-confidence. Afghanistan dissipated for ever the global belief in the invincibility of the Soviet army. Its performance during natural and manmade catastrophes (the earthquake in Armenia and Chernobyl) did nothing to restore this image. (And we can expect further surprises, once the real story of the 'Ussuri war' between Chinese troops and the Soviet army at the end of Mao's cultural revolution is leaked to the press.) The myth of the Soviet army being the bulwark of 'purposive rationality' within an irrationally functioning economy is likewise finished. They evidently need as thorough an overhaul and modernization as society at large, and they can expect it only from *perestroika*.

The situation is, therefore, one of a stalemate between the umpire, the apparatus and the army. This provides some space and a certain amount of time for Gorbachev-Cunctator, but the atmosphere is not conducive to radical change. As far as 'society' is concerned, its internal division is equally thoroughgoing. People (sometimes the same persons) behave in widely different ways insofar as they belong to a certain stratum or to a certain ethnic group. Various ethnic groups, particularly from the Baltic region, display an impressive and constructive spirit of nationbuilding (or rebuilding), but they are, understandably, disruptive of the empire. Some others, especially in the Transcaucasian area, exhibit such reciprocal hatred that it ought to be kept in check by force even by the most liberal central authority. The intelligentsia is still by and large behind *glasnost* and *perestroika*, but their predictable group differences are now surfacing. For many of them, and for different reasons, Gorbachev has become an unacceptable option. At the same time, the same intellectuals, highly critical of the Cunctator, may firmly back him if the domination of the Slav (or merely Russian) nucleus of the empire is endangered. All this suggests that, in addition to the democratic reform of the state and the transformation of the command economy, a third institutional objective has clearly appeared on the horizon: the transformation of the Soviet federation into a confederation (if the historical hour is not already too late for this).

The workers, and the miners above all, slowly embark on strikes and (local) self-organization, but so far, nothing similar to Solidarity has appeared in the USSR. The first free opinion poll made in the Soviet Union on a nationwide sample showed the predictable bifurcation: while over 60 per cent of those interviewed described the economic situation in terms of decline and the fiasco of *perestroika,* more than 70 percent characterized their own economic situation as improving. The seemingly illogical result is perfectly understandable to those who have lived in or studied the old regime. People are still investing, if not their hopes or trust, then at least their urgent demands in the central authority instead of taking the initiative on their own. The latter course would compel them to make a realistic and sober balance sheet of both their private and public affairs. The attitude of a dependent subject, however, calls for hysterical alarm in the public sphere, and for grudging and moderate expressions of relative satisfaction in the private one.

All this can be summed up in two points. First, the present confusion does not offer a single, or even a few, distinct and clear blueprints for reformatory action. In this sense, Gorbachev's 'cunctatorship' is completely understandable. But it cannot remain a *longue durée* strategy because then his anyhow fragile regime is doomed to collapse. The second point comes as no surprise to us: while the East European regimes turn out to be shaky edifices created by military occupation or coups hatched or backed by a foreign army (with the exception of Yugoslavia and, surprisingly, Albania), the ruling apparatus of the USSR has a repressive legitimacy through the chauvinism of the Russian nucleus and by the oppression of all other social conflicts.

THE GERMAN QUESTION

When we published our prediction about a possible and menacing renewal of the Rapallo treaty between Germany and the Soviet Union in the early eighties, the German reaction to it was an almost unanimous combination of hostility and derision. No one, we were advised, thinks seriously of the German reunification; only over-zealous East European dissidents use this discarded historical option as a scarecrow. The West German unilateralist anti-nuclear movement has nothing to do with German nationalism, while the East German pacifist movement's oppositional drive is not targeted on the oppressive character of Honecker's 'workers' and peasants' state'. The latter is economically flourishing and internally solidified. It is not to say much to state that the present East German revolution has thrown out of the window all of these self-delusions.

More important than self-congratulation is the formulation of the very cautious forecast that now can be given. 'Rapallo', as a special deal between the Soviet Union and 'Germany' (in whatever terms we describe this divided entity), is definitely off the agenda. At the same time, German unity is definitely on the agenda. We recommend all East European actors to accept this inevitable course, which would mean – although it is still a long journey – the formal conclusion of the Second World War, as well as of the Cold War, as a relief, not as a threat. 'German nationalism', a fact of history, is neither more nor less dangerous and destructive than Serbian nationalism against Croats and Kosovo-Albanians, Croatian nationalism against Serbs, Romanian nationalism against Hungarians and vice versa. To believe otherwise would be racism with reversed signs. Every nationalism has an inbuilt penchant to become destructive; the question is, in what political context it appears. There is one particular form of German nationalism which presents an *ipso facto* threat to both the Eastern and Western neighbors of Germany: the nationalism of a German Reich. But the mainstream of present German nationalism appears as a result of a democratic German revolution and in the context of a self-unifying Europe. If it lives up to its origins and if it is kept within these limits, there is no more danger in it than in any other European version of nationalism.

If our statement is correct, that certain forms of legitimate German nationalism do not present any more danger to the world than other forms of nationalism, how can we account for the obvious signs of (East and West) European anxiety over a coming German unification? First, it is only fair to admit that there is not just anxiety in the European arena. Parallel to this is the recognition, sometimes stated reluctantly when it comes to Germans but which cannot be overtly questioned, that no nation can be denied the right of self-determination. Second, the world at large is at odds with a question that the Germans also face: What is a German nation which is not a Reich? This apparent preoccupation with history and political theory is in fact a pragmatic political issue of primary relevance, one that has to be clarified before the world can proceed to the issue of German unification. Third, the pace of the East German revolution has caught every actor inside and outside the German states unaware. Raymond Aron once remarked that the governments, but not the peoples, of Europe have accepted the postwar settlement, the end of the war without a peace treaty, as the practically eternal order of things. We have always subscribed to Aron's statement, but its truth has been borne out only by the events of the last months. No one has been politically and theoretically prepared for this truth, particularly not in the German Federal Republic. The essence of social democratic *Ostpolitik* has been that pushing the 'unification issue' will lead the party into the cul-de-sac of Cold War positions. The conservatives, the heirs of Adenauer who *de facto* had abandoned the option of unification in exchange for a partial and limited German sovereignty after the devastating defeat, now find no other way out of their embarrassment except by rehashing the nationalist clichés which earlier served as a mere facade to a bitterly realistic decision and presenting them as a political program. They have also made the grave mistake of adding Kohl's ten points to their slogans of election campaigns which now appear as political blueprints. The Kohl plan, with its silence on future national borders, deliberately disregards the 'shifting Poland westward', a major event of our century engineered by Hitler and Stalin in complicity, which is a *fait accompli* to be held in respect by any German state. This silence even raises French fears about Alsace. The apodictic tone of Kohl's ten points leaves no doubt about the *Anschluss* character of the conservative way of integrating the Eastern into the Western German state. Fourth, an interesting bifurcation of German attitudes seems to have emerged across the board. The West German intelligentsia and the East German 'lower classes' appear to be pushing together for unification in an enthusiastic informal alliance. The former is obviously motivated by cultural nationalism, the latter by the hopes of higher standards of living. At the same time, there is a certain reluctance in the unexpected and equally informal 'alliance' of East German intellectuals (of very different political persuasions), who do not want to be mere pawns in a German–German *Anschluss* and who feel strongly about the birthright of their revolution, *and* the West German 'lower classes', who do not want to relinquish considerable parts of their prosperity on behalf of their poorer Eastern brethren. This now emerging intra-German split may well become the major domestic obstacle of unification. Finally, there is a difference of rhythm between two processes. European integration and German unification run a neck-to-neck race these days, and German nationalists and European integralists are on a collision course, for both believe that their particular cause has priority. All of these are very serious obstacles to putting German unification on the actual political agenda. However, we believe that they can only slow down a process which, with the East German revolution, has become irreversible. As Brandt emphasized, a peaceful, resolute and democratic German movement occupying the streets but not vandalizing anything is a rare phenomenon in German history. In fact, it appeared in pre-Bismarckian times for the last time. Therefore, Germans are now in the historical position of rethinking pre-Bismarckian versions of their gradual unification. A reference to the need for rethinking the options is the deeper meaning of Brandt's other insightful remark in terms of which the problem is not one of reunification but one of unification. In other words, new formulas are needed.

A crucial question is whether Germans find sympathy and understanding for their current cause from East Europeans. The latter, while perfectly entitled to guarantees of their borders and to protection against any possible future German expansionism, would make an irretrievable mistake if they appraised the East German revolution and the perspective of unification exclusively from a position of historical analogies, collective prejudices or the predictable loss of financial support transferred to East Germany, instead of in terms of *unconditional* solidarity. The democratic East German revolution is now gradually demolishing one of the bulwarks of neo-Stalinism (the leaders of which publicly admit that they have been engaged for years in an open conspiracy against Gorbachev). It will put an end to the self-delusion of the overwhelming majority of the West German left and, by its resolutely anti-authoritarian stance, it may bring a most welcome change in German public behavior. The German unification by peace treaty would eliminate an absurd situation, a peace without a peace treaty which has generated Cold War. It could promote the full unification of Europe. It would discard all dangerous scheming with plans of a new Rapallo, because the East Europeans, including the East Germans themselves, now are no longer simple objects of history who can be manipulated at will, but active and fighting subjects. *And above all, it would put an end to the system of Yalta.*

THE COMING DISSOLUTION OF EASTERN EUROPE

We have repeatedly stated throughout this volume that the term 'Eastern Europe' was a Stalinist coinage, a codeword for a region homogenized by sheer violence. We have followed the story of its gradual disintegration, its step by step self-liberation from the Yalta dictation. Evidently, we are writing the last chapter of this long story full of suffering. Short of a historical catastrophe, East Europeans will enter the nineties with the Yalta system behind them. What they then will do with their own history will be overwhelmingly their own responsibility.

Furthermore, all these countries are now passing through the momentous hours of making a document of foundation, a new constitution. The traditions of the region in this regard are, with the exception of Czechoslovakia, meagre, to say the least. And while it goes without saying that feasible constitutions must by definition vary from country to country, a certain collective discussion of the experiences of constitution-making seems to be all the more advisable given that these countries now describe a common passage from totalitarian dictatorship to democracy.

A further dilemma, which also does not remain within national borders, is the restructuring of the economy. Once again, we can expect varying solutions. There will be countries which, in despair over decades of economic frustration, will sell out the national wealth to the first bidder, thus laying the foundation for further internal tensions. Some others in all probability will retain a part of a democratized state property. All of them will establish a mixed economy and, equally, all of them will join new economic partners and communities. But, as its always the case with economic changes, the results will spill over to the political domain.

East-Central Europe bears one major responsibility before the dubious entity called 'History'. Its own democratic writers and theorists have pointed out repeatedly that the turbulence of that particularly unmanageable region was either the cause of, or the pretext for, two cataclysmic world wars. The denizens of this region have to understand that the world would not stand by idly if they embarked again on their traditional little games of mutual animosity which can ignite major explosions.

There are times for history and there are times for politics. Times for history are not 'predictable' in the sense of pollsters, but their major trends can be fathomed and the alternative courses growing out of history can be 'foresensed' and characterized. This kind of premonition is the classic case of self-fulfilling prophecy, for actors of historical trends normally appropriate one or another of these characterizations and follow its proposed patterns. Times for politics are, however, totally unpredictable. In disintegrating, Eastern Europe bids adieu to times for history and enters a political era. Some of its denizens, accustomed to the grandeur of historical periods, will find it difficult to live in more prosaic times. The antidote to tedium can be recalling all the victims of tyranny to whose collective memory this book has been dedicated.

January, 1990

Index